Praise for *Trend Following*

"Michael Covel's Trend Following: *Essential."*

> —Ed Seykota,
> Trend Follower and Original Market Wizard

"Trend Following by Michael Covel? I'm long this book."

> —Bob Spear,
> Developer of Trading Recipes Software

"Michael Covel's Trend Following *is a breakthrough book that captures the essence of what really makes markets tick. Diligently researched and comprehensive in scope, it will replace* Market Wizards *as the must-read bible for a new generation of traders."*

> —Jonathan Hoenig,
> Portfolio Manager, Capitalistpig Hedge Fund LLC,
> Fox News Contributor

"Michael Covel has written the definitive book on Trend Following. With careful research and clear insight he has captured the essence of the most successful of all trading strategies. Michael knows his subject matter and he writes about it with passion, conviction, and enthusiasm. This enjoyable and well written book is destined to become a classic."

> —Charles LeBeau,
> author of *Technical Traders Guide to Computer Analysis of the Futures Markets*

"Trend Following is an engrossing and educational journey through the principles, pitfalls, players, and psychology of aggressive technical trading of the investment markets. Rich in its wisdom and historical study."

> —Gerald Appel,
> President of Signalert Corporation and
> Publisher of Systems and Forecasts Newsletter

Trend Following:

How Great Traders Make
Millions in Up or Down Markets
New Expanded Edition

Michael W. Covel

FT Press
FINANCIAL TIMES

Library of Congress Cataloging-in-Publication Data

Covel, Michael.
   Trend following : how great traders make millions in up or down markets / Michael Covel.— New expanded ed.
      p. cm.
   ISBN 0-13-134550-8
   1. Investments. 2. Stocks. I. Title.
   HG4521.C82 2005
   332.6—dc22

                                    2005021501

Vice President, Publisher: Tim Moore
Executive Editor: Jim Boyd
Editorial Assistant: Pamela Boland
Development Editor: Russ Hall
Associate Editor-in-Chief and Director of Marketing: Amy Neidlinger
Publicist: Amy Fandrei
Marketing Coordinator: Megan Colvin
Cover Designer: Chuti Prasertsith
Managing Editor: Gina Kanouse
Project Editors: Kristy Hart and Michael Thurston
Copy Editor: Deadline Driven Publishing
Senior Indexer: Cheryl Lenser
Senior Compositor: Gloria Schurick
Manufacturing Buyer: Dan Uhrig

© 2007 by Pearson Education, Inc.
Publishing as FT Press
Upper Saddle River, New Jersey 07458

FT Press offers excellent discounts on this book when ordered in quantity for bulk purchases or special sales. For more information, please contact U.S. Corporate and Government Sales, 1-800-382-3419, corpsales@pearsontechgroup.com. For sales outside the U.S., please contact International Sales at international@pearsoned.com.

Printed in the United States of America

Second Printing

ISBN 0-13-613718-0

Pearson Education LTD.
Pearson Education Australia PTY, Limited.
Pearson Education Singapore, Pte. Ltd.
Pearson Education North Asia, Ltd.
Pearson Education Canada, Ltd.
Pearson Educación de Mexico, S.A. de C.V.
Pearson Education—Japan
Pearson Education Malaysia, Pte. Ltd.

For all those investors and traders
who wish they'd done things differently,
now in need of an aha! *moment.*

FINANCIAL TIMES

In an increasingly competitive world, it is quality
of thinking that gives an edge—an idea that opens new
doors, a technique that solves a problem, or an insight
that simply helps make sense of it all.

We work with leading authors in the various arenas
of business and finance to bring cutting-edge thinking
and best-learning practices to a global market.

It is our goal to create world-class print publications
and electronic products that give readers
knowledge and understanding that can then be
applied, whether studying or at work.

To find out more about our business
products, you can visit us at www.ftpress.com.

Contents

Foreword

Charles Faulkner

If you are browsing through this in a bookstore, you are most likely in the investments section. Look around. All of the people near you are also looking for an investing edge. If you are online, you can see by the ratings and recommendations that many other people have been here before you. The other titles in front of you, whether they are actual or virtual, all claim to represent an opportunity to enrich you. Whether you know it or not, you are in a market. You are looking for a winning trade—the information, the edge—that will put you ahead in the markets of stocks, bonds, real estate, or commodities.

When I first modeled the trading strategies of J. Peter Steidlmayer, CBOT trader and the originator of the Market Profile, I had a narrow notion of what makes a market, or how to make money in one. I had heard of George Soros, Jim Rogers, Peter Lynch, and a few others. When I heard the phrase, "buy low and sell high," it made sense to me. It also happened to appeal to me as a former antiques dealer and all round bargain hunter.

I didn't know how little I knew. Somehow I traded my model of the Market Profile—despite my utter ignorance of risk and money management—into a tidy profit. A colleague pointed out to me, "So you're betting on your opinion of other people's opinions." The reality of W.C. Fields' famous retort to Mae West's question (in *My Little Chickade*) sunk in. "Is poker a game of chance?" "Not the way I play it." I was concerned only with market signals—I had a stretch of what you'll learn was "Dumb Luck," instead of the "Poetic Justice" usually dealt to traders with such a lack of preparation. I got out to trade another day.

My chapter in Jack Schwager's *The New Market Wizards* made it possible for me to meet top traders across the industry. Sometimes we appeared on professional panels together. Other times, it was a private conversation. I want to share some of what I learned with you. Before I do, though, I want you to take out a dollar bill. Turn it over. You will see two seals. Look at the one on the left. The one with the words "THE GREAT SEAL" inscribed underneath it, the one with an unfinished pyramid of 13 steps with an eye in a glowing triangle floating above it. It is a wonderful symbol for a successful trader, and represents a trading tool as well.

The stones of the pyramid represent the ways a trader can make money. There's intermediation (brokerage charges), aggregating clients (reducing costs), carry trades, privileged information (insider trading), assessing asset flows (an institutional advantage), advanced technology (particularly for option pricing), models of economic actors and data (fundamentals), models of historical price data (technicals), and others. Some of these are basic—those near the base of the pyramid—and so they offer low returns. Other methods offer high returns. Naturally, as you make your way up on the pyramid, there are fewer stones. No one should be surprised by this. Neither was I.

What did surprise me when meeting and modeling these market wizards was that despite their outward, often dramatic, differences in trading and life style, their thinking about their trading principles was extremely similar. It was like they were floating above the world, seeing it from a different perspective than the rest of the market participants.

What are these differences? Here are a few from the eye of the pyramid:

- It doesn't matter what you think, it's what the market does that matters.
- What matters can be measured, so keep refining your measurements.
- You don't need to know when something will happen to know that it will.
- Successful trading is a probabilistic business, so plan accordingly.
- There is an edge to be gained in every aspect of your trading system.
- Everyone is fallible, even you, so your system must take this into account.
- Trading means losing as well as winning, something you must learn to live with.

Now, you might say to yourself, "Where's the secret sauce in that?" In one sense, you're right. These are extremely simple principles. At the same time they are counterintuitive and take a focused effort to apply. Let me give you an example: I was attending the trading system conference where I first met market wizard Ed Seykota. His table was talking about how successful trading systems could, and should, be simple enough that they could fit on a bumper sticker. Of course, skepticism emanated from other tables. "What about the complexities of the markets?" Their response was that they weren't interested in the markets' complexities; simply in making money on changes in price. Ed and his traders saw through the smokescreen of untested assumptions and beliefs about what you need to know about a market and what it takes to make a successful trading system. This is the difference between knowing a principle and making its market application. Think about adding to a position—also known as "pyramiding." Adding less with each addition to a position actually creates more gain than adding equal amounts each time. It's simple and it's counterintuitive. Another way that image on the dollar is a trading tool.

The book you have in front of you bridges this gap between trading principles and their market application like no other. It may look like a book, but it is really a set of trading tools—a complete and detailed application of these principles and others to the method of trading known as *Trend Following*.

Author and trader Michael Covel has arranged these master lessons so that you can approach them according to your personal preference, or as they call them these days, biases.

The Personalities—In the chapters on Great Trend Followers, you can read the personal histories of leading traders. You'll find there isn't just one type of successful personality; they range from college students to real scientists.

The Performance—For the factually minded, in the chapters on Performance Data and Big Events in Trend Following, there is a succinct summary of historical data from several trend following funds, along with parallel events in the world.

The Psychology—For those who think Human Behavior and Decision Making make the difference, there are chapters on each of these, as well as on Emotional Intelligence—and how to get it—followed by the dangers of Holy Grails.

The Trading Systems—The risk, the reward, the key questions to ask, and the questions Michael is most often asked, along with commentary from the master Trend Followers themselves, encompass these chapters.

The remarkable thing is not that you are looking at this book, but that it exists at all. Conventional wisdom says buy low and sell high. Each of us got our education in bargain hunting somewhere along the line. But what do you do now that your favorite market—be it a stock, bond, or commodity—is at an all-time high...or low? For a completely different perspective, from people who actually make money at this business, take a look inside. Michael Covel has written a timely and entertaining account of Trend Following—how it works, how to do it, and who can do it.

About Charles Faulkner

Charles Faulkner is an international NLP modeler and trainer who has worked with traders since 1986. The co-author of NLP: The New Technology of Achievement, *he was interviewed on* The Psychology of Trading *by Jack Schwager for his book* The New Market Wizards: Conversations with America's Top Traders, *with other interviews appearing in Robert Koppel's* The Outer Game of Trading *and* The Intuitive Trader *and articles in* Futures Magazine *and* Stocks, Futures, and Options Magazine. *A speaker at the F.I.A., The Market Timers Association, the Chicago Board of Trade's Members Only program, and other professional conferences, Charles conducts seminars on the emotions, strategies, beliefs, and design of trading systems.*

Charles consults on human factors in financial risk management to asset management and commodity firms and works with Ed Seykota contributing to his Trading Tribe Process (TTP). He trades stocks and futures when his system signals, and divides his time between the US and the UK where his wife and stepdaughter reside.

Foreword

Larry Hite

When I started trading in the commodity futures markets over 35 years ago, the industry didn't even have a name. Today, the business has grown to the point where there are a myriad of ways to describe the funds that operate and their many styles of investing. The particular discipline of trading that I practiced, even before the nomenclature existed, is now plainly and aptly termed "trend following." In fact, while I have seen many strategies come and go, most of the other managers that I have known to survive and thrive over the past few decades in global futures markets are also trend followers. For having made my living as a trend follower, I've yet to come across a more compelling study, so clearly distilled, than has been offered by Michael Covel in *Trend Following*.

I first met Michael when he was working on this book. I was a little hesitant at first about sharing some of the rather simple secrets of my trade. And, I didn't make it easy on Michael. I started interviewing *him* on his investments and how he managed his risk. He quickly made me realize that he not only understood trend following, but that he embraced it much like me. We delved into the roots of trend following and my investment strategies to explore why they work rather than just accepting the results. In reading *Trend Following*, I now see how well he was able to translate his knowledge, and the perspectives of many of my colleagues, to paper.

A large fraction of traffic accidents are of the type "driver looked but failed to see". Here, drivers collide with pedestrians in plain view, with cars directly in front of them, and even run into trains. That's right—run into trains, not the other way around. In such cases, information from the world is entering the driver's eyes. But at some point along the way this information is lost, causing the driver to lose connection with reality. They are looking but they are not seeing.

Ronald A. Rensink

It's important to have a plan, remain disciplined in executing that plan and pay attention to what is actually happening rather than what you expect to happen. We try to be as objective as possible in our analyses...It's not always easy for people who are involved every day to stay with a plan when misfortune occurs for a time. You always encounter the unexpected and this can push discipline right out of the way in the name of prudence. But prudence almost always dictates staying with the approach that has made you successful. I see that as one of my primary roles. I often encourage everyone during difficult days to remain patient. I don't blame people for the unexpected.

John W. Henry
CME Magazine, Premier Issue

Back in the 1970s, most of the guys I knew traded individual markets. The ones who traded wheat did not talk to the guys who traded sugar. And, the guys who invested stocks did not care to talk to either one, because commodities were for "speculators" and not "investors." Further, the bond crowd thought the stock guys were cowboys. Each group had developed their own superiority complexes and fundamentally believed that only industry experts, like them, could understand the subtle dynamics of their markets. I guess that's part of the reason that no one cared much for trend followers like me—I viewed every market the same way and each represented nothing more than a trade to me. Today, for all the different facets, I believe everyone has come to speak the same language. It's the language of risk.

In my early days, there was only one guy I knew who seemed to have a winning track record year after year. This fellow's name was Jack Boyd. Jack was also the only guy I knew who traded lots of different markets. If you followed any *one* of Jack's trades, you never really knew how you were going to do. But, if you were like me and actually counted *all* of his trades, you would have made about twenty percent a year. So, that got me more than a little curious about the idea of trading futures markets "across the board." Although each individual market seemed risky, when you put them together, they tended to balance each other out and you were left with a nice return with less volatility.

I could always see, after I got to Wall Street, how, for all the confusion, markets were driven by people and their emotions. That was what all of these markets had in common—people—and people just don't change. So, I set out to understand similarities in the way that markets moved. When I added up Jack's trades, only a few very big trades made him all the money. For each of these big winners, I was there when "experts" told Jack that these markets couldn't go any higher. But, they did. Then when I looked at Jack's losses, they tended to be relatively small. While it took me many years to put it all together—remember, there were no books like this back then— these seemingly small observations became the foundation for me of two important, intertwined investment themes: Trend following and risk management. Jack was not so much a trend follower, but he did practice the first rule of trend following: Cut your losers and let your winners run.

Most of the guys that I knew who lost a lot of money actually tended to be more right than wrong. They just lost a lot on a few big losers. I believe that people put too much of a premium on being right. In some ways, it's one of the drawbacks for people who went to the best schools and always got straight A's—they are too used to always being right. It gets back to people and emotions. Everyone is happy to take lots of little winners—it makes them feel good. When their trades go against them, on the other hand, they hold on because they don't want to accept being wrong. Many times, these trades come back and they are able to capture their small profit. To me, that kind of trading is a little bit like picking up nickels in front of a steamroller.

A prudent investor's best safeguard against risk is not retreat, but diversification. [And] true diversification is difficult to achieve by [simply] spreading an investment among different stocks (or different equity managers), or even by mixing stocks and bonds, because the two are not complementary.

David Harding
Winton Capital

Thankfully, the markets don't care about me or you or where we went to school. They don't care if you're short or tall. I was never very good in school and I wasn't a good athlete either. With my background, the way I saw it, I never had any problem with the idea that I could be wrong. So, I have always built in an assumption of wrongness to anything that I do. We now kindly refer to this practice as risk management, but I just wanted to answer the question: "What's the worst thing that could happen to me?" I never wanted to do anything that could kill me. Knowing that I was not likely to be right that often, I had to trade in a way that would make me a lot of money when I was right and not lose me a lot of money when I was wrong. If that wasn't enough, it also had to be simple enough for me to understand.

After many years of searching and learning things the hard way, I evolved my own version of trend following. The idea made sense and I had some good examples to follow. Still, I wanted to prove to myself that it worked without betting real money. I had to test what would have happened had I traded that way in the past. These were the early days of computers and we even had to "borrow" time on university computers to test and prove our theories. It was a painstaking task, but it gave me the comfort that I needed. Now, in reading *Trend Following*, the do-it-yourselfers might argue that having a book that illustrates these same basic principles takes some of the fun out of it.

Actually, Michael, like any good trend follower, has not focused solely on the endpoint. He gives you a deep understanding of the most important part: The path. Unlike so many other books that have been written about investing, *Trend Following* goes beyond the results to explore the journey of this outstanding group of traders.

For my staff at Hite Capital, Michael's *Trend Following* is required reading. For my daughters at home, it has finally settled the question I seemed never to have been able to clearly answer

[Trend following firm] Aspect Capital is aptly named. Its group of physics-trained leaders took it from the aspect ratio of plane design, that is, the wider the wing span, the more stable the plane. As such, Aspect trades not only futures of its early roots but European equities, bonds and currencies in various forms, covering a so-called wider wing span. The London-based hedge fund was the brainchild of Martin Lueck, Eugene Lambert and Anthony Todd. Founded in 1997, the principals were involved in the development of AHL (now owned by Man) with a track record stretching back to 1983. Aspect's disciplined approach has successfully generated returns from both longs and shorts in difficult markets environments.

Futures Magazine and Aspect Capital

myself, "Daddy, what do you do for a living?" This book captures and conveys what so many traders have taken careers and large losses to learn. And lucky for all of us, you don't have to be Phi Beta Kappa to understand it.

We no longer live in that world of wheat guys, sugar guys and stock guys. Trend following trading is an important force in every market and should be a part of any diverse investment portfolio. For me, the discipline of trend following goes beyond trading and money management. Trend following is a way of thinking that can be employed in many parts of life as we all tend to continue to do the things that work for us and stop doing those activities that don't.

The way I see it, you have two choices—you can do what I did and work for thirty-plus years, cobbling together scraps of information, seeking to create a money-making strategy, or you can spend a few days reading Michael's book and skip that three-decade learning curve.

About Larry Hite

Larry founded Mint Investments in 1983. By 1990, Mint Investments had become the largest Commodity Trading Advisor in the world in terms of assets under management. Mint's achievements won Larry Hite and his team industry wide acclaim, and in 1990, Jack Schwager dedicated an entire chapter of his bestselling book, Market Wizards, to Larry's trading and risk management philosophy.

Throughout the 1990's, Larry served as a director at the New York offices of Man Financial as well as managing Mint Investments, the billion-dollar hedge fund company he founded. In 2000, Larry formed Hite Capital Management, LLC. He was joined in this endeavor by former members of the original Mint team, headed by Dr. Alex Greyserman, who continues to serve as the Chief Investment Officer at Hite Capital.

Throughout his career, Larry has been an active participant in numerous philanthropic organizations. He founded his own charitable enterprise, The Hite Foundation, where he continues to act as Chairman. Additionally, he serves as Chairman of the Development Committee for the Institute of International Education's Scholar Rescue Fund, an organization whose goal is to provide safe haven for academics and professionals who are at risk throughout the world.

Preface

"Men wanted for hazardous Journey. Small wages. Bitter cold. Long months of complete darkness. Constant danger. Safe return doubtful. Honor and recognition in case of success."[1]

This book is the result of an eight-year "hazardous journey" for the truth about Trend Following. It fills a void in a marketplace inundated with books about finance and trading but lacking any resource or, for that matter, practically any reference to what we believe is the best strategy to consistently make money in the markets. That strategy is known as **Trend Following**:

"Let's break down the term 'Trend Following' into its components. The first part is 'trend.' Every trader needs a trend to make money. If you think about it, no matter what the technique, if there is not a trend after you buy, then you will not be able to sell at higher prices . . . 'Following' is the next part of the term. We use this word because trend followers always wait for the trend to shift first, then 'follow' it."[2]

Trend Following seeks to capture the majority of a trend, up or down, for profit. It trades for profits in the major asset classes—stocks, bonds, currencies, and commodities. However simple the basic concepts about Trend Following are, they have been widely misunderstood. Our desire to correct this state of affairs is what, in part, launched our research. We wanted to be as objective as possible, so we based our writing on the available data:

- Trend followers' month-by-month performance histories.
- Trend followers' published words and comments over the last 30 years.

When it is a question of money, everyone is of the same religion.

Voltaire

Education rears disciples, imitators, and routinists, not pioneers of new ideas and creative geniuses. The schools are not nurseries of progress and improvement, but conservatories of tradition and unvarying modes of thought.

Ludwig von Mises

- News accounts of financial disasters.
- News accounts of the losers in those financial disasters.
- Charts of markets traded by trend followers.
- Charts of markets traded by losers in the financial disasters.

If we could have developed a book comprised of only numbers, charts, and graphs of Trend Following performance data, we would have. However, without any explanation, few readers would have appreciated all of the ramifications of what the data showed. Therefore our approach to writing *Trend Following* became similar to the one Jim Collins describes in *Good to Great*, in which a team of researchers generated questions, accumulated data in their open-ended search for answers, and then energetically debated it.

Trend followers we studied form a sort of underground network of relatively unknown traders who, except for an occasional article, the mainstream press has virtually ignored. What we have attempted to do is lift the veil, for the first time, on who these enormously successful traders are, how they trade, and what is to be learned from their approach to trading that we might apply to our own portfolios.

Trend Following challenges much of the conventional wisdom about successful trading. We were determined to avoid being influenced by knowledge institutionalized and defined by Wall Street. We were adamant about fighting "flat earth" thinking. During our research, we tried to avoid starting with an assumption and then finding the data to support it. Instead we asked the question and then, objectively, doggedly, and slowly, let the answer reveal itself.

If there was one factor that motivated us to work in this manner, it was simple curiosity. The more we uncovered about trend followers, the more we wanted to know. For example, one of our earliest questions was who profited when Barings Bank collapsed in 1995. Our search unearthed Barings Bank–related performance data including that of trend follower John W. Henry (now the majority owner of the Boston Red Sox). His track record generated new questions, such as, "How did he discover Trend Following in the first place?" and "Has his approach changed in any significant way in the past 20 years?"

We were also curious about who won the $1.9 billion Long Term Capital Management lost during August and September 1998. We wanted to know why the biggest banks on Wall Street would invest $100 billion in an options pricing model, Nobel prize–winning or not. Further, considering what mutual fund managers have lost in the past few years and what successful trend followers have earned during the same time period, we could not understand why so few investors know anything about Trend Following. We also became interested in:

The important thing in science is not so much to obtain new facts as to discover new ways of thinking about them.

Sir William Bragg

- How trend followers win in the zero-sum game of trading.
- Why Trend Following has been the most profitable style of trading.
- The philosophical framework of trend followers' success.
- Timeless principles of Trend Following.
- The Trend Following worldview of market behavior.
- Reasons why Trend Following is so enduring.

Many of the trend followers we studied are reclusive and extremely low key. Some discovered Trend Following on their own and used it to make their fortunes out of home offices. Bill Dunn, a successful trend follower who has beaten the markets for over 25 years, works out of a quiet, spartan office in a Florida coastal town. For Wall Street, this approach to trading is tantamount to sacrilege. It goes against all the customs, rituals, trappings, and myths we have grown accustomed to associating with Wall Street success. In fact, it is our hope that our profiles of trend followers will correct the public's misconception of a successful trader as a harried, intense workaholic who spends 24/7 in the labyrinth of a Wall Street trading firm, surrounded by monitors and screaming into a phone.

We've assembled the first comprehensive look at Trend Following, but this is neither a course nor the only resource you will ever need. It is to be used in conjunction with our Web site at *www.trendfollowing.com*. We have tried to be comprehensive with our definitions. However, if we mention an unfamiliar word, name or reference a source you haven't heard of, please go to Google (*www.google.com*).

We have tried to make the material accessible and interesting enough so it might give you an occasional "aha" experience. However, if you're looking for trading "secrets," you need to look elsewhere. There are none. If you're in the mood for stories about what it's like inside a typical Wall Street firm or how greedy traders

Fish see the bait, but not the hook; men see the profit, but not the peril.

Chinese Proverb

To be aware how fruitful the playful mood can be is to be immune to the propaganda of the alienated, which extols resentment as a fuel of achievement.

Eric Hoffer

sow the seeds of their destruction, like in *Den of Thieves*, or *Barbarians at the Gate*, we will not meet your needs.

You may have noticed that I use "we" instead of "I" when describing the process of writing this book. That's because it could not have been written without the generosity of the traders, professors, investors, colleagues, and friends who graciously shared their wisdom and trading experiences with me. Without their support, hard work, long hours, and creativity, *Trend Following* would still be an ongoing hazardous journey. So if there is any "honor and recognition" to be given, it is to everyone who participated, not just the person whose name appears on the cover.

Acknowledgments

It is a pleasure to recognize the traders, colleagues, mentors, finance writers, and friends who contributed directly and indirectly to the original and expanded editions.

Justin Vandergrift and William W. Noel, III must be singled out for special mention. They were the core members of our original *Trend Following* research team. The book would not have come together without their hard work. Justin also gave great time and energy on the performance data appendix in this expanded edition.

I am particularly grateful to those traders—Ed Seykota, Bill Dunn, Daniel Dunn, Mark Rzepczynski, Pierre Tullier, Jason Russell, Easan Katir, Jonathan Hoenig, and Paul Mulvaney—who were generous with their feedback under tight writing deadlines. And thanks also to Martin Bergin of Dunn Capital Management for an initial introduction to Bill Dunn.

The support of Charles Faulkner must be acknowledged as well. He shared his intellect, enthusiasm, and most of all, his time, reading and critiquing various drafts. Franklin Gold, Volker Knapp, Dion Kurczek, Jose Cruset, Teresa Coffey-Gordon, and Jennifer Hill of Fidelity/Wealth-Lab provided great content and support for this expanded edition—thank you.

I also want to thank Peter Borish of Twinfields Capital, Bill Miller of Legg Mason, Michael Mauboussin of Legg Mason, Richard Cripps of Legg Mason, David Harding of Winton Capital, William Fung of PI Asset Management, Toby Crabel of Crabel Capital, Grant Smith of Millburn Corporation, Salem Abraham of Abraham Trading, Mark Abraham of Quantitative Capital Management, Bernard Drury of Drury Capital, Larry Hite of Hite Capital Management, Michael Clarke of Clarke Capital Management, Mark Rosenberg of SSARIS Advisors, LLC, Jon Sundt of Altegris, Christian Baja of Superfund, David Beach of Beach Capital, and Alejandro Knoepffler of Cipher Investment Management for their generous personal time and consideration over 2004 and 2005. I want to especially thank Jerry Parker of Chesapeake Capital for answering questions early in my career.

Celia Straus acted as my better half during the entire writing process. Her efforts were invaluable. Jerry Mullins, Molly Alton Mullins, Beneva Schulte, Withers Hurley, Elizabeth

Ellen, Justice Litle, Barry Ritholtz, Mark Rostenko, Arthur Maddock, Brett Steenbarger, and Bob Spear also made valuable contributions.

Throughout years of research, I've benefited repeatedly from the trading wisdom and experience of John W. Henry, Jonathan Craven, Mark Hawley, John Hoade, Shaun Jordan, Carol Kaufman, Jane Martin, Leo Melamed, Larry Mollner, Kim Hunter, Gibbons Burke, Chuck LeBeau, and Leon Rose. A sincere thank you also goes out to Oliver Alliker, James Altucher, Gerald Appel, Aspect Capital, Hunter Baldwin, Tom Basso, John Boik, Bob Brooks, Wade Brorsen, Ursula Burger, Jake Carriker, Celeste Cave, Art Collins, Cory Colvin, Allan Como, Larry Connors, Chip Dempsey, Tim Dempsey, Rolf Dobelli, Edward Dobson, David Dolak, Woody Dorsey, David Druz, Patrick Dyess, Stephen Eckett, William Eckhardt, Marc Faber, Mark Fitzsimmons, Ed Foster, Nelson Freeburg, Mitsuru Furukawa, Dave Goodboy, Jayanthi Gopalakrishnan, Stephanie Haase, Scott Hicks, James Holter, Scott A. Houdek, Robert (Bucky) Isaacson, Christian Jund, MaryAnn Kiely, Eddie Kwong, Pete Kyle, Eric Laing, Elina Manevich, Bill Mann, Jon Markman, Michael Martin, John Mauldin, Timothy M. McCann, Lizzie McLoughlin, James Montier, Georgia Nakou, Peter Navarro, Gail Osten, Michael Panzner, Bob Pardo, Baron Robertson, Jim Rogers, Murray Ruggiero, Michael Seneadza, Takaaki Sera, Tom Shanks, Howard Simons, Barry Sims, Aaron Smith, Michael Stephani, Richard Straus, Nassim Nicholas Taleb, Stephen Taub, Ken Tower, Ken Tropin, Tomoko Uchiyama, Thomas Vician, Jr., Robert Webb, Kate Welling, Cole Wilcox, Gabriel Wisdom, Brent Wood, and Patrick L. Young for all of their efforts and support over 2004 and 2005.

And thank you to the following publications and writers who generously allowed us to quote from their work: Sol Waksman and Barclay Managed Futures Report, *Futures Magazine*, Managed Account Reports, Michael Rulle of Graham Capital Management, and *Technical Analysis of Stocks and Commodities Magazine*.

I am also indebted to the following authors whose works continue to be treasure troves of information and insight: Morton Baratz, Peter Bernstein, Clayton Christensen, Jim Collins, Jay Forrester, Tom Friedman, Gerd Gigerenzer, Daniel Goleman, Stephen Jay Gould, Alan Greenberg, Larry Harris, Robert Koppel, Edwin Lefevere, Michael Lewis, Jesse Livermore, Roger Lowenstein, Ludwig von Mises, Lois Peltz, Ayn Rand, Jack Schwager, Denise Shekerjian, Robert Shiller, Van Tharp, Edward Thorp, Peter Todd, Brenda Ueland, and Dickson Watts.

This book could only have come to fruition with the editorial guidance of Jim Boyd at Financial Times Prentice Hall, as well as the able assistance and attention to detail of Dennis Higbee, who copy edited. I also want to thank Donna Cullen-Dolce, Lisa Iarkowski, Stephen Crane, and John Pierce for their remarkable production and marketing skills. Kristy Hart, Sarah Kearns, Gina Kanouse, Jim Schachterle, Lucy Petermark, and Pablo Rendina provided critical support. To Paul Donnelly at Oxford University Press, I owe a special debt of gratitude for seeing the potential of my initial proposal. And to Lisa Berkowitz, a big thank you for making "it" happen.

—Michael Covel
November, 2005

Part I

Trend Following

1

"Speculation is dealing with the uncertain conditions of the unknown future. Every human action is a speculation in that it is embedded in the flux of time."
—Ludwig von Mises[1]

The Market

A market is simply a place where buyers and sellers gather to trade and exchange goods, buying and selling for any number of reasons. The market performs the essential role of connecting financial and real economies. The New York Stock Exchange and the National Association of Securities Dealers Automated Quotation System (you hear it called NASDAQ on the news) are two markets. There are also futures exchanges like the Chicago Board of Trade or the Chicago Mercantile Exchange. All of these exchanges are markets where trend followers do their buying and selling.

It is the markets' ability to give a "price" that buyers and sellers can rely on as fact. Ludwig von Mises, the great Austrian economist, offered:

"It is the very essence of prices that they are the offshoot of the actions of individuals and groups of individuals acting on their own behalf. The catallactic concept of exchange ratios and prices

The people that I know who are the most successful at trading are passionate about it. They fulfill what I think is the first requirement: developing intuitions about something they care about deeply, in this case, trading. They are the people who study years of charts, or commodity annuals . . . They develop a deep knowledge of whatever form of analysis they use. Out of that passion and knowledge, their trading ideas, insights, and intuitions emerge.

Charles Faulkner[2]

3

precludes anything that is the effect of actions of a central authority, of people resorting to violence and threats in the name of society or the state or of an armed pressure group. In declaring that it is not the business of the government to determine prices, we do not step beyond the borders of logical thinking. A government can no more determine prices than a goose can lay hen's eggs."[3]

Winning and Losing

The joy of winning and the pain of losing are right up there with the pain of winning and the joy of losing. Also to consider are the joy and pain of not participating. The relative strengths of these feelings tend to increase with the distance of the trader from his commitment to being a trader.

Ed Seykota[4]

Between the corporate and market scandals of the past few years, it is understandable that the general public equates winning with abusing the market system. However, there are disciplined men and women trading in the markets with the utmost integrity who achieve spectacular returns year after year. We urge you to examine their market philosophies and strategies so that you will understand what makes them successful. We ask you to examine their beliefs and self-perceptions so you understand what keeps them honest. However, before we examine other's perspectives, we want you to take a moment to consider your own. How do you approach investing?

For example, does this describe you? At the end of the Nineties, just when you were feeling good about yourself because you were more secure financially, the dot-com bubble burst, and by the time it was over, you had lost a significant amount of money. You found yourself angry with the analysts, experts, brokers, or money managers whose advice you had taken. You didn't do anything wrong except follow their advice. Now you doubt that that you will ever meet your investment goals. You've held on to your remaining investments believing that the market will eventually turn around, but deciding what to do with your 401k money has become stressful. You still believe that buying at the bottom is the way to go. You've now begun to think that what winning in the markets really requires is just plain dumb luck.

If you think education is expensive, try ignorance.

Derek Bok

Or maybe you might view your financial world like this: Sure, you lost some money in the bear market but, win or lose, you enjoy the thrill of investing in a stock in the hopes of making a profit. Investing is entertainment for you. Plus, you like to boast about your investments to garner the admiration of others. You know you can be depressed and angry when you lose, but you also know that when you win, you feel terrific. It's a great high. Since your main goal is to invest for quick profits, you're going to keep on doing what you've always done, bear or bull. After all, there was one time a few years ago when trading off a "hot tip" made you a nice profit.

There is a much better way to think about investing. How would you feel about embracing this perspective? Your approach is objective and rational. You have enough confidence in your own decision-making that you don't seek out investment recommendations from others. You're content to wait patiently until the right opportunity comes along. Yet, you're never too proud to buy a stock that is making new highs. For you, buying opportunities are usually market breakouts. Conversely, when you recognize that you are wrong, you exit immediately. You view a loss as an opportunity to learn and move on. What good is obsessing on the past going to do you? You approach your trading as a business, making note of what you buy or sell and why in the same matter-of-fact way that you balance your checkbook. By not personalizing your trading decisions, you're able to look forward to making them.

What a stark contrast in perspectives. The first is that of a potential loser; the latter is that of a potential winner. Don't be in such a hurry to choose the winning approach until you've found out just what making such a choice entails. On the other hand, we hope you'll find, in *Trend Following*, the inspiration to step up to the plate and go for it:

The perfect speculator must know when to get in; more important he must know when to stay out; and most important he must know when to get out once he's in.

"Profit-seeking speculation is the driving force of the market."—Ludwig von Mises[5]

Investor v. Trader: How Do You See the World?

Do you consider yourself an investor or a trader? Most people think of themselves as investors. However, if you knew that big winners in the markets call themselves traders, wouldn't you want to know why? Simply put, they don't invest, they trade.

Investors put their money, or capital, into a market, like stocks or real estate, under the assumption that the value of the entity they invest in will increase over time. As the value increases, so does the person's "investment." Investors typically do not have a plan for when their investment value decreases. They hold on to their investment, hoping that the value will reverse itself and go

Nothing has changed during the 21 years we've been managing money. Government regulation and intervention have been, are, and will continue to be present for as long as society needs rules by which to live. Today's governmental intervention or decree is tomorrow's opportunity. For example, governments often act in the same way that cartels act. Easily the most dominant and effective cartel has been OPEC, and even OPEC has been unable to create an ideal world from the standpoint of pricing its product. Free markets will always find their own means of price discovery.
Keith Campbell[6]

Trend followers are traders, so we generally use the word "trader" instead of "investor" throughout.

back up. Investors typically succeed in bull markets and lose in bear markets.

This is because investors anticipate bear, or down, markets with fear and trepidation and therefore are unable to plan how to respond when they're losing. They chose to "hang tight," so they continue to lose. They have some idea that a different approach to losing involves more complicated trading transactions like "selling short," of which they know little and don't care to learn. If the mainstream press continually positions investing as "good" or "safe" and trading as "bad" or "risky," people are reluctant to align themselves with traders or even seek to understand what trading, as opposed to investing, is all about.

A trader has a defined plan or strategy to put capital into a market in order to achieve a single goal: profit. Traders don't care what they own or what they sell as long as they end up with more money than they started out with. They are not investing in anything. They are trading. It is an important distinction.

Tom Basso, a longtime trend follower, has often said that a person is a trader whether or not they are actually trading. Some people think they must be in and out of the markets every day to call themselves a trader. What makes someone a trader has more to do with their perspective on life than with making a given trade. For example, a trend follower's perspective includes patience. Like the African lion waiting for days for the right moment to strike its unsuspecting prey, a trend follower can wait weeks or months for a trend.

Ideally, traders go short as often as they go long, enabling them to make money in both up and down markets. However, a majority of "traders" won't or can't go short. They resemble investors in that they struggle with the concept of making money when a market declines. We hope that after reading *Trend Following*, the confusion and hesitation associated with making money in down markets will dissipate.

Fundamental v. Technical: What Kind of Trader Are You?

There are two basic theories of trading. The first theory is fundamental analysis, the study of external factors that affect the supply and demand of a particular market. Fundamental analysis pays attention to factors like weather, government policies, domestic and foreign political and economic events, price-earnings ratios, and balance sheets. By monitoring supply and demand factors, or "fundamentals" for a particular market, it is supposedly possible to predict a change in market conditions before that change has been reflected in the price of the market.

The vast majority of Wall Street are proponents of fundamental analysis. They are the academics, brokers, and analysts who spoke highly of the "new economy," predicting that all dot-com stocks would rise forever due to an assortment of fundamental forecasts. Millions bought into their rosy projections and rode the dot-com bubble straight up with no clue how to exit when the bubble burst.

Has anyone changed their investment strategies, or do they still need their daily fix of fundamental headlines? Evidence that nothing has changed can be found in Yahoo! Finance's commentary outlining a single day of trading in the fall of 2003:

"It started off decent, but ended up the fourth straight down day for stocks . . . early on, the indices were in the green, mostly as a continuation from the bounce Monday afternoon . . . but as the day wore on and the markets failed to show any upward momentum, the breakdown finally occurred . . . The impetus this time was attributed to the weakness in the dollar, even though the dollar was down early in the day while stocks were up . . . also, oil prices popped higher on wishful thinking statements from a Venezuelan official about OPEC cutting production . . . whether or not these factors were simply excuses for selling, or truly perceived as fundamental factors hardly matters . . . The tone is fragile and the chartists are becoming increasingly concerned about a more significant correction . . . the late, quick dip in the indices at the close didn't help . . . the corporate news was generally good . . . Home Depot (HD 34.95 -0.52) had an excellent earnings report but lost early stock gains . . . Agilent (A 27.77) also had good earnings . . . General Electric (GE 28.44 +0.63) was upgraded to 'buy' at Merrill Lynch."

Millions of readers still log on to Yahoo! Finance every day, so on their behalf we ask the following questions:

- Why aren't four straight down days a good thing if you are short?
- Please define with a precise formula the term *bounce*.

Whenever we get a period of poor performance, most investors conclude something must be fixed. They ask if the markets have changed. But trend-following presupposes change.

John W. Henry[7]

One of our basic philosophical tendencies is that change is constant, change is random, and trends will reappear if we go through a period of non-trending markets. It's only a precursor to future trends and we feel if there is an extended period of non-trending markets, this really does set up a base for very dynamic trends in the future.

Former Head of Research at John W. Henry[8]

- Please define with a precise formula the term *upward momentum*.
- Who attributed the impetus to weakness in the dollar? How did they do this?
- Please define with a precise formula the term *fragile tone*.
- What does *the corporate news was generally good* mean?
- What does it say for fundamental analysis that Home Depot reported good earnings, but the stock dropped?
- Merrill Lynch has issued a *buy* for GE. Will there ever be a *sell*? How much does Merrill Lynch say we should buy of GE?

Where are the facts in Yahoo!'s commentary? Where is the objectivity? One of the greatest trend followers, Ed Seykota, nails the problem of fundamental analysis with his typical good humor:

"One evening, while having dinner with a fundamentalist, I accidentally knocked a sharp knife off the edge of the table. He watched the knife twirl through the air, as it came to rest with the pointed end sticking into his shoe. 'Why didn't you move your foot?' I exclaimed. 'I was waiting for it to come back up,' he replied."[9]

But I think our ace in the hole is that the governments usually screw things up and don't maintain their sound money and policy coordination. And about the time we're ready to give up on what usually has worked, and proclaim that the world has now changed, the governments help us out by creating unwise policy that helps produce dislocations and trends.

Jerry Parker[11]

Don't we all know an investor who is waiting for "their" market to come back? Motley Fool's home page reflects the folly of literally "banking on" fundamental analysis as a solution:

"It all started with chocolate pudding. When they were young, brothers David and Tom Gardner learned about stocks and the business world from their father at the supermarket. Dad, a lawyer and economist, would tell them, 'See that pudding? We own the company that makes it! Every time someone buys that pudding, it's good for our company. So go get some more!' The lesson stuck."[10]

David and Tom Gardner's pudding story may be cute but it is not complete. Their plan gets you in, but it doesn't tell you when to get out of the pudding stock or how much of the pudding stock you must buy. Unfortunately, many people believe their simple story is a good strategy for making money.

The second theory, technical analysis, operates in stark contrast to fundamental analysis. This approach is based on the belief that, at any given point in time, market prices reflect all known factors affecting supply and demand for that particular market. Instead of evaluating fundamental factors outside the market, technical analysis looks at the market prices themselves. Technical traders believe that a careful analysis of daily price action is an effective means of capitalizing on price trends.

Now here is where the understanding of technical analysis gets tricky. There are essentially two forms of technical analysis. One form is based on an ability to "read" charts and use "indicators" to divine the market direction. These so-called technical traders use methods designed to attempt to predict a market direction. Here is a great example of the predictive view of technical analysis:

"I often hear people swear they make money with technical analysis. Do they really? The answer, of course, is that they do. People make money using all sorts of strategies, including some involving tea leaves and sunspots. The real question is: Do they make more money than they would investing in a blind index fund that mimics the performance of the market as a whole? Most academic financial experts believe in some form of the random-walk theory and consider technical analysis almost indistinguishable from a pseudoscience whose predictions are either worthless or, at best, so barely discernably better than chance as to be unexploitable because of transaction costs."[12]

This is the view of technical analysis held by the majority—that it is some form of superstition, like astrology. Technical prediction is the only application of technical analysis that the majority of Wall Streeters are aware of as evidenced by equity research from Credit Suisse First Boston:

"The question of whether technical analysis works has been a topic of contention for over three decades. Can past prices forecast future performance?"[13]

However there is another type of technical analysis that neither predicts nor forecasts. This type is based on price. Trend followers form the group of technical traders that use this type of analysis. Instead of trying to predict a market direction, their strategy is to react to the market's movements whenever they occur. Trend followers respond to what has happened rather than anticipating what will happen. They strive to keep their strategies based on statistically validated trading rules. This enables them to focus on the market and not get emotionally involved.

While a fundamental analyst may be able to properly evaluate the economics underlying a stock, I do not believe they can predict how the masses will process this same information. Ultimately, it is the dollar-weighted collective opinion of all market participants that determines whether a stock goes up or down. This consensus is revealed by analyzing price.

Mark Abraham
Quantitative Capital Management, L.P.

Markets aren't chaotic, just as the seasons follow a series of predictable trends, so does price action.

Stocks are like everything else in the world: They move in trends, and trends tend to persist.

Jonathan Hoenig
Portfolio Manager,
Capitalistpig Hedge Fund LLC

It is not the strongest of the species that survive, nor the most intelligent, but the ones most responsive to change.

Charles Darwin

However, price analysis never allows trend followers to enter at the exact bottom of a trend or exit at the exact top of the trend. Second, with price analysis they don't have to trade every day. Instead, trend followers wait patiently for the right market conditions instead of forcing the market. Third, there are no performance goals with price analysis. Some traders might embrace a strategy that dictates, for example, "I must make $400 dollars a day." Trend followers would ask them, "Sure, but what if the markets don't move on a given day?"

One trend follower summarized the problem:

"I could not analyze 20 markets fundamentally and make money. One of the reasons [Trend Following] works is because you don't try to outthink it. You are a trend follower, not a trend predictor."[14]

Discretionary v. Mechanical: How Do You Decide?

It is when the unimaginable occurs that the systematic trader remains calm, presciently knowing when to buy, sell, or adjust their exposure.

Mark Abraham
Quantitative Capital Management, L.P.

We have established the idea that you can be an investor or trader. We have established that trading can be fundamentally or technically based. Further, technical trading can be predictive or reactive. And we've explained how trend followers are traders who use a reactive technical approach based on price. However, there is one more distinction. Traders can be discretionary or mechanical.

John W. Henry, one of the best trend followers over the last 20 years, thinks it's important for clients to know his approach and he makes a clear distinction between the two strategies: "JWH believes that an investment strategy can only be as successful as the discipline of the manager to adhere to the requirements in the face of market adversity. Unlike discretionary traders, whose decisions may be subject to behavioral biases, JWH practices a disciplined investment process."[15]

When Henry speaks of decisions that may be subject to behavioral biases, he is referring to the legions of traders who make their buy and sell decisions based on the sum of their market knowledge, their view of the current market environment, or any number of other factors. In other words, they use their discretion—hence the use of "discretionary" to describe their approach to trading.

Decisions made at the "discretion" of the trader are subjective and therefore can be changed or second-guessed. There are no ironclad assurances that these discretionary trading decisions are based on reality, and not colored by personal bias. Of course, a trader's initial choices to launch the system are discretionary. You must make discretionary decisions like choosing a system, selecting your portfolio, and determining a risk percentage. However, once you've decided on the basics, you can then choose to systematize these discretionary decisions and from that point on rely on a mechanical trading system.

Mechanical trading, used by trend followers, is based on an objective and automated set of rules. The rules are derived from their market view or philosophy. Traders rigidly follow these trading rules (often putting them into computer programs) to get themselves in and out of the market. A mechanical trading system makes life easier by working to eliminate emotion from trading decisions and forcing you stick to the rules. It enforces discipline. If you break your own rules with a mechanical trading system, you can go broke.

The trend is your friend except at the end when it bends.

Ed Seykota[18]

John W. Henry speaks to the downsides of discretionary trading:

"Unlike discretionary traders, whose decisions may be subject to behavioral biases, JWH practices a disciplined investment process. By quantifying the circumstances under which key investment decisions are made, the JWH methodology offers investors a consistent approach to markets, unswayed by judgmental bias."[16]

I feel sorry for the traders who watch CNBC all day, every day. They hope to eek out some competitive advantage from the comments of some guy who has never traded an S&P contract in his life. Even if the media happened to have something relevant to say, the news is already reflected in the open, high, low, close, open interest and daily volume.

Christian Baha
CEO Superfund

It seems a bit rigid to say you can't even use just a little discretion when faced with a trading decision, doesn't it? After all, where's the "fun" if all you ever do is follow a mechanical model? But then Trend Following isn't about fun. It's about winning. The Director of Research of Campbell and Company, one of the oldest and most successful Trend Following firms, is adamant about avoiding discretion:

"One of our strengths is to follow our models and not use discretion. This rule is written in stone at Campbell."[17]

You will see that, like Campbell's Director of Research, trend followers use their words carefully and deliberately. It was encouraging to us to find that there are few if any instances when their words don't reflect their performance data.

Timeless

Trend Following is not new. The strategy is simply discovered by new generations of traders at different times:

"[Salem Abraham, a trend follower,] began researching the markets by asking a simple question: Who is making money? The answer was trend followers and his journey began."[19]

Defining a trend is like defining love. We know it when we see it, but we are rarely sure exactly what it is. Fung and Hsieh's paper goes a long way to doing for trends what poets have been trying to do for love since time immemorial. They give us a working model that quantitatively defines their value for us. Traders will not be surprised to learn that Trend Following advisors performed best during extreme market moves, especially during bad months for equities.[20]

Few people have made the journey with Salem Abraham. During the dot-com era of the late 1990s, so many investors and traders with so little strategy were making so much money that trend followers disappeared from the radar screen even though they kept right on making money.

Since Trend Following has nothing to do with short-term trading, cutting edge technologies, or Wall Street Holy Grails, its appeal was negligible during the stock market bubble. If investors could jump on the bandwagon of practically any "long only" hedge fund manager or turn a profit trading themselves by simply buying internet stocks and holding on to them, what need was there to adopt a strategy such as Trend Following?

However, when we look at how much money trend followers have made since the bubble has popped, Trend Following becomes far more relevant. The following chart (Chart 1.1) shows a hypothetical index of three longtime Trend Following firms compared against the S&P stock index. The chart combines Dunn Capital Management, Campbell and Co., and John W. Henry and Co. into an equally-weighted index:

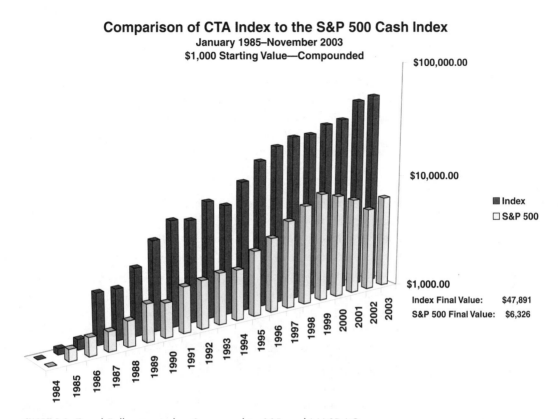

Comparison of CTA Index to the S&P 500 Cash Index
January 1985–November 2003
$1,000 Starting Value—Compounded

$100,000.00

$10,000.00

■ Index
☐ S&P 500

$1,000.00

Index Final Value: $47,891
S&P 500 Final Value: $6,326

CHART 1.1: Trend Following Index Compared to S&P and NASDAQ

Yet even when Trend Following success is brought to their attention, investors are still often skeptical. They say the markets have changed and that Trend Following no longer works. Their concern usually stems from a random press story of a trend follower who "blew up" and lost all of his and his clients' money. But the truth is that Trend Following hasn't changed, even though a single trend follower may have. That is a big difference.

Let's put change and Trend Following in perspective. Markets behave the same as they did 300 years ago. In other words, markets are the same today because they always change. This is a philosophical underpinning of Trend Following. A few years ago, for example, German mark trading had significant trading volume. Now the Euro has replaced the German mark. This was a huge, yet typical, change. If you are flexible, market changes, like changes in life, don't have to impact you negatively.

Change is not merely necessary to life—it is life.
Alvin Toffler

Accepting the inevitability of change is the first step to understanding Trend Following philosophy. John W. Henry describes the benefits of understanding change:

"But what won't change? Change. When a period of difficult performance continues, however, most investors' natural conclusion is that something must be done to fix the problem. Having been through these drawdowns before, we know that they are unpleasant, but they do not signal that something is necessarily wrong with the future. During these periods almost everyone asks the same question in these exact words: 'Have the markets changed?' I always tell them the truth: 'Yes.' Not only have they changed, but they will continue to change as they have throughout history and certainly throughout our 19 years. Trend Following presupposes change. It is based on change."[21]

Markets go up, down, and sideways. They trend. They flow. They surprise. No one can forecast a trend's beginning or end until it becomes a matter of record, just like the weather. However, if your trading strategy is designed to adapt to change, you can take advantage of the changes to make money:

"If you have a valid basic philosophy, the fact that things change turns out to be a benefit. At least you can survive. At the very least, you will survive over the long term. But if you don't have a valid basic philosophy, you won't be successful because change will eventually kill you. I knew I could not predict anything, and that is why we decided to follow trends, and that is why we've been so successful. We simply follow trends. No matter how ridiculous those trends appear to be at the beginning, and no matter how extended or how irrational they seem at the end, we follow trends."—John W. Henry[22]

The people who excel in any field are people who realize that the moment is there to be seized—that there are opportunities at every turn. They are more alive to the moment.

Charles Faulkner[23]

What does Henry mean by "a valid basic philosophy"? He is talking about a trading strategy that can be defined, quantified, written down, and measured in terms of numbers. Do you have one of those? Does your broker have one? Does your mutual fund manager have one? Does your high-flying hedge fund have one? Trend followers do not guess if they must buy or sell. They know what to do, because they have their "valid basic philosophy" set in a plan.

Has Trend Following Changed?

There are plenty of people who ignore Trend Following's tremendous track record and argue that it is outdated or inferior or that it plain doesn't work.

"Has Trend Following changed?" was the topic of a panel at the Managed Fund Association's Network 2001 conference. Dr. Patrick L. Welton, CEO and Chairman of Welton Investment Corporation, said that there is no evidence that Trend Following has changed. In order to prove this fact, he constructed 120 trend-following models. Some were reversal-based, and others were not. Some were breakout-based on price with others on volatility and band-style breakouts. The average holding periods ranged from two weeks to one year. The results gave almost identical performance characteristics in periods covering the late 1980s, early 1990s, and late 1990s.

Welton also addressed the misconception that the sources of return for Trend Following had changed, saying that there was no evidence to support that perception. He pointed out that starting from first principles, it was a fact that the source of return for Trend Following resulted from sustained market price movements. Human reaction to such events, and the stream of information describing them, takes time and runs its course unpredictably. Welton went on to state that the resulting magnitude and rate of change of price could not be reliably forecast. This is the precise reason why Trend Following works.[24]

Burt Kozloff, a consultant in the hedge fund industry, also confronted skeptics. Here is an excerpt from a presentation he gave:

"In February 1985, on a tour of Germany sponsored by the Deutsche Terminborse, several advisors and pool operators were making a presentation to a group of German institutional investors. Among them were two trend-based traders, Campbell & Co. and John W. Henry & Co. During the question-and-answer period, one man stood and proclaimed: 'But isn't it true that Trend Following is dead?' At this point, the moderator asked that slides displaying the performance histories for Campbell and Henry be displayed again. The moderator marched through the declines, saying: 'Here's the

The four most expensive words in the English language are "this time it's different."

Sir John Templeton

While conceding tacitly or explicitly that over the long run daily price movements are serially independent (move randomly) technical analysts focus on recurring short term patterns and trends. They are like surfboard riders, who study the movements of the waves, not in order to understand why they behave as they do, but simply in order to be on hand whenever they surge, to catch them at their crest, or as soon thereafter as possible to ride them as far as they possible can, and to dissemble before they change direction.

Morton S. Baratz[25]

first obituary for trend-based trading. Here's the next one . . . and the next but these traders today are at new highs, and they consistently decline to honor the tombstones that skeptics keep erecting every time there's a losing period.' Campbell and JWH have made their investors hundreds of millions of dollars since that time. It might, therefore, be a mistake to write yet another series of obituaries."[26]

A new Trend Following obituary will be written every few years despite the incredible amounts of money made by its practitioners. Perplexed at Wall Street's lack of acceptance, John W. Henry once responded to Trend Following critics:

By honest I don't mean that you only tell what's true. But you make clear the entire situation. You make clear all the information that is required for somebody else who is intelligent to make up their mind.

Richard Feynman

"How can someone buy high and short low and be successful for two decades unless the underlying nature of markets is to trend? On the other hand, I've seen year-after-year, brilliant men buying low and selling high for a while successfully and then going broke because they thought they understood why a certain investment instrument had to perform in accordance with their personal logic."[27]

Trend followers generally seem to be oblivious to those who question the validity of their strategy. Why spend energy constantly defending yourself when you are producing monster returns year after year?

Trend Following Modus Operandi:
Follow Price

Trend followers generate phenomenal returns because their decisions are ultimately based on one piece of core information: price. In an increasingly uncertain and, these days, downright unfriendly world, it is extremely efficient and effective if our decision-making is based on this single, simple, reliable truth. The constant barrage of fundamental data, such as price-earnings ratios, crop reports, and economic studies, plays into traders' tendencies to make trading more complicated than it needs to be. Yet, factoring in every possible fundamental still does not tell a trader how much and when to buy, or how much and when to sell.

It is not unusual for many traders to become familiar with and focus on only one market (usually in their own country) to the exclusion of all other global opportunities. Seeking to maintain the maximum degree of comfort, they follow this one familiar market's movements faithfully. If they specialize in stocks, they wouldn't dream of branching out into currencies or futures. How can a stock trader know anything about currencies? The idea that you could know enough about Cisco and soybeans to trade them both seems unfathomable to some. But think about what cotton, crude oil, Cisco, Sun, GE, the U.S. dollar, the Australian dollar, soybeans, wheat, Microsoft, EMC, and Oracle all have in common. Price.

Market prices are the objective data. You can compare and study prices and measure price movements, even if you know nothing about the markets themselves. You can look at individual price histories and charts without knowing which market is which and trade them successfully.

Follow the Trend

Don't try to guess how far a trend will go. You can't. Peter Borish, former second-in-command for Paul Tudor Jones, lays bare the only concern a trader must have:

"Price makes news, not the other way around. A market is going to go where a market is going to go."[28]

The concept of price as the trading cue is just too darn simple for people to accept. This is demonstrated by the mainstream press, who always emphasize all the wrong numbers:

"At some point investing is an act of faith. If you can't believe the numbers, annual reports, etc., what numbers can you believe?"—Bill Griffith, Anchor, CNBC

Bill Griffith misses the point when he asks what numbers you can believe if you can't believe a company's annual report. It doesn't matter whether you can or cannot believe the earnings statement. All of these numbers can be doctored. The traded price can't be fixed. It's the only number to believe. However, this simple fact does not diminish the confusion. Alan Sloan, by all accounts a fine finance reporter, searches for numbers to trust:

"If some of the smartest people on Wall Street can't trust the numbers you wonder who can trust the numbers."

What numbers is Sloan talking about? Balance sheets? Price-earnings ratios? You can't ever trust those numbers. Someone can

[Trend Following] is motivated by a very broad interpretation of the universe. The underlying belief is that economic systems adjust to changes in fundamentals gradually and over long periods of time, and that the consequent trends are evident everywhere in human history and commerce. Political, economic and social regime changes trigger price adjustments in markets that don't happen instantaneously. For example, the growth and decline of the Roman Empire took place, not in a day, but over hundreds of years. A major problem, of course, is that markets don't move from one state to another in a straight line: there are periods of countertrend shock and volatility. We spend most of our time trying to find ways to deal with those unsettling but inevitable events. That being said, it is really not difficult to put together a simple trend-following system that can generate positive returns over a realistic holding period ñ and there are many, many commercial systems that have been generating strong, albeit volatile, returns for a long time. So there are definitely firm grounds for believing in Santa Claus.

Paul Mulvaney
CIO of
Mulvaney Capital Management Ltd.

Ed Seykota is a genius and a great trader who has been phenomenally successful. When I first met Ed he had recently graduated from MIT and had developed some of the first computer programs for testing and trading technical systems. . . .Ed provided an excellent role model. For example, one time, he was short silver and the market just kept eking down, a half penny a day. Everyone else seemed to be bullish, talking about why silver had to go up because it was so cheap, but Ed just stayed short. Ed said, "The trend is down, and I'm going to stay short until the trend changes." I learned patience from him in the way he followed the trend.
Michael Marcus[31]

always alter them. Beyond that, even if you knew accurate balance sheet numbers, they can never help you determine when or how much to buy or sell. John W. Henry drives home the critical lesson:

". . . [P]olitical uncertainty is one reason why John W. Henry & Company, Inc. (JWH) investment decisions are not driven by discretionary judgements. How, for example, do you measure the impact of statements from Messrs. Greenspan, Rubin, Summers, Miyazawa, or Sakakibara? Even if JWH knew all the linkages between fundamentals and prices, unclear policy comments would limit our ability to generate returns...trying to interpret the tea leaves in Humphreys-Hawkins testimony or the minds of Japanese policy authorities does not lend itself to disciplined systematic investing. Instead of trying to play a losers game of handicapping policy statements our models let market prices do the talking. Prices may be volatile but they do not cloud the truth in market reactions. Our job is to systematically sift price data to find trends and act on them and not let the latest news flash sway our market opinions."[29]

You can't read tea leaves. John W. Henry can't. Ed Seykota can't. Nobody can. William Eckhardt, a longtime trend follower and former partner of trend follower Richard Dennis, builds off Henry's wisdom by describing how price is what "traders live and die by." The moment you add any other variables to the decision-making process, you've diluted price:

"An important feature of our approach is that we work almost exclusively with price, past and current . . . Price is definitely the variable traders live and die by, so it is the obvious candidate for investigation . . . Pure price systems are close enough to the North Pole that any departure tends to bring you farther south."[30]

How does a trend follower perceive the trading process? A well-known trend follower relates this story about trading sugar. He had been buying sugar—thousands of sugar contracts. Every day, the market was closing limit up. Every day, the market was going higher and higher. This trend follower just kept buying more and more sugar each day limit up. A broker was watching all this. One day the broker called after the market was closed because he had extra contracts of sugar that were not balanced out, and he said to this trend follower, "I bet you want to buy these other 5,000 contracts of sugar." The trend follower replied, "Sold."

Think about that: After the market has closed limit up for days in a row, this trader says, "Sure, I'll buy more sugar contracts at the absolute top of the market." Why is this an important lesson? Everybody instinctively wants to buy sugar on the dip. Let it come down low. Let me get a bargain. Trend Following works by doing the opposite, by buying higher prices.

Be less curious about people and more curious about ideas.

Marie Curie

Let's say you saw a stock go from 5 to 100. When it was at 5, you didn't know it was going to go to 100. And trend followers didn't know it was going to go to 100 either. But they were buying all along, *knowing* that it could go to 100 even though it might not. So did it make sense to miss out on this trade that went to 100 because you did not enter at 5? Would you have avoided the trade if you had had the chance to get in at 20 instead of 5? If you got in at 20 and it went to 100, you made a great trade. You can't time the trade. No one can pick a top or bottom.

Even Good Traders Confuse Price

The trading histories of Julian Robertson and Louis Bacon, two famous hedge fund managers, underscore the importance of price for decision making.

In the last few years, Julian Robertson shut his long running hedge fund down. He was a global macro trader who relied on fundamentals for decision-making. He had a close relationship with another global macro trader, Louis Bacon. Bacon is extremely secretive to the extent that it's nearly impossible to find out his performance numbers unless you are a client. We do know from the little bit of writing available on Bacon that he's pulled hundreds of millions, if not billions, of profit from the marketplace. While Bacon does not advertise himself as a trend follower, the following excerpt leaves no doubt that he is focused on price action just as much as John W. Henry:

"If a stock goes from 100 to 90, an investor who looks at fundamentals will think maybe it's a better buy," explains one source. "But with Louis [Bacon], he will figure he must have been wrong about something and get out." Contrast that, say, with [Julian] Robertson, who, even after shutting down his firm, was doggedly holding on to massive positions in such stocks as US Airways Group and United Asset Management Corp... [Bacon

The wisest Trend Follower we know has said that every 5 years some famous trader blows up and everyone declares Trend Following to be dead. Then 5 years later some famous trader blows up and everyone declares Trend Following to be dead. Then 5 years later . . . well, was the problem Trend Following or the trader?

[Trend Following] is similar to being long options because the stop loss creates a limited downside, and the continuation of the trend creates the large upside. This is why the phrase for this approach to trading is to 'cut losses' and to 'let profits run.' Of course, if trends continually fail to materialize, these limited losses can accumulate to large losses. This is also true for any option purchase strategy. For trend followers, the 'option premium' is 'paid' for after an unsuccessful trade is closed when a stop loss has been reached. The premium can also be 'paid' after markets have moved a great deal, profits have been made, and a reversal causes a trailing stop to be hit, and some of the profits reversed.

Michael S. Rulle,
President,
Graham Capital Management[34]

You will also find additional research from Duke University on our Web site, www.trendfollowing.com, that takes Rulle's point to an academic proof.

also offered] in a recent investor letter: Those traders with a futures background are more 'sensitive' to market action, whereas value-based equity traders are trained to react less to the market and focus much more on their assessment of a company's or situation's viability."[32]

Today, Louis Bacon is still trading and following the price. But Julian Robertson is out of the game, due in part, perhaps, to his refusal to accept "price" as his decision-making cue.

Trend followers are in the moment. They know that attempting to pinpoint the beginning of a trending market is futile. When trends begin, they often arise from a flat market that doesn't appear to be trending in any direction. The idea is to take small bets early on in a market to see if the trend does, indeed, mature and get big enough to make big money. How do Trend Following strategies succeed? Michael Rulle, President of Graham Capital Management and a trend follower, states:

"The ability of Trend Following strategies to succeed depends on two obvious but important assumptions about markets. First, it assumes that price trends occur regularly in markets. Secondly, it assumes that trading systems can be created to profit from these trends. The basic trading strategy that all trend followers try to systematize is to 'cut losses' and 'let profits run.'"[33]

We asked Charles Faulkner, a modeler of top traders and an expert in Neuro-Linguistic Programming, to expand upon this, at first glance, simple idea:

"Many traders have told me the first rule of trading is to, 'Cut your losses, and let your profits run.' And then, that it's the hardest thing to do. Seldom do any of them wonder why, and yet this is exactly where the efficient market hypothesis breaks down, and the psychological nature of the markets shows through. When we lose or misplace something we expect to find it later. The cat comes back. We find our car keys. But we know a dollar on the street will not be there with the next person who passes by. So experience teaches us that losses are unlikely and gains are hard. 'A bird in the hand is worth two in the bush.' This is when I tell them that they earn their trading profits by doing the hard thing—by going against human nature. This is where the discipline comes in, the psychological preparation, the months of system testing that give the trader the confidence to actually trade against his natural tendencies."

If cutting losses and letting profits run is the trend follower's mantra, it is because harsh reality dictates that you can't play the game if you run out of money. Nor can you predict the trend direction, as Christopher Cruden, Managing Director of the trend follower Tamiso and Co., points out:

"I would prefer to finish with a certain currency forecast, based upon my own fundamental reading of the market and one which underpins my personal investment philosophy . . . The only problem is I can't tell you when this will happen or which event will be first. On that basis alone, it seems best to stay with our systematic approach."[35]

Cruden knows a potential forecast will give uncertain investors a feeling of confidence, but he also knows forecasting is impossible. Why pretend?

A good example of not letting profits run can be seen in trading strategies that take profits off the table before a trend is over. For example, a broker revealed to us that one of his strategies was to ride a stock up for a 30 percent gain and then exit. That was his strategy. Let it go up 30 percent and get out. Sounds reasonable. However, a strategy that uses profit targets is problematic. The biggest problem is that it goes against the math of getting rich, which is to let your profits run. Trend followers ride trends as far as they can instead of taking their profits as soon as they make them. If you can't predict the end or top of a trend, why get out early and risk leaving profits on the table?

For example, you start with $50,000. The market takes off and your account swells to $80,000. You could, at that point, quickly pull your $30,000 profit off the table. Your misconception is that if you don't take those profits immediately, they will be gone. Refusing to risk those accumulated profits is a big mistake.

Trend followers realize that a $50,000 account may go to $80,000, back to $55,000, back up to $90,000, and from there, perhaps, all the way up to $200,000. The person who took profits at $80,000 is not around to take the ride up to $200,000. Letting your profits run is tough psychologically. But understand that in trying to protect every penny of your profit, you actually prevent yourself from making big profits.

In Patton my favorite scene is when U.S. General George S. Patton has just spent weeks studying the writing of his German adversary Field Marshall Erwin Rommel and is crushing him in an epic tank battle in Tunisia. Patton, sensing victory as he peers onto the battle field from his command post, growls, "Rommel, you magnificent bastard. I read your book!"

Paul Tudor Jones
as quoted in the Foreword to
The Alchemy of Finance

Are you a bull market baby? Can you survive in any situation?

Handling Losses

You are going to have ups and downs in your trading account. Losses are a part of the trading game. You're going to have losses with Trend Following:

"You can't make money if you are not willing to lose. It's like breathing in, but not being willing to breathe out."—Ed Seykota[36]

If you don't have losses, you are not taking risks. If you don't risk, you won't win big. Losses aren't the problem. It's how you deal with them. Ignore losses with no plan and they will come back to haunt you. Trend Following works to handle loss with stops. This sensible approach allows you to continue to trade:

"Theoretically, really big losses rarely befall a trend follower since he decides to eliminate or reverse his position as soon as the market goes against him. A lot of little losses are inevitable . . . The rationale for hanging in is that any price move could be the beginning of a trend, and the occasional big breakout justifies a string of small losses."[37]

Conclusion

A wise trend follower once told me a story about when he was in Bermuda, with a new trader who wanted to learn the "secrets." "Just give me the quick and dirty version," the neophyte said. The experienced trader took the newbie out to the beach. They stood there watching the waves break against the shoreline. The neophyte asked, "What's your point?" The old trader said, "Go down to the shoreline where the waves break. Now begin to time them. Run out with the waves as they recede and run in as the waves come in. Can you see how you could get into rhythm with the waves? You follow the waves out and you follow them in. You just follow their lead.

In our search for the facts about Trend Following, we learned that its basic tenets, its philosophical underpinnings, are relevant not only to trading, but also to our lives in general, from business to personal relationships. We also found in our conversations with the old pro trend followers that Trend Following works best when pursued with an unbridled passion.

How important is passion? Brett Steenbarger, Ph.D., an Associate Professor of Psychiatry and Behavioral Sciences at SUNY Upstate Medical University in Syracuse, NY, puts it in perspective:

"Find your passion: the work that stimulates, fascinates, and endlessly challenges you. Identify what you find meaningful and rewarding, and pour yourself into it. If your passion happens to be the markets, you will find the fortitude to outlast your learning curve and to develop the mastery needed to become a professional. If your passion is not the markets, then invest your funds with someone who possesses an objective track record and whose investment aims match your own. Then go forth and pour yourself into those facets of life that will keep you springing out of bed each morning, eager to face each day."[38]

Many people would sooner die than think; in fact, they do so.

Bertrand Russell

As we assembled *Trend Following*, we found that when used within the context of passion, the term "Trend Following" could also be substituted throughout for other activities in life. Our insight occurred when rereading this passage from a 1938 book on creative writing by Brenda Ueland:

"Whenever I say writing in this book I also mean anything that you love and want to do or to make. It may be a six act tragedy in blank verse, it may be dressmaking or acrobatics, or inventing a new system of double entry accounting . . . but you must be sure that your imagination and love are behind it, that you are not working just from grim resolution, i.e., to impress people."[39]

Among people who take the trouble to understand what the business is about instead of assuming it involves speculating on live cattle, it is readily understood.

Bruce Cleland,
Campbell and Co.[40]

Trend followers do not trade with grim resolve or with an intention to impress others. They are playing the game to win and enjoying every moment of it. Like other high level performers, such as professional athletes and musicians, they understand how critical it is to maintain a winning attitude if you want success.

Key Points

- Ed Seykota: "All profitable systems trade trends; the difference in price necessary to create the profit implies a trend."

- Trend Following is based on simple universal laws we can all learn.

- No one knows how high or how low a market will go. No one knows when a market will move. You can't undo the past, and

If you take emotion—would be, could be, should be—out of it, and look at what is, and quantify it, I think you have a big advantage over most human beings.
John W. Henry[41]

you can't predict the future. Prices, not traders, predict the future.

- Trend followers buy high and sell low. This is counterintuitive for most people.

- Using "common sense" is not a good way to judge or trade markets.

- Losses are a cost of doing business. No one can be right all the time. No one can make money all the time. Trend followers expect and handle losses with objectivity and detachment. If you don't have losses, you are not taking risks. If you don't risk, you won't win.

- Trend Following is a classic targeting of an opportunity. Bill Dunn, a trend follower for over 25 years, named one of his funds "T.O.P.S." for "targets of opportunity systems." Don't mistake Dunn's terminology. He is not predicting.

- Price must go either up, down, or sideways. No advances in technology, leaps of modern science, or radical shifts in perception will alter this fact.

A trend is a trend is a trend, Gertrude Stein would have said if she were a trader . . . Once you have a game plan, the differences are pretty idiosyncratic.
Richard Dennis[42]

- What if they told you that the best way to get to point B, without bumping into walls, would be to bump into the walls and not worry about it. Don't worry about getting to point B, but just enjoy bumping into the walls.[43]

- "If you take emotion-would be, could be, should be-out of it, and look at what is, and quantify it," says John W. Henry, pontificating from the owner's box at Fenway Park on a perfect Sunday afternoon, a bottle of spring water at his side, "I think you have a big advantage over most human beings."

Great Trend Followers

2

"Most of us don't have the discipline to stay focused on a single goal for
five, ten, or twenty years, giving up everything to bring it off, but that's
what's necessary to become an Olympic champion, a world class
surgeon, or a Kirov ballerina. Even then, of course, it may be all in vain.
You may make a single mistake that wipes out all the work. It may ruin
the sweet, lovable self you were at seventeen. That old adage is true:
You can do anything in life, you just can't do everything. That's what
Bacon meant when he said a wife and children were hostages to fortune.
If you put them first, you probably won't run the three-and-a-half-
minute-mile, make your first $10 million, write the great American
novel, or go around the world on a motorcycle. Such goals take
complete dedication."
—Jim Rogers[1]

The best way to understand Trend Following is not by only
reading formulas that make up the strategy, but by meeting the men
and women who use it. Investors today are reluctant to concede
that they might do better when it comes to their finances with some
mentoring or guidance. While they will sign up for a cooking course,
they won't take advantage of the wisdom of either their
predecessors or their peers about money. They prefer "reinventing
the wheel" to modeling their behavior after proven excellence.
However, since we consider role modeling to be critical to learning,
this chapter profiles excellent trend followers.

As observers of Trend Following, we've come to realize that if you take historical and current trend following performance data seriously, you must make a choice. You can accept the data as fact, make an honest assessment of yourself and your approach to investing, and make a commitment to change. Or you can pretend the performance data doesn't exist. If you think you're likely to make the latter choice, you'll want to reconsider whether Trend Following is for you.

Trend followers are generalists when it comes to their strategy. Tom Friedman, a noted author in the field of international relations, explains:

"The great strategists of the past kept forests as well as trees in views. They were generalists, and they operated from an ecological perspective. They understood the world is a web, in which adjustments made here are bound to have effects over there—that everything is interconnected. Where might one find generalists today? The dominant trend within universities and the think tanks is toward ever-narrower specialization: a higher premium is placed on functioning deeply within a single field than broadly across several. And yet without some awareness of the whole—without some sense of how means converge to accomplish or to frustrate ends—there can be no strategy. And without strategy, there is only drift."[2]

The men we profile see the whole. They see the connections. They also know themselves and how to separate their emotions from their financial decision-making. One of our favorite "Market Wizards," Charles Faulkner, explained to us how crucial it is to know who you are.

"Being able to trade your system instead of your psychology means separating your self from your trading. This can begin with your language. "I'm in the trading business" and "I work as a trader" are very different from "I'm a trader" or "I own a few stocks and bonds" (from a major east coast speculator). The market wizards I've met seem to live by William Blake's phrase, "I must make my own system or be enslaved by another's." They have made their own systems—in their trading and in their lives and in their language. They don't allow others to define them or their terms. And they are sometimes considered abrupt, difficult, iconoclastic, or full of themselves as a result. And they know the greater truth—they are themselves and they know what works for them."

Technical trading is not glamorous. It will rarely tell that you bought at the lows and sold at the highs. But trading should be a business, and a systematic program is a plan to profit over time, rather than from a single trade. High expectations are essential to success, but unrealistic ones just waste time. Computers do not tell the user how to make profits in the market; they can only verify our own ideas. We consider using a computer to develop trading programs to be a sensible, conservative approach.

Cognitrend GMBH

Bill Dunn

Who is Bill Dunn? He is a trend follower. He's made a fortune. And frankly, he doesn't care if you know who he is. He made 50 percent in 2002 when the majority of investors were losing big. He never hesitates to swing for the home run, for Bill Dunn, it can be all or nothing. He has produced 24 percent a year for 28 years. We started with a profile of Bill Dunn because his performance data is a clear, consistent, and *dramatic* demonstration of Trend Following.

Whenever you can, count.
Sir Francis Galton[4]

Bill Dunn is founder and chairman of Dunn Capital Management, Inc. In the spring of 2003, more than $1 billion was invested in his managed programs, and for good reason: During a period of spectacularly unimpressive stock market returns, Dunn Composite was up nearly 50 percent for the past 12 months. Bill Dunn is one of the purest trend followers ever, because he trades his trading system full throttle. Dunn Capital Management has no defined "target" per annum return for its clients (other than positive). There is nothing in Dunn Capital Management's risk management that precludes annual returns approaching 100 percent. There is no policy that if, for example, a Dunn Capital Management program were to be up 50 percent by mid-year that the company would "rest on its laurels," so to speak, and dial back trading for the rest of the calendar year. Further it is not surprising to see Dunn down 20 percent or more every three or four years, but whatever the level of volatility, this independent, self-disciplined long-term trend follower never deviates from his core strategy:

"We have a risk budgeting scheme that certainly was ahead of its time in 1974 and is still—in our opinion—state of the art in 2003."—Daniel Dunn, son of Bill Dunn and Executive Vice-President of Dunn Capital Management[3]

It may not be so difficult to believe that Bill Dunn *truly* adheres to the principles he set forth 25 years ago if you have read Jim Collins' latest work *Good to Great*:

"Essentially, whatever you find will be as true 10 years from now, 20 years from now, 30 or 50 years from now as it is today and as it was 50 years ago. And if you can put your finger on those truths, then you've made a contribution."[5]

Bill Dunn's contribution was made when he put his finger on "those truths" about Trend Following. He has always believed that in order to make money, you must be able to live with a certain amount of volatility. Clients who invest their money with Dunn Capital Management are required to make a serious financial commitment and must have absolute, "no questions asked" trust in Dunn's decision-making. This trend follower has no patience for anyone who questions his ability to sustain losses. He is not a role model for the faint-hearted. His "full throttle" approach has proven itself for 30 years, making Dunn himself and the clients of Dunn Capital Management rich.

His "risk budgeting scheme" or money management is based on objective decision-making. "Caution is costly" could be his motto. At a certain point he enters a market, and, if the market goes down, at a certain point he exits that market. To Bill Dunn, trading without a predefined exit strategy is a recipe for disaster.

Dunn's risk management system allows him to balance the overall volatility of his portfolio—something the average or even professional investor ignores. The more volatile a market, the less he trades. The less volatile a market, the more he trades. For Dunn Capital Management, if risk-taking is a necessary means to profit-taking, then position size should always be titrated to maintain the targeted risk constraint, which in turn should be set at the maximum level acceptable to the investor. Dunn Capital Management's system of risk management ensures that they exit a market when the trade goes against them:

"One of our areas of expertise in the risk-budgeting process is how risk is going to be allocated to say a yen trade and how much risk is going to be allocated to an S&P trade and what is the optimal balance of that for a full 22 market portfolio. The risk parameters are really defined by their buy and sell signals so it is just a matter of how much are you going to commit to that trade so that if it goes against you, you are only going to lose x%."—Daniel Dunn[8]

Extreme Performance Numbers

Like Bill Dunn, this chart (Chart 2.1) assumes an "in your face" attitude. The performance data compares the returns if you had hypothetically invested $1000 with Dunn Capital Management and $1000 with the S&P. The data demands a choice—either put your

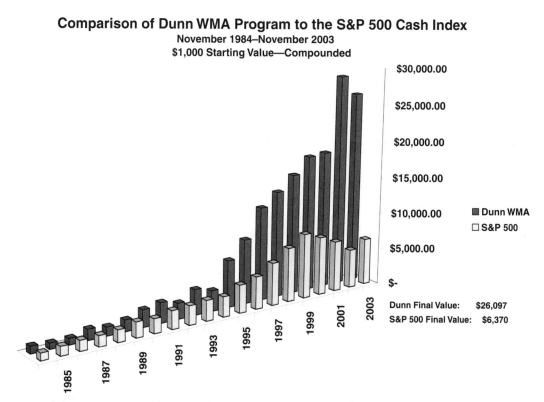

Comparison of Dunn WMA Program to the S&P 500 Cash Index
November 1984–November 2003
$1,000 Starting Value—Compounded

Dunn WMA
S&P 500

Dunn Final Value: $26,097
S&P 500 Final Value: $6,370

CHART 2.1: Dunn Capital Management: Composite Performance 1974–2003

money with Dunn Capital Management, learn to trend follow yourself, or pretend Trend Following does not exist.

How does Dunn do it? Here are two charts that reflect different periods of Dunn Capital Management's trading history, but tell the same story about Dunn's approach to trading. The first one (Chart 2.2) is the Japanese Yen trade from December 1994 to June 1996, where Dunn made a killing.

1995 was a great year for Bill Dunn. He made a fortune trading the Japanese Yen. In 2003, for the first time, he publicly walked through his thought processes—his Trend Following process—with an audience of investors, who came away with an invaluable lesson:

"This is 18 months of the Japanese Yen and as you can see it went up and down and there was some significant trends so we should have had an opportunity to make some money and it turns out we did. Since the WMA is a reversal system it's always in the market, it's either long or short, trying to follow and identify the

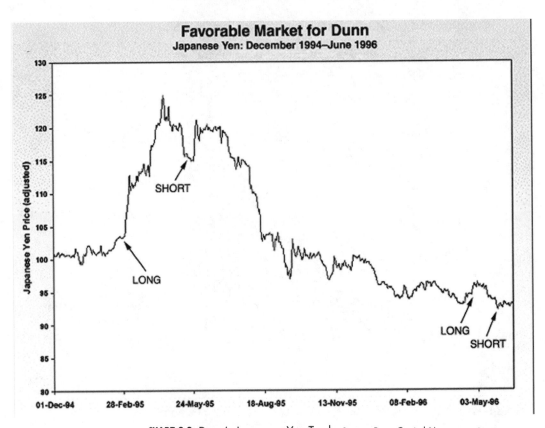

Favorable Market for Dunn
Japanese Yen: December 1994–June 1996

CHART 2.2: Dunn's Japanese Yen Trade *Source:* Dunn Capital Management

major trends. So while this is the first signal . . . that's shown on the chart and is long, we obviously must have been short coming in [to this] big rise. [The rise] was enough to tell us we should quit being short and start being long and it seemed like a pretty smart thing do . . . after we saw that [big rise up]."[9]

The beginning is the most important part of the work.

Plato

Dunn is riding the trend up that first big hill of the yen in March 1995. He is making his decisions within the context of his mechanical system. He continues:

"Then we have significant retracement which caused a short signal for the WMA program; our model has always incorporated near term volatility and this volatility [as we went long] was far less than the volatility that was going on [when we went short]."[10]

Dunn summarizes the trade:

"Now also because the volatility was very high here . . . this rise was—not enough to give us a long signal and as a result we rode this short position for nearly a year all the way down—where we got a long signal which was wrong and we reversed and went down to short. Now that was a very, very good market for our program, but some markets are not so good . . . "[11]

If you visit our Web site at *www.trendfollowing.com*, you can follow a link to listen to Dunn talk about this very yen trade. The confidence of his tone and delivery cannot be replicated in print.

Be Nimble

"The recent volatility in the energy complex has been quite exciting and potentially rewarding for the nimble."—Bill Dunn[12]

What exactly does Dunn mean by using the word "nimble"? He means he is ready to go. When an opportunity to get on a potential trend appears, he is prepared. He takes the leap. We see that he is nimble when, relying on his system, he reacts to the Japanese yen move with alacrity because he trusts his trading plan and his management of risk.

The second chart is the British pound (Chart 2.3) where, unlike the Japanese yen, the market proved unfavorable for Dunn. It was a typical whipsaw market, which is always difficult for trend followers because there is no clear trend. You can see how Dunn entered and was stopped out; then entered and was stopped out again. Remember, trend followers don't predict markets, they react to them—so the small losses were part of the game. He managed the small losses since the British pound was only a portion of his portfolio. His yen trade more than made up for his losses on the British pound trade, because, no matter how uncomfortable others are with his approach, for Bill Dunn, winners have always offset losers over the long run.

If you told Bill Dunn that his approach made you feel uncomfortable he would say:

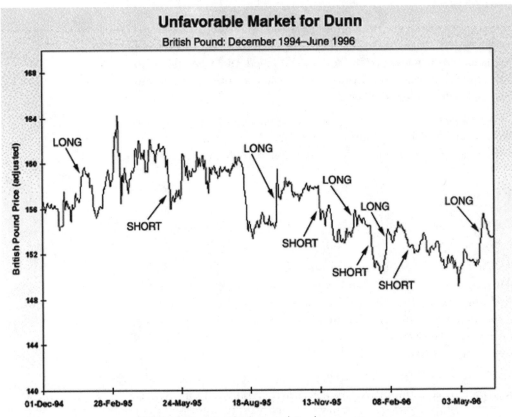

CHART 2.3: Dunn's British Pound Trade *Source:* Dunn Capital Management

"We don't make market predictions. We just ride the bucking bronco."—Bill Dunn[13]

Dunn's failed trades on the British pound—the up and down, go nowhere trend—is exactly what he means when he says, "We just ride the bucking bronco." In hindsight, you might be asking yourself why Dunn was trading the British pound if he was losing. The simple answer is that neither he nor anyone else could have predicted whether or not the British pound would be the next great home run. The real question is, "Do you stay out of the game because you can't predict how the game is going to unfold?"

About Bill Dunn

Now in his 60s, Bill Dunn grew up in Kansas City and Southern California. After graduating from high school, he served three years with the U.S. Marine Corps. In the ensuing years, he received a bachelor degree in engineering physics from the University of Kansas in 1960 and a doctorate in theoretical physics from Northwestern University in Chicago in 1966. For the next two years, he held research and faculty positions at the University of California and Pomona College. From 1968 to 1974, he worked for research organizations near Washington, D.C., developing and testing logistical and operational systems for the Department of Defense. Bottom line: Dunn enjoyed the "R&D" side of things, but also understood the real world's need for applications that worked. The markets are his real world.

Around the age of 35, Bill Dunn "got it." At the time he was working out of his home in suburban Fairfax, Virginia:

"In 1970, Dunn came across a newsletter touting a commodities trading system, 'which almost sounded too good to be true.' Upon testing it, that turned out to be the case . . . Using daily data, Dunn's system looked for big trends, as defined by a percentage of a price move from a recent low or high. It traded each market three to five times a year, automatically reversing if the trend moved in the other direction. [Dunn determined] position size by risking 2% to 6% of equity under management on each trade."[14]

It's not uncommon for great long-term trend followers to have trades in place for well over a year, hence the term "long." If you want day trading insanity or the feeling of exhilaration in Las Vegas, Dunn is not the person you should choose as a role model:

"Following his computerized trading system, Dunn holds long term positions in major trends typically trading only two to five times per year in each market. The original system was and still is a reversal system, whereby it is always in the market, either long or short. Dunn says he's held winning positions for as long as a year and half."[15]

Bill Dunn believed in his Trend Following system enough to start Dunn Capital Management the year before he made that initial 35 percent return. But he needed more capital to execute his particular plan of attack. He found it, in the person of Ralph Klopenstein: "Ralph Klopenstein . . . helped launch trading advisor William Dunn of Dunn Capital Management by giving him a $200,000 house account to manage. Dunn, a Defense Department systems analyst . . . realized his trading hobby would require a whole lot of other people's money to use a promising system he developed."[16]

I made the decision [to concentrate on managing money] four or five years ago when I realized that I would make far more money—with the skill set that I have—with a whole lot less work than with anything else," Pardo says. That is when he entered into a fee-sharing agreement with CTA Dunn Capital Management. Pardo calls his relationship with Dunn a match made in heaven. Dunn funds his CTA with the company's proprietary capital and does the execution and the paperwork. For that, they share in the fees and participate equally in the technology. It also frees Pardo to continue building models that Dunn can eventually use for excess capacity.[17]

Ed Seykota, another trend follower profiled in this chapter, is fond of pointing out that when you stop trying to please others and concentrate on pleasing yourself, you gradually become aware of what you are passionate about in life. And when that happens, all sorts of people will come out of the woodwork to help you achieve your goals. Dunn is proof positive.

Life at Dunn Capital Management

Several years ago, through family and friends' connections, a variation on "six degrees of separation," I had an opportunity to visit Stuart, Florida, and spend a day at Dunn Capital Management.

Bill Dunn's office is on a quiet street, located off a waterway in the heart of Stuart, Florida, a quiet retirement community 30 miles from West Palm Beach. Dunn shares the two-story white building with an assortment of doctors and other small business owners. There is no receptionist at Dunn Capital Management, so once you've entered the office, your only recourse is to saunter down a hallway to see if anyone is in. It feels more like an accountant's office than a high powered trading firm. In fact, the atmosphere is so casual and laid-back that there is no atmosphere. Dunn Capital Management is a shining example of why location, pretentious offices, and intense activity have little to do with over-the-top trading success.

There are only a handful of employees at Dunn because it doesn't take many employees to run his $1 billion-plus fund. Plus, these employees are not all traders, because the hardest thing to deal with when running a hedge fund is not the trading decisions, but the accounting and regulatory concerns. No one at Dunn Capital Management is tied to screens watching the market, because trades are entered only after an alarm at a lonely PC goes off indicating a buy or sell signal and thus the need to call a broker.

Another reason Dunn has so few employees is because he has a relatively few well-chosen clients. In fact, he's fond of saying, "If people want to invest with me, they know where to find me." Dunn Capital Management's investors benefit from the fact that there is no disconnect between its bottom line as a hedge fund manager and the investor's bottom line—to wit, trading profits.

Bill Dunn's fund is different because he compounds absolute returns. He leaves his money on the table by reinvesting in the fund. As a result, Dunn's trading capital is not only made up of recently added money from new clients but rather the result of systematically reinvesting profits over a long period of time. Dunn assumes his clients' trust. He will indulge clients only once when it comes to second-guessing or questioning Dunn Capital Management's investment strategies. After that he sends their money back.

Instead of looking for a quick hit, Dunn keeps a good portion of his clients' profits in the market. By focusing on profits and incentive fees, Dunn only makes money when the fund makes money. He doesn't charge a management fee. With no management fee, there is no incentive to constantly raise capital. The only incentive is to make money. If Dunn makes money he gets a portion of the profits. Compounding, or reinvesting your profits, makes sense if you're serious about making money, and Bill Dunn is serious.

Confidence comes from success, to be sure, but it can also come from recognizing that a lot of carefully examined failures are themselves one path to success.

Denise Shekerjian[18]

He's also direct. In the short time I spent with him, I was impressed with his matter-of-fact, "no b.s." attitude. He was polite without being effusive; interested without being encouraging. He was wearing a pair of khakis and a Hawaiian shirt, and he made it clear, since we both knew I was job-hunting, that he was looking for loyal soldiers who would stay for the long term.

No Profit Targets

Bill Dunn doesn't say to himself, "Okay, I want 15 percent a year." The market can't be ordered to give a trader a steady 15 percent rate of return, but even if it could, is a steady 15 percent the right way to approach trading in the first place? If you started with $1,000, what rate of return would you rather have over a period of three years? +15%, +15%, and +15% or the unpredictable -5%, +50%, and +20%? At the end of three years the first hypothetical investment opportunity would be worth $1520 but the second investment would be worth $1710. The second one would be a stream of returns representative of a Bill Dunn type trading style.

Profit targets imply a trader can predict the future. Profit targets are profit-limiting. Trend followers stay in the moment of now, avoid prognostication, and let markets run as far as they go.

Thomas Vician, Jr.
Student of Ed Seykota's

Trend followers have no desire to force some preconceived return. You can't dial in a certain amount return for some given year. There are no profit targets that work:

"We only have two systems. The first system is the one I started with in 1974. The other system, we developed and launched in 1989. The major strategic elements of these two models—how and when to trade, how much to buy and sell—have never changed in almost 30 years. We expect change. None of the things that have happened in the development of new markets over the past 30 years strike us as making the marketplace different in any essential way. The markets are just the markets. I know that is unusual. I know in the past five years a lot of competitors have purposefully lowered the risk on their models i.e. they are de-leveraging them or trying to mix them with other things to reduce the volatility. Of course, they have also reduced their returns."—Bill Dunn[19]

Dunn addresses a critical issue here: reducing risk to reduce volatility to appeal to nervous clients. The result is always lower absolute returns. If you remain fixated on volatility as your enemy, instead of correctly realizing volatility is the actual source of profit, you will never "get" Bill Dunn's game.

"Money management is the true survival key."

Bill Dunn[20]

Bill Dunn is one of the best at using risk management—more commonly called money management (see Chapter 10). His superior money management routinely allows him to score big. In June, 2002, Dunn Capital Management returned +24.26%, then followed with +14.84% for the month of July. By that time, he was up +37% for the same year in which buy-and-holders of the NASDAQ for this period were crushed. He finished 2002 up more than 50 percent.

How does Bill Dunn do it?

- **He cuts his losses.**
- **He never changes his core strategy:** His performance is not a result of human judgment. Dunn's Trend Following is quantitative and systematic, with no discretionary overrides of his system-generated trade signals. This is a foreign concept to those investors who watch CNBC for stock tips. His trading style doesn't drift.
- **Long-term holding:** For holding periods of approximately 3.75 years and beyond, all returns are positive for Dunn Capital

Management. Lesson? Stay with a system for the long haul and you do well. Quick hit traders and day traders suffer by jumping around, looking for the unreachable quick bucks.

- **Compounding:** Dunn compounds relentlessly. He plows profits back into his trading system and builds upon fresh gains.
- **Recovery:** Dunn had losing years of 27.1 percent in 1976 and 32.0 percent in 1981 followed by multiyear gains of 500 percent and 300 percent, respectively. You must be able to accept drawdowns and understand that recovery is, by the nature of trends, around the corner.
- **Going Short:** Dunn goes short as often as long. In general buy-and-holders never consider the "short side." If you are not biased to trend direction, you can win either way.

Drawdowns Are Part of Success

Dunn Capital Management has had its share of drawdowns as well as monster returns, but losses don't seem to bother the firm or its clients much. This may be because Bill Dunn's approach to losses is clear and calm:

"Some experience losses and then wait for gains, which they hope will come soon . . . But sometimes they don't come soon and sometimes they don't come at all. And [the traders] perish."—Bill Dunn[21]

But don't think for a second that you are not going to suffer pain, either by trading like Bill Dunn or letting Bill Dunn manage your money. Because drawdowns—a.k.a. your account going down—will make you feel like you need an extra dose of Prilosec.

Dunn Capital Management in Print

There are great lessons to be learned from the performance data of trend followers like Bill Dunn, but you can find equal insight from their writings as well. The Dunn Capital Management monthly newsletter adopts a brutally honest tone when communicating with clients, as evidenced by the following excerpts from monthly newsletters throughout the spring of 2003:[22]

1. "As global monetary, fiscal, and political conditions grow increasingly unsustainable, the trend-following strategy that DUNN steadfastly employs, may possibly be one of the few beneficiaries."

2. "The only thing that can be said with certainty about the current state of the world economy is that there are many large, unsustainable imbalances and structural problems that must be corrected. Perhaps the equity markets are correctly predicting a rapid return to more stable and prosperous times. Perhaps not. Regardless, there seems to be more than ample fodder for the creation of substantial trends in the coming months."

Change is not merely necessary to life—it is life.
Alvin Toffler

3. "It seems that Mr. Greenspan's twin bubbles, equities and housing, working along side the federal, municipal, and external deficits, will make the coming weeks and months more interesting than anyone may really care to witness. If this all seems a bit too grim, do not forget that California, on its own, would be the fifth largest economy in the world. Currently, the state has a thirty-three billion dollar budget gap, which seems almost certain to result in the peaceful overthrow of the state's chief executive in November. Also remember that the analysis presented here may be nothing more than an incorrect interpretation of the facts. On the truly bright side, it is comforting to know that the opinions expressed in this letter will have absolutely no bearing on the time-tested methods that DUNN uses to generate trading profits and manage risk."

We love the fact that even though Dunn Capital Management has strong political opinions, they know that their opinions mean zilch when it comes to properly trading the market. Their political and or economic opinions do not form the basis of when they decide to buy or sell.

Clients

Bill Dunn trades one way—his way. What problems can prevent clients from seeing Bill Dunn's way?

• Clients usually do not understand the nature of Trend Following. They will often panic and pull out just before a big move makes them a lot of money.

- Clients may start asking for the trader to change his approach. Although they may not have articulated this directly to the fund manager, they really wanted the Trend Following strategy customized for them before investing their money in the first place. The manager is then faced with a difficult decision: Take the client's money and make money through management fees (which can be lucrative) or trade their capital as originally designed. Trading a Trend Following system as originally designed is the optimal path in the long run.

If clients try to change or adjust how Dunn Capital Management trades, he either lets them go or doesn't take them on as a client in the first place:

"A person must be an optimist to be in this business, but I also believe it's a cyclical phenomenon for several other reasons. In our 18 years of experience we've had to endure a number of long and nasty periods during which we've asked ourselves this same question. In late 1981 our accounts had lost about 42% over the previous 12 months, and we and our clients were starting to wonder if we would ever see good markets again. We continued to trade our thoroughly researched system, but our largest client got cold feet and withdrew about 70% of our total equity under management. You guessed it. Our next month was up 18% and in the 36 months following their withdrawal our accounts made 430%!"—Bill Dunn[23]

This observation always made me wonder why Bill Dunn and Dunn Capital Management are not studied in MBA programs. Are Harvard MBAs aware of Bill Dunn when they graduate?

Passing the Torch

Daniel Dunn, son of Bill Dunn, first joined Dunn Capital Management as a programmer and analyst in 1975. He also earned a doctorate in immunology in 1988 and a medical degree in 1990 from the University of Chicago. Immunology has no apparent relationship to trading, but Daniel Dunn's background serves to reinforce the fact that Trend Following is a learnable science, as well as the old axiom that the apple doesn't fall far from the tree.

We are afforded a glimpse into how little is understood about Trend Following when Daniel Dunn was asked at a recent managed money conference (although it's hard to fathom how he could have kept a straight face) if he had a crystal ball projection for where the gold market was headed. He replied:

"Absolutely we have no crystal balls and anyone bringing one to work would be thrown out summarily."[24]

Why on earth would you ever even contemplate asking a trend follower, with such a publicly known tradition of not being able to predict anything, this question?

Check Your Ego at the Door

What is it like to work at Dunn? Dunn Capital Management recently posted a job wanted ad on the Monster.com job board. Part of it read:

"Candidates . . . must NOT be constrained by any active non-compete agreement and will be required to enter into a confidentiality and non-compete agreement. Only long-term, team players need apply (no prima donnas). Salary: competitive base salary, commensurate with experience, with bonus potential and attractive benefits, beginning at $65,000."[25]

Notice how Dunn says, "[N]o prima donnas." This man owns the vast majority of his company. He states, "[O]nly long-term team players need apply." In other words, readers of this ad can choose either to work for Bill Dunn or attempt to be Bill Dunn on their own, but they cannot have both. Trend Following demands taking personal responsibility for one's actions, and Bill Dunn makes it clear that he is responsible for Dunn Capital Management.

One of the interesting traits of the many trend followers we spoke with personally or observed from afar is their honesty. If you listen closely to their words and review their performance data, they are more than happy to tell you exactly what they are doing and why.

Key Points

- Bill Dunn's attitude captures the essence of Trend Following. His performance data is one of the clearest, most consistent, most dramatic demonstrations of Trend Following success available.

- Dunn Capital Management goes short as often as they go long.

- Dunn Capital Management's average rolling 60-month period has yielded a return of about 231 percent.

- For holding periods of approximately 3.75 years and beyond all returns are positive at the firm.

- Dunn Capital Management's designed risk is a 1 percent chance of a 20 percent or greater loss in a month.

- On a dollar-weighted composite basis, a hypothetical investment of $1000 in Dunn Capital Management from October 1974 through April 2003 would have grown to $439,004, a compound annual return of 23.72 percent after all fees and expenses. The S&P 500 grew to $38,119 over the same period.[26]

"Men's expectations manifest in trends."
John W. Henry[27]

John W. Henry

The performance data of Bill Dunn and John W. Henry show them to be trend followers cut from similar cloth. They are both astonishingly successful self-made men who started without formal association to Wall Street. They developed trading systems in the 1970s that have made them millions of dollars again and again. Their correlated performance data shows that they both trade for absolute returns and often trade in the same trends at the same time. Today, John W. Henry manages over two billion dollars in client assets.

John W. Henry's performance is listed in the following chart (Chart 2.4):

Another big winner was John W. Henry & Co.'s dollar fund, which returned 50% through the end of August, mostly by betting the dollar would weaken against the euro and the yen. "We really caught the trend from April through July when the dollar kept losing ground against other currencies," says Mark Rzepczynski, chief investment officer at Henry in Boca Raton, Fla. Both Rzepczynski and Dunn hope to profit from movements in global currencies and stock indexes as uncertainty continues over Iraq.[28]

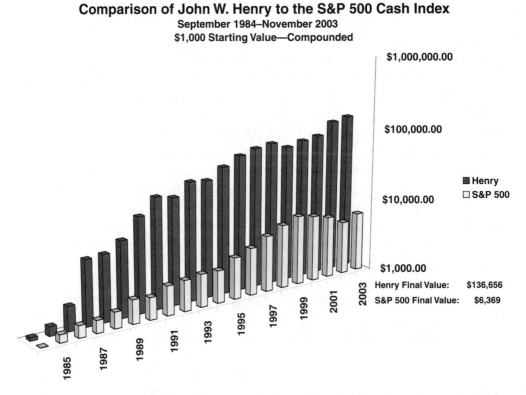

Comparison of John W. Henry to the S&P 500 Cash Index
September 1984–November 2003
$1,000 Starting Value—Compounded

Henry Final Value: $136,656
S&P 500 Final Value: $6,369

CHART 2.4: $1000 Growth of Financials and Metals as of September 30, 2003

John W. Henry has captured some of the great trends of our generation. By all available evidence, John W. Henry was on the other side of the Barings Bank blowout in 1995. In the zero-sum game, he won what Barings Bank lost. More recently, in 2002, Henry was up 40 percent while the NASDAQ was spiraling downwards. He, like Dunn, doesn't have a strategy that could be remotely considered "active or day trading," but when his trading system tells him, "It's time," he can literally blow the doors off the barn with spectacular returns in short order.

There are, of course, differences between Henry and Dunn. Bill Dunn manages the investments of only a few large clients, while John W. Henry has worked over the years with large brokerage firms like Morgan Stanley, who raise money from smaller retail clients. Over time, the differences in their client bases may have lessened, but the point is that trend followers may approach their businesses differently but still end with similar results.

You can't help but notice that, as the new owner of the Boston Red Sox, John W. Henry is now applying the basic tenets of Trend Following—simple heuristics for decision-making, mathematics, statistics, and application of a system—to the world of sports. Henry and baseball are connected clearly in Chapter 5.

Prediction Is Futile

"I don't believe that I am the only person who cannot predict future prices. No one consistently can predict anything, especially investors. Prices, not investors, predict the future. Despite this, investors hope or believe that they can predict the future, or someone else can. A lot of them look to you to predict what the next macroeconomic cycle will be. We rely on the fact that other investors are convinced that they can predict the future, and I believe that's where our profits come from. I believe it's that simple."—John W. Henry

Because Trend Following is primarily based on a single piece of data—the price—it can be difficult to paint the true story of what that really means. Henry is always able to articulate clearly and consistently how he trades, year after year to those willing to listen carefully. To generate his profits, he relies on the fact that other traders think they can predict where the market will go and often end up as losers. John W. Henry will tell you that he routinely wins the losses of the market losers in the great zero-sum trading game.

There is no Holy Grail. There is no perfect way to capture that move from $100/ounce to $800/ounce in gold.

John W. Henry[29]

About John W. Henry

John W. Henry was born in Quincy, Illinois to a successful farming family. For a midwest farm boy in the Fifties there was nothing in the world like baseball, and from the time nine-year-old John W. Henry went to his first major league game, he was hooked. In the summer, he would listen in rapt attention to the great St. Louis Cardinals broadcaster Harry Caray night after night. John W. Henry has described himself as having average intelligence but a knack for numbers, and like many young baseball fans, he crunched batting averages and ERAs in his head.

Henry attended community colleges and took numerous night courses, but never received his college degree. It wasn't for lack of

How are we able to make money by following trends year in and year out? I think it's because markets react to news, but ultimately major change takes place over time. Trends develop because there's an accumulating consensus on future prices, consequently there's an evolution to the "believed true price value" over time. Since investors are human and they make mistakes, they're never 100% sure of their vision and whether or not their view is correct. So price adjustments take time as they fluctuate and a new consensus is formed in the face of changing market conditions and new facts. For some changes this consensus is easy to reach, but there are other events that take time to formulate a market view. It's those events that take time that form the basis of our profits.

John W. Henry

interest, however. When he was attending a class taught by Harvey Brody at UCLA, they collaborated on and published a strategy for beating the odds at blackjack. When his father died, John took over the family farms, teaching himself hedging techniques. He began speculating in corn, wheat, and soybeans. And it wasn't long before he was trading for clients. In 1981, he founded John W. Henry and Company, Inc., in Newport Beach, California.[30]

If John W. Henry's first managed account was staked with $16,000 and he now owns the Boston Red Sox, don't you think the best question to ask is, "How?" John W. Henry & Co.'s president, Mark Rzepczynski, paints what appears to be at first glance a simplistic portrait depicting their firm's success:

"There has been surprisingly little change. Models we developed 20 years ago are still in place today. Obviously, we trade a different mix of markets. We've also added new programs over the last 20 years, but relative to many of our peers, we have not made significant adjustments in our trading models. We believe that markets are always changing and adjusting, and the information that's important to investors will also change. In the 1980s, everyone was interested in the money supply figures . . . everyone would wait by their phones until that number came out. In the 1990s, the information du jour was unemployment numbers. But people's reactions to the markets are fairly stable. Uncertainty creates trends and that's what we're trying to exploit. Even if you have better and faster dissemination of information, the one thing we haven't really improved is people's ability to process information. We're trying to exploit people's reaction, which is embedded in prices and leads to trends. These reactions are fairly stable and may not require major adjustments of models."[31]

Rzepczynski reiterates an important philosophical tenet of Trend Following: In looking at the long term, change is constant. And because change is constant, uncertainty is constant. From uncertainty, trends emerge. It is the exploitation of these trends that forms the basis of Trend Following profit. All of the cutting edge technology and news-gathering capabilities in the world are not going to help you trade trends. That stuff is white noise.

When I spoke with Mark Rzepczynski he offered insight regarding all aspects of the trading business at John W. Henry and Co.:

- "We stick to our knitting."
- "Most people don't have the discipline to do what they need to do.
- "We like to keep it sophisticatedly simple."
- "Our best trading days are when we don't trade."
- "We make more money the less we trade."
- "Some of our best trades are when we are sitting on our hands doing nothing."
- "We don't want to be the smartest person in the market. Trying to be the smart person in the market is a losing game."

We have made our business managing risk. We are comfortable with risk and we get our reward from risk.

John W. Henry[33]

Mark was not being flippant. He was direct and gracious. His tone was matter of fact. He wanted people to understand why John W. Henry and Co. does what it does. A few years ago, Mark gave a great analogy about the emotional ups and downs you must cope with to reach Trend Following success:

"Looking at the year as a mountain ride . . . Anyone who has ridden the trains in mountainous Switzerland will remember the feeling of anxiety and expectations as you ascend and descend the rugged terrain. During the decline, there is anxiety because you often do not know how far you will fall. Expectations are heightened as you rise out of the valley because you cannot always see the top of the mountain."[32]

Life is a school of probability.

Walter Bagehot[34]

A World-View Philosophy

Trend followers John W. Henry and Bill Dunn could not have developed their systems without first deciding how they were going to view the world. Each, through experience, education, and research, came to an understanding of how markets work before they determined how to trade them. What each of them found, separately, was that market trends are more pervasive than people think, and could have been traded in the same way 200 years ago as they are today.

John W. Henry spent years studying historical price data from the 18th and 19th centuries in order to prove to himself that there was only one successful way to approach trading. When he explains his investment philosophy, he is crystal clear about what it is and what it is not:

- **Long-term trend identification:** Trading systems ignore short-term volatility in the attempt to capture superior returns during major trending markets. Trends can last as long as a few months or years.
- **Highly disciplined investment process:** Methodology is designed to keep discretionary decision-making to a minimum.
- **Risk management:** Traders adhere to a strict formulaic risk management system that includes market exposure weightings, stop-loss provisions, and capital commitment guidelines that attempt to preserve capital during trendless or volatile periods.
- **Global diversification:** By participating in more than 70 markets and not focusing on one country or region, they have access to opportunities that less diversified firms may miss.

As we have seen, some traders dismiss Trend Following as simply predictive technical analysis. John W. Henry is not some "technical indicator guru" trying to make predictions:

". . . Trend followers like JWH don't try to anticipate reversals or breakouts. They respond to them. They are not prognosticators, 'Some people call what we do technical analysis, but JWH just identifies and follows trends. It's like, if you are in the fashion world, you have to follow trends, or you're yesterday's news.' But as with technical analysis, trend followers believe that markets are smarter than any of their individual participants. In fact, they make it their business not to try to figure out why markets are going up or down or where they're going to stop."[35]

John W. Henry's use of fashion as a metaphor for Trend Following hits the nail on the head and goes beyond the obvious comparison between trends in clothing and trends in markets. He explains that to be fashionable you have no choice but to follow stylistic trends of the moment. Likewise, trend followers have no choice but to react to trends, and like those who dictate fashion, successful trend followers are exploiting trends long before the general public seems to know they exist.

Trend followers would agree with H. L. Mencken when he said, "We are here and it is now. Further than that, all human knowledge is moonshine." They understand that attending to what is taking place in the market from moment to moment isn't a technique, it is what is and that is all. The moment, the here and now, is the only place that is truly measurable. John W. Henry demonstrates how he applies this philosophy in a past coffee trade:

"He strongly backs pure technical and mechanical trading. He zeros in on the folly of fundamental trading by telling a story about a coffee trade he made in 1985. All fundamentals were bearish: The International Coffee Organization was unable to agree on a package to support prices, there was an oversupply of coffee, and the freeze season was over in Brazil . . . his system signaled an unusually large long position in coffee. He bought, placing 2% of the portfolio on the trade. The system was right. Coffee rallied to $2.75 per lb. from $1.32 in the last quarter of the year, and he made a 70% return. 'The best trades are the ones I dislike the most. The market knows more than I do. The most opportunities are in areas that are not exploited.'"[36]

We don't predict the future, but we do know that the next five years will not look like the last five years. That just doesn't happen. Markets change. And our results over the next three years will not replicate the last three. They never do.

John W. Henry[38]

It's What You Think You Know That Gets You Into Trouble

Trend Following, culled down to its core essentials, is remarkably simple to explain. Henry points out that the complicated, difficult elements of Trend Following are not about what you must master, but what you must eliminate from your market view.

On why the long-term approaches work best over decades:

"There is an overwhelming desire to act in the face of adverse market moves. Usually it is termed 'avoiding volatility' with the assumption that volatility is bad. However, I found avoiding volatility really inhibits the ability to stay with the long-term trend. The desire to have close stops to preserve open trade equity has tremendous costs over decades. Long-term systems do not avoid volatility, they patiently sit through it. This reduces the occurrence of being forced out of a position that is in the middle of a long-term major move."[37]

On stocks:

"The current thinking is that stocks have outperformed everything else for 200 years. They may have a little relevance for the next 25 years. But there is no one in the year 2000 that you can convince to jettison the belief that 200 years of performance will not cause stocks to grow to the sky. Right now people believe in

Let's take a look at the type of markets we face around the world. There is a constant barrage of information; but often this information can be conflicting and, in some cases, does not come out with the frequency that we would like. For example, monetary policy can serve as a simple case. There are only a limited number of Fed meetings a year; however, this is supposed to help us infer the direction of interest rates and help us manage risk on a daily basis. How do you manage risk in markets that move 24 hours a day, when the fundamental inputs do not come frequently? In the grain markets, crop reports are fairly limited, and demand information comes with significant lags, if at all. How can this information be best incorporated in the daily price action? Under these types of conditions, simple approaches, such as following prices, may be better.

Mark S. Rzepczynski,
President & Chief Investment Officer,
John W. Henry & Co.[40]

data that supports the inevitable growth in prices of stocks within a new landscape or new economy. What will be new to them is an inevitable bear market."[39]

For all his talk about avoiding predictions, John W. Henry is making one here. He is predicting that stocks can't go up forever because eventually trends reverse themselves. He is also pointing out that as a trend follower, he will be prepared whenever they do to take action.

It Starts with Research

John W. Henry has influenced many traders. One of his former employees presented observations in his new firm's marketing materials:

- The time frame of the trading system is long-term in nature, with the majority of profitable trades lasting longer than six weeks and some lasting for several months.
- The system is neutral in markets until a signal to take a position is generated.
- It is not uncommon for markets to stay neutral for months at a time, waiting for prices to reach a level which warrant a long or short position.
- The system incorporates predefined levels of initial trade risk. If a new trade turns quickly unprofitable, the risk control parameters in place for every trade will force a liquidation when the preset stop-loss level is reached. In such situations, a trade can last for as little as one day.

This same former employee participated in a conference seminar while working at John W. Henry and Co. The conference was sparsely attended, and as happens when someone speaks to a small audience, the conversation became more informal and more revealing of the early years at John W. Henry and Company:

"We are very well aware of the trends that have taken place in the last 20 years and we are just curious to see are we in a period in this century that Trend Following seems to work? Have we lucked out that we happen to be in this industry during trends for the last decade or two? We went back to the 1800s and looked at interest rates, currency fluctuations and grain prices to see if there was as much volatility in an era that most people don't know much about as there has been this decade. Much to our relief and maybe also surprise, we found out that there were just as many trends, currencies, interest rates, and grain prices back in the 1800s as there has been exhibited this last decade. Once again we saw the trends were relatively random, unpredictable and just further supported our philosophy of being fully diversified and don't alter your system to work in any specific time period."

"Hours and hours were spent in the depths of the university library archives. They gave us Xerox burns on our hands, I think, photo copying grain prices and interest rate data. Not only in the U.S., but also around the world. We looked at overseas interest rates back to that time period. A lot of it is a little bit sketchy but it was enough to give us the fact that things really jumped around back then as they do now."[41]

It reminded us of the scene in the Wizard of Oz when Toto pulls back the curtain to reveal who the wizard really is. It was clear that there were no secret formulas or hidden strategies with John W. Henry. There were no short cuts. This was slow, painstaking trench warfare in the bowels of a library, armed only with a photocopying machine to archive price histories for their analysis.

Years later, I was inspired to do my own price data research. My objective was not to use price data at that time in a trading system but to see instead how little markets had changed. One of the best places to research historical market data in newspapers and magazines from over 100 years ago is the U.S. National Agricultural Library. Don't be misled by the word "Agricultural." You can review the stacks at this library and spend hours pouring over magazines from the 1800s. Like John W. Henry's firm, I discovered that markets were indeed basically the same then as now.

John W. Henry on the Record

John W. Henry spoke at an FIA Research Division Dinner held in New York City on April 20, 1995. This was only months after the Barings Bank debacle. During the Q&A moderated by Mark Hawley of Dean Witter Managed Futures (now Morgan Stanley), Henry revealed some of the qualities shared by all successful trend followers. This small excerpt from the post-dinner Q&A shows

We can't always take advantage of a particular period. But in an uncertain world, perhaps the investment philosophy that makes the most sense, if you study the implications carefully, is trend-following. Trend-following consists of buying high and selling low. For 19 years we have consistently bought high and sold low. If trends were not the underlying nature of markets, our type of trading would have very quickly put us out of business. It wouldn't take 19 years or even 19 months of buying high and selling low ALL of the time to bankrupt you. But trends are an integral, underlying reality in life. How can someone buy high and sell low and be successful for two decades unless the underlying nature of markets is to trend? On the other hand, I've seen year-after-year, brilliant men buying low and selling high for a while successfully and then going broke because they thought they understood why a certain investment instrument had to perform in accordance with their personal logic.

John W. Henry[42]

Henry at his best, full of grace and good humor. He refuses to waste time discussing fundamentals and offers a genuine appreciation of the nature of change:

Mark Hawley: The question that always comes up for technicians is: do you believe the markets have changed?

John W. Henry: It always comes up whenever there are losses especially prolonged losses. I heard it, in fact, when I started my career 14 years ago. They were worrying, "Is there too much money going into Trend Following?" You laugh, but I can show you evidence in writing of this. My feeling is that markets are always changing. But if you have a basic philosophy that's sound, you're going to be able to take advantage of those changes to greater or lesser degrees. It is the same with using good, sound business principles—the changing world is not going to materially hurt you if your principles are designed to adapt. So the markets HAVE changed. But that's to be expected and it's good.

Female Voice: John, you're noted for your discipline. How did you create that, and how do you maintain that?

Everything flows.

Heraclitus

John W. Henry: Well, you create discipline by having a strategy you really believe in. If you really believe in your strategy, that brings about discipline. If you don't believe in it, in other words, if you haven't done your homework properly, and haven't made assumptions that you can really live with when you're faced with difficult periods, then it won't work. It really doesn't take much discipline, if you have a tremendous confidence in what you're doing.

Male Voice: I'd like to know if your systems are completely black box.

John W. Henry: We don't use any black boxes. I know people refer to technical Trend Following as "black box," but what you have is really a certain philosophy of trading. Our philosophy is that there is an inherent return in Trend Following. I know CTAs that have been around a lot longer than I have, who have been trading trends: Bill Dunn, Millburn, and others, who have done rather well over the last 20 to 30 years. I don't think it's luck year after year after year.

Successful trend followers are often described as simply profiting from their "good luck," when in fact, it is not luck but discipline that enables them to win absolute returns. They don't have secret strategies or inside information. Their black box, if there ever was one, is price action.

What this transcript cannot recreate on the page is the audience's reaction. I remember looking around at all the John W. Henry fans jammed into that Wall Street hotel suite and thinking, "Everyone in this room is far more interested in viewing John W. Henry as a personality—a rock star—instead of figuring out what he does to make money." John is one of the best traders around. He is exceptional. But shouldn't the goal be to try and find similar success in whatever walk of life you pursue rather than only applaud John W. Henry's?

Change Is Overrated

Often more vocal than other trend followers, John W. Henry has been publicly forthright about Trend Following for years. For instance, his presentation in Geneva, Switzerland, could have been a semester course in Trend Following for anyone open to the message:

"We began trading our first program, the JWH Original Program, in 1981 and this was after quite a bit of research into the practical aspects of a basic philosophy of what drives markets. The world was frighteningly different in those days than it is today, when I was designing what turned out to be a Trend Following system. That approach—a mechanical and mathematical system—has not really changed at all. Yet the system continues to be successful today, even though there has been virtually no change to it over the last 18 years."[43]

We can't help but notice that the "we haven't changed our system" chorus is sung by not only Bill Dunn but John W. Henry and numerous other trend followers as well. And how does this timeless system work? Here is an example of a winning chart for Henry (Chart 2.5):

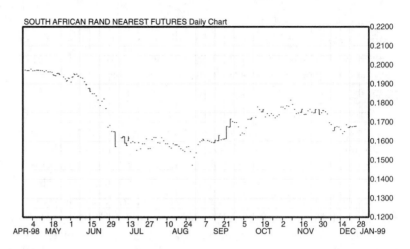

CHART 2.5: Henry's South African Rand Trade, 1998 *Source: Barchart.com*

"We took a position around March or April 1998 in the South African rand, short (which would be this particular chart, this is the dollar going up against the rand). You can see it takes time for these things and if you're patient, you can have huge profits, especially if you don't set a profit objective."—John W. Henry[44]

Moreover, just like Dunn Capital Management, John W. Henry did well in the 1995 Japanese yen (Chart 2.6).

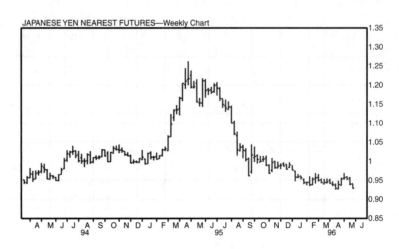

CHART 2.6: Henry's Japanese Yen Trade, 1994–1996 *Source: Barchart.com*

"You can see that in this enormous move, when the dollar/yen went from 100 to 80 in that particular month we were up 11% just in the Japanese yen that quarter."—John W. Henry[45]

Fade the Fed

The regular overreaction to Federal Reserve announcements, no matter how offhanded, is part of Wall Street life. Some so-called pros take the Fed's or Alan Greenspan's words and act on them even if there is no real way to know what any of it even means. Does it make logical sense to worry about what the Fed is going to do if there is no clear way to decipher their actions to begin with? The Fed, to the best of our knowledge, has never offered any statement you could rely on that would dictate, "Buy 1000 share of MSFT today."

I always know what's happening on the court. I see a situation occur, and I respond.

Larry Bird

John W. Henry and Dunn Capital Management's Trend Following systems are predicated on price action, not Greenspan's words. They are ready for a change in price at all times. A moving market has no impact if your trading style has been developed from the ground up to respond to change:

"I know that when the Fed first raises interest rates after months of lowering them, you do not see them the next day lowering interest rates. And they don't raise rates and then a few days later or a few weeks later lower them. They raise, raise, raise, raise . . . (PAUSE) . . . raise, raise, raise. And then once they lower, they don't raise, lower, raise, lower, raise, lower. Rather they lower, lower, lower, lower. There are trends that tend to exist, whether they are capital flows or interest rates . . . if you have enough discipline, or if you only trade a few markets, you don't need a computer to trade this way."—John W. Henry[46]

Henry makes it sound simple, doesn't he? That is because trading is generally explained in ways that make it sound harder than it needs to be. John W. Henry prepares for Fed actions, wars, rumors of war, elections, scandals, embargoes, treaties, droughts, floods, and market crashes—before they happen. Henry knows our minds can create anxiety by conjuring up terrifying future market scenarios, so he relies on his system to keep him focused in the present.

Key Points

- John W. Henry's first managed fund was staked with $16,000 in 1981. He now owns the Boston Red Sox baseball team.
- John W. Henry has a four-point investment philosophy: long-term trend identification, highly disciplined investment process, risk management, and global diversification.
- Henry understands change. This understanding gives him a distinct advantage.

Ed Seykota

"Win or lose, everybody gets what they want out of the market. Some people seem to like to lose, so they win by losing money."

Ed Seykota[47]

Fortune tellers live in the future. So do people who want to put things off. So do fundamentalists.

Ed Seykota[48]

Once you enter the world of markets and investing, you will eventually run across the book *Market Wizards* by Jack Schwager. Of all the trader interviews in *Market Wizards*, the most memorable is the one with Ed Seykota. While you may perceive Ed Seykota's manner as extremely direct, you will agree Seykota is unique in the way he thinks. One profound, and now famous, statement of his was, "[E]verybody gets what they want out of the market." This was a response to a question about trading, but we feel certain that Seykota would say it also applies to life.

Although almost completely unknown to both traders and laymen alike, Ed Seykota's achievements rank him as one of the best trend followers (and traders) of our time. I first met Ed Seykota at a small beachside cafe. I had received an invitation from Seykota to get together to discuss the outreach possibilities of the Internet. During our first meeting, he asked me what I thought Richard Dennis was looking for when he hired his student traders. My reply was to say I thought Dennis was looking for students who could think in terms of odds. Seykota's response was to ask me if my reply was my own thinking or something I was told by someone else. This was my first indoctrination to Seykota's "direct nature."

The following story passed along from an associate is "pure Ed Seykota":

"I attended a day long seminar in February 1995 in Toronto, Canada where Seykota was one of the guest speakers. The WHOLE audience peppered Seykota with questions like: Do you like gold?, Where do you think the Canadian $ is headed?, How do you know when there is a top?, How do you know when the trend is up?, etc. To each of these he replied: I like gold—it's shiny, pretty—makes nice jewelry or I have no idea where the Canadian dollar is headed or the trend is up when price is moving up, etc. His replies were simple, straight forward answers to the questions asked of him. Later I learned through the event organizer that a large majority of the audience (who paid good money, presumably to learn the 'secrets' of trading from a Market Wizard) were not impressed. Many felt they had wasted their time and money listening to Seykota. Seykota's message couldn't be clearer to anyone who cared to listen. The answers were found in the very questions each person asked. Don't ask: how do you know the trend is moving up?, instead ask: what is going to tell me the trend is up? Not: what do you think of gold?, instead ask: am I correctly trading gold? Seykota's answers effectively placed everyone in front of a huge mirror, reflecting their trading self back at them. If you don't even know the question to ask about trading, much less the answers, get out of the business and spend your life doing something you enjoy."[49]

How would you have reacted to Seykota's speech?

Pyramiding instructions appear on dollar bills. Add smaller and smaller amounts on the way up. Keep your eye open at the top.

Ed Seykota[51]

Performance Second to None

What are Seykota's performance numbers? "Seykota earned, after fees, nearly 60% on average each year from 1990 to 2000 managing proprietary money in his managed futures program."[50]

Ed Seykota is different than John W. Henry and Bill Dunn. He literally has been a one-man shop his entire career. There is no fancy office or other employees. He does not hold himself out as a public money manager and he is extremely selective of his clients. He doesn't really care whether people have money that they want him to trade or not. I've had the chance to review his monthly performance data for the decade of the 1990s. The month-by-month numbers are eye popping. Seykota takes big risks, and he gets big rewards.

About Ed Seykota

Edward Seykota was born in 1946. He earned his Bachelor of Science from MIT in 1969 and by 1972 had embarked on the trading career he pursues to this day—investing for his own account and the accounts of a few select others. Ed was self-taught, but influenced in his career by Amos Hostetter and Richard Donchian.

Early on Seykota was hired by a major brokerage firm. He conceived and developed the first commercial computerized trading system for client money in the futures markets. According to Jack Schwager's *Market Wizards*, he increased one client's account from $5,000 to $15,000,000 in just 12 years.

Ed Seykota once told me that he taught a college course in trading that lasted 10 weeks. He spent the first week of the class teaching basic information about trading. He then spent another week teaching the class Donchian's 5&20 trading system. However, he needed the remaining 8 weeks of the class to convince people to use the system he had taught—to get them to work on themselves enough to accept the losses that it would generate.

Van K. Tharp[53]

For the past few years, Seykota has worked from an office in his house on Lake Tahoe. His trading is largely confined to the few minutes it takes to run his internally written computer program, which generates trading signals for the next day. He also mentors traders through his Web site and his Trading Tribe, a widespread community of like-minded traders. He has served as a teacher and mentor to some great traders, including Michael Marcus, David Druz, Easan Katir and Jim Hamer. Seykota's Trading Tribe is discussed further in Chapter 6.

The Seykota "Secret"

Ed Seykota's style is direct. He enjoys debunking market ignorance with terse, Zen-like statements that force the listener to look inward:

"The biggest secret about success is that there isn't any big secret about it, or if there is, then it's a secret from me, too. The idea of searching for some secret for trading success misses the point."[52]

Ed Seykota's self-deprecating responses often emphasize process over outcome, but don't be misled by his modesty, because Seykota gets impatient with hypocrisy and mindlessness. He is a fearless trader and does not suffer fools gladly. Yet when he remembers his first trade, we see how early he uncovered his passion for what he does:

"The first trade I remember, I was about five years old in Portland, OR. My father gave me a gold-colored medallion, a sales promotion trinket. I traded it to a neighbor kid for five magnifying lenses. I felt as though I had participated in a rite of passage. Later, when I was 13, my father showed me how to buy stocks. He explained that I should buy when the price broke out of the top of a box and to sell when it broke out of the bottom. And that's how I got started."[54]

On how he first started trading:

"I saw a letter published by Richard Donchian, which implied that a purely mechanical Trend Following system could beat the markets. This too seemed impossible to me. So I wrote computer programs (on punch cards in those days) to test the theories. Amazingly, his [Donchian] theories tested true. To this day, I'm not sure I understand why or whether I really need to. Anyhow, studying the markets, and backing up my opinions with money, was so fascinating compared to my other career opportunities at the time, that I began trading full time for a living."[55]

Chauncey DiLaura brokered stocks for about 20 years when he met Ed Seykota in 1989. After attending some of Seykota workshops, he quit the brokerage business and started trading for his own account.[58]

Trading was in his blood at a young age: "So at age 23, I went out on my own with about a half-dozen accounts in the $10,000–25,000 range."[56]

Ed Seykota found an alternative to a Wall Street career built only on commissions. From the beginning, he worked for incentive fees alone. If he made money for his clients, he got paid. If he did not make money, he did not get paid. He shares in the profits only if money is made for the client account. Does your broker, mutual fund manager, or hedge fund work like that?

Amos Hostetter: "Never Mind the Cheese"

As a new trader, Ed Seykota passed through Commodities Corp, sort of a trader training ground, in Princeton, New Jersey. One of his mentors was Amos Hostetter. Amos Hostetter made phenomenal amounts of money trading. According to an article by Shawn Tully in *Fortune Magazine*, when a market's supply-and-demand prospects looked promising, Hostetter would put up one-third of his ultimate position. If he lost 25 percent of that stake, he'd get out. "Never mind the cheese," he'd crack, "let me out of the trap." But when the market swung his way, he'd add another third, taking a final position when prices climbed half as high as he thought they'd go. Hostetter's strategies were so successful that they were computerized so other traders could learn to duplicate his success.[57]

His "get out of the trap" strategies influenced many top traders of the last 30 years. Who else passed through Commodities Corporation? Traders with names like Paul Tudor Jones, Bruce

If a gambler places bets on the input symbol to a communication channel and bets his money in the same proportion each time a particular symbol is received, his capital will grow (or shrink) exponentially. If the odds are consistent with the probabilities of occurrence of the transmitted symbols (i.e., equal to their reciprocals), the maximum value of this exponential rate of growth will be equal to the rate of transmission of information. If the odds are not fair, i.e., not consistent with the transmitted symbol probabilities but consistent with some other set of probabilities, the maximum exponential rate of growth will be larger than it would have been with no channel by an amount equal to the rate of transmission of information.

J. L. Kelly, Jr[61]

Kovner, Louis Bacon, and Michael Marcus paid their dues at Commodities Corp. Interestingly, in the mid-1990s, long after the majority of the trend followers had moved on to their own firms, I visited Commodities Corporation's offices. Midway through our tour, we bumped into a stressed-out energy trader. After a few minutes of conversation, he and I began to chat about his trading style, which was based on fundamentals. Throughout our entire conversation, he was glued to the monitor. When I brought up Trend Following, he assured me that it did not work. I was surprised that a trader working for a famous firm, known for training brilliant trend followers, was completely blinded to even the possibility that Trend Following worked. I realized then that even the people closest to Trend Following may never have an appreciation for it.

Jay Forrester: System Dynamics

Along with Amos Hostetter, Jay Forrester, a professor of Seykota's at M.I.T., was a strong influence:

"One of my mentors, Jay Forrester, was a stickler for clear writing, a sign of clear thinking."[59]

Jay Forrester taught Ed about System Dynamics. "It is a method for studying the world around us. Unlike other scientists, who study the world by breaking it up into smaller and smaller pieces, system dynamicists look at things as a whole. The central concept to system dynamics is understanding how all the objects in a system interact with one another. A system can be anything from a steam engine, to a bank account, to a basketball team. The objects and people in a system interact through "feedback" loops, where a change in one variable affects other variables over time, which in turn affects the original variable, and so on. An example of this is money in a bank account. Money in the bank earns interest, which increases the size of the account. Now that the account is larger, it earns even more interest, which adds more money to the account. This goes on and on. What system dynamics attempts to do is understand the basic structure of a system, and thus understand the behavior it can produce. Many of these systems and problems which are analyzed can be built as models on a computer. System dynamics takes advantage of the fact that a computer model can be of much greater complexity and carry out more simultaneous calculations than can the mental model of the human mind."[60]

This type of thought process and computer modeling is not only a foundation of Seykota's success, but it can be seen across the trend following landscape.

Seykota.com

Seykota gives visitors ample amounts of wisdom and whimsy in answers to the emails he receives. Here are some examples of Seykota's "clear" responses, selected by both him and us from his website:[62]

"To avoid whipsaw losses, stop trading."

Lesson: You will have losses. Accept them.

"Here's the essence of risk management: Risk no more than you can afford to lose, and also risk enough so that a win is meaningful. If there is no such amount, don't play."

Lesson: Money management is crucial. This is reviewed in Chapter 10.

"Trend Following is an exercise in observing and responding to the ever-present moment of now. Traders who predict the future, dwell upon a non-existent place, and to the extent they also park their ability to act out there, they can miss opportunities to act in the now."

Lesson: All we have is now. It is much better to react to the fact of market movements in present time than a future time that doesn't exist.

"Markets are fundamentally volatile. No way around it. Your problem is not in the math. There is no math to get you out of having to experience uncertainty."

Lesson: You can crunch all the numbers you like, but your "gut" still has to handle the ups and downs. You have to live with and feel the uncertainty.

"I recall, in the old days, people showing a lot of concern that markets are different and Trend Following methods no longer work."

Lesson: Today or yesterday, skeptics abound. They sound like broken records in their desire to see trend following debunked.

"It can be very expensive to try to convince the markets you are right."

For a system trader it's way more important to have your trading size down than it is to fine tune your entry and exit points.

David Druz[63]

I'd say the most important benefit I attained from my time in the Incline Tribe was how I learned to incorporate my feelings around uncertainty into my trading. Ed and I worked on it until I finally got the Aha: that my need for uncertainty is a natural part of my emotional constitution. And if my clients don't eventually get it, I may need new clients, or they may need T-Bills. Their money-drama is not part of my system.

Michael Martin
Student of Ed Seykota's

Lesson: Go with the flow. Leave your personal or fundamental opinions at the door. Do you want to be right or make money? The losers profiled in Chapter 4 tried to convince everyone that they were right and lost big time.

"When magazine covers get pretty emotional, get out of the position. There's nothing else in the magazine that works very well, but the covers are pretty good. This is not an indictment of the magazine people, it's just that at the end of a big move there is a communal psychological abreaction which shows up on the covers of magazines.[64]

Lesson: Crowd psychology is real, and the price reflects all.

Seykota Students

Easan Katir: Seykota Student #1

Ed's track record is incredible, but one of his students, Easan Katir, offered us a warning when it comes to making comparisons:

"Journalists, interviewers and such like to hedge their praise and use phrases such as 'one of the best traders' etc. If one looks at Ed Seykota's model account record, and compares it with anyone else, historical or contemporary, he is the best trader in history, period. Isn't he? Who else comes close? I don't know of anyone. Livermore made fortunes but had drawdowns to zero. There are numerous examples of managers with a few years of meteoric returns who subsequently blow up. The household names, Buffet and Soros, are less than half of Ed's return each year. One might apply filters such as Sharpe ratios, AUM, etc., and perhaps massage the results. But as far as the one central metric—raw percentage profit—Ed is above anyone else I know, and I've been around managing money for 20 years."

Jason Russell: Seykota Student #2

Jason Russell of J. Russell Capital is a student of Ed Seykota's. He provided us a glimpse into the process of training with Ed:

"Through working with Ed I have learned many things in the past couple of years, one of the most important being: Apply Trend Following to your life as well as to your trading. Freeing yourself from the need to understand "why" is as useful when dealing with family, friends and foes as it is when entering or exiting a trade. It also has the added benefit of making you a much better trader."

Most traders cannot recognize how simple life really is. This is similar to what Russell describes as Seykota's view of simplicity:

"There is simplicity beyond sophistication. Ed spends a lot of time there. He listens, he feels, he speaks with clarity. He is a master of his craft. Before working with Ed, I spent years learning, reading, and earning various designations. All of this has been useful as it provides me with a high level of technical proficiency. However, somehow through this whole process, I have gained a strong appreciation for simplifying. Miles Davis was once asked what went through his mind when he listened to his own music. He said: 'I always listen to what I can leave out.' That sounds like Ed."

David Druz: Seykota Student #3

In a published interview, David Druz once described what it was like to work with Ed Seykota:

"It was one of the most incredible experiences of my life. He is the smartest trader I have ever seen. I don't think anybody comes close. He has the greatest insights into how markets work and how people operate. It's almost scary being in his presence. It was tough surviving working with him because of the mental gymnastics involved. If you have a personality weakness, he finds it—fast. But it's a positive thing because successful traders must understand themselves and their psychological weaknesses. My time with Ed was one of the greatest times of my life and gave me tremendous confidence—but I don't trade any differently because of it. A guy like Ed Seykota is magic."[65]

The difference between a successful person and others is not a lack of strength, not a lack of knowledge, but rather a lack of will.

Vince Lombardi

Ed would be the first to say that he is no magician. While it may be human nature to attribute phenomenal trading success to magical powers, Trend Following is really a form of trial and error. The errors are all the small losses incurred while trying to find those big trends.

Jim Hamer: Seykota Student #4

We asked yet another of Seykota's students for insight into his trading, but Jim Hamer, a trend follower based out of Williamburg, Virginia, felt it was important to tell us about Ed's life beyond the markets:

"I lived with Ed and his family for a little over two months in early 1997. One of the more amazing things I observed about Ed is that he has gifts in so many areas, trading being just one of them. He showed me a music video that he produced many years ago. It was an excellent production. He also recorded an album several years before the video. He is a very talented musician. My favorite song was "Bull Market" which he used to play for me on his acoustic guitar. During the time I was with him, he was very involved in

I cut my trading teeth during a year-long apprenticeship with Ed in 1994. The experience is invaluable to my subsequent trading success. Apprenticing with Ed is like getting a drink of water at a fire hydrant.

Thomas Vician, Jr.
Student of Ed Seykota's

experiments that attempted to redefine airflows as they relate to the Bernoulli Principle. He spent an enormous amount of time putting together academic papers and sending them to several experts in the field concerning this work. He is the consummate scientist. One day we took a 'field trip' to visit Ed's state legislator to discuss Charter School legislation and the impact on Ed's children and the students of Nevada. Not long after I left, Ed ran for the local school board. He has a keen interest in and knowledge of education. Ed Seykota will never be defined solely by trading. He has a love of learning and is a modern day Renaissance man."

Charles Faulkner, profiled in Chapter 6, once said to me that, in his opinion, if Seykota had wanted to stay in academia, he would have won a Nobel prize. However we both knew that Seykota would have abhorred life in an ivory tower. This is a man who relishes the here and now, where he can confront real problems and provide real solutions. He chooses to live his trading, not admire it. He has passion.

Key Points

- Ed Seykota: "Win or lose, everybody gets what they want out of the market. Some people seem to like to lose, so they win by losing money."
- Ed Seykota: "To avoid whipsaw losses, stop trading."
- Ed Seykota: "Risk no more than you can afford to lose, and also risk enough so that a win is meaningful."
- Ed Seykota: "Trend Following is an exercise in observing and responding to the ever-present moment of now."
- Ed Seykota: "Fundamentalists and anticipators may have difficulties with risk control since a trade keeps looking 'better' the more it goes against them."
- Ed Seykota: "Until you master the basic literature and spend some time with successful traders, you might consider confining your trading to the supermarket."
- Ed Seykota: "I don't predict a nonexisting future."

Keith Campbell

Considering he's one of the largest (in terms of client assets) and oldest trend followers, Keith Campbell and his company, Campbell and Company, are nearly nonexistent in terms of visibility. Do an Internet search and you'll find almost no information about their trading. You would think that with $5 billion in client capital (before leverage), Campbell & Co. would be as well known as Fidelity.

When you have a very reclusive trader, access to his monthly performance data since the mid-1970s makes up for the lack of information due to any self-imposed anonymity. The data (Chart 2.7) speaks the truth about the success of a trend follower such as Keith Campbell even if he's reluctant to do so.

You've got to have a longer perspective and confidence in the veracity of the approach that you're using.
Bruce Cleland,
President and Chief Executive Officer at
Campbell & Co. in Towson, Md.[66]

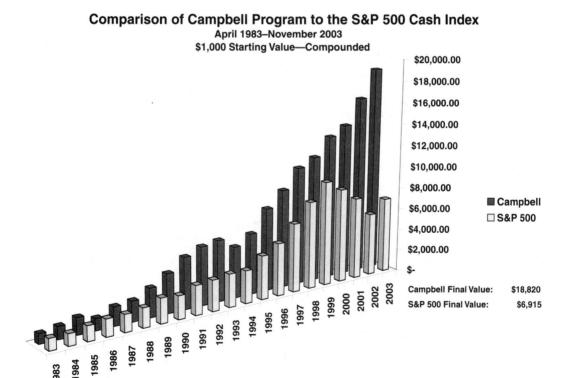

Comparison of Campbell Program to the S&P 500 Cash Index
April 1983–November 2003
$1,000 Starting Value—Compounded

Campbell Final Value: $18,820
S&P 500 Final Value: $6,915

CHART 2.7: Hypothetical $1000 Growth Chart for Campbell & Co.

About Keith Campbell

Measure what is measurable, and make measurable what is not so.
Galileo Galilei[67]

Perhaps one reason trend followers respect the unexpected is because many of them did not set out to become traders. When unexpectedly exposed to trading, they realized how well suited they were for the world of finance and eventually came upon Trend Following as their ideal strategy. In the 1960s, Keith Campbell took a job in California where he could both ski and surf. When his roommate moved out of their California apartment, Campbell advertised for a replacement and ended up with Chet Conrad, a commodity broker. In an interview, Campbell recalls that, "(Conrad) got me into trading as a customer. But he was always moaning he didn't have enough money to trade." In an interview, Campbell describes how, in 1971, he put together $60,000 from 12 investors to form his first futures fund with three advisors—a fundamentalist, a bar chartist, and a point-and-figure advocate. When that fund struggled, he started the Campbell Fund and then took it over on January 1, 1972. A few years later, Campbell and Conrad went their separate ways. Conrad relocated to Lake Tahoe, Nevada on a gutsy sugar trade that turned a borrowed $10,000 into $3 million. Campbell remained with his fund, which today is the oldest commodity fund still trading.[68]

There was a time when a lot of people thought that the models or algorithms that we used were king— that everything else was ancillary to the mathematics. I think today as an industry we have a much more realistic and a better balanced approach. The mathematics are very important, but it's only one piece of the puzzle. The most important thing overall is the total investment process, of which the signal generator is an important part. Portfolio structuring, risk management, execution strategies, capital management, and leverage management may not be directly connected to the algorithm that generates the buy and sell signals, but they are all hugely important.
Bruce Cleland,
President and CEO,
Campbell and Co.[70]

However, it is unfair to refer to Campbell and Co. as a "commodity fund" because Campbell trades more than just commodities. Jim Little of Campbell and Co. makes this clear when he describes the widely diverse markets they trade, which include stocks:

"We always are looking for non-correlated absolute return strategies that can produce higher quality risk adjusted returns; whether that is more managed futures strategy models or long/short equities or whatever. We have 30 years of experience doing long/short stock indexes, bond futures and currencies; to do it in individual equities (stocks) isn't that much different."

But, like John W. Henry, trading diverse markets doesn't translate into complicated trading strategies. Campbell also believes in keeping it simple:

"I'm very uncomfortable with black box trading where I'm dealing with algorithms I don't understand. Everything we do we could do on the back of an envelope with a pencil."[69]

Campbell's "back of an envelope" remark must be a revelation to those people who imagine trading to be wildly complex. The real story with Keith Campbell like other great trend followers is his discipline to stick to his rules in the toughest of times.

Campbell Compared to Benchmarks

While we are no proponent of benchmarking, the following chart (Chart 2.8) shows drawdown comparisons across asset classes:

CHART 2.8: Worst Case Cumulative Percentage Decline, Jan. 1972–Dec. 1995

- S&P–43% (12/72–9/74)
- Fidelity Magellan–63% (6/72–9/74)
- Campbell's Oldest Fund–36% (9/74–3/76)
- Lehman Brothers Government Bond Index–12% (1/94–10/94)

Many skeptics like to think trend followers are the only ones with drawdowns. The chart shows the truth of drawdowns across several indexes and fund types.

It is a fact that drawdowns happen. The key is to accept that and be able to manage them when they occur. Otherwise, you are left watching the NASDAQ drop 77 percent peak to trough over 2000–2002 with no plan on what to do next. Buy and hope?

Still, Keith Campbell's strategies are doubted by many on Wall Street, especially the "old guard," who like to point out how risky Trend Following is. Campbell refutes the notion that financial instruments such as futures are "risky":

"A common perception is that futures markets are extremely volatile, and that investing in futures is therefore very risky, much riskier than equity investments. The reality is that generally futures prices are less volatile than common stocks prices. It is the amount of leverage available in futures which creates the perception of high risk, not market volatility. The actual risk involved in futures trading depends, among other things, upon how much leverage is used."[71]

Campbell & Company analyzes only technical market data, not any economic factors external to market prices.[72]

Trend followers like Campbell manage their leverage precisely. Handling leverage is a crucial component of their risk management. It is part of the strategy that allows them to keep coming back day after day, year after year to trade and win. This is covered in greater depth in Chapter 10.

Correlation and Consistency

Most trend followers earn their returns at different times than common benchmark measures, such as the S&P stock index. Campbell (Chart 2.9), like John W. Henry & Company and other longtime trend followers, is not correlated with stock market indexes.

CHART 2.9: Correlation Analysis Between Campbell Composite and S&P 500 Index, Jan. 1980–Nov. 2003. Source: Campbell & Co.

Both Positive	96 of 287 Months
Opposite	150 of 287 Months
Both Negative	41 of 287 Months

Even more remarkable than his lack of correlation to the S&P benchmark, Keith Campbell's performance (Chart 2.10) is consistent over total months, total years, and 12-, 24-, 36-, 48-, and 60-month rolling time windows:

CHART 2.10: Past Consistency of the Campbell Composite, Jan. 1972–Nov. 2003 (estimates). *Source:* Campbell & Co.

January 1980–November 2003 (estimates)	Number of Time Periods	Number of Profitable Periods	Number of Unprofitable Periods	Percentage Profitable
Total Months	287	161	126	56.10%
Total Years	31	26	5	83.87%
12-Month Rolling Windows	276	217	59	78.62%
24-Month Rolling Windows	264	228	36	86.36%
36-Month Rolling Windows	252	226	26	89.68%
48-Month Rolling Windows	240	240	0	100.00%
60-Month Rolling Windows	228	228	0	100.00%

Are you any more knowledgeable about Campbell & Co. now? Qualitatively perhaps not, but quantitatively their performance "numbers" demonstrate, yet again, the validity of Trend Following.

Key Point

- Campbell & Co.: "Everything we do we could do on the back of an envelope with a pencil."

Jerry Parker

I first visited Jerry Parker's original office in Manakin-Sabot, Virginia in 1994. Manakin-Sabot is a rural Richmond suburb. It's in the "sticks." Why make that point? Because a few months before, I was in Salomon Brothers' office in lower Manhattan gazing across, for the first time, their huge trading floor, which seemed like the epicenter of all trading. The lightbulb went off when I saw Parker's unpretentious offices in Manakin-Sabot for the first time. You never would have guessed that this was where the thoughtful, laid-back CEO of Chesapeake Capital Management managed over $1 billion. For Jerry Parker, like Bill Dunn, trappings are meaningless.

Parker grew up in Lynchburg, Virginia, graduating from the University of Virginia. He was working as an accountant in Richmond when he applied to Richard Dennis' training program and was the first student Dennis accepted. Pragmatic and consistent, he went on to start his own money management firm, Chesapeake Capital, in 1988. He made the decision to risk less and make less for clients, so he took the turtle trading approach, a Trend Following strategy, and ratcheted it down a degree. In other words, he took a very aggressive system for making money and customized it to investors who were comfortable with a lower percentage of risk and lower returns.

Even though he was shooting for lower risk, he returned 61.82 percent on his money in one incredible year, 1993, that put his firm on the map (Chart 2.11). However, he is generally in the 12–14 percent return range today. His more conservative approach to Trend Following is different from Bill Dunn or Ed Seykota, for example, who have always developed their systems for absolute

Our trend-following methods do not pretend to determine the value of what we are trading, nor do they determine what that value ought to be, but they do produce absolute returns fairly consistently.

Jim Little,
Campbell & Co.[73]

Comparison of Chesapeake to the S&P 500 Cash Index
February 1988–November 2003
$1,000 Starting Value—Compounded

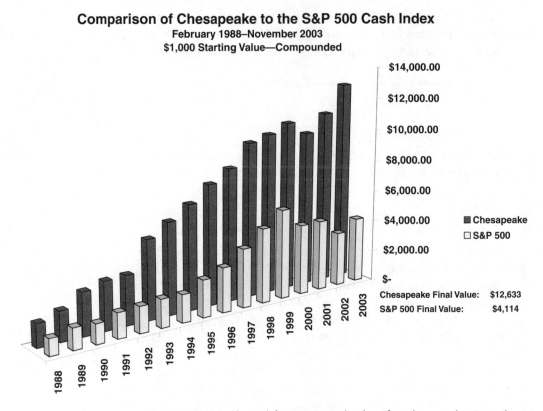

CHART 2.11: Hypothetical $1000 Growth Chart for Chesapeake Capital

returns. Parker does it a little differently, but no less successfully. I met Parker in 1995 and then again in early 2000 and walked away impressed each time at how straightforward and unassuming he was.

The Virginia Gentleman

Technical traders do not need to have a particular expertise in each market that they trade. They do not need to be an authority on meteorological phenomena, geopolitical occurrences or the economic impact of specific worldwide events on a particular market.

Jerry Parker[74]

In the Fall of 1998, Jerry Parker spoke at the annual Futures and Options Expo in Chicago. At the height of the dot-com bubble, Trend Following seemed stodgy, especially when the speaker was as self-deprecating and thoughtful as Parker. His address covered a full range of Trend Following philosophies. He left half his allotted time for Q&A, however, and this is where attendees were able to gain some insight into his firm's trading techniques. However skeptical Parker's audience, it did not prevent him from offering simple, direct, and solid advice about trading to those willing to accept it.

On the dangers of a buy-and-hold mentality:

"The strategy of buy and hold is bad. Hold for what? A key to successful traders is their ability to leverage investments . . . many [traders] are too conservative in their willingness to leverage."[75]

On the folly of predicting where markets may be headed:

"I don't know nor do I care. The system that we use at Chesapeake is about the market knowing where it's going."[76]

On his Trend Following trading system:

"This flies in the face of what clients want: fancy schools, huge research, an intuitive approach that knows what's going to happen before it happens, e.g., be overweight in the stock market before the rate cut. But obviously you can't know what's going to happen before it happens, and maybe the rate cut is the start of a major trend, and maybe it's o.k. to get in after. That's our approach. No bias short or long."[77]

On counter-trend or day trading:

"The reason for it is a lot of traders as well as clients don't like Trend Following. It's not intuitive, not natural, too long term, not exciting enough."[78]

On the wishful thinking of victims of recent market disasters:

"They said 'the market's wrong, it'll come back'. The market is never wrong."[79]

Ask yourself if you want to be right or do you want to win. They are different questions.

I participated in the Richard Dennis "Turtle Program." The methods we were taught and the trading experience received were all a technical approach to trading the commodity markets. The most important experience that led me to utilize a technical approach was the amount of success that I experienced trading Rich's system.

Jerry Parker[81]

Parker Downplays Intelligence

Trend Following success is much more predicated on discipline than pure academic achievement. Parker is candid about the intelligence required at his firm:

"We have a system in which we do not have to rely on our intellectual capabilities. One of the main reasons why what we do works in the markets is that no one can figure out what is happening."[80]

The best trend followers, such as Jerry Parker, are willing to admit that pure I.Q. is not the key. They also know that the latest news flash of the day is not information that figures into their decisions about when to buy, when to sell, or how much to buy or sell at any time:

"Our pride and opinions should not interfere with sound trading approaches."[82]

Parker has also trained and influenced other traders. For a great example of the Trend Following "under the radar" network in action, look no further than Jerry Parker's associate, Salem Abraham.

Salem Abraham:
Texas Pioneer

Salem Abraham does it differently than most trend followers. He truly proves physical location is meaningless for success:

"It would be hard to find a financial firm in the United States as removed from Wall Street, geographically and culturally, as the Abraham Trading Company. Housed in the same building where his grandfather, Malouf Abraham, once chewed the fat with local politicians and ranchers while building a sizable land-speculation business, the company has evolved into one of the nation's most unusual trading operations."[83]

It was while he was a student at Notre Dame University that Salem Abraham found he had a natural ability for and interest in trading. Like Greg Smith, one of Ed Seykota's students, he researched which traders were the most successful and discovered Trend Following. Abraham returned home to the family ranch in Canadian, Texas, after graduating and discussed the idea of trading for a living with his "Granddad," who cautiously agreed to help him get started. According to Abraham, he was to "try it out for six months," and then discard the idea ("throw the quote machine out the window") if he failed.[84]

There was no failure for Abraham. He quickly developed a Wall Street business in the most anti-Wall Street way. Abraham's culture is astonishingly different than what you might expect from a top trader:

"No one at the company has an Ivy League degree. Most of the employees at Abraham Trading have backgrounds working at the area's feedlots or natural-gas drilling and pipeline companies. Their training in the complexities of trading and arbitrage is provided on the job by Mr. Abraham, 37. "This beats shoveling manure at 6 in the morning," said Geoff Dockray, who was hired as a clerk for Mr. Abraham after working at a feedlot near Canadian. "The financial markets are complicated but they're not as relentless as dealing with livestock all the time."[85]

Abraham outlines his "meat and potatoes" approach to trading:

"The underlying premise of ATC's trading approach is that commodity interests will, from time to time, enter into periods of major price change to either a higher or lower level. These price changes are known as trends, which have been observed and recorded since the beginning of market history. There is every reason to believe that in free markets prices will continue to trend. The trading approach used by ATC is designed to exploit these price moves."[86]

When asked about his relationship with Jerry Parker, Abraham gave a terrific example of six degrees of separation:

"We do in fact know Jerry Parker with Chesapeake Capital. The shortest version I can give you is he is my dad's sister's husband's brother's daughter's husband. I'm not sure you can call that related but something like that. I first learned about the futures industry by talking to him while he visited in-laws in Texas."

Jerry Parker knows Abraham's age (and success) can cause problems:

"Sometimes people have a tendency to resent a young guy who's making so much money," said Jerry Parker, himself a hedge fund manager from Richmond, Virginia, who has been an investor in Mr. Abraham's fund for the last five years. "I just think he has a lot of guts."[88]

Here is Abraham's performance (Chart 2.12):

I think the only cardinal evil on earth is that of placing your prime concern within other men. I've always demanded a certain quality in the people I liked. I've always recognized it at once--and it's the only quality I respect in men. I chose my friends by that. Now I know what it is. A self-sufficient ego. Nothing else matters.

Ayn Rand[87]

Abraham Trading was up +74.65% for 2003.

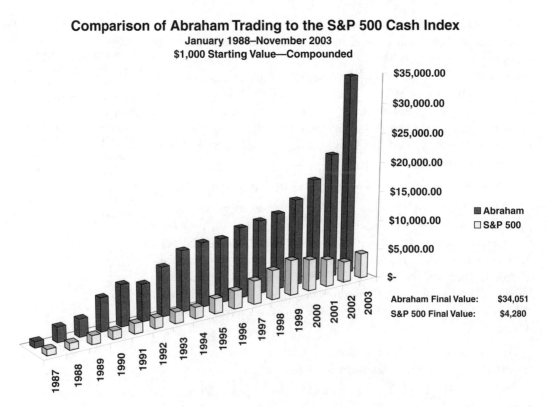

Comparison of Abraham Trading to the S&P 500 Cash Index
January 1988–November 2003
$1,000 Starting Value—Compounded

| Abraham Final Value: | $34,051 |
| S&P 500 Final Value: | $4,280 |

CHART 2.12: Hypothetical $1000 Growth Chart for Abraham Trading Company

If there is a lesson to be learned from Salem Abraham, it is simply that, if you want to become a trend follower, it doesn't hurt to get out there and meet the players.

Parker and Abraham are ultimately realists. They play the zero-sum game hard in different ways and excel at it, but they have also found a way to balance key components of their lives. Without compromising integrity, they have found a way to apply their trading philosophy and at the same time please demanding clients for the benefit of all.

Key Points

- Jerry Parker: "A key to successful traders is their ability to leverage investments . . . many [traders] are too conservative in their willingness to leverage."

- Jerry Parker: "A lot of traders as well as clients don't like Trend Following. It's not intuitive, not natural, too long term, not exciting enough."
- Jerry Parker: "The market is never wrong."
- Trend Following success is not predicated on academic achievement.

Richard Dennis

Richard Dennis is retired from trading. Unfortunately, his exit has been misinterpreted by some in the press as sounding the death-knell of Trend Following. It is true that Dennis' career had big ups and downs, but Trend Following itself is doing just fine.

Trading was even more teachable than I imagined. In a strange sort of way, it was almost humbling.
Richard Dennis[90]

Richard Dennis was born and raised in Chicago in close proximity to the exchanges. He began trading as a teenager with $400 saved from his pizza delivery job. Because he was too young to qualify for membership on the exchange, he would send signals to his father, who would do the actual trading. At 17, he finally landed a job in the pit as a runner on the exchange floor and started trading.[89]

Dennis' Students: The Turtles

Eventually, Dennis would achieve fantastic wealth with profits in the hundreds of millions of dollars. However, his real fame would come from his experiment in teaching trading to new traders.

In 1984 he made a bet with his partner William Eckhardt. Dennis believed that trading could be taught. Eckhardt belonged to the "you're born with it or you're not" camp. They decided to experiment by seeing whether they could teach novices successful trading. Twenty-plus students were accepted into two separate training programs. Dennis called his students "Turtles," after a turtle breeding farm he had visited in Singapore.

How did it start? Dennis ran classified ads saying "Trader Wanted" and was immediately overwhelmed by some 1,000 queries from would-be traders. He picked 20+ novices, trained them for two weeks, and then gave them money to trade for his firm. The new traders included two professional gamblers, a fantasy-game designer, an accountant, and a juggler. Jerry Parker, the former

I agree with the metaphysics of technical analysis that the fundamentals are discounted. You don't get any profits from fundamental analysis; you get profit from buying and selling. So why stick with the appearance when you can go right to the reality of price and analyze it better?

Richard Dennis[92]

accountant who now manages more than $1 billion dollars, was one of several who went on to become top money managers.[91]

While Richard Dennis appears to own the mantle of Trend Following teaching professor, there are many other trend followers, including Seykota, Dunn, and Henry, who have served as teachers to a number of very successful traders. Also keep in mind that not all the Turtles turned out to be winners. Once they left Dennis' tutelage and traded on their own, there were several Turtles who failed dismally. Their root problems were often poor personal discipline coupled with an incomplete understanding of the psychology needed to win. Perhaps, once some Turtles went out on their own, they could not cope without the safety net of being under Dennis' wing. Of course, Jerry Parker is a monster exception to this theory.

This is not a criticism of the system Dennis taught his students. It is rather an acknowledgement that some people could not stick with the trading system as it was taught them or perhaps were never really comfortable with it to begin with. In stark contrast, Bill Dunn was completely unknown to the general public when the Turtles burst onto the scene in the 1980s. Since that time, Bill Dunn has slowly and forcefully overtaken most, if not all, trend followers in terms of absolute performance. It would be a mistake if you called him a Turtle. You have to wonder if something about the initial small one-man shop of Bill Dunn set in motion the very habits that enabled him to roar past the Turtles that seemingly had the superior head start. For years many of the Turtles also refused to acknowledge they were even trend followers while Bill Dunn was always candid. Did the hype and mystery of the Turtles set forward in the Market Wizards books help most of them in the long run?

All this said, the story of the Turtles is so wide spread that the criteria Dennis used to select his students is still insightful.

Turtle Selection Process

Dale Dellutri, a former executive at Dennis' firm managed the Turtle group. He said they were looking for "smarts and for people who had odd ideas." Ultimately, they selected several blackjack players, an actor, a security guard, and a designer of the fantasy game Dungeons and Dragons. One of the ways they screened candidates was by having them answer true or false questions.

If you were a candidate faced with the question, "Do you favor being long or short, whichever you're comfortable with?" for example, you might have answered, "True," figuring that the statement reflected Dennis' approach. Or, you might have said, "Yeah, it makes sense that Dennis would think that on initiation I must know precisely at what price to liquidate if a profit occurs." Your answers would have been incorrect.

You might have figured that his strategy included rules like "one should trade the same number of contracts in all markets" or "when one has $100,000 to risk, one ought to risk $25,000 on every trade," or that traders can never go broke taking profits. You would have been wrong, however, since these statements are the wrong way to go about Trend Following.

It might make sense to you that Dennis would think a high percentage of trades should be profits and that needing and wanting money are good motivators to good trading. You might have even told yourself that Dennis follows hunches in trading. If you came to these conclusions, you wouldn't have been chosen, because they are all false.

On the other hand, if you were answering the questions and agreed that on initiation you probably should know precisely where to liquidate if a loss occurs or that ideally, average profits should be about three or four times average losses, you'd stand a chance, since these statements are true. You'd also be in the running if you supported Dennis' statement that a trader should be willing to let profits turn into losses and that he learns more from his losses than his profits.

Not all the questions were true or false. Dennis also asked candidates to write short paragraphs explaining why they would like to work for him, and how they once made a decision under pressure and why they made it. Candidates also had to describe something risky they did and why they took the risk. At first glance these questions might seem simplistic, but Dennis would not care what you think:

"I suppose I didn't like the idea that everyone thought I was crazy or going to fail, but it didn't make any substantial difference because I had an idea what I wanted to do and how I wanted to do it."[94]

Richard Dennis placed the passion to achieve at the top of his list. You have to wake up with that inner drive and desire to make

There's nothing quite as good or bad as trading. They give you a number every day. That's what's good about it, and that's what's bad about it. That's what makes it hard. That's what makes it worth doing.

Richard Dennis[93]

it happen. You have to go for it. Dennis also outlined the problem with profit targets (a key lesson taught to the Turtles):

"When you have a position, you put it on for a reason, and you've got to keep it until the reason no longer exists. Don't take profits just for the sake of taking profits."[95]

Dennis makes it clear that if you don't know when a trend will end, but you do know it can go significantly higher, then why get off?

Dennis, Clients, and Blowups

While some of his students have had successful money management careers (some not), Dennis seems to especially not do well when trading for clients. If Dennis just traded for himself, he might be fine (and much richer). His problems seem to arise when he trades for clients who do not truly understand the nature of Trend Following trading. His most recent stab at managing money for others, which ended in the fall of 2000, resulted in a compounded annual return of 26.9 percent (after fees), including two years when performance exceeded 100 percent. But, he stopped trading for clients after a drawdown in 2000. His clients pulled their money right before his trading would have gone straight up. Doubt us that he would have gone up? Use Dunn Capital Management, and just about any other trend follower, as a proxy and you will see what happened in the fall of 2000. If those impatient clients had stayed with Rich Dennis from the fall of 2000 to the present, they would have been richly rewarded far surpassing stock market buy and hold gains by comparison.

One of the biggest lessons a trader can learn is that trading for your own account and trading for clients are two different things. John W. Henry has said that it never gets easy losing money for clients. Traders who concentrate on expanding just their own capital often have a great advantage over money managers. Money managers must deal with the pressure and expectations of clients at all times.

There might have been other reasons for Dennis's problems beyond the pressure and expectations of his clients. For example, Dennis said that he could not program a computer if it walked in and bit him. He outsourced his programming, as many people do. But there is something to be said about knowing how everything under the hood works. Ed Seykota is generally acknowledged to have programmed the first computerized trading system. Bill Dunn and his staff wrote their original programming for their trading systems. In other words, there may be value in learning C++ if you are going to trade a trend following trading system.

Key Points

- Richard Dennis: "Trading was even more teachable than I imagined. In a strange sort of way, it was almost humbling."

- Richard Dennis: "When you have a position, you put it on for a reason, and you've got to keep it until the reason no longer exists. Don't take profits just for the sake of taking profits. You have to have a strategy to trade, know how it works and follow through on it."

- Richard Dennis: "You don't get any profits from fundamental analysis; you get profit from buying and selling."

Richard Donchian

The Father of Trend Following

While Richard Donchian is no longer with us, his influence resonates among trend followers. He is known as the father of Trend Following. His original technical trading system became the foundation on which later trend followers would build their systems. Where do you think the Turtle system evolved from? He is noteworthy among traders in general, as he was the originator of the managed money industry. From the time he started the industry's first managed fund in 1949 until his death, he shared his research and served as a teacher and mentor to numerous present-day trend followers.

About Richard Donchian

Richard Donchian was born in 1905 in Hartford, Connecticut. He graduated from Yale in 1928 with a BA in economics. He was so fascinated by trading that even after losing his investments in the 1929 stock market crash, he returned to work on Wall Street.

I don't think trading strategies are as vulnerable to not working if people know about them, as most traders believe. If what you are doing is right, it will work even if people have a general idea about it. I always say that you could publish trading rules in the newspaper and no one would follow them. A key is consistency and discipline.

Richard Dennis[97]

I became a computer applicant of Dick's (Donchian) ideas. He was one of the only people at the time who was doing simulation of any kind. He was generous with his ideas, making a point to share what he knew; it delighted him to get others to try systems. He inspired a great many people and spawned a whole generation of traders, providing courage and a road map.

Ed Seykota[98]

In 1930, he managed to borrow some capital in order to trade shares in Auburn Auto, what William Baldwin in his article on Donchian called, "the Apple Computer of its day." The moment after Donchian made several thousand dollars on the trade, he became a market "technician," charting prices and formulating buy and sell strategies without concern for an investment's basic value.[99]

From 1933 to 1935, Donchian wrote a technical market letter for Hemphill, Noyes & Co. He stopped his financial career to serve as an Air Force statistical control officer in World War II, but returned to Wall Street after the war and he became a market letter writer for Shearson Hamill & Company. Then, in 1960 he joined Hayden, Stone to become VP and Director of Commodity Research. He began to keep detailed, technical records on futures prices, recording daily price data in a ledger book. Barbara Dixon, one of his students, observed how he computed his moving averages, posted his own charts by hand, and developed his market signals—without the benefit of an accurate database, software, or any computing capability. His jacket pockets were always loaded down with pencils and a pencil sharpener.[101]

Much of Donchian's work went unnoticed by the numerous stars of finance that followed him. Dixon makes it clear that her mentor's work preceded and prefigured that of the academic theorists who developed the foundations of the modern theory of finance. Long before Harvard's John Litner published his quantitative analysis of the benefits of including managed futures in a portfolio with stocks and bonds, Donchian had made the exact same points in his weekly newsletter, *Trend Timing Comments*. Plus Donchian used concepts like diversification and risk control, key elements of modern portfolio theory that won William Sharpe and Harry Markowitz Nobel prizes in economics in 1990.[102]

Donchian: The Personification of Persistence

Was Donchian an "overnight sensation"? After 42 years, Donchian was still only managing $200,000, despite his detailed graphs of price charts for stocks and commodities. Then, in his mid-60s, everything came together, and a decade later, he was managing $27 million at Shearson/American Express. He was making $1 million a year in fees and commissions and another million in trading profits on his own money.[103]

Mid-60s? What patience and persistence! Like all the other trend followers, Donchian lauds the importance of price:

"Donchian doesn't predict price movements, he just follows them. His explanation for his success is simple and as old as the Dow Theory itself: 'Trends persist.' 'A lot of people say things like: 'Gold has got to come down. It went up too fast.' That's why 85% of commodities investors lose money,' he says. Donchian strives never to be distracted from his system. 'The fundamentals are supposed to be bullish in copper,' he says. 'But I'm on the short side now because the trend is down.'"[105]

Donchian's Student

Barbara Dixon was one of the more successful female traders in the business. Dixon graduated from Vassar College in 1969, but because she was a woman and a history major, no one would hire her as a stockbroker. Undaunted, she finally took a job at Shearson as a secretary for Richard Donchian. Dixon received three years of invaluable tutelage in Trend Following under Donchian. When Donchian moved to Connecticut, she stayed behind to strike out on her own in 1973. Before long, she had some 40 accounts, ranging from $20,000 to well over $1 million.

Dixon is still a devoted practitioner of Donchian's trading approach:

"I'm not a mathematician. I believe that the simple solution is the most elegant and the best. Nobody has ever been able to demonstrate to me that a complex mathematical equation can answer the question, 'Is the market moving in an uptrend, downtrend or sideways.' Any better than looking at a price chart and having simple rules to define those three sets of circumstances. These are the same rules I used back in the late 70s."[106]

Richard Donchian was, once again, ahead of his time when he taught the critical importance of fast and simple decision-making, a subject covered in Chapter 7.

In another published account, Dixon points out that a good system is one that keeps you alive and keeps your equity intact when there are no trends. She explains that the reason for any system is to get you into the market when a trend establishes itself. Her message is clear: "[D]on't give up the system, even after a string

I remember in 1979 or 1980 at one of the early MAR conferences being impressed by the fact that I counted 19 CTAs who were managing public funds, and I could directly identify 16 of the 19 with Dick Donchian. They had either worked for him or had had monies invested with him. To me, that's the best evidence of his impact in the early days. Dick has always been very proud of the fact that his people have prospered. He also was proud that after too many years in which his was the lone voice in the wilderness, his thinking eventually came to be the dominant thinking of the industry.

Brett Elam,
Elam Management Corp.[104]

Losing an illusion makes you wiser than finding a truth.

Ludwig Borne

of losses." She says that is important because that's just when the profits are due.[107]

Dixon doesn't attempt to predict price moves, nor expect to be right every time. They "hop on board" once a trend has begun, and let [their] profits run. She is clear that you can't attempt to forecast the top or bottom of a price move. You hope that it will continue indefinitely because you expect to make money over the long run, but on individual trades, you admit when you're wrong and move on.[108]

Today most people fixate on the new and fresh, yet we still find almost every word Donchian (or Dixon) wrote newer, fresher, and more honest than anything currently written under the heading of "finance" in today's print. Our favorite Donchian wisdom:

"It doesn't matter if you're trading stocks or soybeans. Trading is trading, and the name of the game is increasing your wealth. A trader's job description is stunningly simple: Don't lose money. This is of utmost importance to new traders, who are often told, Do your research. This is good advice, but should be considered carefully. Research alone won't insure a profit, and at the end of the day, your main goal should be to make money, not to get an A in How to Read a Balance Sheet."

Donchian's blunt talk may explain why Wharton's finance curriculum does not include mention of Bill Dunn, John W. Henry, Ed Seykota, Keith Campbell, Jerry Parker, or Richard Donchian.

Key Points

- Donchian's account dropped below zero following the 1929 stock market crash.
- He was one of the Pentagon whiz kids in World War II. He served as a cryptanalyst and worked closely with Robert McNamara during his Air Force tenure.
- Donchian did not start his Trend Following fund until age 65. He traded into his 90s. He personally trained legions in the art of Trend Following. He trained women at a time when women had little respect on Wall Street.
- Richard Donchian: "Nobody has ever been able to demonstrate to me that a complex mathematical equation can answer the question, 'Is the market moving in an up trend, downtrend or sideways.'"

Jesse Livermore and Dickson Watts

Ed Seykota found wisdom and inspiration through the work of Richard Donchian. Who else influenced trend followers? How long ago did this style of trading all start? Trend followers would point to Jesse Livermore, an early 20th century stock and commodity trader who was a trend follower before the term even existed.

Jesse Livermore was born in South Acton, Massachusetts in 1877. At the age of 15, he went to Boston and began working in Paine Webber's Boston brokerage office. He studied the price movements and began to trade on their price fluctuations. When Jesse was in his 20s, he moved to New York City to speculate in trading in the stock and commodities market. Over 40 years of trading, he developed a knack for speculating on price movements. One of his foremost rules was, "Never act on tips."

The unofficial biography of Jesse Livermore was *Reminiscences of a Stock Operator*, published in 1923. Written by journalist Edwin Lefevre, who readers reasonably assumed was a pseudonym for Livermore himself, *Reminiscences of a Stock Operator* has become a Wall Street classic. Numerous quotes from the book are so embedded in more than a century of trading lore that traders today do not have the slightest idea where they originated. We've selected a few of his great lessons:[109]

Can one know absolutely when price will trend? No. Does one have to know absolutely in order to have a profitable business? No. In fact, a great number of businesses are based on the probability that a time based series will trend. In fact, if you look at insurance, gambling, and other related businesses, you will come to the conclusion that even a small positive edge can mean great profits.

Chat Forum Post

1. "It takes a man a long time to learn all the lessons of his mistakes. They say there are two sides to everything. But there is only one side to the stock market; and it is not the bull side or the bear side, but the right side."

2. "I think it was a long step forward in my trading education when I realized at last that when old Mr. Partridge kept on telling the other customers, Well, you know this is a bull market! he really meant to tell them that the big money was not in the individual fluctuations but in the main movements— that is, not in reading the tape but in sizing up the entire market and its trend."

3. "The reason is that a man may see straight and clearly and yet become impatient or doubtful when the market takes its time about doing as he figured it must do. That is why so many men in Wall Street, who are not at all in the sucker class, not even in the third grade, nevertheless lose money. The market does

not beat them. They beat themselves, because though they have brains they cannot sit tight. Old Turkey was dead right in doing and saying what he did. He had not only the courage of his convictions but the intelligent patience to sit tight."

4. " . . . The average man doesn't wish to be told that it is a bull or bear market. What he desires is to be told specifically which particular stock to buy or sell. He wants to get something for nothing. He does not wish to work. He doesn't even wish to have to think. It is too much bother to have to count the money that he picks up from the ground."

5. "A man will risk half his fortune in the stock market with less reflection than he devotes to the selection of a medium-priced automobile."

We love volatility and days like the one in which the stock market took a big plunge, for being on the right side of moving markets is what makes us money," "A stagnant market in any commodity, such as grain has experienced recently, means there's no opportunity for us to make money.

Dinesh Desai[110]

Think about the wild speculation that took place during the dot-com bubble of the late 1990s, and then remember Livermore was referring to the market environment of 75 years ago.

Jesse Livermore did write one book himself: *How to Trade in Stocks: The Livermore Formula for Combining Time, Element and Price*. It was published in 1940. The book is rare and difficult to find. Livermore was by no means a perfect trader. He was not a role model. His trading style was bold and often extremely volatile. He went broke several times. He made and lost millions. That being said, his personal trading performance does not detract from the wisdom of his words.

Was Livermore the first trend follower? We doubt it. One trader who had an influence on Livermore was Dickson Watts. Watts was President of the New York Cotton Exchange between 1878 and 1880, a long time before the CNBC daily hype machine of today, yet his words are as relevant as ever:

"What is Speculation? All business is more or less speculation. The term speculation, however, is commonly restricted to business of exceptional uncertainty. The uninitiated believe that chance is so large a part of speculation that it is subject to no rules, is governed by no laws. This is a serious error. Let us first consider the qualities essential to the equipment of a speculator:

1. Self-reliance. A man must think for himself, must follow his own convictions. Self-trust is the foundation of successful effort.

2. Judgement. That equipoise, that nice adjustment of the facilities one to the other, which is called good judgement, is an essential to the speculator.

3. Courage. That is, confidence to act on the decisions of the mind. In speculation there is value in Mirabeau's dictum: Be bold, still be bold; always be bold.

4. Prudence. The power of measuring the danger, together with a certain alertness and watchfulness, is important. There should be a balance of these two, Prudence and Courage; Prudence in contemplation, Courage in execution. Connected with these qualities, properly an outgrowth of them, is a third, viz: promptness. The mind convinced, the act should follow. Think, act, promptly.

5. Pliability. The ability to change an opinion, the power of revision. 'He who observes,' says Emerson, 'and observes again, is always formidable.'

"The qualifications named are necessary to the makeup of a speculator, but they must be in well-balanced combination. A deficiency or an over plus of one quality will destroy the effectiveness of all. The possession of such faculties, in a proper adjustment is, of course, uncommon. In speculation, as in life, few succeed, many fail."[111]

Ultimately people want to know why does trend following keep working. Livermore's words from another time answer that question for our time:

"Wall Street never changes, the pockets change, the suckers change, the stocks change, but Wall Street never changes, because human nature never changes."

Key Points

- Trend followers are not lucky; they are consistently prepared.
- Trend followers take what the market offers in the moment. They don't predict the future.
- To make money, you must be able to live with and accept volatility.

Part II

Performance Data 3

Anyone can tell you they have a successful trading method or system, but ultimately the only objective measurement that matters at the end of the day is raw performance. Consider all of the presented data to be scientific proof of Trend Following. If a claim is to be made it must be supported. The numbers in this chapter and at our Web site, *www.trendfollowing.com* don't lie.

In reviewing the performance histories from the trend followers profiled in Chapter 2, we zeroed in on five key concepts that help explain the data:

1. Absolute Returns
2. Volatility
3. Drawdown
4. Correlation
5. Zero-Sum

Absolute Returns

An absolute return trading strategy means you are trying to make the most money possible without being limited to comparison to a typical index such as the S&P:

"An absolute return manager is essentially an asset manager without a benchmark. . .Bench marking can be viewed as a method of restricting investment managers so as to limit the potential for surprises, either positive or negative."—Alexander M. Ineichen[2]

Trend followers never attempt to track any particular index— ever. If trend followers like Bill Dunn, John W. Henry, and Ed Seykota had a coat of arms, "Absolute Returns" would be emblazoned upon it. They thrive and profit off the "surprises" that benchmarking so forcefully and artificially tries to stop.

Are all trend followers shooting for absolute returns? No, not all play the game full tilt. Jerry Parker, an exceptionally gifted trend follower, purposefully aims for lower returns to cater to a different client base. Although today Parker does trade some of his portfolios for absolute return as well.

This ain't clipping coupons. No risk, no return.

Anonymous

John W. Henry articulates the strong case for an absolute return strategy:

"JWH's overall objective is to provide absolute returns. JWH is an absolute return manager, insofar as it does not manage against a natural benchmark. Relative return managers, such as most traditional equity or fixed income managers, are measured on how they perform relative to some pre-determined benchmark. JWH has no such investment benchmark, so its aim is to achieve returns in all market conditions, and is thus considered an absolute return manager."[3]

Shoot for a benchmark in return, and you run with the crowd. The benchmark is a crutch for those who do not want to ponder alternatives. Benchmarks like the S&P make people feel safe, even if that feeling is artificial. Trend followers understand that trading for absolute returns and not from blind adherence to benchmarks is the best way to handle uncertainty:

"The concept of indexing and benchmarking is very useful in the world of traditional, long-only investing, but we believe that it has limited usefulness for absolute return investing. Again, it gets back to the notion of what it takes to achieve an absolute return—

portfolio managers need to have an enormous amount of latitude and freedom in the execution of their trading strategy to ensure capital preservation and achieve a positive return. At its core, this concept of absolute return investing is almost antithetical to benchmarking, which encourages traditional managers to have similarly structured portfolios and look at their performance on a relative basis. Frankly, the reason many hedge fund managers became hedge fund managers was to get away from the institutionally-driven, relative performance world, and into an environment where they could be judged by—and prosper from—their investing talents and profitability."[4]

If your trading strategy is based on benchmark comparisons, it won't matter whether you are a talented trader, since your decisions are limited to boundaries defined and set by the averages. Why would any trading skill be relevant?

Fear of Volatility; Confusion with Risk

There are organizations that rank and track trend follower's monthly performance numbers. One organization, International Traders Research (ITR), gives them a 'star ranking' (not unlike the more famous Morningstar):

The class of those who have the ability to think their own thoughts is separated by an unbridgeable gulf from the class of those who cannot.
Ludwig Von Mises[6]

"The quantitative rating system employed by ITR to rank and rate the performance of all commodity trading advisors (CTAs) rated in the database are relative to the performance of all other CTAs. Ratings are given in four categories: a) Equity, b) Performance, c) Risk exposure, and d) Risk-adjusted returns. In each category, the highest possible rating is five stars and the lowest possible rating is one star. The actual statistics on which the percentiles are based are as follows:

1. Performance: ROR

2. Risk: Standard Deviation

3. RiskAdj: Sharpe Ratio

4. Equity: Assets"[5]

Dunn Capital receives one star for "Risk," the implication being that an investment with Bill Dunn is risky. However, do these kinds of rankings really give us accurate information on Dunn Capital

Volatility is the tendency for prices to change unexpectedly. [1]

Management's risk? ITR uses standard deviation as their measure for "Risk." This is a measure of volatility and not risk. High volatility alone does not necessarily mean higher risk as a percent of equity traded.

It's doubtful that Bill Dunn is concerned about being unfairly penalized with such a measurement, but for someone who is accustomed to comparing traders by using standard deviation as a risk measurement, the story is inaccurate.

A great example of the star system weakness is demonstrated by the ranking of infamous former trader Victor Niederhoffer. At the time of Victor Niederhoffer's public trading demise in 1997 (more on Victor Niederhoffer's dance with the Asian Contagion in Chapter 4), he was rated as four stars for "Risk." Based on the past performance of Niederhoffer, the rankings were saying that he was a much "safer bet" than Dunn Capital Management. Obviously, the star system failed for people who believed Niederhoffer was less "risky." Standard deviation as a risk measure has done trend followers and anyone who wishes to learn about them or from them an injustice. One of our goals is to dispel the simplistic notion that Trend Following is "just risky" or that they "all have high standard deviations" which means they are "bad."

Where does proper analysis begin? Examine the following chart of various trend following performances from January 1993 to June 2003 (Chart 3.1):

CHART 3.1: Absolute Return: Annualized ROR (Jan. '93–Jun. '03)

Trading Managers	Annualized ROR	Compounded ROR
1 Eckhardt Trading Co. (Higher Leverage)	31.14%	1622.80%
2 Dunn Capital Management, Inc. (World Monetary Asset)	27.55%	1186.82%
3 Dolphin Capital Management Inc. (Global Diversified I)	23.47%	815.33%
4 Eckhardt Trading Co. (Standard)	22.46%	739.10%
5 KMJ Capital Management, Inc. (Currency)	21.95%	703.59%
6 Beach Capital Management Ltd (Discretionary)	21.54%	675.29%

CHART 3.1: Absolute Return: Annualized ROR (Jan. '93–Jun. '03) Continued

Trading Managers		Annualized ROR	Compounded ROR
7	Mark J. Walsh & Company (Standard)	20.67%	618.88%
8	Saxon Investment Corp. (Diversified)	19.25%	534.83%
9	Man Inv. Products, Ltd (AHL Composite Pro Forma)	17.66%	451.77%
10	John W. Henry & Company, Inc. (Global Diversified)	17.14%	426.40%
11	John W. Henry & Company, Inc. (Financial & Metals)	17.07%	423.08%
12	Dreiss Research Corporation (Diversified)	16.47%	395.71%
13	Abraham Trading Co. (Diversified)	15.91%	371.08%
14	Dunn Capital Management, Inc. (Targets of Opportunity System)	14.43%	311.66%
15	Rabar Market Research (Diversified)	14.09%	299.15%
16	John W. Henry & Company, Inc. (International Foreign Exchange)	13.89%	291.82%
17	Hyman Beck & Company, Inc. (Global Portfolio)	12.98%	260.18%
18	Campbell & Company (Fin. Met. & Energy—Large)	12.73%	251.92%
19	Chesapeake Capital Corporation (Diversified)	12.70%	250.92%
20	Millburn Ridgefield Corporation (Diversified)	11.84%	223.88%
21	Campbell & Company (Global Diversified—Large)	11.64%	217.75%
22	Tamiso & Co., LLC (Original Currency Account)	11.42%	211.29%
23	JPD Enterprises, Inc. (Global Diversified)	11.14%	203.03%

At some point, just saying a trader is volatile makes no sense if you look at the absolute return performance of Bill Dunn or John W. Henry (Chart 3.1). Raw absolute return must count for something.

However, volatility (what standard deviation really measures) is a four-letter word for most market participants. Volatility scares them silly, even though a freshman algebra student could quickly analyze any historical data series of any market or trend follower and see that volatility is to be expected, plenty of investors run away from even a hint of volatility. Of course, some markets and traders are more volatile than others, but degrees of volatility are a basic fact of life. To trend followers, volatility is the precursor to profit. No volatility equals no profit.

The press is also usually confused by the concept of volatility as seen in this excerpt from *Business Week*:

"Trend followers are trying to make sense out of their dismal recent returns. 'When you look past the superficial question of how we did, you look under the hood and see immense change in the global markets,' says John W. Henry's president. 'Volatility is just a harbinger of new trends to come.' Maybe. But futures traders are supposed to make money by exploiting volatility. Performance isn't a 'superficial question' if you were among the thousands of commodity-fund customers who lost money when the currency markets went bonkers."[8]

Unfortunately, this reporter is confused about volatility. High volatility doesn't necessarily mean high risk. Additionally, focusing on one time period in isolation while ignoring a complete performance history does not present the full picture. We wondered if he had written a follow-up article correcting his observations about Trend Following since the following year Bill Dunn produced a 60.25 percent return and Jerry Parker produced a 61.82 percent return. It didn't surprise us when our search of all *Business Week* articles revealed nothing remotely resembling a follow-up article or correction.

What Is Volatility for Trend Followers?

Some people suggested a few years ago that Trend Following had been marginalized. The answer is we haven't been marginalized—[Trend Following] has played a key role in helping protect a lot of people's wealth this year.

Mark Rzepczynski,
President and Chief Investment Officer
of John W. Henry & Co, 2003[9]

Nicola Meaden, a hedge fund researcher, compared monthly standard deviations (volatility as measured from the mean) and semi-standard deviations (volatility measured on the downside only) and found that while trend followers experience a lot of volatility, it is concentrated on the upside, not the downside.

Because, generally speaking, trend followers' volatility is consistently on the plus side, they are unfairly penalized by Sharpe Ratio aficionados. The Sharpe Ratio does not show whether volatility is on the plus or the minus side because it does not account for the difference between the standard deviation and the semi-standard deviation. The actual formula for calculating them is identical, with one exception: The semi-standard deviation looks only at observations below the mean. If the semi-standard deviation is lower than the standard deviation, the historical pull away from the mean has to be on the plus side. If it is higher, the pull away from the mean is on the minus side. Meaden points out the huge difference that puts Trend Following volatility on the upside if you compare monthly standard (12.51) and semi-standard (5.79) deviation.[10]

Here is another way of understanding upside volatility: Think about a market that is going up. You enter at $100 and the market goes to $150. But then the market drops down to $125. Should you panic? No. Because after going from $100 to $150, then dropping back to $125, the market then zooms up to $175. This is Trend Following volatility in action.

You entered at $100. Why are you feeling bad about yourself when your position is at $125, even though you got up to a high of $150? You are still up $25, right? Far too many investors get tied up in knots trying to control or constrain how your profits move forward. Everybody wants a trade that allows you to enter at $100 and be at $120 at the end of a year. Ideally, at the end of the second year it would be at $140. Then at the end of the next year it would be at $160; the next year at $180, and so on. The real world doesn't work like that. Your position may go from $100 to $150 to $125 to $175 to $225.

Trading is a zero-sum game in an important accounting sense. In a zero-sum game, the total gains of the winners are exactly equal to the total losses of the losers.[12]

Trend followers have greater upside volatility and less downside volatility than traditional equity indices such as the S&P, because they exit their losing trades quickly. This results in many small loses. On the other hand, trend followers stay with profitable trends for a long time, even if there is upside volatility. When trend followers do well, they make money in sudden bursts, hence the high upside volatility.

Michael Rulle, President of Graham Capital, adds:

"A trend follower achieves positive returns by correctly targeting market direction and minimizing the cost of this portfolio. Thus, while Trend Following is sometimes referred to as being 'long volatility,' trend followers technically do not trade volatility, although they often benefit from it."[11]

Invariably, the best trend followers are high volatility traders. High rewards come with high volatility. If you can stay price driven and react to the moment with a precise set of rules, there is no need to obsess on preserving open profits or engineering new ways to lower volatility. The question, then, is not how to reduce volatility, but how to manage it through proper investment size or money management.

That being said you must be accustomed to never seeing a smooth growth curve for your money. You will have to get used to riding the bucking bronco. Jerry Parker, John W. Henry, and Bill Dunn don't see straight up equity curves in their accounts either, so you are in good company.

John W. Henry makes the clear distinction between volatility and risk:

". . . Risk is very different from volatility. A lot of people believe there is no difference, but there's a huge difference and I can spend an hour on that topic. Suffice it to say that we embrace both volatility and risk and, for us, risk is that we're going to lose if we risk two tenths of one percent on a particular trade. That is, to us, real risk. Giving back a profit to you probably seems like risk, to us it seems like volatility."

Some people seem to like to lose, so they win by losing money.

Ed Seykota[14]

Henry's long-term world-view doesn't avoid high volatility. He patiently sits though it. The last thing he wants to experience is volatility forcing him out of a major trend before he can garner the big profits. Dinesh Desai, a trend follower from the 1980s who is now retired, was fond of saying that he loved volatility. He was clear that being on the right side of a moving market was the source of his profits.

But the skeptics mistakenly view high volatility, the engine that drives Trend Following's spectacular returns, as negative. For example, in the May 2001 *Managed Accounts Reports*, a fund manager who manages about $1.5 billion in assets remains on the sidelines refusing to believe in trend following:

"My biggest source of hesitancy about the asset class [Trend Following] is its reliance on technical analysis. Trading advisors do seem to profit, but since they rarely incorporate economic data, they simply ride price trends until they reverse. The end result of this crude approach is a subpar return to risk ratio." Another manager opines, "Why should I give money to a AA baseball player when I can hire someone in the major leagues?"[13]

How can one look at the absolute performance of Bill Dunn or John W. Henry and call it AA baseball? If you can get beyond the majority's irrational fear of volatility, you can learn when volatility really matters. Trend follower Jason Russell, President of J. Russell

Capital and student of Ed Seykota's, knows when volatility kicks in for him:

"Volatility matters when you feel it. All the charts, ratios and advanced math in the world mean nothing when you break down, vomit or cry due to the volatility in your portfolio. I call this the vomitility threshold. Understanding your threshold is important, for it is at this point that you lose all confidence and throw in the towel. Traders, portfolio managers and mathematicians seem well equipped to describe risk with a battery of formulas and ratios they use to measure volatility. However, even if you can easily handle the math, it can be a challenge to truly conceptualize it. The simple fact is that for the investor, the act of truly working through the thoughts and feelings that accompany losing money is hard. It is about as enjoyable as working through the thoughts and feelings associated with your death when preparing a will. There is no mathematical formula for vomitility because it is different for each person . . . For the [trader] who wants anything other than an interest-paying deposit at the bank, I think I can sum it up as follows: Surrender to the reality that volatility exists or volatility will introduce you to the reality that surrender exists."

If you were to put all the Trend Following models side by side, you would probably find that most made profits and incurred losses in the same markets. They were all looking at the same charts and obtaining the same perception of opportunity.

Marc Goodman
Kenmar Asset Allocation[16]

Drawdowns

With volatility comes the inevitable drawdown. "A Drawdown is any losing period during an investment record. It is defined as the percent retrenchment from an equity peak to an equity valley. A Drawdown is in effect from the time an equity retrenchment begins until a new equity high is reached. (i.e., In terms of time, a drawdown encompasses both the period from equity peak to equity valley (Length) and the time from the equity valley to a new equity high (Recovery).)"[15]

For example, if you start from $100,000 and drop to $50,000, then you are in a 50 percent drawdown. (You can also say that you have lost 50 percent.) Thus drawdown is a reduction in account equity.

Unfortunately, poorly educated clients and regulators have made drawdown a dirty word similar to how they vilify volatility. Traders are often forced to talk about their drawdowns in a highly negative manner, as if they must make excuses for these losses. Take this excerpt from Bill Dunn's marketing materials for example:

Dunn Capital Management's documents include a "summary of serious past losses." The summary explains that the firm has suffered through seven difficult periods of losses of 25% or more. Every potential investor receives a copy. Dunn says the summary communicates that this is what happened before and it will happen again. "If the investor is not willing to live through this, they are not the right investor for the portfolio," Dunn says."[18]

"Investors should be aware of the volatility inherent to DUNN's trading programs. Because the same portfolio risk profile is intrinsic to all DUNN programs, investors in any DUNN program can be expected to experience volatility similar to DUNN's composite record. During 26+ years of trading, the composite record, on a month-to-month basis, has experienced eight serious losses exceeding 25%. The eighth such loss equaled 40%, beginning in September 1999 and extending through September 2000. This loss was recovered in the three-month period ending in December 2000. The most serious loss in DUNN's entire history occurred over a four-month period which ended in February 1976 and equaled 52%. Clients should be prepared to endure similar or worse periods in the future. The inability (or unwillingness) to do so will probably result in serious loss, without the opportunity for subsequent recovery."[17]

Unless you truly understand how Dunn Capital Management trades, you might refuse to even consider investing with them, even though their 28-year track record is spectacular on an absolute return basis.

Obviously you don't want to over-haul a program in response to one year just because something didn't work. That's when you're almost guaranteed that it would have worked the next year had you kept it in there.

Examine the Dunn drawdown history (Chart 3.2):

*James Klingler
Eclipse Capital
MAR, April 2002, Issue No. 278*

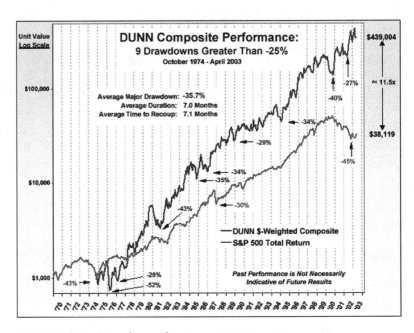

CHART 3.2: Dunn Drawdown Chart. *Source:* Dunn Capital Management

Imagine that the valleys between the peaks are filled with water. First, place a piece of paper over the chart and then very slowly move the paper to the right and uncover the chart. Imagine that you have made a very large investment in the fund. How do you feel as you move the page? How long can you remain underwater? How deep can you dive? Do you pull out the calculator and figure out what you could have earned at the bank? Do you figure out that you lost enough to buy a vacation, car, house, castle or perhaps solve the hunger crisis in a small country?

To the smart investor, the Dunn drawdown chart (Chart 3.2) is entirely acceptable because of his absolute returns over the long term, but of course that doesn't make these numbers necessarily easy to live with.

A proper discussion of drawdown and Trend Following must lead to the recovery process (which means bringing your capital to the point where your drawdown first started). Historically, trend followers quickly make money back during their recovery from drawdown.

The 25 or 50 biggest trend followers are essentially going to make money in the same places. What differentiates them from one another are portfolio and risk management.[19]

However, we must not neglect the math associated with losing money and then making it back. What if you start with $100 and it drops to $50. You are now in a 50 percent drawdown. How much do you have to make just to get back to break-even (Chart 3.3)? 100 percent. That's right, when you go down 50 percent, you need to make 100 percent to get back to break-even.

Notice that as your drawdown increases (Chart 3.3), the percent gain necessary to recover to the breakeven point increases at a much faster rate. Trend followers live with this chart day in and day out. Their strategy is designed with these numbers in mind.

CHART 3.3: Drawdown Recovery Chart

Size of drawdown	Percent gain to recover
5%	5.3%
10%	11.1%
15%	17.6%
20%	25.0%
25%	33.3%
30%	42.9%

CHART 3.3: Drawdown Recovery Chart Continued

Size of drawdown	Percent gain to recover
40%	66.7%
50%	100%
60%	150%
70%	233%
80%	400%
90%	900%
100%	Ruin

We have not made any changes because of a drawdown. While we have made minor changes since the program started trading in 1974, over the course of the years the basic concepts have never changed. The majority of the trading parameters and the buy and sell signals largely have remained the same.

Bill Dunn[21]

Unfortunately, the investment community uses drawdown numbers to paint an incomplete and unfair picture of Trend Following. David Harding of Winton Capital offered us insight.

"A key measure of track record quality and strategy "riskiness" in the managed futures industry is drawdown, which measures the decline in net asset value from the historic high point. Under the Commodity Futures Trading Commission's mandatory disclosure regime, managed futures advisors are obliged to disclose as part of their capsule performance record their 'worst peak-to-valley drawdown.' As a description of an aspect of historical performance, drawdown has one key positive attribute: it refers to a physical reality, and as such it is less abstract than concepts such as volatility. It represents the amount by which you are less well off than you were; or, put differently, it measures the magnitude of the loss an investor could have incurred by investing with the manager in the past. Managers are obliged to wear their worst historical drawdown like a scarlet letter for the rest of their lives."[20]

We recognize that traders must wear their worst drawdowns like a scarlet letter, but if the entire story of an absolute return trading strategy such as Trend Following is revealed, no one need ever fear a drawdown. For example, here is John W. Henry's drawdown and recovery in action (Chart 3.4):

CHART 3.4: JWH Financial and Metals Portfolio, Jan. 1, 1989 through Oct. 31, 1999

Source: John W. Henry and Company[22]

	-10% or More	-15% or More	-20% or More	-25% or More	-30% or More
# Month-End Occurrences	28	18	10	7	3
Average Drawdown	-19.7%	-24.0%	-29.2%	-31.7%	-37.5%
# Profitable 12 Months Later	25	17	All	All	All
Average Profit 12 Months Later	+52.4%	+58.6%	+73.5%	+74.8%	+96.1%
Average Time to New Peak through Trough	4 months	4 months	4 months	4 months	4 months

Henry's historical recovery bolsters our words with cold, hard numbers. But there is no getting around it: You can't eliminate catastrophic risk, much less drawdowns, from your trading. But you can manage drawdowns with Trend Following techniques.

Interestingly, there is another perspective on drawdowns that few people consider. When you look at Trend Following performance data—for example, Bill Dunn's track record—you can't help but notice that some times for becoming an investor in Dunn Capital Management are better than others.

Smart clients of Bill Dunn will look at the performance chart of Dunn Capital Management and buy in when the fund is experiencing a drawdown. Why? Because if Dunn is down 30 percent, and you know from your analysis of his past performance data that his recovery from drawdowns is typically quick and impressive, then why not "buy" Bill Dunn while he is on sale? This is commonly referred to as equity curve trading. Tom Basso makes the case:

"I haven't met a trader yet that wouldn't say privately that he would tend to buy his program on a drawdown, particularly systematic traders. But, investors seem to not add money when, to traders, it seems to be most logical to do so . . . Why don't investors

You have to keep trading the way you were before the drawdown and also be patient. There's always part of a trader's psyche that wants to make losses back tomorrow. But traders need to remember you lose it really fast, but you make it up slowly. You may think you can make it up fast, but it doesn't work that way.

David Druz[23]

"Correlation coefficient: A statistical measure of the interdependence of two or more random variables. Fundamentally, the value indicates how much of a change in one variable is explained by a change in another."[25]

Maryland-based Campbell & Company, a trend-following managed futures firm with almost $3 billion in assets under management, has returned 17.65% since its inception in 1972, proving that performance can be sustainable over the long-term.[26]

The Millburn Diversified Portfolio has a 10% allocation which has historically exhibited superior performance characteristics coupled with an almost zero correlation of monthly returns to those of traditional investments. If an investor had invested 10% of his or her portfolio in the Millburn Diversified Portfolio from February 1977 through August 2003 he or she would have increased the return on his or her traditional portfolio by 73 basis points (a 6.2% increase) and decreased risk (as measured by standard deviation) by 0.26 of a percent (an 8.2% decrease).

www.millburncorp.com

invest on drawdowns? I believe the answer to that question lies in the investing psychology of buying a drawdown. The human mind can easily extrapolate 3 months of negative returns into 'how long at this rate will it take to lose 50% or everything?' Rather than seeing the bargain and the positive return to risk, they see only the negative and forecast more of the same into the future."[24]

Not only do trend followers tell clients to buy into their funds during a drawdown, they buy into their own funds with their own capital during their drawdowns. We know of employees at top trend followers that are almost giddy when they are in a drawdown since they know what is around the corner. This is a strong indication of the faith they have in their ability to recover.

Correlation

Correlation comparisons not only prove that Trend Following is a legitimate style, but also demonstrate the similarity of performances among trend followers. Correlation is not only important in assembling the portfolio you trade (see Chapter 9), but it is your critical tool to analyze and compare performance histories of trend followers. Unlike misguided comparisons using standard deviations, we find correlation comparisons of performance data extremely useful.

Julius A. Staniewicz, of John W. Henry and Co, in *Learning to Love Non-Correlation*, defines correlation as "a statistical term giving the strength of linear relationship between two random variables. It is the historical tendency of one thing to move in tandem with another." The correlation coefficient is a number from -1 to +1, with -1 being the perfectly opposite behavior of two investments (e.g., up 5% every time the other is down 5%). +1 reflects identical investment results (up or down the same amount each period). The further away from +1 one gets (and thus closer to -1), the better a diversifier one investment is for the other. But since John W. Henry's firm is keenly aware of keeping things simple, they also provide us with another description of correlation: The tendency for one investment to "zig" while another "zags."[27]

We took the monthly performance numbers of trend followers and computed their correlation coefficients. Comparing correlations provided the evidence that trend followers trade typically the same markets in basically the same way at the same time.

Look at the correlation chart (Chart 3.5) and ask yourself why two trend followers who don't work in the same office—who are on opposite sides of the continent—have the same three losing months in a row with very similar percentage losses. Then ask why they have the same winning month, then the same two losing months, and then the same three winning months in a row. The relationship is there because these trend followers can only respond to what the market offers. The market offers trends to everyone equally. They're all looking at the same market aiming for the same target of opportunity.

Does this chart (Chart 3.5) mean trend followers are using similar techniques? Absolutely.

CHART 3.5: Correlation among Trend Followers

	AbrDiv	CamFin	CheDiv	DUNWor	EckSta	JohFin	ManAHL	MarSta	RabDiv
AbrDiv	1.00	0.56	0.81	0.33	0.57	0.55	0.56	0.75	0.75
CamFin	0.56	1.00	0.59	0.62	0.60	0.56	0.51	0.57	0.55
CheDiv	0.81	0.59	1.00	0.41	0.53	0.55	0.60	0.72	0.75
DUNWor	0.33	0.62	0.41	1.00	0.57	0.62	0.61	0.51	0.45
EckSta	0.57	0.60	0.53	0.57	1.00	0.57	0.58	0.74	0.71
JohFin	0.55	0.56	0.55	0.62	0.57	1.00	0.53	0.55	0.50
ManAHL	0.56	0.51	0.60	0.61	0.58	0.53	1.00	0.57	0.59
MarSta	0.75	0.57	0.72	0.51	0.74	0.55	0.57	1.00	0.68
RabDiv	0.75	0.55	0.75	0.45	0.71	0.50	0.59	0.68	1.00

AbrDiv: Abraham Trading Co.
CamFin: Campbell & Company
CheDiv: Chesapeake Capital Corporation
DUNWor: DUNN Capital Management, Inc.
EckSta: Eckhardt Trading Co.
JohFin: John W. Henry & Company, Inc.
ManAHL: Man Inv. Products, Ltd
MarSta: Mark J. Walsh & Company
RabDiv: Rabar Market Research

Surprisingly, correlation can be a touchy subject for some trend followers. The Turtles (Chapter 2) were all grateful to Richard Dennis for his inspiration and mentoring, but some seemed to become ambivalent over time, obviously indebted to Dennis but struggling to achieve their own identity:

"[Hawksbill] says his system is 95% Dennis' system and the rest his 'own flair . . . I'm a long way from someone who follows the system mechanically . . . but by far, the structure of what I do is based on Richard's systems, and certainly, philosophically, everything I do in terms of trading is based on what I learned from Richard.'"[28]

Even when correlation data still shows similar patterns of trading among many of Dennis' students, the desire of some to differentiate themselves from each other is stronger than their need to address the obvious similarity in Turtle return streams:

"There no longer is a turtle trading style in my mind. We've all evolved and developed systems that are very different from those we were taught, and that independent evolution suggests that the dissimilarities to trading between turtles are always increasing."[29]

The correlation chart comparing Hawksbill to other Turtle trend followers paints a clear picture. The relationship is solid. The data (Chart 3.6) is the real judge:

CHART 3.6: Correlation among Turtle Traders

	Chesapeake	Eckhardt	Hawksbill	JPD	Rabar
Chesapeake	1	0.53	0.62	0.75	0.75
Eckhardt	0.53	1	0.7	0.7	0.71
Hawksbill	0.62	0.7	1	0.73	0.76
JPD	0.75	0.7	0.73	1	0.87
Rabar	0.75	0.71	0.76	0.87	1

Correlation coefficients gauge how closely an advisor's performance resembles another advisor. Values exceeding 0.66 may be viewed as having significant positive performance correlation. And consequently, values exceeding -0.66 may be viewed as having significant negative performance correlation.

Chesapeake Capital Corporation
Eckhardt Trading Co.
Hawksbill Capital Management
JPD Enterprises Inc.
Rabar Market Research

Of course, there is more to the story than just correlation. While correlations show the Turtles still trade in similar ways, their returns can also differ because of their individual leverage choices. Some traders use a lot of leverage while others, like Jerry Parker, use less in order to increase the comfort level of some institutional investors. Parker explains, "The bigger the trade, the greater the returns and the greater the drawdowns. It's a double-edged sword."[30]

The Zero-Sum Nature of the Markets

"Zero-sum" or "zero-sum trading" is arguably the most important concept in this chapter. Larry Harris, the Chair in Finance at the Marshall School of Business at University of Southern California and the current Chief Economist of The Securities and Exchange Commission, gets to the crux of the matter:

"Trading is a zero-sum game when gains and losses are measured relative to the market average. In a zero-sum game, someone can win only if somebody else loses."[31]

If you get people asking the wrong questions, you don't have to worry about the answers.

Hunter S. Thompson

Another good explanation of the zero-sum concept is found in "The Winners and Losers of the Zero-Sum Game: The Origins of Trading Profits, Price Efficiency and Market Liquidity," a white paper also authored by Larry Harris. In speaking with Harris he told us he was amazed at how many people came from the TurtleTrader.com Web site seeking to download his white paper and or find more information on the topics it addressed.

In brief, Harris examines what factors determine who wins and who loses when trading. He does this by categorizing traders by type and then evaluating their trading styles to determine whether the styles lead to profits or losses. Harris was direct in his analysis:

"Winning traders can only profit to the extent that other traders are willing to lose. Traders are willing to lose when they obtain external benefits from trading. The most important external benefits are expected returns from holding risky securities that represent deferred consumption. Hedging and gambling provide other external benefits. Markets would not exist without utilitarian traders. Their trading losses fund the winning traders who make prices efficient and provide liquidity."[32]

There are individuals who absolutely will not accept that there must be a loser for them to be a winner. They cannot live with the idea that life is unfair and they can't have it both ways with everyone winning. Although they want to win, they do not want to live with the guilt that by their winning, someone else had to lose. This is a poorly thought out, yet all too common, view of the situation.

What separates winners from losers? Harris offers: "On any given transaction, the chances of winning or losing may be near even. In the long run, however, winners profit from trading because they have some persistent advantages that allow them to win slightly more often (or occasionally much bigger) than losers win."[33]

For anyone who has ever played blackjack or poker, or read about "edges" in gambling, Harris' words will ring a bell:

"To trade profitably in the long run, you must know your edge, you must know when it exists, and you must focus your trading to exploit it when you can. If you have no edge, you should not trade for profit. If you know you have no edge, but you must trade for other reasons, you should organize your trading to minimize your losses to those who do have an edge. Recognizing your edge is a prerequisite to predicting whether trading will be profitable."[34]

These observations will save your skin if you're willing to accept the zero-sum game, but as you will see throughout this chapter and the next, many traders are either ignorant of zero-sum thinking or choose to ignore it.

George Soros Refutes Zero-Sum

The success of famed trader George Soros is well-known:

"Soros is the best-known [of the] hedge fund investors. In 1992 he was called 'the man who broke the pound' for placing $10 billion in bets against the British pound that netted him at least $1 billion in profit."[35]

George Soros appeared on *Nightline*, the ABC news program, a few years ago. The following exchange between Soros and host Ted Koppel goes straight to the core of zero-sum:

Ted Koppel:. . . as you describe it, it [the market] is, of course, a game in which there are real consequences. When you bet and you win, that's good for you, it's bad for those against whom you have bet. There are always losers in this kind of a game.

George Soros: No. See, it's not a zero-sum game. It's very important to realize . . .

Ted Koppel: Well, it's not zero-sum in terms of investors. But, for example, when you bet against the British pound, that was not good for the British economy.

George Soros: Well, it happened to be quite good for the British economy. It was not, let's say, good for the British treasury because they were on the other side of the trade . . . It's not—your gain is not necessarily somebody else's loss.

Ted Koppel: Because—I mean put it in easily understandable terms—I mean if you could have profited by destroying Malaysia's currency, would you have shrunk from that?

George Soros: Not necessarily because that would have been an unintended consequence of my action. And it's not my job as a participant to calculate the consequences. This is what a market is. That's the nature of a market. So I'm a participant in the market.

Soros opens his own personal can of worms here with his view on zero-sum. Here's an online weblog post that incorrectly analyzes the importance of Soros' interview. The poster argues:

"Cosmetically, Koppel wipes the floor with Soros. He's able to portray Soros as a person who destroys lives and economies without a second thought, as well as simplify, beyond belief, something that should not be simplified."[36]

This is nonsense. The fact that Soros is a player in the market does not establish him as a destroyer of lives. You may disagree with Soros' ever-changing political ideology, but you can't question his morality for participation in the market. Do you have a 401k plan designed to generate profits from the market? Of course you do, just like Soros.

Others, such as Lawrence Parks, a union activist, correctly states that Soros is in a zero-sum game, but then get sidetracked by bias such as deeming the concept of zero-sum unfair and harsh for the "working man":

What objectivity and the study of philosophy requires is not an "open mind," but an active mind—a mind able and eagerly willing to examine ideas, but to examine them critically.

Ayn Rand[37]

I believe the answer lies in coming to terms with what Heisenberg's research uncovered in the field of physics: that we cannot expect to accurately predict the future given this present environment. There are quite simply too many mixed signals, and too much uncertainty. In my view, we just cannot expect to understand the present situation with any exactness. Perhaps a more reasonable approach would be to embrace the uncertainty. Once we embrace the uncertainty, we may be able to use it to our advantage.

Jon C. Sundt
President
Altegris Investments
2nd Quarter 2004 Commentary

"Since currency and derivative trading are zero-sum games, every dollar "won" requires that a dollar was "lost." But who are the losers that not only sustain but continue to tolerate these enormous losses year after year? Who could be so wealthy or so ignorant that $50 billion each year doesn't matter? Haven't they realized what a losing proposition this has been? What's more, why do they keep playing at a losing game? The answer is that the losers are all of us. And, while neither rich nor stupid, we've been given no choice but to continue to lose. Every time we, on behalf of our businesses or ourselves, change one currency into another, we lose transaction costs. Every time we hedge a payment from or to a foreign land, the cost of that hedge represents a loss of wealth. And every time one of these fiat currencies cannot be "defended," the workers, seniors, and business owners of that country—folks like us—suffer big time. Indeed, as their currencies are devalued, workers' savings and future payments, such as their pensions, denominated in those currencies lose purchasing power. Interest rates increase. Commercial relationships predicated upon lower interest rates unravel, and businesses go out of business. Through no fault of their own, working people lose their jobs in addition to their savings. There have been press reports that, after a lifetime of working and saving, people in Indonesia are eating bark off the trees and boiling grass soup. While not a secret, it is astonishing to learn how sanguine the beneficiaries have become of their advantage over the rest of us. For example, famed financier George Soros in his recent The Crisis of Global Capitalism plainly divulges: 'The Bank of England was on the other side of my transactions and I was taking money out of the pockets of British taxpayers.' To me, the results of this wealth transfer are inescapable."[38]

Parks argues that the only choice he has been given is to lose. He loses; his union loses; everyone apparently loses in the zero-sum game. Of course there are winners and he knows that. The zero-sum game is, indeed, a wealth transfer. The winners profit from the losers. Parks correctly describes the nature of the zero-sum game but then positions the game in terms of morality. Life is not fair. If you don't like being a loser in the zero-sum game, perhaps it is time to consider how the winners (trend followers) play the game.

While it may appear that we are defending Soros, we're not. The market is a zero-sum game. Trying to fathom Soros' reasons for denying this would be pure speculation on our part. Soros is not always a zero-sum winner either. Soros was on the losing side of the zero-sum game during the Long Term Capital Management fiasco in 1998. He lost $2 billion. (We discuss this in more detail in Chapter 4). He also had severe trouble in the 2000 tech meltdown:

It's all a matter of perspective. What some consider a catastrophic flood, others deem a cleansing bath.

Gregory J. Millman[42]

"With bets that went sour on technology stocks and on Europe's new currency, the five funds run by Soros Fund Management have suffered a 20 percent decline this year and, at $14.4 billion, are down roughly a third from a peak of $22 billion in August 1998."[39]

These wins and losses seem to have taken a toll on Soros: "Maybe I don't understand the market. Maybe the music has stopped but people are still dancing. I am anxious to reduce my market exposure and be more conservative. We will accept lower returns because we will cut the risk profile."[40]

We don't see evidence that the market has changed. Nor has the zero-sum game changed. However, something may have changed within George Soros.

Dot-Com Meets Zero-Sum

Judge Milton Pollack's 2003 ruling dismissing class action suits against Merrill Lynch clearly illustrates the concept of zero-sum again. He minces no words in warning whiners about the zero-sum game they are playing:

"Seeking to lay the blame for the enormous Internet Bubble solely at the feet of a single actor, Merrill Lynch, plaintiffs would have this Court conclude that the federal securities laws were meant to underwrite, subsidize, and encourage their rash speculation in joining a freewheeling casino that lured thousands obsessed with the fantasy of Olympian riches, but which delivered such riches to only a scant handful of lucky winners. Those few lucky winners, who are not before the Court, now hold the monies that the unlucky plaintiffs have lost, fair and square, and they will never return those monies to plaintiffs. Had plaintiffs themselves won the game instead of losing, they would have owed not a single penny of their winnings to those they left to hold the bag (or to defendants)."[41]

A 96-year-old judge bluntly telling the plaintiffs to take responsibility for their own actions may have been painful reading for investors who were following the case. Pollack chastises the losers for trying to circumvent the zero-sum market process by using the legal process basically telling them this time there would be no free lunch.

The harsh reality of the markets is that, if you are a trader or investor, ultimately, you have only yourself to blame for the decisions you make with regard to your money. You can make losing decisions or winning decisions. It's your choice.

David Druz, a student of Ed Seykota and a longtime trend follower, takes the Judge Pollack's ruling a step further and spells out the practical effects of the market's zero-sum nature:

"Everyone who enters the market thinks they will win, but obviously there are losers as well. Somebody has to be losing to you if you are winning, so we always like to stress that you should know from whom you're going to take profits, because if you're buying, the guy that's selling thinks he's going to be right, too."

The market is a brutal place. Forget trying to be liked. Need a friend, get a dog. The market doesn't know you and never will. If you are going to win, then someone else has to lose. You don't like these "survival of the fittest" rules? Stay out of the zero-sum game.

If all it took to beat the markets was a Ph.D. in mathematics, there'd be a hell of a lot of rich mathematicians out there.
Bill Dries[43]

Key Points

- Trend followers always prepare for drawdowns after strong periods of performance.
- An absolute return strategy means you are trying to make the most money possible.
- The fact that markets are volatile (go up and down) is not a problem. The problem is you if that volatility scares you.
- Trading is a zero-sum game in an important accounting sense. In a zero-sum game, the total gains of the winners are exactly equal to the total losses of the losers.
- Trend followers go to the market to trade trends. However, not all market players are trying to do the same thing. Fannie Mae could be making a change in their bond portfolio. A major investment bank could be trading a strategy that will not tolerate volatility. Bottom line people trade for different goals. George Crapple, a trend follower with 25+ years in experience, makes the point: "So while it may be a zero some game, a lot of people don't care. It's not that they're stupid; it's not speculative frenzy; they're just using these markets for a completely different purpose."

Big Events in
Trend Following

4

"I have noticed that everyone who ever told me that the markets are efficient is poor."
—Larry Hite, Mint Investment Management Company

"Rare events are always unexpected, otherwise they would not occur."
—Nassim Taleb[1]

To comprehend Trend Following's impact, you have to look at the performance data of great trend followers to understand why they were the winners in some of the biggest trading events of our generation. This chapter focuses on high profile trading events where trend followers won huge profits in the zero-sum game.

Wall Street is famous for events, such as corporate collapses or mutual fund blow-ups, that transfer capital from winners to losers and back again. But interestingly, the winners always seem to be missing from the after the fact analysis. The mainstream press by and large is fascinated with losers. Taking their lead from the press, the general public also gets caught up in the drama of the losers, oblivious to the other equal interesting story of the winners.

Occasionally, a writer such as Herb Greenberg does ask the right question:

An investment in DUNN acts as a hedge against unpredictable market crises.

Dunn Capital Management
Marketing Materials

I'd say that Proctor and Gamble did what their name says, they proctored and gambled. And now they're complaining.

Leo Melamed

"Each time there's a derivatives disaster, I get the same question: If Barings was the loser, who was the winner? If Orange County was the loser, who was the winner? If Procter & Gamble was the loser, who was the winner?"[2]

But the Herb Greenbergs of the world never identify the winners. Prominent academics in the field of finance searching for winners also come up short, as Christopher Culp of the University of Chicago laments:

"It's a zero-sum game. For every loser there's a winner, but you can't always be specific about who the winner is."[3]

When the big trading events happen, people know the losses are going somewhere, but once the obvious is stated, they stop thinking about it. Reflecting on the unknown is not pleasant, as Alexander Ineichen demonstrates:

"Fear is still in the bones of some pension fund trustees. . .after Mr. Leeson brought down Barings Bank. The failure of Barings Bank is probably the most often cited derivatives disaster. While the futures market had been the instrument used by Nick Leeson to play the zero-sum game [and] someone made a lot of money being short the Nikkei futures Mr. Leeson was buying."[4]

It often seems that trends create events more than events create trends. The event itself is usually a reflection of everyone "getting it" as Ed [Seykota] calls it, "an aha." By this time, the trend followers usually have well-established positions.

Jason Russell[6]

Someone did indeed make a lot of money trading short to Leeson's long, as we discuss later in the chapter. Perhaps Wall Street has been looking at the issue through the wrong lens. Michael Mauboussin and Kristen Bartholdson, of Credit Suisse First Boston, point out that standard finance theory comes up blank when explaining how to win during the high impact events:

"One of the major challenges in investing is how to capture (or avoid) low-probability, high-impact events. Unfortunately, standard finance theory has little to say about the subject."[5]

The unexpected events that Greenberg, Culp, Ineichen, and Mauboussin refer to are the source of big profits for trend followers. Big unexpected events made Bill Dunn, John W. Henry, and Jerry Parker rich. Michael Rulle, President of Graham Capital Management, lays out the case from his trend following perspective:

"For markets to move in tandem there has to be a common perception or consensus about economic conditions which drives it. When a major "event" occurs in the middle of such a consensus, such as the Russian debt default of August 1998, the terrorist attacks of September 11, 2001, or the corporate accounting scandals of 2002, it will often accelerate existing trends already in place . . . 'events' do not happen in a vacuum. . . This is the reason Trend Following rarely gets caught on the wrong side of an 'event.' Additionally, the stop loss trading style will limit exposure when it does. . . When this consensus is further confronted by an 'event,' such as a major country default, the 'event' will reinforce the crisis mentality already in place and drive those trends toward their final conclusion. Because Trend Following generally can be characterized as having a 'long option' profile, it typically benefits greatly when these occurrences happen."[7]

However, big events also generate plenty of misguided analysis by focusing on unanswerable questions like those posed by Thomas Ho and Sang Lee, authors of *The Oxford Guide to Financial Modeling*:[8]

1. "What do these events tell us about our society?"

2. "Are these financial losses the dark sides of all the benefits of financial derivatives?"

3. "Should we change the way we do things?"

4. "Should the society accept these financial losses as part of the 'survival of the fittest' in the world of business?"

5. "Should legislation be used to avoid these events?"

It is not unusual to see people frame market wins and losses as the classic morality tale. These questions are designed to absolve the guilt of all those who lost. The market is no place for political excuses or social engineering. No law will change human nature. If you don't like losing, it might be time to examine the strategy of the winners.

The performance histories of trend followers during the 1992–2002 Stock Market Bubble, the 1998 Long Term Capital Management (LTCM) crisis, the Asian Contagion (Victor Niederhoffer), Barings Bank in 1995, and the German firm Metallgesellschaft help to answer the question: "who won?"

On Saturday, February 25, 1995, Mike Killian, who almost single-handedly built Barings Far East customer brokerage business over the past seven years, was awakened at 4:30 a.m. in his Portland, Ore., home. It was Fred Hochenberger from the Barings Hong Kong office.
"Are you sitting down?" Hochenberger asked a sleepy Killian.
"No, I'm lying down."
"Have you heard any rumors?"
Killian, perplexed, said no.
"I think we're bust."
"Is this a crank call?" Killian asked.
"There's a really ugly story coming out that perhaps Nick Leeson has taken the company down."[9]

Event #1:
Stock Market Bubble

Conventional capital market theory is based on a linear view of the world, one in which investors have rational expectations; they adjust immediately to information about the markets and behave as if they know precisely how the structure of the economy works. Markets are highly efficient, but not perfectly so. Inefficiencies are inherent in the economy or in the structure of markets themselves . . . We believe inefficiencies in markets can be exploited through a combination of trend detection and risk management.

John W. Henry & Company, Inc.[10]

The period from 1999–2002 was littered with volatile up-and-down markets. While the prime story for that three-year period was the NASDAQ meltdown, there were several subplots, ranging from September 11 to Enron to Trend Following drawdowns and their subsequent recoveries to new highs.

How did trend followers, for example, do compared to the S&P and NASDAQ for 2002 (Chart 4.1)?

CHART 4.1: 2002 Performance Histories for Trend Followers

Bill Dunn: +54.23%

Salem Abraham +21.37%

John W. Henry: +45.06%

Jerry Parker: +11.10%

Jim Hamer (Ed Seykota Student): +16.06%

David Druz (Ed Seykota Student): +33.17%

Bill Eckhardt (Richard Dennis' Partner): +14.05%

Mulvaney Capital: +19.37%

S&P: -23.27

NASDAQ: -31.53%

Dow: -16.76

Charts 4.2 through 4.9 show what trends they were riding to produce this performance.

Drawdowns and Recoveries

It's no secret that for the majority of 2000, trend followers were in a nasty drawdown. They were down significantly heading into the last few months of the year. The press and skeptics were calling the strategy finished.

I was not surprised when a *Barrons* reporter contacted TurtleTrader.com for an opinion. She had it in for John W. Henry

CHART 4.2: Trend Followers and the S&P Chart, Jan. 2002–Dec. 2002 *Source:* Barchart.com

CHART 4.3: Trend Followers and the Dollar Chart, Jan. 2002–Dec. 2002 *Source:* Barchart.com

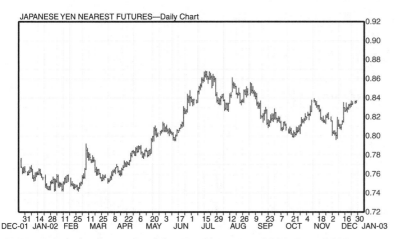

CHART 4.4: Trend Followers and the Yen Chart, Jan. 2002–Dec. 2002 *Source:* Barchart.com

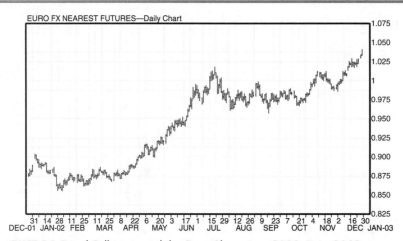

CHART 4.5: Trend Followers and the Euro Chart, Jan. 2002–Dec. 2002 *Source: Barchart.com*

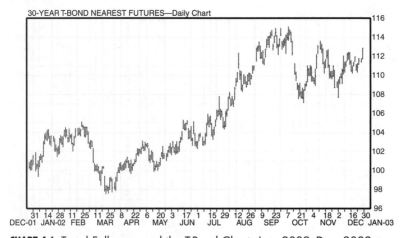

CHART 4.6: Trend Followers and the T-Bond Chart, Jan. 2002–Dec. 2002 *Source: Barchart.com*

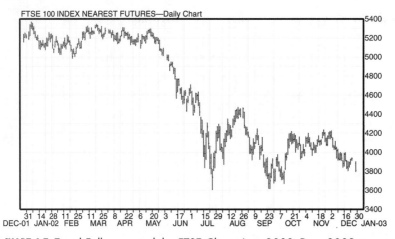

CHART 4.7: Trend Followers and the FTSE Chart, Jan. 2002–Dec. 2002 *Source: Barchart.com*

CHART 4.8: Trend Followers and the Euro-Bund, Jan. 2002–Dec. 2002 *Source:* Barchart.com

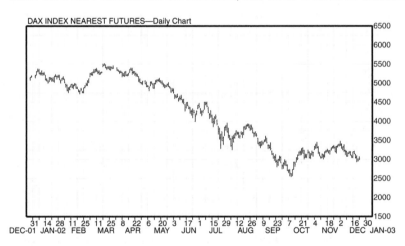

CHART 4.9: Trend Followers and the DAX, Jan. 2002–Dec. 2002 *Source:* Barchart.com

and Bill Dunn and was looking for confirmation that Trend Following was dead. It was pointed out to her that drawdowns had occurred in the past and were not uncommon. But, over the long haul, trend followers made tremendous amounts of money trading for the absolute return. She ignored those facts. Here's an excerpt from the piece she wrote:

"John W. Henry isn't alone in experiencing hard times. But the firm's losses are among the most staggering . . . The company's hardest-hit trend-following trading program, called Financial & Metals, was down 18.7% in 1999 . . . Henry, whom one rival calls

Convergent styles
• *World knowable*
• *Stable world*
• *Mean-reverting*
• *Short volatility*
• *Arbitrage-based*

Divergent styles
• *World uncertain*
• *Unstable world*
• *Mean-fleeing*
• *Long volatility*
• *Trend Following*

Mark S. Rzepczynski[11]

'our industry's Dave Kingman,' definitely swings for the fences. (Kingman hit 442 home runs during his 16 seasons in the majors, but he also struck out more than 1,800 times.) It's unclear whether John W. Henry will make changes to his trading program, one he cooked up decades ago while on a vacation to Norway."[12]

You have to wonder if this *Barrons* reporter had taken the time to read John W. Henry's speech from November of 2000 before writing her December article. Henry seems to have been hinting at a huge success just around the corner:

"Unfortunately, markets do not step to a drummer that we control. The period we have just been through has been terrifically painful for investors, brokers, general partners and trading advisors. Drawdowns affect everyone emotionally, psychologically and physically when they persist. It becomes very easy to envision a scenario in which things never get better. However, at JWH, experience tells us that things inevitably look bleakest before the tide turns."[13]

John W. Henry knew the tide was turning.

On January 10, 2001, this same reporter sent me an email stating that she was doing a follow-up story to the one in December, and wanted comment. I was impressed that she was essentially acknowledging her mistake and was even willing to set the record straight. Because for the record Bill Dunn made 28 percent in November of 2000 and 29 percent in December of 2000. John W. Henry made 13 percent in November of 2000 and 23 percent in December. Here's an excerpt of her follow-up piece:

"Wall Street's biggest commodity-trading advisers posted a dramatic turnaround in the fourth quarter, turning last year's heart-stopping losses into gains for the year. Will it last? . . . In the October–December period, CTAs benefited from pricing trends in global bond markets and rising prices in the natural-gas and oil sectors. Also, December's steady rise in the euro proved to be a boon for currency traders. 'This rebound is not a surprise,' says Michael Covel, of TurtleTrader.com, which tracks trend followers. . . John W. Henry, a high-profile commodities-trading firm in Boca Raton, Florida, profiled by Barron's last month posted a 20.3% return last year in its largest trading program which was down 13.7% for the first nine months of the year, powered back 39.2% in the fourth quarter."[14]

Don't be fooled by the calm. That's always the time to change course, not when you're just about to get hit by the typhoon. The way to avoid being caught in such a storm is to identify the confluence of factors and to change course even though right now the sky is blue, the winds are gentle, and the water seems calm ... After all look how calm and sunny it is outside.

Thomas Friedman
The World is Flat

How was John W. Henry able to "power back 39.2%" in the fourth quarter of 2000 after posting a loss of 13.7 percent for the first nine months of the year? What trends did he ride? Where was his target of opportunity? The answers can be found in Enron, California, and Natural Gas.

Enron, California, & Natural Gas

If you examine the natural gas market over the last few months of 2000 and almost all of 2001, you can see the trading opportunity. For trend followers the natural gas market's great trend up and great trend down were big wins.

The losers were Enron and the state of California. Enron's collapse is a classic case of greed, fear, and ultimately, incompetence at work. From Enron's upper management's manipulation of the facts to the employees who purposefully ignored the manipulations to the state of California's inept attempts to play the energy markets, everyone was accountable. In the zero-sum game, everyone is responsible, whether they admit it or not.

The Enron debacle is stunning when you consider the losers. The number of investors who deluded themselves into thinking they were on a path to quick riches is incalculable. From the portfolio managers of pension funds and university endowments to individual investors, everyone was caught up in the exhilaration of a company that seemed to go in only one direction—up. Owners of Enron stock saw an instant pot of gold. They were quite willing to look the other way and suspend their disbelief to celebrate a zooming share price guilt-free.

But there was a problem: They had no strategy to sell when the time came and the trend turned. All good bulls die—whether people admit it or not. The Enron stock chart (Chart 4.10) is now famous.

There was only one key piece of data needed to judge Enron: the share price. At its peak, the company's stock traded at $90 a share, but it collapsed to 50¢ a share. Why would anyone hold onto a stock that goes from $90 to 50¢? Even if Enron was the biggest scam ever propagated, must we not take to task the hopeful investors who held on all the way down to 50¢ a share? Don't the investors bear the responsibility for *not* selling? The chart was telling them the trend had changed.

After having experienced a 40.0% decline through September 2000, Dunn Capital Management finished 2000 with a 17.3% asset weighted composite return. Dunn's 75.5% gain in the fourth quarter delivered $590 million to its investors; its annualized composite compound return since the firm's inception over 26 years ago is now 24.3%.[15]

Q: Why didn't Wall Street realize that Enron was a fraud?
A: Because Wall Street relies on stock analysts. These are people who do research on companies and then, no matter what they find, even if the company has burned to the ground, enthusiastically recommend that investors buy the stock.

Dave Barry,
Humor Columnist

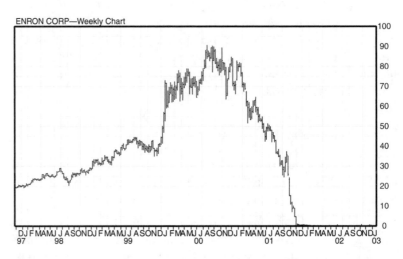

CHART 4.10: Enron Stock Chart *Source:* Barchart.com

They say patience is a virtue. For me patience is synonymous with discipline. You must have the discipline to know that markets change and poor periods are followed by good period. Longevity in this business—I have seen it again and again—is measured by discipline.

John W. Henry[16]

Not only were there massive winners and losers in trading just Enron stock, but the zero-sum game sprang into full force during the California energy crisis in late 2000 and over the course of 2001. Enron was a primary supplier of natural gas to California. California, bound by its own flawed deregulation schemes, freely signed long-term contracts with energy trading firms and bought natural gas from Enron to generate electricity.

Not surprisingly, with inexperienced players and bad agreements in place, Enron and the state of California all but forgot that natural gas was just another market. Like any market, it was subject to go up and down for any number of fundamental reasons. Eventually, natural gas spiked up and down in ferocious trends. Unfortunately, neither Enron nor California had a plan in place to deal with price changes.

Feeling abused, California complained loudly. California Senator Diane Feinstein maintained that they had no culpability in the game. In a January 2002 press release she argued:

"I am writing to request an additional hearing to pursue what role Enron had in the California energy crisis with respect to market manipulation and price gouging. Enron's ability to deal in complex unregulated financial derivatives in the natural gas market

CHART 4.11: Natural Gas Stock Chart *Source:* Barchart.com

while controlling a tremendous share of the gas trading market, provided Enron the ability to manipulate market prices. This was very likely a key factor in driving up gas and electricity prices leading to the California energy crisis."

It has been said that the energy crisis involving Enron and natural gas cost California $45 billion over two years in higher electricity costs and slowed economic growth. When you look at the charts of natural gas (Chart 4.11) and Enron (Chart 4.10), you have to question Feinstein's statements.

Why did California lock itself into stringent agreements with firms like Enron? Why did California, through its own deals, trade outside typical market structures? Why couldn't they deal with a changing natural gas price? California itself must accept blame for its decisions.

Anyone at any time can trade natural gas at the New York Mercantile Exchange. Anyone can hedge a natural gas position. The opportunity to speculate and hedge is there for everyone. It is not a novel concept. Of course, trend followers were playing the natural gas game too, riding it up and down for profit as Chart 4.12 demonstrates.

Among the hottest funds this year [2002] are Dunn Capital Management, which is up more than 50%. Daniel Dunn, who runs the firm from Stuart, Fla., profited on trades on Japan's Nikkei, Germany's DAX, and Britain's FTSE stock indexes, as well as on bond and eurodollar interest-rate futures offered on the Chicago exchanges.[17]

CHART 4.12: Trend Followers' Performance

Dunn Capital Management WMA

October 2000: +9.12%

November 2000: +28.04%

December 2000: +29.39%

January 2001: +7.72%

John W. Henry Financials and Metals

October 2000: +9.39%

November 2000: +13.33%

December 2000: +23.02%

January 2001: +3.34%

Graham Capital Management K4

October 2000: +1.44%

November 2000: +7.41%

December 2000: +9.37%

January 2001: +2.37%

Man Investments

October 2000: +4.54%

November 2000: +10.30%

December 2000: +10.76

January 2001: +1.49%

Campbell and Company Financials and Metals

October 2000: +3.19%

November 2000: +5.98%

December 2000: +2.38%

January 2001: -1.09%

CHART 4.12: Trend Followers' Performance *Continued*

Chesapeake Capital

October 2000: -0.62%

November 2000: +7.42%

December 2000: +8.80%

January 2001: -0.43%

Abraham Trading

October 2000: +9.51%

November 2000: +8.58%

December 2000: -0.18%

January 2001: +2.28

One Enron employee was frustrated by the entire sordid affair: "My fellow (former) colleagues have no one to blame other than themselves for allowing such disastrous losses to occur in their retirement accounts. An abdication of personal responsibility should not be rewarded. It is a sad consequence but it is reality."[18]

From private mutual fund companies like Janus to retirement funds managed by state governments, no one had a plan for exiting Enron. They all bought the stock, but selling was never in the picture. The Enron story is much more profound than a tale of one company's journey to disaster. It is the story of inept individuals managing billions of retirement wealth.

How much did the losers lose? Losses in Enron were staggering:

- Japanese Banks lost $805.4 million.
- Abbey National Bank lost £95 million.
- John Hancock Financial Services lost $102 million.
- British Petroleum retirement lost $55 million on Enron debt.

David Brady, Stein Roe Focus Fund manager, admits to owning Enron: "'Where did I go wrong? If I learned anything, I learned the same old lessons . . . The numbers just didn't add up. If you had looked at the numbers, the balance sheet would have showed you the real problems.'"

Public retirement accounts recklessly bet on Enron too:

- The Kansas Public Employees Retirement System had about $1.2 million invested in about 82,000 shares of Enron stock, "It was based on (Enron's) spectacular earnings growth, and many analysts recommended it as a hot stock," said David Brant, Kansas securities commissioner.
- The retirement fund for the City of Fort Worth lost nearly $1 million in Enron.
- The Teacher Retirement System of Texas first invested in Enron in June 1994. It has realized a net loss of approximately $23.3 million from its Enron stock holdings and $12.4 million in net unrealized losses from its current bond holdings in Enron. Jim Simms of Amarillo, a board member for six years and Chairman of the Board, said: "We're human beings—when you're investing money, you'll have some winners and some losers . . . You can't protect yourself when you're being fed inaccurate information . . . We had all the precautions in place."

Enron's fall from grace is no different from other corporate implosions, although the losers (such as those in Chart 4.13) may need to call it "new" to rationalize their losses. But the game doesn't change, even if the names of the companies do.

The best way I can explain it is that many investors believed that [our] returns were in some way inferior to the returns of many other hedge fund strategies, because of a perception of higher volatility, and lower absolute returns. The additional. . .benefits of low correlation, transparency, liquidity, and effective regulation somehow escaped their attention. What 2002 has demonstrated is that in fact the returns of many of those other strategies are not as "absolute" as had been perceived, and many of them appear to actually have a strong upside bias.

Bruce Cleland
Campbell & Co.[19]

CHART 4.13: Largest Shareholders in Enron (% fund in Enron shares):

Alliance Premier Growth (4.1%)

Fidelity Magellan (0.2%)

AIM Value (1%)

Putnam Investors (1.7%)

Morgan Stanley Dividend Growth (0.9%)

Janus Fund (2.9%)

Janus Twenty (2.8%)

Janus Mercury (3.6%)

CHART 4.13: Largest Shareholders in Enron (% fund in Enron shares) Continued

---

Janus Growth and Income (2.7%)

Rydex Utility (8%)

Fidelity Select Natural Gas (5.7%)

Dessauer Global Equity (5.6%)

Merrill Lynch Focus Twenty (5.8%)

AIM Global Technology (5.3%)

Janus 2 (4.7%)

Janus Special Situations (4.6%)

Stein Roe Focus (4.2%)

Alliance Premier Growth (4.1%)

Merrill Lynch Growth (4.1%)

[A]ll the intensive research these firms performed did not protect them, or their investors, from massive losses. It is particularly noteworthy [that] Janus, whose commercials tout their superior research efforts and skills, [held] over 16 million shares. On April 30, 2001, the last time it reported individual fund holdings, 11 Janus funds collectively owned more than 5 percent of Enron. As of Sept. 30, Janus still owned more than 5 percent of Enron. Another touter of their superior stock-picking skills is the Fidelity family of funds. As of September 30, 2001, together they owned 154 million shares. So much for the value or research [of Janus and Fidelity].

Larry Swedroe
Buckingham Asset Management[20]

An interesting aspect of the Enron fiasco was the close relationship between the Enron share price and natural gas. To lose money in Enron stock was essentially to lose money in natural gas. They were connected at the hip. It appears that Enron was serving as nothing more than a derivative for natural gas. The company presented mutual funds and pension funds an opportunity to get into natural gas speculation even if their mission statement may have limited them to stock speculation. Using Enron as a proxy, mutual and pension funds were able to ride natural gas to the top. Not only was everyone buying and holding Enron, they were, for all intents and purposes, buying and holding natural gas. The data makes the case.

September 11, 2001

September 11, 2001, demonstrates the unpredictable on a grand scale. How could anyone know in advance where the safe place to be in the market was? Before considering September 11th specifically, consider Ed Seykota's words in general:

"A surprise is an event that catches someone unaware. If you are already on the trend, the surprises seem to happen to the other guys.[21]

We don't see things as they are. We see things as we are.

Anaïs Nin

No one could have predicted that a terrorist attack would close Wall Street for four days. While it was difficult to stay focused on the rigors of everyday life, trend followers maintained their sense of balance. Unlike those investors who made trading decisions they would not have made before September 11th, trend followers confronted the market as always. They dealt with it as they always had—with a plan set in motion long before the event happened.

Trend followers were short stocks and long bonds ahead of the attack, because that was where those markets were already headed. For example, Marty Ehrlich of Sunrise Capital Partners said how lucky they were to be well-positioned ahead of the September 11 attack. Jim Little, executive vice president for Campbell & Co. makes the case that currency markets also followed through with continued trends. "The (U.S.) dollar had already begun to weaken before the attacks, hence Campbell was short that market." He also noted that Campbell had been long bonds and short a number of global stock index futures contracts ahead of the attack as a result of established trends.[22]

Their entries into positions were not triggered by actions on September 11th. Their decisions to be in or out of the market were set in motion long before the unexpected event of September 11th happened. Although Enron, the California energy crisis, and September 11 are vivid illustrations of the zero-sum game with trend followers as the winners, the story of Long Term Capital Management in the summer of 1998 is the epitome of a Trend Following case study.

Event #2:
Long Term Capital Management Collapse

Long Term Capital Management (LTCM) was a hedge fund that went bust in 1998. The story of who lost has been told repeatedly over the years; however, since trading is a zero-sum game, we thought it would be educational to explore who the winners were. LTCM is a classic saga of the zero-sum game played out on a grand scale with trend followers as the winners.

"Trillion Dollar Bet," a PBS special describes how LTCM came to be. In 1973, three economists, Fischer Black, Myron Scholes, and Robert Merton, discovered an elegant formula that revolutionized modern finance. This mathematical holy grail, the Black-Scholes Option Pricing Formula, was sparse and deceptively simple. It earned Scholes and Merton a Nobel Prize and attracted the attention of John Meriweather, the legendary bond trader of Salomon Brothers.

Long Term Capital Management promised to use mathematical models to make investors wealthy beyond their wildest dreams. LTCM attracted the elite of Wall Street's investors and initially reaped fantastic profits managing their money. Ultimately, their theories collided with reality, and sent the company spiraling out of control.[23]

Needless to say, this was not supposed to happen:

"They were immediately seen as a unique enterprise. They had the best minds. They had a former vice chairman of the Federal Reserve. They had John Meriwether . . . So they were seen by individual investors, but particularly by banks and institutions that went in with them, as a ticket to easy street."[24]

In order to understand the LTCM fiasco, we first need to take a quick look at the foundations of modern finance. Merton Miller and his colleague Eugene F. Fama, two scholars at the University of Chicago, launched what became known as the Efficient Market Hypothesis:

"The premise of the hypothesis is that stock prices are always right; therefore, no one can divine the market's future direction, which in turn, must be 'random.' For prices to be right, of course, the people who set them must be both rational and well informed."[26]

In other words, Miller and Fama believed that perfectly rational people would never pay more or less than any financial instrument was actually worth. A fervent supporter of the Efficient Markets Hypothesis, Myron Scholes was certain that markets could not make mistakes. His associate, Robert Merton, took it a step further with his continuous-time finance theory, which essentially wrapped the finance universe in a tidy ball.[27]

"Merton's markets were as smooth as well brewed java, in which prices would flow like cream. He assumed . . . that the price of a share of IBM would never plunge directly from 80 to 60 but would always stop at 79 3/4, 79 1/2 and 79 1/4 along the way."[28]

The most damaging consequence of the LTCM episode is therefore the harm done by the perception that Federal Reserve policy makers do not really have the faith to take their own medicine. How can they persuade the Russians or the Japanese to let big institutions fail, if they are afraid to do the same themselves? [25]

If LTCM's universe was supposed to be "in a tidy ball," it may have been because where Merton and Scholes pioneered their theories, academic life was pretty tidy. LTCM's founders believed the market was a perfect normal distribution with no outliers, no fat tails, and no unexpected events. Their problems began the moment they accepted these assumptions.

Once Merton, Scholes, and Meriwether had Wall Street convinced that the markets were a nice, neat, and continuous normal distribution, and there was no risk worth worrying about, LTCM began using mammoth leverage for supposedly risk-free big returns.

Approximately 55 banks gave LTCM financing, including Bankers Trust, Bear Stearns, Chase Manhattan, Goldman Sachs, J.P. Morgan, Lehman Brothers, Merrill Lynch, Morgan Stanley, and Dean Witter. Eventually LTCM would have $100 billion in borrowed assets and more than $1 trillion worth of exposure in markets everywhere. This type of leverage was not a problem initially or so it seemed. Robert Merton was even said to have remarked to Merton Miller that you could think of LTCM's strategy like a gigantic vacuum cleaner sucking up nickels across the world.

But it was too complicated, too leveraged, and devoid of any real risk management. The Organization for Economic Cooperation and Development described a single trade that exemplified LTCM's overall trading strategy. It was a bet on the convergence of yield spreads between French bonds (OATs) and German bonds (bunds). When the spread between the OATs and the bunds went to 60 basis points in the forward market, LTCM decided to double its position. That deal was "only one leg of an even more complex convergence bet, which included hedged positions in Spanish peseta and Italian lira bonds."[30]

UBS said last week it would take a SFr950m ($686m) charge reflecting losses relating to its equity investment in LTCM, which was linked to an options deal that the former Union Bank of Switzerland had done with the hedge fund before merging with Swiss Bank Corporation to create the new UBS.[29]

The result of all these "complex convergences" was that no one had a clue what LTCM was really up to, risk-wise. The LTCM professors ran a secretive and closed operation so convoluted that the regulators, much less the investors, had no idea what, when, or how much they were trading. Not being able to price an instrument or trade freely in and out of it on a daily basis ignores what Wall Street calls "transparency." Trend follower Jerry Parker thought the differences in transparency between LTCM and his own trading firm were worth noticing:

We've always had 100% transparency . . . The good thing about CTAs is their strategies are usually straightforward, not something that only a few people in the world can understand. We're Trend Following and systems-based, something you can easily describe to a client . . . People who aren't willing to show clients their positions are in trouble . . . One of the problems was that people put too much money in these funds [such as Long Term Capital]. We ask for just 10% of risk capital, and clients know they may make 10% one month and lose 10% the next month. The ultimate error is to put a ton of money with geniuses who 'never lose money.' When all hell breaks loose, those guys lose everything."[31]

Even more than LTCM's lack of transparency, a bigger failure involved "lightning":

"I don't yet know the balance between whether this was a random event or whether this was negligence on theirs and their creditors' parts. If a random bolt of lightning hits you when you're standing in the middle of the field, that feels like a random event. But if your business is to stand in random fields during lightning storms, then you should anticipate, perhaps a little more robustly, the risks you're taking on."[33]

The Black-Scholes option pricing formula did not factor in the randomness of human behavior—only one example of the negligence that ultimately would cause the lightning bolts of August and September 1998. When lightning struck LTCM, trend followers were assessing the same markets—playing the zero-sum game at the same time. In hindsight, the old-guard Chicago professors were clearly aware of the problem:

"Models that they were using, not just Black-Scholes models, but other kinds of models, were based on normal behavior in the markets and when the behavior got wild, no models were able to put up with it."—Nobel Laureate Professor Merton Miller[34]

If only the principals at LTCM had remembered Albert Einstein's quote that elegance was for tailors, part of his observation about how beautiful formulas could pose problems in the real world. LTCM had the beautiful formulas; they were just not for the real world. Eugene Fama, Scholes' thesis advisor, had long held deep reservations about his student's options pricing model:

"If the population of price changes is strictly normal [distribution], on the average for any stock . . . an observation more

Last month [August 1998], during one of the most stressful points in market performance, our largest portfolio, Financial and Metals, was up [an estimated] 17.7%. Of the $2.4 billion that we manage, I think just slightly over half of it is in the Financial and Metals Portfolio. This was not a direct result of the decline in the U.S. market—as I said we don't trade in the S&P 500—but rather an example of the typical predictable investor behavior in the face of trouble. In reverting to rules of thumb, in this case the flight to quality, global bonds rose, global stock markets plunged, and a shift in foreign exchange rates occurred. However, the magnitude of the moves was the only real surprise for us. The trends which were demonstrated during late August had been in place for weeks or months beforehand.

John W. Henry[32]

For most investors, August was the month from hell. Not for William Dunn, though. His firm, Dunn Capital Management, with $900 million under management, had one of its best runs in years. He's up 25.4% so far this year, and 23.7% in August alone.[36]

than five standard deviations from the mean should be observed about once every seven thousand years. In fact such observations seem to occur about once every three to four years."[35]

LTCM lost 44 percent of their capital, or $1.9 billion, in August 1998 alone. In a letter to LTCM's 100 investors dated September 1998, John W. Meriwether wrote:

"As you are all too aware, events surrounding the collapse of Russia caused large and dramatically increasing volatility in global markets throughout August. We are down 44% for the month of August and 52% for the year to date. Losses of this magnitude are a shock to us as they surely are to you, especially in light of the historical volatility of the fund."[37]

At the time of Meriwether's letter, Long Term Capital Management's history consisted of only four short years, and although its "losses of this magnitude" may have shocked LTCM, its clients, and the lender banks to whom it owed over $100 billion, those trading losses became the source of profits for trend followers. Amazingly, Scholes still seemed, years later, to have a problem with accepting personal responsibility for his action in the zero-sum game:

"In August of 1998, after the Russian default, you know, all the relations that tended to exist in a recent past seemed to disappear."[38]

Ultimately, the Fed, along with major world banks, most of which were heavily vested in LTCM, bailed the firm out.

Who Lost?

CNN Financial offered the following losers on October 2, 1998:

- Everest Capital, a Bermuda-based hedge fund, lost $1.3 billion. The endowments of Yale and Brown Universities were invested in Everest.
- George Soros' Quantum Fund lost $2 billion.
- High Risk Opportunity Fund, a $450 million fund run by III Offshore Advisors, went bust.

- The Tiger Fund run by Julian Robertson lost $3.3 billion in August and September of 1998.
- Liechtenstein Global Trust lost $30 million.
- Bank of Italy lost $100 million.
- Credit Suisse lost $55 million.
- UBS lost $690 million.
- Sandy Weill lost $10 million.
- Dresdner lost $145 million.

Who Won?

As dramatic as the LTCM blowout story is the real lessons we can learn are from the winners. Bruce Cleland, of trend follower Campbell and Company, candidly summed up LTCM and his firm's strategy:

"If you look back to the early part of 1998, you will see it was a similar period in terms of industry returns. It was a very sad time all the way through July. And then out of nowhere it came, the collapse or the near-collapse of Russia in August and the LTCM (Long-Term Capital Management) crisis. All of a sudden, August was up 10% and September and October were up 4% or 5%, and many CTAs pulled down an 18% or 20% year out of nowhere. It's very hard to put your head back where you were three months before that and say it looked like a very gloomy business without much of a future and all of a sudden we're the place it's all at. The hedge fund world had fallen apart, equities had gone into the toilet and managed futures were king and on the front page of *The Wall Street Journal*. So some of this is the psychology of what we do."[39]

Trend followers know they will not behave the same way as the majority of traders when faced with an unexpected event. Their "way" is set in motion long before the event ever happens.

The performance data for trend followers in August and September of 1998 looks like one continuous credit card swipe from LTCM. During the exact same period that LTCM lost $1.9 billion in assets, the aggregate profits (Chart 4.14) of five long-term trend followers; Bill Dunn, John W. Henry, Jerry Parker, Keith Campbell, and Man exceeded $1 billion in profit.

"There are two kinds of people who lose money: those who know nothing and those who know everything." With two Nobel prize winners in the house, Long-Term Capital clearly fits the second case.[40]

The Fed's intervention was misguided and unnecessary because LTCM would not have failed anyway, and the Fed's concerns about the effects of LTCM's failure on financial markets were exaggerated. In the short run the intervention helped the shareholders and managers of LTCM to get a better deal for themselves than they would otherwise have obtained.[41]

CHART 4.14: Trend Following Profits Aug.–Sept. 1998

Dunn Capital Management WMA

July 1998: -1.37%, 575,000,000

August 1998: +27.51%, 732,000,000

September 1998: +16.8%, 862,000,000

Dunn Capital Management TOPS

July 1998: -1.08%, 133,000,000

August 1998: +9.48%, 150,000,000

September 1998: +12.90%, 172,000,000

John W. Henry Financials and Metals

July 1998: -0.92%, 959,000,000

August 1998: +17.50, 1,095,000,000

September 1998: +15.26, 1,240,000,000

Campbell and Company Financials and Metals

July 1998: -3.68, 917,000,000

August 1998: +9.23, 1,007,000,000

September 1998: +2.97, 1,043,000,000

Chesapeake Capital

July 1998: +3.03, 1,111,000,000

August 1998: +7.27, 1,197,000,000

September 1998: -0.59, 1,179,000,000

Man Investments

July 1998: +1.06, 1,636,000,000

August 1998: +14.51, 1,960,000,000

September 1998: +3.57, 2,081,000,000

Percent returns for each month and total money under management in that fund.

. . .[O]ne of the former top executives of LTCM [gave] a lecture in which he defended the gamble that the fund had made. "What he said was, Look, when I drive home every night in the fall I see all these leaves scattered around the base of the trees,?. . .There is a statistical distribution that governs the way they fall, and I can be pretty accurate in figuring out what that distribution is going to be. But one day I came home and the leaves were in little piles. Does that falsify my theory that there are statistical rules governing how leaves fall? No. It was a man-made event." In other words, the Russians, by defaulting on their bonds, did something that they were not supposed to do, a once-in-a-lifetime, rule-breaking event. . . [this] is just the point: in the markets, unlike in the physical universe, the rules of the game can be changed. Central banks can decide to default on government-backed securities.

Malcolm Gladwell[42]

Crunch the numbers for yourself on Dunn Capital Management's World Monetary Assets (WMA) fund. Their fund made nearly $300 million for the months of August and September 1998 alone. What markets (Charts 4.15–4.22), for example, did trend followers profit from?

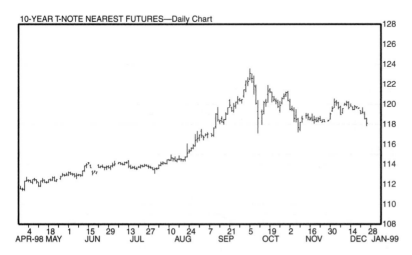

CHART 4.15: Trend Followers and the 10 Year T-Note May 1998–Dec. 1998 *Source: Barchart.com*

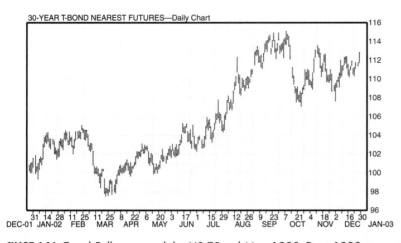

CHART 4.16: Trend Followers and the US T-Bond May 1998–Dec. 1998 *Source: Barchart.com*

CHART 4.17: Trend Followers and the German Bund May 1998–Dec. 1998 *Source:* Barchart.com

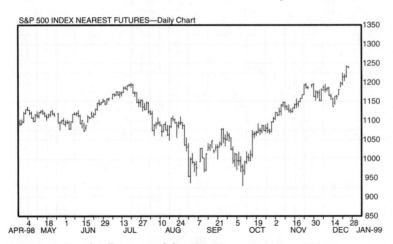

CHART 4.18: Trend Followers and the S&P May 1998–Dec. 1998 *Source:* Barchart.com

CHART 4.19: Trend Followers and the Swiss Franc May 1998–Dec. 1998 *Source:* Barchart.com

CHART 4.20: Trend Followers and the Eurodollar May 1998–Dec. 1998 *Source:* Barchart.com

CHART 4.21: Trend Followers and the Yen May 1998–Dec. 1998 *Source:* Barchart.com

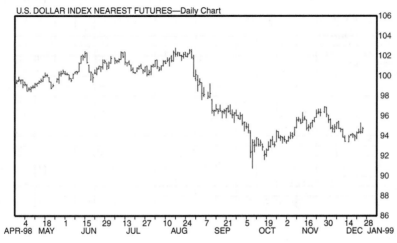

CHART 4.22: Trend Followers and the Dollar Index May 1998–Dec. 1998 *Source:* Barchart.com

It isn't that they can't see the solution. It is that they can't see the problem.

G. K. Chesterton[43]

What "lessons learned" do business school professors teach when analyzing LTCM's failure today? We are guessing that one thing they don't teach are the crucial points Jerry Parker made when he differentiated his firm from LTCM:

1. Transparent—By and large, trend followers trade markets on regulated exchanges. They are not cooking up new derivatives in their basement. Trend followers typically trade on freely traded markets, where there is a price that everyone can see that allows anyone to buy or sell. Trend followers have nothing in common with the derivatives fiascos that damaged Orange County or Proctor and Gamble.

2. Understandable—Trend Following strategies can be understood by just about anybody. There is no high-level math that only PhDs can comprehend.

3. No Rock Stars—There are individuals who not only want to make money, but also want a rock star as their portfolio manager. They want to think that the strategy being used to make them money is exciting and state-of-the-art. Trend followers are not in the game for notoriety, just to win.

Debate still continues as to whether it was proper for the government to step in and save LTCM. Indeed, what would have happened (and how much more money would trend followers have made) if LTCM had been allowed to properly implode?

We asked Dunn Capital Management whether they thought it was proper that the Fed helped bail out LTCM. Daniel Dunn replied with a one-word answer: "No." When we asked Bill Dunn, he opined:

"I believe the Long Term Capital Management collapse was caused by:

1. Their trading approach was based on the theory that prices and relationships between prices tend to vary, but they also tend to return to their mean value over long periods of time. So in practice, they probably looked at a market (or a spread between markets) and determined what its mean value was and where the current price was in relation to their estimate of its

'true mean' value. If the current price was below the mean, a 'buy' was indicated, and if it was above the mean, a 'sell' was indicated. (I don't know what their exit strategy was.)

2. The main problem with the above is that as market prices move further against your position, you will be experiencing losses in your open positions and your above trading approach would suggest that adding to the current position will prove to be even more profitable than originally expected. Unless this market very quickly turns and starts its anticipated return to its mean, additional losses will be suffered and the potential for profit will seem to become even greater, although elusive.

3. This problem can only be overcome by either adopting a strict entry and exit strategy that is believed to promote survivability or by having a nearly unlimited amount of capital/credit to withstand the occasional extreme excursions from the mean, or better yet, adopt both of these ideas.

4. But the situation became even more unstable when LTCM ventured into highly illiquid investment vehicles and also became a very major part of these very thin markets.

5. In the end, they became overextended and they ran out of capital before any anticipated reversion to the mean could bail them out."—Bill Dunn

Investors who cannot or will not learn from the past could be setting themselves up for another August–September 1998. Another LTCM fiasco may be in the offing if the Black-Scholes way of life where the world is a normal distribution is still considered a viable approach to investing. Philip Anderson, a Nobel Prize Recipient in Physics, reminds us of the dangers that come from thinking in terms of normal distributions:

"Much of the real world is controlled as much by the 'tails' of distributions as by means or averages: by the exceptional, not the mean; by the catastrophe, not the steady drip; by the very rich, not the 'middle class.' We need to free ourselves from 'average' thinking."[44]

Breaking out from average thinking results in hitting home runs (trend followers) instead of attempting and failing to slap those supposed sure-fire singles (LTCM).

We make a lot more money trading at the level we do. The trade-off is volatility, but if it doesn't cause you to perish, then you're better off in the long run.

Pierre Tullier[46]

Event #3:
Asian Contagion and Victor Niederhoffer

The Asian crisis of 1997, also referred to as the Asian Contagion, was yet another big event where trend followers won. One of the biggest losers during the fall of 1997 was the infamous trader Victor Niederhoffer. Always opinionated, bombastic, and for most of his trading career, exceptionally successful, Niederhoffer's trading demise was swift and complete.

Victor Niederhoffer played a big game, whether at speculating, chess, or squash. He challenged grandmasters in chess and won repeated titles as a national squash champion. He regularly bet hundreds of millions of dollars and consistently won until Monday, October 27, 1997. That day he lost an estimated $50 to $100 million, and his three hedge funds, Limited Partners of Niederhoffer Intermarket Fund L.P., Limited Partners of Niederhoffer Friends Partnership L.P., and Niederhoffer Global Systems S.A., bellied up.[45]

Imagine receiving this letter, which was faxed to clients of Victor Niederhoffer on Wednesday, October 29, 1997:

On Wednesday Niederhoffer told investors in three hedge funds he runs that their stakes had been "wiped out" Monday by losses that culminated from three days of falling stock prices and big hits earlier this year in Thailand.[47]

To:

Limited Partners of Niederhoffer Intermarket Fund, L.P.

Limited Partners of Niederhoffer Friends Partnership, L.P.

Shareholders of Niederhoffer Global Systems, S.A.

Dear Customers:

As you no doubt are aware, the New York stock market dropped precipitously on Monday, October 27, 1997. That drop followed large declines on two previous days. This precipitous decline caused substantial losses in the fund's positions, particularly their positions in puts on the Standard & Poor's 500 Index. As you also know from my previous correspondence with you, the funds suffered substantial losses earlier in the year as a result of the collapse in the East Asian markets, especially in Thailand.

The cumulation [sic] of these adverse developments led to the situation where, at the close of business on Monday, the funds were unable to meet minimum capital requirements for the maintenance of their margin accounts. It is not yet clear what is the precise extent (if any) to which the funds' equity balances are negative. We have been working with our broker-dealers since Monday evening to try to meet the funds' obligations in an orderly fashion. However, right now the

> *indications are that the entire equity positions in the funds has been wiped out.*
>
> *Sadly, it would appear that if it had been possible to delay liquidating most of the funds' accounts for one more day, a liquidation could have been avoided. Nevertheless, we cannot deal with "would have been." We took risks. We were successful for a long time. This time we did not succeed, and I regret to say that all of us have suffered some very large losses.*[48]

Niederhoffer seems unable to acknowledge that he, alone, was to blame for his losses in the zero-sum game. He did it. No one else did it for him and he can't use the unexpected as his excuse.

Niederhoffer's trading performance was long heralded as low-risk. He made money almost every month. Compared to trend followers, he was the golden boy. Who would want to place money with Bill Dunn or John W. Henry and potentially tolerate a bigger drawdown when they could put their money with Victor Niederhoffer, who seemed to combine similar performance with what appeared to be far less risk and almost no drawdown?

The notion that Niederhoffer was devoid of risk sank with his trading firm in 1997. Let's examine Niederhoffer's performance numbers during the year (Chart 4.23):

I felt there were very definite economic trends that were established from knowledge and the ability to know what events meant. I was looking for a way to participate in [those] major trends when they occurred, even though they were unexpected.

Bill Dunn[50]

CHART 4.23: Niederhoffer 1997 Performance[49]

Date	VAMI	ROR	Quarter ROR	Yearly ROR	Amount Managed
Jan-97	11755	4.42%			
Feb-97	11633	-1.04%			
Mar-97	10905	-6.26%	-3.13%		$130.0M
Apr-97	11639	6.73%			
May-97	11140	-4.28%			
Jun-97	10296	-7.58%	-5.58%		$115.0M
Jul-97	11163	8.42%			
Aug-97	5561	-50.18%			
Sep-97	7100	27.67%	-31.04%		$88.0M
Oct-97	1	-99.99%			
Nov-97	1	0.00%			
Dec-97	1	0.00%	-99.99%	-99.99%	0

[Victor Niederhoffer] looked at markets as a casino where people act as gamblers and where their behavior can be understood by studying gamblers. He regularly made small amounts of money trading on that theory. There was a flaw in his approach, however. If there is a . . . tide . . . he can be seriously hurt because he doesn't have a proper fail-safe mechanism.

George Soros[54]

As you review Niderhoffer's 1997 performance meltdown (Chart 4.23), keep in mind that in the last issue of The Stark Report (International Traders Research's former name) where his performance was still listed, his ranking is as follows:

Return: 4 stars
Risk: 4 stars
Risk Adj: 4 stars
Equity: 5 stars[51]

These star rankings give the impression that Victor Niederhoffer was risk-free. Niederhoffer's trading, like LTCM's, was predicated on a world of normal distributions. Measuring him with standard deviation as the risk measure gave an imperfect view of what Niederhoffer's true risk actually was. Of course there were some observers who were well aware of the inherent problems in Niederhoffer's contrarian style long before his blowout. Frank J. Franiak spoke out 6 months earlier in spring 1997:

"It's a matter of time before something goes wrong."[52]

But Niederhoffer loyalists were only concerned with whether the profits were coming in, even if his strategy was deeply flawed and potentially dangerous. His clients were enamored with his ability to rebound: "Whatever voodoo he uses, it works."—Timothy P. Horne, chairman of Watts Industries Inc. (Niederhoffer customer since 1982)[53]

Unfortunately, the vast majority of Niederhoffer clients did not realize until after their accounts were toast that voodoo doesn't work.

Niederhoffer Confuses Trend Following

Oddly, five years after his blowout, Niederhoffer ripped Trend Following:

"Granted that some users of Trend Following have achieved success. Doubtless their intelligence and insights are quite superior to our own. But it's at times like this, when everything seems to be coming up roses for the trend followers' theories and reputations, that it's worthwhile to step back and consider some fundamental questions:

1. Is their central rule, The trend is your friend, valid?

2. Might their reported results, good or bad, be best explained as due to chance?

"But first, a warning: We do not believe in trend-following. We are not members of the Market Technicians Association or the International Federation of Technical Analysts or the TurtleTrader Trend Followers Hall of Fame. In fact, we are on the enemies list of such organizations."[55]

We have a hard time understanding how, after reviewing the month by month performance histories of Keith Campbell, Jerry Parker, John W. Henry, and Bill Dunn, that their "numbers" are "due to chance" as Niederhoffer says.

Niederhoffer goes on to question the objective nature of Trend Following: "No test of 'The trend is your friend' is possible, because the rule is never put forward in the form of a testable hypothesis. Something is always slippery, subjective, or even mystical about the rule's interpretation and execution."[56]

Even though the performance data is clear, in his most recent book Niederhoffer still didn't "get it":

"In my dream, I am long IBM, or priceline.com, or worst of all, Krung Thai Bank, the state owned bank in Thailand that fell from $200 to pennies while I held in 1997. The rest of the dream is always the same. My stock plunges. Massive margin calls are being issued. Related stocks jump off cliffs in sympathy. Delta hedges are selling more stocks short to rebalance their positions. The naked options I am short are going through the roof. Millions of investors are blindly following the headlines. Listless as zombies, they are liquidating their stocks at any price and piling into money market funds with an after tax yield of -1 percent. 'Stop you fools!' I scream. 'There's no danger! Can't you see? The headlines are inducing you to lean the wrong way! Unless you get your balance, you'll lose everything—your wealth, your home!'"[57]

Niederhoffer seems to have a difficult time accepting blame. He is the one non-trend-follower who should be profiled in two of our chapters. Not only does his zero-sum wealth transfer during the 1997 Asian Contagion make him critical to Chapter 4, but his inconsistent thinking and refusal to take responsibility for his actions place him squarely in our chapter on Holy Grails.

In statistical terms, I figure I have traded about 2 million contracts . . . with an average profit of $70 per contract. This average profit is approximately 700 standard deviations away from randomness, a departure that would occur by chance alone about as frequently as the spare parts in an automotive salvage lot might spontaneously assemble themselves into a McDonald's restaurant.

Victor Niederhoffer[58]

Most important, Niederhoffer is an inveterate contrarian. He feeds off panic, making short-term bets when prices get frothy. He condemns the common strategy of trend-following, which helped make his buddy George Soros super-rich. "A delusion," he declares.[59]

Despite his envy and admiration, he did not want to be Victor Niederhoffer—not then, not now, and not even for a moment in between. For when he looked around him, at the books and the tennis court and the folk art on the walls—when he contemplated the countless millions that Niederhoffer had made over the years—he could not escape the thought that it might all have been the result of sheer, dumb luck.

Malcolm Gladwell[60]

Cumulative losses continued to mount through 1994. By 31 December 1994, they stood at yen;25.5 billion (S$373.9 million) and after the collapse of the Baring Group, amounted to Yen;135.5 billion (S$2.2 billion). In retrospect, it seems probable that until February 1995, the Baring Group could have averted collapse by timely action."[61]

Event #4:
Barings Bank Meltdown

The first few months of 1995 must go down as one of the most eventful periods in the history of speculative trading. The market events of that time period, by themselves, could be the subject of a graduate course in finance at Harvard Business School. Only a few years later, despite the significance of what happened, the events have been forgotten.

A rogue trader, Nick Leeson, overextended Barings Bank in the Nikkei 225, the Japanese equivalent to the American Dow, by speculating that the Nikkei 225 would move higher. It tanked, and Barings, the Queen's bank, one of the oldest, most well-established banks in England, collapsed, losing $2.2 billion.

Who won the Barings Bank sweepstakes? That question was never asked by anyone—not the *Wall Street Journal* nor *Investor's Business Daily*. Was the world only interested in a story about failure and not in the slightest bit curious about where that $2.2 billion went? Trend followers were sitting at the table devouring Leeson's mistakes. They saw, in Barings, an opportunity to win as Barings lost.

The majority of traders do not have the discipline to plan three, six, and twelve months ahead for unforeseen changes in markets. But planning ahead for the unexpected is an essential ingredient of Trend Following. Big moves are always on the horizon if you are simply reacting to the market and not trying to predict it.

Why do many people miss the big events and consequently the big trends? Most traders make decisions on their perception of what the market direction will be. Once they make their directional choice, they become blinded to any other option. They keep searching for any type of validation to support their analysis even if they are losing money—just like Nick Leeson. Before the Kobe earthquake in early January 1995, with the Nikkei trading in a range of 19,000 to 19,500, Leeson had long futures positions of approximately 3,000 contracts on the Osaka Stock Exchange. After the Kobe earthquake of January 17, his build-up of Nikkei positions intensified and Leeson just kept buying as the Nikkei sank.[62]

Who Won?

Observe the Nikkei 225 (Chart 4.24) from September 1994 until June 1995. Barings' lost assets padded the pockets of disciplined Trend Following traders.

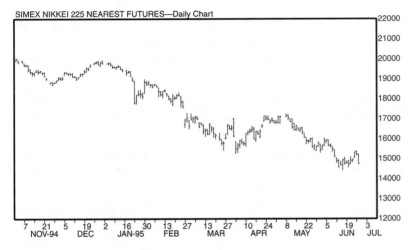

CHART 4.24: Nikkei 225 Sep. 1994–Jun. 1995 *Source:* Barchart.com

A few months after Barings, John W. Henry's performance (Chart 4.25) makes the case clear:

CHART 4.25: John W. Henry Trading Programs

Name of Program	01-95	02-95	03-95
Financials and Metals	$648	$733	$827
	-3.8	15.7	15.3
Global Diversified	$107	$120	$128
	-6.9	13.5	8.5
Original	$54	$64	$73
	2.1	17.9	16.6
Global Financial	$7	$9	$14
	-4.1	25.6	44.4

All dollars are in millions under management.

Dean Witter (now Morgan Stanley) was John W. Henry's broker at the time:

"I have over $250 million with John W. Henry. . .I have been pleased to see how well the Original [John W. Henry] Program has done so far in 1995: up over 50 percent through April 18th [1995]."—Mark Hawley, Dean Witter Managed Futures[63]

Other trend followers brought home huge gains in February and March of 1995 (Chart 4.26) as well. However, their winnings arguably were more the result of the fantastic Japanese Yen trend up and down.

What about luck? In my opinion, luck is far and away the most important determinant in our lives. Various events of infinitesimal probability—where you are born, to whom you are born, who you marry, where you take your first job, which school you choose—have enormous impact on our lives. People tend to deny that luck is an important determinant. We like explanations. For instance, during a basketball game there are innumerable random events. If a guy hits three in a row, he's really hot. Most of the time, it's random. Of course, the announcer doesn't want to say, "Oh my! Another random event!" That's not exciting, so he'll give a reason. But it's just luck. Not all of our luck is good, but there is more good luck behind our performance than even I like to acknowledge.

James Simons
The Greenwich Roundtable
June 17, 1999

CHART 4–26: 1995 Trend Following Performance

Name	01-95	02-95	03-95
Chesapeake	$549	$515	$836
	-3.2	-4.4	8.6
Rabar	$148	$189	$223
	-9.4	14.0	15.2
Campbell Fin/Metals	$255	$253	$277
	-4.53	5.85	9.58
Mark J. Walsh	$20	$22	$29
	-16.4	17.0	32.3
Abraham	$78	$93	$97
	-7.9	1.2	6.6
Dunn (WMA)	$178	$202	$250
	0.5	13.7	24.4
Dunn (TOPS)	$63	$69	$81
	-7.6	9.9	22.7
Millburn Ridgefield	$183	$192	$233
	-6.5	8.7	19.4

Monthly percent returns with total money under management. All dollars are in millions under management.

There may be slight differences in leverage and signal timing, but even from a quick glance it is clear: Big trends equaled big profits at the same time for all trend followers. John W. Henry confirmed in 1998, albeit cryptically, his zero-sum Barings win:

"The inflation story, of course, is not the most dramatic example. More recently Asia is another example of how one-time big events can lead to trends that offer us opportunity, and really shape our world. Whether you believe the causal story of banking excesses in Asia or not, there was a clear adjustment in the Asian economies that has been, and will continue to be, drawn out. Under these situations, it's natural that trends will develop, and recognizing these trends allows us to capitalize on the errors or mistakes of other market participants. Because, after all, we're involved in a zero-sum game."[64]

John W. Henry and Nick Leeson were involved in a zero sum game. They both ponied up to the table. However, there was one big difference—John W. Henry had a strategy. What Nick Leeson had nobody really knows, but as long as Leeson was making money his bosses and higher-ups in England did not much care.

There is no profit taking per se. We only exit on stop-losses, because profit taking would interfere with the unlimited upside potential we have, in theory, on every position. Our stop-loss policy is an actuarial model that analyzis the probability and consequences of hitting stops placed at various prices relative to the current market level. This allows us to estimate the expected loss associated with each possible exit point and hence to construct an optimal liquidation schedule.

Paul Mulvaney,
CIO of
Mulvaney Capital Management, Ltd.

Event #5:
Metallgesellschaft

Metallgesellschaft now has a new name and a new identity as a specialty chemicals, plant, and process engineering concern. But for 119 years, the German company was a metals, trading, and construction conglomerate, best known for the high-profile mess it was involved in after a New York arm, MG Refining Marketing Inc. (MGRM), produced what its chief lenders considered reckless losses in its energy-trading operations. In 1993, steep margin debt calls contributed significantly to Metallgesellschaft's loss of $1.5 billion (2.3 billion Deutsche marks at the time). Just before collapsing, the company was bailed out by German banks.[65]

What happened?

Metallgesellschaft (MG), was long crude oil futures on the New York Mercantile Exchange (NYMEX) through most of 1993. Over that time period, MG lost, depending on the estimate or source, $1.3 to $2.1 billion. Because trading is a zero-sum game, those traders in short crude oil futures made the money MG lost. They were the winners, and they were trend followers.

But in the course of the next 12 months, it became more and more obvious that other traders were formulating trading strategies that exploited MG's need to liquidate its expiring long position. At the end of each trading month, as MG tried to liquidate its long positions by buying the offsetting shorts, other traders would add their short positions to MG's, creating the paper market equivalent of a glut in supply that initially exceeded the number of longs, driving prices down until the market reached equilibrium. The combined force of MG's selling its long position in the prompt contract and other traders increasing their short positions was severe downward pressure on crude prices as the prompt month contract neared expiration.[66]

During the course of 1993, crude oil futures (Chart 4.27) slowly declined from May through December.

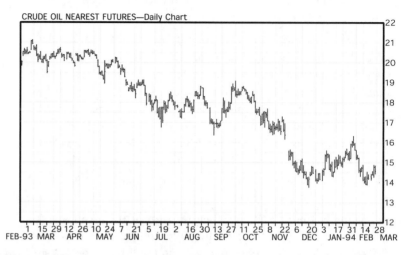

CHART 4.27: Crude Oil Futures Feb. 1993–Feb. 1994 *Source: Barchart.com*

There is always someone on each side of a trade. The difficulty lies in determining who is on the opposite side of a position if one side is known. That MG lost was known, but who won and how? In the aftermath of the MG losses, a variety of explanations developed. The financial world was treated to academic mumbo jumbo from MBA students analyzing why MG lost money, as well as numerous articles condemning energy futures. The actual explanation is simply that MG had a bad plan and lost big.

Trend followers played a major role in MG's defeat. The job of explaining this is made easy by their performance data (Chart 4.28):

CHART 4.28: Trend Followers' Performances Jun. 1993–Jan. 1994

	6-93	7-93	8-93	9-93	10-93	11-93	12-93	1-94
Abraham	-1.2	6.6	-5.3	1.2	-6.6	3.5	12.5	-1.45
Chesapeake	1.0	9.5	5.8	-2.7	-0.1	1.1	5.8	-3.33
JPD	-6.9	10.2	-2.1	-4.1	-2.0	2.7	8.6	-3.9
Rabar	-1.3	14.8	-3.9	-4.1	-6.0	5.6	10.1	-10.5
Saxon	-2.7	20.5	-14.3	-2.1	-1.1	6.6	17.1	-10.8

The key to explaining Chart 4.28 lies in the months of July 1993, December 1993, and January 1994. Those months do not require much more than a glance at the correlation data to confirm the similarity in strategies used by trend followers. Trend followers all made money in July and December, and they all lost money in January.

The academics, the media, and everyone, it seems, figured out that professional traders were shorting the energy market and putting extensive pressure on MG. What the academics never found out or never seemed to be interested in finding out was who those professional traders were. The performance data was out there for everybody to look at. It wasn't a secret.

Every day, trend followers knew how many contracts or shares to trade based on total capital at that time. For example, after they initiated positions and were rewarded with strong profits in July, they were willing to risk those profits again, which is what they did. In August, with nice profits in hand, they were willing to risk all of those profits and still lose a fixed percentage based on their original stops. They were willing to let profits on the table turn into losses. They let the market tell them when the trend was over (i.e. January 1994).

In Fall 1993, trend followers continued to hold their established short positions in crude oil futures. MG was long crude oil futures and desperately trying to stay afloat while trend followers waited like predators. But trend followers were not just short; they were aggressively short, reinvesting their profits back into additional short crude oil positions as the market decreased more and more.

On the losing side of this zero-sum game, MG had no apparent strategy. They refused to take a loss early on. In fact, the whole MG affair would have been a footnote in trading history if they had simply exited after the July price decline. However, instead, MG stayed in the game in hopes of an upward trend to make up for losses. But MG had no inkling of the steely discipline of their opponents. Not one of the trend followers was going to exit anytime soon. The price told them the trend was down. An exit would have violated one of their most fundamental rules: Let winners run.

Crude oil began its final descent in late November into December. At this time, MG management liquidated all positions and further fueled the November and December crude price drop. Ultimately all good trends must come to an end. Trend followers would eventually begin their crude oil futures exit in January 1994. If you look at the

One of the few things the post-mortems seem to have glossed over is the trap that MG had gotten itself into by becoming the dominant participant in the futures markets. By the fall of 1993, some traders had come to anticipate the rollovers of MG's positions. As long as its huge position was in the market, MG hung there like a big piñata inviting others to hit it each month. The self-entrapping nature of its positions is what is missing from Edwards and Canter's, and even Culp and Miller's, defenses of MG.[67]

According to the NYMEX, MGRM held the futures position equivalent of 55 million barrels of gasoline and heating oil.[68]

"Can you do addition?" the White Queen asked. "What's one and one and one and one and one and one and one and one and one and one?" "I don't know," said Alice. "I lost count."

Lewis Carroll[69]

performance of trend followers in January 1994 (Chart 4.28), you can see what they lost for the month as they extricated themselves from their history-making profits of 1993 (Chart 4.29).

CHART 4.29: 1993 Trend Following Returns

Name	% Return
Abraham Trading	+34.29%
Chesapeake Capital	+61.82%
Man Investments	+24.49%
Rabar Market Research	+49.55%
Dunn WMA	+60.25%
John W. Henry Financials and Metals	+46.85%
Mark J. Walsh	+74.93%
Eckhardt Trading	+57.95%

Final Thoughts

There is no shortage of big events in the past three decades demonstrating how trend followers whipped the competition. But there are still skeptics who think they have uncovered the Achilles heel of Trend Following.

The S&P lost 29.6% of its value during the 1987 crash and took until May 1989 to recover. EAFE Index, Jaguar and Quantum performance was highly correlated to that of the broad market. Over the full period, Financial and Metals Portfolio earned nearly 260% on a composite basis.

John W. Henry[70]

The 1987 Stock Crash

One of our favorite questions from skeptics is: "How did the trend followers do during the 1987 stock crash?" Their tone always gives away what they think the answer will be (or what they hope it will be). The fall of 1987, as the data proves (Chart 4.30 and Chart 4.31), produced historic gains for trend followers:

CHART 4.30: Oct.–Nov. 1987 Stock Market Crash

Name	% Return
S&P 500	-28%
John W. Henry Original Investment Program	+58.2%
John W. Henry Financials and Metals Portfolio	+69.7%

CHART 4.31: Trend Following Performance 1987

Name	% Return
Chesapeake Capital	+38.78%
JPD	+96.80%
Rabar	+78.20%
John W. Henry Financials and Metals	+251.00%
Campbell and Company Financials and Metals	+64.38%
Millburn Ridgefield	+32.68%
Dunn Capital Management WMA	+72.15%
Mark J. Walsh	+143%
Man Investments	+42.54%

Success demands singleness of purpose.

Vince Lombardi

The First Gulf War

Skeptics also assume that the first Gulf War was probably a time period in which trend followers incurred losses. The data from John W. Henry shows otherwise:

"During the 1990 market decline and subsequent recovery, Financial and Metals Portfolio generated returns of 38.1% against the S&P 500's 4.4%. While Jaguar and Quantum performed better than the broad market, they did not perform as well as Financial and Metals Portfolio."[71]

Jerry Parker offers a clear and coherent view of why fundamental analysis played no role in the trading of trend followers during this time period:

"Fundamental analysis that excluded the possibility of an Iraqi invasion of Kuwait in the summer of 1990 would have been incomplete and possibly unprofitable, or worse. This was the only 'fundamental' that was worth knowing, yet was the very one that almost no one could have known. Technical analysis relies upon the idea that smart money will move into a market and give advance warning that a position should be taken. This often occurs when the true major fundamentals are unknown."[72]

The events presented in this chapter should leave you with one inescapable conclusion: Trend Following is successful because it

A speculative mania is a wonderful thing for our program. We do as much of that as possible. Unfortunately, in saying that, I sound a little bit anti-common man, man on the street. What's bad for the general public is very good for our program.

Toby Crabel, Crabel Capital
The Greenwich Roundtable
November 20, 2003

When you have eliminated the impossible, what ever remains, however improbable must be the truth.
Sir Arthur Conan Doyle[73]

has no quarterly performance constraints. What do we mean? Both Wall Street and Main Street measure their success on the artificial constraints of the calendar. For example, looking back at the end of 2000, you can see that without November and December offering such huge home runs, trend followers would have had a terrible year. For those people who judge trading success by "quarters," trend followers were dead the better part of 2000.

The whole idea of quarterly performance reporting implies you can predict the market or successfully shoot for profit targets. Quarters may not be real, but they provide a comfortable structure for investors who mistakenly believe they can demand nice, consistent profits. This demand for consistency can lead to the constant search for the Holy Grail or "hot hand" to the detriment of ever winning.

Blaming derivatives for financial losses is akin to blaming cars for drunk driving fatalities.
Christopher L. Culp[74]

Imagine playing a football game where there are four quarters, and you have to score in each quarter to win. Imagine placing more importance on scoring in each quarter than winning the game. Now Bill Dunn says, "I might score 28 points in any of the four quarters. I might score at any point in the game, but the object, at the end of the game is to win." So if Bill Dunn scores 28 points in the first quarter and no points in the next three quarters, and wins, who cares when he scored? Wall Street's misguided emphasis on quarterly performance puts more importance on scoring each quarter than it does on winning the game.

The alternative is to become a home run hitter and take what the market gives no matter when it arrives. Absolute return players like Bill Dunn have no profit targets. They view their world as a "rolling return." We asked Dunn Capital Management how they address the quarterly performance measures so popular on Wall Street. We wanted to know how they educated clients to appreciate "big event hunting." Their response was clear: "Clients must already have an appreciation for the pitfalls of relying on short-term performance data before they can appreciate us."

Blunt talk for a serious game. On the other hand, after he retired from trading, Julian Robertson publicly lamented quarterly performance constraints, comparing them to a necessary but incompetent baseball umpire: "One of the great investors likened it to a batter not having an umpire. If you don't have an umpire, you can wait for the fat pitch. The trouble with investing for other people, particularly in a hedge fund, is that you do have an umpire—called quarterly performance."

The Coming Storm

What will be the next big event? No one can know for sure. However, there is strong evidence that the lessons of Long Term Capital Management are long forgotten. February 2004 commentary from the *Economist* sounds like a replay:

"The size of banks' bets is rising rapidly the world over. This is because potential returns have fallen as fast as markets have risen, so banks have had to bet more in order to continue generating huge profits. The present situation "is not dissimilar" to the one that preceded the collapse of LTCM . . . banks are 'walking themselves to the edge of the cliff'. This is because—as all past financial crises have shown—the risk-management models they use woefully underestimate the savage effects of big shocks, when everybody is trying to wriggle out of their positions at the same time . . . By regulatory fiat, when banks' positions sour they must either stump up more capital or reduce their exposures. Invariably, when markets are panicking, they do the latter. Since everyone else is heading for the exits at the same time, these become more than a little crowded, moving prices against those trying to get out, and requiring still more unwinding of positions. It has happened many times before with more or less calamitous consequences . . . It could well happen again. There are any number of potential flashpoints: a rout in the dollar, say, or a huge spike in the oil price, or a big emerging market getting into trouble again. If it does happen, the chain reaction could be particularly devastating this time."[75]

When the chain reaction happens, as it always does, guess who will be the winners?

The success of options valuation is the story of a simple, asymptotically correct idea, taken more seriously than it deserved, and then used extravagantly, with hubris, as a crutch to human thinking.

Emanuel Derman[76]

It seems LTCM could have survived one Nobel prize-winner, but with two, they were doomed.

Frederic Townsend[77]

Key Points

- Ed Seykota: "Trends become more apparent as you step further away from the chart."

- Surprise makes prices move.

- Trend followers are generally on the right side of big moves.

- The most interesting aspect of the Barings Bank blowout was who won. Everyone knew the Queen's bank lost. Barings' losses were won by trend followers in the zero-sum game.

Corporations make good and bad decisions every day" offers one dealer. P&G made a bad decision. But if they came in with a Pampers line that flopped, you wouldn't have hearings in Congress, would you?[78]

When the mind is in a state of uncertainty the smallest impulse directs it to either side. [Lat., Dum in dubio est animus, paulo momento huc illuc impellitur.]

Terence (Publius Terentius Afer)
Source: Andria (I, 5, 32)

- People place too much emphasis on the short-term performance of trend followers. They draw conclusions about one month's performance and forget to look at the long term. Just like a batting average, which can have short-term streaks over the course of a season, trend followers have streaks. Trend Following performance does deviate from averages, but over time there is remarkable consistency.

- Value-at-risk (VAR) models measure volatility, not risk. If you rely on VAR as a risk measure you are in trouble.

- Hunt Taylor, Director of Investments, Stern Investment Holdings, states: "I'm wondering when statisticians are going to figure out that the statistical probability of improbable losses are absolutely the worst predictors of the regularity with which they'll occur. I mean, the single worst descriptor of negative events is the hundred-year flood. Am I wrong? How many hundred-year floods have we lived through in this room? Statistically maybe we should have lived through one and we lived through seven now at this point."

- 2004-2005 crude oil and natural gas price shocks. European Union squabbles. Hurricane Katrina hitting the United States Gulf coast. Are you prepared for and protected from the unexpected? Do you have a plan?

Baseball: Thinking Outside the Batter's Box

5

"How to hit home runs: I swing as hard as I can, and I try to swing right through the ball . . . The harder you grip the bat, the more you can swing it through the ball, and the farther the ball will go. I swing big, with everything I've got. I hit big or I miss big. I like to live as big as I can."
—Babe Ruth

"What is striking is that the leading thinkers across varied fields—including horse betting, casino gambling, and investing—all emphasize the same point. We call it the Babe Ruth effect: even though Ruth struck out a lot, he was one of baseball's greatest hitters."
—Michael J. Mauboussin and Kristen Bartholdson[1]

The concepts that make up Trend Following should be experienced to be understood completely, a tough prerequisite. We found it helpful to compare Trend Following to baseball, a sport all of us have experienced either passively or actively to one degree or another. Baseball has always been a passion of mine. My playing career went from Little League into college, and I've watched more baseball than I care to admit. I've always known that baseball and Trend Following have much in common, but it wasn't until the past few years that sportswriters and financial writers started acknowledging their similarities. Not surprisingly, this was about the time that John W. Henry bought the Boston Red Sox. Henry makes the connection in Michael Lewis' *Moneyball*:

The point about Dykstra, at least to Billy, was clear: Dykstra didn't let his mind mess him up. Only a psychological freak could approach a 100-m.p.h. fastball aimed not all that far from his head with total confidence. "Lenny was so perfectly designed, emotionally, to play the game of baseball," Beane said. "He was able to instantly forget any failure and draw strength from every success. He had no concept of failure. I was the opposite."

Moneyball[2]

The general complacency of baseball people—even those of undoubted intelligence—toward mathematical examination of what they regard properly and strictly as their own dish of tea is not too astonishing. I would be willing to go as far as pretending to understand why none of four competent and successful executives of second-division ball clubs were most reluctant to employ probabalistic methods of any description . . . but they did not even want to hear about them!

Earnshaw Cook[6]

"People in both fields [stock market and baseball] operate with beliefs and biases. To the extent that you can eliminate both and replace them with data, you gain a clear advantage. Many people think they are smarter than others in the stock market and that the market itself has no intrinsic intelligence as if it's inert. Many people think they are smarter than others in baseball and that the game on the field is simply what they think through their set of images/beliefs. Actual data from the market means more than individual perception/belief. The same is true in baseball."[3]

Are you smarter than the market? If you could find the data that would prove otherwise but still enable you to win, would you be able to set aside your ego and play the game by a set of rules? If so, you might be on the same path as John W. Henry.

The Home Run

Ed Seykota, Bill Dunn, and John W. Henry swing for the fence. They hit home runs in their trading performance. They are the Babe Ruths of Trend Following. If any of them coached a baseball team, they would approach it like the former manager of the Baltimore Orioles:

"Earl Weaver designed his offenses to maximize the chance of a three-run homer. He didn't bunt, and he had a special taste for guys who got on base and guys who hit home runs."[4]

Ed Seykota uses a clever baseball analogy to explain his view of absolute returns (and home runs): "When you're up to bat, it doesn't pay to hedge your swing . . . True for stocks & true for [Barry] Bonds."[5]

If you are going to play, you might as well play hard. Isn't that Seykota's insight? Swing hard and if you miss, so be it.

Life is too dynamic to remain static.

John W. Henry[7]

George Herman Ruth, hero of New York, hero of baseball, and arguably one of the greatest sports legends of all time, will always be known for his hard swings and home runs. But he had another habit that isn't talked about much: striking out. In fact, with a lifetime batting average of .342, the Babe spent almost two-thirds of his time trudging back to the dugout. From a pure numbers perspective, he saw more failure at the plate than success. But when he got a piece of one, well, it was enough to give any pitcher nightmares.

There's a reason why "Ruthian" is still a well-known adjective in sportswriting, conveying the awe and power of a mighty blast that sails far over the fence, up and away into the very highest reaches of stands. Ruth understood full well that the hits help a whole lot more than the strikeouts hurt. He summarized his philosophy in a nutshell: "Every strike brings me closer to the next home run."

Richard Driehaus, a hugely successful trader who has made millions trading trends, hits the nail on the head:

"A third paradigm [in the financial press] is don't try to hit home runs—you make the most money by hitting a lot of singles. I couldn't disagree more. I believe you can make the most money hitting home runs. But, you also need a discipline to avoid striking out. That is my sell discipline. I try to cut my losses and let my winners run."8

But swinging for the fence is often characterized as reckless by the uninitiated:

"One anonymous competitor said Henry is our industry's Dave Kingman, referring to the ex-ballplayer famous for either hitting home runs or striking out. Henry says such talk is unfair. 'I've been doing this for 20 years, and every time there's a change in the market, they say I should change my ways. But every time there's a period when we don't do well, it's followed by one in which we do extraordinarily well.'"9

An anonymous competitor thinks Henry is Dave Kingman? John W. Henry's performance is much closer to Babe Ruth's than Dave Kingman's. Let's examine the actual hitting statistics of Ruth and Kingman (Chart 5.1):

CHART 5.1: Babe Ruth v. Dave Kingman [30]

	Babe Ruth:	**Dave Kingman:**
At Bats	8399	6677
Hits	2873	1575
Runs	2174	901
Home Runs	714	442
Batting Average	.342	.236
Slugging	.690	.478

Even before he trained with commodities legend Richard Dennis, Jim DiMaria had learned an important trading principle in the less lucrative arena of baseball statistics: The players who score the most runs are home run hitters, not those with consistent batting records. "It's the same with trading," the 28-year-old DiMaria says. "Consistency is something to strive for, but it's not always optimal. Trading is a waiting game. You sit and wait and make a lot of money all at once. The profits tend to come in bunches. The secret is to go sideways between the home runs, not lose too much between them."10

And if you step back from American society and ask "What kind of people are getting rich these days?" the answer is increasingly "People like John W. Henry." That is, people on the nerdly end of the spectrum, who have a comfort with both statistical analysis and decision-making in an uncertain environment. And these people, increasingly, will demand that their teams be run along rational lines.

Michael Lewis[11]

Compare the slugging percentages. There is no comparison. Kingman could not be considered a great run producer by any measure. On the other hand, Henry's performance numbers are top-flight production. Henry has a great slugging percentage.

People want it both ways. John W. Henry supposedly strikes out too much (we all know that's not relevant by now, right?), but he's made himself enough money to buy the Boston Red Sox for $700 million. Where do you think he got that money from? John W. Henry has said that he knows of numerous institutional investment managers, primarily in Europe, who manage billions of dollars for clients, who have spent more than 20 years watching him and waiting for him to fail.

The lesson for traders is this: If you have confidence in your method and yourself, then temporary setbacks don't matter, because you will come out ahead in the long run. So go ahead and commit. Go for the home run.

To further illustrate the point, consider a modern day example: the blue-collar Joe v. the entrepreneur. The blue-collar Joe is paid the same lump sum every two weeks like clockwork (with the occasional miniscule raise paced to keep up with inflation). In terms of winning percentage, blue collar is king: his ratio of hours worked to hours paid is one to one, a perfect 100 percent. He has a steady job and a steady life. Of course, the security he feels is something of an illusion—his paycheck comes at the whim of his local economy, his industry, and even the foreman of his plant. And the pay isn't exactly impressive. It gives him a solid, livable life, but not much more.

In contrast, consider the entrepreneur. His paydays are wildly irregular. He frequently goes for months, sometimes years, without seeing tangible reward for his sweat and toil. His winning percentage is, in a word, pathetic. For every 10 big ideas he has, seven of them wind up in the circular file. Of the remaining three, two of those fizzle out within a year—another big chunk of time, money and effort down the drain. But we can't feel too sorry for the poor entrepreneur who spends so much time losing. He has a passion for life, he controls his own destiny, and his last idea paid off with a seven-figure check.

Moneyball and Billy Beane

Billy Beane is the General Manager of the Oakland A's baseball team. He does things differently than the stodgy old-line baseball managers. He makes his baseball decisions on the "numbers."

Billy Beane doesn't have a fancy stadium or a wealthy owner. In fact, this small-market team's payroll is one-third that of the New York Yankees. However, the Oakland A's are routinely among the best teams in major league baseball, having reached the playoffs four years in a row (2000–2003). What happened? Billy Beane became the Oakland A's general manager. In "The Buffett of Baseball," the old school perspective on what constitutes a winning baseball team (familiar truisms about talent, character, and chemistry) is compared with the new scientific approach based on numbers. This new approach is based on extensive scientific research into baseball statistics. It is often called sabermetrics, after SABR, the Society for American Baseball Research, and has proved almost all of the old truisms to be false. The genius behind sabermetrics was a mechanical engineer named Earnshaw Cook, who, in the early 1960s, compiled reams of data that overturned baseball's conventional wisdom. But when he presented the data to executives at a handful of struggling teams, they shooed him away. So Cook wrote a book called *Percentage Baseball,* based on statistics that were irrefutable.[13]

The performance data of trend followers is likewise irrefutable. Beane-ball and Trend Following apply science (the precision of numbers) to what heretofore has been always layered in subjective opinion, myth, and feeling.

What are some examples of Billy Beane's "by the numbers" approach to baseball? "Beane uses actuarial analysis to figure out, say, the odds of a high-school pitcher's becoming a major leaguer. And, in drafting and acquiring talent, he relies on sabermetric truths. For instance, if your team draws a lot of walks and hits a lot of home runs while giving up few of each, it will win a lot of ballgames. So Beane has stocked his team with sluggers who take walks, and control pitchers who rarely give up home runs."[16]

Billy Beane says, "Get me the runs." In his world, he neither wants nor needs a team full of Lance Johnsons, who only slap singles and never hit home runs.

You know, there are a core of institutional investment managers, primarily in Europe, who manage billions of dollars for clients, who have waited for me to fail for more than twenty years. They have an inherent bias against the notion that data or mechanical formulas can lead to success over time in markets. They have personally watched my success now for more than twenty years. Yet, if anything, they are now no more convinced than they were twenty years ago that I am going to be successful in the future using data over analysis. I am not legendary (on Wall Street or off). Bill is, and I assume the inherent bias against him within baseball will increase now that he has taken sides.

John W. Henry[14]

Even while managing $1.1 billion using quantitative analysis, which he calls "quant," Henry knew that the same, dispassionate statistical investigation could be used to help shape a baseball team and its budget. "It is remarkably similar," "I just happened to apply 'quant' to an area that's extremely lucrative."[15]

The nature of markets is to trend. The nature of life is to trend.

John W. Henry[18]

John W. Henry Enters the Game

Many trend followers started trading on their own with small accounts. They grew slowly as independents and were often renegades, unlike the more conventional traders on Wall Street who still "earn their spurs" at Goldman Sachs or Morgan Stanley. Their nature and their strategies are polar opposites of the traders who inhabit a Wall Street world built on commissions. Like Billy Beane's view of baseball players, trend followers realize that large amounts of cash do not guarantee wins. Strategy and smarts beats capital nine times out of ten.

Trend Following's connection with baseball and numbers picked up even more steam with John W. Henry's hiring of Bill James, the quintessential baseball "quant," or numbers guy, for over 20 years. Bill James, the consummate outsider, was brought on to enrich Henry's Red Sox club with his unique numbers-based view of baseball. James' views might be too harsh for the majority of professionals and fans in the baseball world. For example, he is excruciatingly blunt in his negative assessment of folks like Don Zimmer, the loveable-looking former bench coach for the Yankees:

Usually when making investments, it is implicit that investors believe they have some degree of knowledge about the future. So Wall Street has more fortune tellers than any other industry. I feel I've had an advantage over the years because I am clear about a couple of things: 1) it is part of the nature of life itself (and markets are simply manifestations of people's expectations) to trend, and 2) I will never have a complete or full understanding of anything. Therefore, all investment decisions should be based on what can be measured rather than what might be predicted or felt.

John W. Henry[19]

"[A]n assortment of half-wits, nincompoops, and Neanderthals like Don Drysdale and Don Zimmer who are not only allowed to pontificate on whatever strikes them, but are actually solicited and employed to do this."[17]

Unfortunately, Zimmer might just have added fuel to James' fire with his boneheaded attack on Pedro Martinez during the 2003 American League Championship Series with the Yankees. Zimmer may have, in fact, exhibited a hint of Neanderthal behavior. However, the bad feelings Bill James has about the establishment seem to be mutual:

"'A little fat guy with a beard who knows nothing about nothing,' is how Hall of Fame manager Sparky Anderson once described James, who's neither short nor fat."[20]

How unique is the Bill James perspective of baseball? Extremely:

"I keep thinking, however, about an e-mail that James sent me after I visited him in Kansas, in which he tried to explain the connection between his obsession with crime stories and baseball.

'I feel a need to be reminded, day in and day out, how easy it is for a fantasy to grab hold of your foot like a rope, and dangle your life upside down while brigands go through your pockets,' he wrote. 'The essential message of crime books is: Deal with the life you've got. Solve the problems you have, rather than fantasizing about a life without them.'"[21]

When James says solve the problems you have as opposed to fantasizing about what your life would be like without them, I am reminded of Trend Following's reliance on price. Price is a collective perception. You can accept it or ignore it. That brings us back to John W. Henry's love of numbers. Even when he owned the Florida Marlins, Henry knew he had to change:

"By the time he sold the Marlins to buy the Red Sox, Henry was convinced that baseball was putting too much emphasis on tools—baseball jargon for athletic ability—and not enough on performance. The on-the-field success of the Oakland A's, then the only team using sabermetrics, confirmed Henry's view. 'The Marlins would draft athletes,' he says, 'while the A's would draft baseball players.'[22]

Part of the problem, from John W. Henry's perspective, is the baseball old guard's love of the Adonis athlete over pure production—hitting, power, plate discipline. Would you rather have the ripped stud who looks the part, but swings and misses at every curveball, or do you notice that short fat guy who can't run and looks ridiculous, but never swings at a bad pitch and produces runs by the bushel? "Producing" is the John W. Henry goal in both his baseball and his trading. To reach his production goal requires clarity as Henry states:

"People in both baseball and the financial markets operate with beliefs and biases. To the extent you can eliminate both and replace them with data, you gain a clear advantage. Many people think they are smarter than others in the stock market, and that the market itself has no intrinsic intelligence—as if it's inert. Similarly, many people think they are smarter than others in baseball, and that the game on the field is simply what they think it is, filtered through their set of images and beliefs. But actual data from the market means more than individual perception/belief. And the same is true in baseball."[24]

For nearly 25 years, there's been a huge food fight in baseball. The argument was basic: How do you evaluate a player? On one side were general managers, scouts and managers. For the most part, they evaluated players the old-fashioned way—with their eyes, stopwatches and radar guns and by looking at statistics which were popularized in the 19th century. Their mind-set was always, "How fast does he run? How hard does he throw? What's his batting average? Does he look like a major leaguer should look?" On the other side—led by statistical gurus such as Bill James and Pete Palmer, and assisted by countless lesser "seamheads" (including, at times, me)—were the geeks, the outsiders, mere fans, who thought they knew better.

Thomas Boswell,
Washington Post[23]

Thinking about baseball in terms of "numbers" was not done when I played the sport, nor do I have any memory of my coaches preaching the Bill James or John W. Henry gospel.

Red Sox 2003–2004

Red Sox Nation will forever debate whether or not Pedro Martinez should have been lifted in the 8th inning of Game 7 of the 2003 American League Championship Series against the Yankees. But he was left in, and the Yankees rallied from three runs down to win the series. Grady Little, the Red Sox manager, was blamed for Boston's loss and fired soon thereafter. Many people wondered if he wasn't being unfairly scapegoated for a decision others would have made. After all, Pedro was his ace, and Little's gut told him to stay with his ace.

It's like any field. There's a vested interest in maintaining the status quo so you don't have to learn anything new.

Robert Neyer, ESPN[25]

Perhaps in this situation, Pedro gets through the 8th nine times out of ten. After all, the percentage of innings in which a pitcher gives up three or more runs is small, and Pedro is an exceptional pitcher. However, a look at the numbers says that leaving him in was the wrong decision. After 105 pitches in a given start, his batting average against rises to .370. He ended up throwing 123 pitches in Game 7.

Little's dismissal was summed up in *The Brown Daily Herald*:

"Grady isn't a stats guy, plain and simple. He's an old school manager who goes with his gut and defers to his partially informed conscience when making decisions. Contrast this with the front office, which has transformed itself into a sabermetric, number-crunching machine, and the divide is clear as day . . . Fast forward to the eighth inning of Game 7 of the ALCS. Grady sends Pedro back onto the mound to the surprise of many who assumed he would be yanked after throwing exactly 100 pitches. Opponents hit .364 off Pedro this year after his 105th pitch—even Tony Clark could hit Pedro in the late innings."[26]

By the end of the 2003 baseball season I had learned something from publishing Moneyball. I'd learned that if you look long enough for an argument against reason, you will find it.

Michael Lewis[27]

The late, great Stephen Jay Gould, a numbers man (and lifelong baseball fan), offered some insight into the decision-making process that may have left Pedro in the game:

"Everybody knows about hot hands. The only problem is that no such phenomenon exists. The Stanford psychologist Amos Tversky studied every basket made by the Philadelphia 76ers for more than a season. He found, first of all, that probabilities of making a second basket did not rise following a successful shot. Moreover, the number of 'runs,' or baskets in succession, was no greater than what a standard random, or coin-tossing, model would predict. Of course Larry Bird, the great forward of the Boston Celtics, will have more sequences of five than Joe Airball—but not because he has greater will or gets in that magic rhythm more often. Larry has longer runs because his average success rate is so much higher, and random models predict more frequent and longer sequences. If Larry shoots field goals at 0.6 probability of success, he will get five in a row about once every thirteen sequences (0.6^5). If Joe, by contrast, shoots only 0.3, he will get his five straight only about once in 412 times. In other words, we need no special explanation for the apparent pattern of long runs. There is no ineffable 'causality of circumstance' (if I may call it that), no definite reason born of the particulars that make for heroic myths—courage in the clinch, strength in adversity, etc. You only have to know a person's ordinary play in order to predict his sequences."[28]

Gould's friend, Ed Purcell, a Nobel laureate in Physics, did research on baseball streaks. He concluded that nothing ever happened in baseball above and beyond the frequency predicted by coin-tossing models. The longest runs of wins and losses are as long as they should be.[29]

Had Grady Little played the numbers in 2003, the Red Sox might not have had to wait until 2004 to finally win the World Series. For there is no doubt that an analysis of numbers, as evidenced by Bill James, Billy Beane, and John W. Henry, works as strategy for playing baseball.

Key Points

- John W. Henry: "Life is too dynamic to remain static."

- If you have realistic confidence in your method and yourself, then temporary setbacks don't matter. Going for the home run can allow you to come out ahead in the long run.

- Thinking in terms of odds is a common denominator of baseball and Trend Following.

When Grady Little let Pedro continue pitching into the eighth in Game 7 of the ALCS against the Yankees, he provided the perfect demonstrator of why the Red Sox fired him after his second winning season in Boston. Little explained his move (which allowed the Yankees to tie and eventually win) after the game: "We trained him to work just like that deep into a game. When he tells me he has enough in the tank to keep going, that's the man I want out there. That's no different than what we've done the last two years." In fact, the stats said just the opposite. Pedro pitched into the eighth only five times in his 29 regular-season starts, and simply didn't pitch well after he'd thrown 100 pitches, the number he'd tossed before taking the mound in the eighth. In fact, during 2003, opponents' batting averages went up .139 after Pedro tossed his 105th pitch—strong evidence that he'd continue to weaken. That it would turn out badly was likely, as most everyone knew—and as the Red Sox computers knew. [30]

The truth of a theory is in your mind, not in your eyes.

Albert Einstein[31]

Part III

Human Behavior 6

Today, trend followers such as John W. Henry and Ed Seykota spend as much time observing and understanding human behavior as they do trading. Understanding human behavior in relation to the markets is commonly referred to as behavioral finance.

Behavioral finance is the study of why and how human beings and markets behave in relation to each other. It evolved out of the contradiction between classical economic theory and reality. Economic theory is based on the assumption that people are able to act rationally, have identical values and access to information, and use rational decision-making. The truth is that we are irrational to varying degrees and seldom make completely rational decisions

We understand the distinction between simple and easy. Simple, robust solutions are easier to find than robust people or firms willing to apply them.

Jason Russell[2]

History does not repeat itself: people just keep forgetting it. No matter how many stock market bubbles there have been, or will be, investors and their advisors always treat the current one as permanent, sometimes even calling it a "new era." In the meantime, others, myself included, have abandoned all hope of people permanently remembering the lessons of history.[3]

even if we think we do. Charles Faulkner clarifies core issues associated with behavioral finance:

"The current proliferation of electronic technologies—computers, the Internet, cellphones, 24 hour news and instant analysis—tend to distract us from the essentially human nature of markets. Greed, hope, fear, and denial, herd behavior, impulsiveness and impatience with process ('Are we there yet?') are still around, and if anything, more intensely so. Few people have absorbed the hard neuroscience research that reasons arrive afterwards. That given the choice between a simple, easy to understand, explanation that works and a difficult one that doesn't, people tend to pick the latter. People would rather have any story about how a series of price changes happened than that there is no rational reason for it. Confusing hind-sight with foresight, and complexity with insight are a few more 'cognitive illusions' of Behavioral Finance."

Faulkner is absolutely correct, but that doesn't make his words easy to accept. The problem is, not accepting the truth is always going to get you into trouble one way or another, as Carl Sagan points out:

"It is far better to grasp the Universe as it really is than to persist in delusion, however satisfying and reassuring."

Prospect Theory

Investment bubbles have always been a part of market history. For example, speculators in the Netherlands in the 17th century drove up the prices of tulip bulbs to absurd levels. The inevitable crash followed. Since then, from the Great Depression to the recent dot-com implosion, people can't seem to steer clear from speculative manias. They make the same mistakes over and over again.

Daniel Kahneman, the Princeton professor who was the first psychologist to win the Nobel Prize in Economics, for studies he conducted with Amos Tversky, attributed market manias partly to investors' "illusion of control," calling the illusion "prospect theory." Kahneman studied the intellectual underpinnings of investing—how traders estimate odds and calculate risks—in order to prove how often we act from the mistaken belief that we know more than we do. Kahneman's stark conclusion is that we are victims of our own overconfidence.

Kahneman and Tversky found that a typical person acts on what they christened the "law of small numbers"—basing broad predictions on narrow samples of data. For instance, we buy a fund that's beaten the market three years in a row, convinced it's "on a hot streak." People seem to be unable to stop themselves from overgeneralizing the importance of a few supporting facts. Limited statistical evidence seems to satisfy our intuition no matter how inadequate the depiction of reality.[4]

Further, Kahneman and Tversky determined we dislike losses so much that we will make irrational decisions in vain attempts to avoid them. This helps explain, why some investors sell their winning stocks too early, but hold on to losers for too long. It is human nature to take the profit from a winner quickly on the assumption our win won't last for long, and stick with a loser in the futile hope it will bounce back.[5]

However, trend followers know if you don't cut your losses short, there's a good chance the losses will get larger. The more you struggle with your small loss, the larger it may become and the harder it may be to deal with if your decision-making is delayed. The problem we have with accepting a loss is that it forces us to admit we are wrong. We human beings just don't naturally like to be wrong.

Any discussion of why investors are their own worst enemies, when it comes to being wrong, must start with sunk costs. A sunk cost is an investment of money and time that has already been incurred and that you can't recoup. Thinking in terms of sunks lets you see a loss for what it actually is—a loss. While we all know that sunk costs must not influence our present decisions, we have a hard time forgetting the past. A person may buy more of a stock even though it is tanking simply because of the initial decision to buy it. The person can then say proudly, "I bought on a discount!" Of course if the price of the stock never goes up again, as is often the case, this theory implodes.

Trend followers ignore sunk costs. If they buy and the market goes against them, they exit. "Take your small loss and go home" is their mantra. However, most of us are ambivalent when we have to deal with sunk costs. Although intellectually we know that there is

Knowing others is wisdom; Knowing the self is enlightenment. Mastering others requires force; Mastering self needs strength.

Lao Tsu[6]

If there is one trait that virtually all effective leaders have, it is motivation. They are driven to achieve beyond expectations—their own and everyone else's. The key word here is achieve. Plenty of people are motivated by external factors such as a big salary or the status that comes from having an impressive title or being part of a prestigious company. By contrast, those with leadership potential are motivated by a deeply embedded desire to achieve for the sake of achievement.

Daniel Goleman[8]

nothing we can do about money already spent and we must move on, emotionally we dwell in the past.

An experiment with a $10 theater ticket demonstrates our irrationality when it comes to sunk costs. Kahneman and Tversky told one group to imagine they have arrived at the theater only to discover they have lost their ticket. "Would you pay another $10 to buy another ticket?" A second group was told to imagine that they are going to the play but haven't bought a ticket in advance. When they arrive at the theater, they realize they have lost a $10 bill. Would they still buy a ticket? In both cases, the subjects were presented with essentially the same simple question: Would you want to spend $10 to see the play? 88 percent of the second group, which had lost the $10 bill, opted to buy the ticket. But the first group, the ticket losers, focusing on sunk costs, tended to ask the question in a different way: Am I willing to spend $20 to see a $10 play? Only 46 percent said yes.[7]

There are a number of behaviors that will almost guarantee losses in the markets. These behaviors, the antithesis of the way trend followers operate, include:

- **Lack of discipline:** It takes an accumulation of knowledge and sharp focus to trade successfully. Many would rather listen to the advice of others than take the time to learn for themselves. People are lazy when it comes to the education needed for trading.

- **Impatience:** People have an insatiable need for action. It may be the adrenaline rush they're after, their "gambler's high". Trading is about patience and objective decision-making, not action addiction.

- **No objectivity:** We tend not to cut our losses fast enough. It goes "against the grain" to sell. At the same time, we often get out of winners too soon. In both cases, we are unable disengage emotionally from the market. We marry our positions.

- **Greed:** Traders try to pick tops or bottoms in hopes they'll be able to "time" their trades to maximize their profits. A desire for quick profits can blind traders to the real hard work needed to win.

- **Refusal to accept truth:** Traders do not want to believe the only truth is price action. As a result, they act contrary to the trend, and set the stage for the losses that almost always arrive.

- **Impulsive behavior:** Traders often jump into a market based on a story in the morning paper. Markets discount news by the time it is publicized. Thinking that if you act quickly, somehow you will beat everybody else in the great day-trading race is a grand recipe for failure.

- **Inability to stay in the present:** To be a successful trader, you can't spend your time thinking about how you're going to spend your profits. Trading because you have to have money is not a wise state of mind in which to make decisions.

- **Avoid false parallels:** Just because the market behaved one way in 1930, does not mean a similar pattern today will give the same result.

If you try to bridge the gap between the present and the future with predictions about the market direction, you're guaranteed to be in a continual state of uncertainty whether you admit to it or not. Scientists have now begun to investigate the impact of extended uncertainty on human beings. The conclusion? We react the same way to uncertainty that other animals do when faced with a threat, by shifting into "fight or flight" mode.

But unlike the animal's environment, where the threat passes quickly one way or another, our lives are spent in constant stressful situations, many of which never go away or never arrive. According to neuroscientist Robert Sapolsky, human beings, unlike other animals, can—and often do—experience stress simply by imagining stressful situations. "For 99 percent of the beasts on this planet, stressful situations include about three minutes of screaming terror, after which the threat is over or you are over. We humans turn on the exact same stress response thinking about 30-year mortgages," Sapolsky says. Yet, while thinking about a mortgage is not life-threatening, the stress is probably going to last much longer than three minutes. So what do researchers like Sapolsky think the biggest public health problem in the developed world 50 years from now will be? Depression.[9]

Traders can definitely get depressed when they lose. Usually, they look everywhere else, blaming others or events to avoid taking responsibility for their actions. Instead of working out their own motivations and emotions in order to understand why they make the decisions they do, they chase after yet one more Holy Grail or

NLP is short for Neuro-Linguistic Programming. The name sounds high tech, yet it is purely descriptive. Neuro refers to neurology, our nervous system—the mental pathways our five senses take which allow us to see, hear, feel, taste and smell. Linguistic refers to our language ability; how we put together words and phrases to express ourselves, as well as how our "silent language" of movement and gestures reveals our states, thinking styles and more. Programming, taken from computer science, refers to the idea that our thoughts, feelings and actions are like computer software programs. When we change those programs, just as when we change or upgrade software, we immediately get positive changes in our performance. We get immediate improvements in how we think, feel, act and live.

Charles Faulkner[10]

Fat, drunk and stupid is
no way to go through life,
son.

                         Animal House[12]

Self-Knowledge Keys
1. Know what you want.
   Know who you are, not
   who you think you
   should be. Self-
   awareness gives you the
   power to pursue what
   really feeds your soul
   and the belief that you
   deserve it.
2. Know the cost of getting
   what you want. Realize
   the trade-offs of every
   choice. People often
   think if they are clever
   they can make choices
   without experiencing
   any downside. Any road
   you choose means there
   is a road you won't
   experience.
3. Be willing to pay the
   cost. People often try to
   negotiate to win a choice
   without cost. Every
   choice involves a price;
   we get to decide what
   cost we want to pay.[13]

fundamental forecast, hoping to discover the ironclad "winning" strategy.

Another reason uncertainty looms so large is because we are often ambivalent about money to begin with. Some of us would like to have more money but feel guilty about admitting it. A few of us have lots of money, but want even more and still feel guilty. Take a moment to think through your motivations for trading. If you have any reason for trading other than to make money, find something else to do and avoid the stress from the beginning. There is nothing good or bad about money. Money is just a tool—nothing more, nothing less.

Is money a legitimate reason for us to feel anxious or guilty? Ayn Rand articulates a nonjudgmental and rational attitude about money in her classic *Atlas Shrugged*:

"'So you think that money is the root of all evil?' said Francisco d'Anconia. 'Have you ever asked what is the root of money? Money is a tool of exchange, which can't exist unless there are goods produced and men able to produce them. Money is the material shape of the principle that men who wish to deal with one another must deal by trade and give value for value. Money is not the tool of the moochers, who claim your product by tears, or of the looters, who take it from you by force. Money is made possible only by the men who produce. Is this what you consider evil?'"[11]

According to any number of economic theories, conflicted feelings about money shouldn't exist. Human behavior should reflect a rational approach to money and not assign different values to the same products and the same values to different products. We are supposed to refuse to pay too much for a watch because of the social cache of a label. We are supposed to make intelligent objective choices that maximize our wealth and financial security.

But then what is the motivation behind the person who runs up credit card debt at 14 percent interest, but would never think of dipping into their savings account to pay off the debt? What is the explanation for people who spend time researching a new car or designer kitchen, but when it comes time to invest their retirement funds, refuse to learn or engage in any research? Charles Faulkner thinks there is more at play in these situations:

"Some problems run deeper, springing from limiting, unconscious beliefs. For instance, a trader who has labeled himself a one-for-trader, or who learned as a child the biblical story it's easier for a camel to pass through the eye of a needle than for a rich man to enter the kingdom of God, may subconsciously sabotage his trading to respect his beliefs. They're deeply ingrained in us . . . but if all the ethical people think money is bad, who's going to get the money?"[14]

If we think money is bad, how are we going to make more? How do trend followers think about money? What advice can we trust to help us reprogram our responses so that we trade rationally, objectively, and mindfully?

Here are three experts on human behavior, who have studied these questions and come to the same conclusions.

Emotional Intelligence: Daniel Goleman

Many traders mindlessly repeat the same actions over and over again, day after day hoping for better results. They want to believe that if they are able to discern patterns they will win. As a result they are continually making connections and drawing parallels that are not valid. They miss seeing the differences. Seeing those differences separate the winners and losers.

Ironically, the real pattern they miss is the one common to all successful traders. This is the pattern of acting with complete confidence in their ability to make decisions, right or wrong, in the face of change. You must become fearless:

"They have confidence in their ability to make (investment) decisions, and to persist in the face of adversity to revise their thinking and their action in light on new information and insight, and abiding confidence in their ability to learn. In a phrase, they have the confidence to change."—Charles Faulkner

The less confident you are, the more you will create frustrating and demoralizing experiences for yourself. The more you learn about the markets and yourself, the more confident you become. The more confident you become, the more effective you are as a trader.

In 1995, psychologist Daniel Goleman published his best-seller, *Emotional Intelligence*, a thoroughly researched and powerful case

It may readily be conceived that if men passionately bent upon physical gratifications desire greatly, they are also easily discouraged; as their ultimate object is to enjoy, the means to reach that object must be prompt and easy or the trouble of acquiring the gratification would be greater than the gratification itself. Their prevailing frame of mind, then, is at once ardent and relaxed, violent and enervated. Death is often less dreaded by them than perseverance in continuous efforts to one end.

Alexis de Tocqueville[15]

for broadening the meaning of intelligence to include our emotions. Drawing on brain and behavioral research, Goleman demonstrated why people with high IQs often flounder, while people with modest IQs often do extremely well. According to Goleman, the factors that influence how well we do in life include self-awareness, self-discipline, intuition, empathy, and an ability to enter the flow of life, character traits most traders would not consider particularly useful for garnering profits from the markets. But trend followers would agree with Goleman, since these are exactly the traits at the core of their trading success. Trend followers are self-aware; therefore they are able to monitor and manage their true emotions. In other words, they can separate what they feel from how they trade and make trading decisions objectively.[16]

Goleman points out that being self-aware also means understanding what you want out of life. You know what your goals and values are and you are able to stick to them. For instance, if you're offered a high-paying job that doesn't square with your values or your long-term goals, you can turn it down promptly and without regret. If you are faced with a breach of corporate ethics by one of your employees, you deal with it instead of either ignoring it or making a half-hearted response because you pretend to yourself it won't happen again.[17]

Emotional self-control makes anyone more productive. However, Goleman is not saying we should repress our feelings of anxiety, fear, anger, or sadness. We must acknowledge and understand our emotions for what they are, so that we are able to behave in ways that make us effective at what we do. Goleman goes on to say that, like animals, biological impulses drive our emotions. There is no way to escape them, but we can learn to self-regulate our feelings and, in so doing, manage them. Self-regulation is like an ongoing inner conversation that the emotionally intelligent engage in to free themselves from being prisoners of their own feelings. Goleman hastens to add that if we are able to engage in such a conversation, we still feel bad moods and emotional impulses just as everyone else does, but we are able to control them and even to channel them in useful ways.[18]

Trend followers' ability to delay gratification, stifle impulsiveness, and shake off the market's inevitable setbacks and upsets, makes them not only successful traders, but also leaders. Goleman found that effective leaders all had a high degree of emotional intelligence along with the relevant IQ and technical skills. And that while these other "threshold capabilities" were the entry-level requirements for executive positions, emotional intelligence was the "sine qua non" of leadership. Without emotional intelligence, someone can have superior training, an incisive, analytical mind, and infinite creativity, but still won't make a great leader.[21]

If you look at how trend followers like Bill Dunn, Ed Seykota, and John W. Henry developed, you'll see that they were all self-starters, motivated from the beginning to achieve. But perfecting the strategy of Trend Following, applying it to new markets, teaching others how to trend follow, and expanding their own knowledge of trading is what keeps them in the game.

Just as important as managing your own feelings is being able to recognize the feelings of others. Few of us live, or trade for that matter, in a vacuum. The sense of being cut off from the world, of being isolated with no one to turn to, is a common consequence of traders who feel the pressure but have only their computer to relate to. This doesn't necessarily mean you need a group of colleagues to hang out with around the water cooler every couple of hours, but objectivity comes from having a balanced life.

Charles Faulkner

Why have men like Richard Donchian and Ed Seykota (Chapter 2) been able to teach Trend Following? One answer is found in the field of Neuro-Linguistic Programming, or NLP. One of the best teachers of NLP is Charles Faulkner who speaks with an authority and clarity gained from having taught hundreds of traders how to gain the "mental edge":

"NLP's techniques involve moving out negative mental beliefs and replacing them with positive ones. Think of an unpleasant trade . . . As you do that, what happens if you take a breath and go 'aaah,' push it out and then trade with it? Much better. People go through fifths of scotch trying to get that feeling. When you get agitated, go 'whoosh' and just step out of it that way and you'll find that it's less. Do it again and you'll be at zero real fast."—Charles Faulkner[22]

I first met Charles Faulkner at a trading seminar. Since then, we've continued to maintain a friendship. Faulkner has a natural

When popular opinion is nearly unanimous, contrary thinking tends to be most profitable. The reason is that once the crowd takes a position, it creates a short-term, self-fulfilling prophecy. But when a change occurs, everyone seems to change his mind at once.

Gustave Le Bon[23]

Walk into the college classroom, and you will hear your professors teaching your children that man can be certain of nothing; that his consciousness has no validity whatsoever; that he can learn no facts and no laws of existence; that he's incapable of knowing an objective reality.

Ayn Rand[24]

"I model human excellence."

Charles Faulkner[25]

gift for teaching how to envision the big picture. He always urges traders to take matters into their own hands:

"He wants traders to believe that, 'I am competent to be confident. I know what's going on in these markets. If I don't know, I get out.'"[26]

Like many master teachers Faulkner uses simple stories to illustrate complex lessons. I found, for example, Faulkner's "Swiss skiing" example from *The New Market Wizards* to be especially insightful. He used skiing to explain how NLP works. He pointed out that until the 1950s, most people thought skiing was a matter of natural talent that you had or you didn't have. Then films were made of some of Europe's greatest skiers to identify all the movements that characterized them. It was found that they all had certain techniques in common. All kinds of people could learn to be very good skiers if the movements that made a great skier, the essence of their skills, could be identified so they could be taught to others. Faulkner observed that this essence of skills was called a model, and that the model (or set of basic principles) could be applied to any endeavor.[27]

Ed Seykota's Trading Tribe

Profiled in Chapter 2, Ed Seykota has long served as a mentor to traders. His natural inclination to teach and mentor has evolved into his Trading Tribe, a global network of groups of traders who meet monthly to "work through challenges":

"The trading tribe is an association of traders who commit to excellence, personal growth, and supporting and receiving support from other traders."[28]

Ed Seykota's Trading Tribe works on the psychological and emotional issues Seykota believes are crucial for successful trading (and life for that matter). Charles Faulkner tells a story about Seykota's finely honed intuition when it comes to trading:

"I am reminded of an experience that Ed Seykota shared with a group. He said that when he looks at a market, that everyone else thinks has exhausted its up trend, that is often when he likes to get in. When I asked him how he made this determination, he said he just put the chart on the other side of the room and if it looked like it was going up, then he would buy it . . . Of course this trade was seen through the eyes of someone with deep insight into the market behavior."[31]

Seykota doesn't pretend to have all the answers but he is extremely good at reflecting the mirror back to his students so they will focus on where the issues really lie. His precision with language, like Faulkner's, makes you pay attention to what he is saying. One of Seykota's students Chauncey DiLaura breaks Seykota's teachings down:

"The mind is a filter, letting only some information in . . . When you're designing systems or setting stops, it's an ever-present part of what you do. My goal is to get in touch with those subconscious processes. A lot of what [Seykota does is] a breathing technique to achieve an altered state of consciousness where you somehow relax your conscious filters. We did it both unstructured and in a structured way, with ideas to concentrate on, such as, 'Why do I always do this when I'm trading?'"[32]

Here are some of my favorite insights from my conversations with Seykota:

- One use of the Trading Tribe Process is to locate and dissolve the feelings that stand between you and following your system.

- When you notice all things happen now, and when you take responsibility for your experience, you notice that even "noise" results from your intention. At that point you can clarify your intention and remove the noise. The entire length of the chain of events exists in the ever evolving moment of now—and at all points of now, you may choose to see your result equals your intention. Alternatively, you may choose to avoid responsibility, especially for the noise, and then try to find exogenous "causes."

- Analysis leads to solving and fixing. The Trading Tribe Process leads to dis-solving and noticing things already work right. Incontrovertible solvers tend to use TTP as an analytical tool— until they happen to experience their own feelings of wanting to solve things.

- Take responsibility for your experience and you can see that intentions equals results. Deny responsibility for your

"My life has stopped, but I continue to age," deadpans Karen Levine, a Wharton School MBA who has worked at General Mills (GIS), Unilever, Deloitte Consulting, Condé Nast, and Hearst. But in real terms, Levine made more in 1988 fresh out of Harvard College than she earns today. During her two years of battling unemployment, Levine has worked for $8 an hour at Pottery Barn and for $18 an hour as a temp for a Wall Street trading firm. "I can't even afford a dog," she says.[33]

The illiterate of the 21st century will not be those who cannot read and write, but those who cannot learn, unlearn, and relearn.

Alvin Toffler

Human beings never think for themselves, they find it too uncomfortable. For the most part, members of our species simply repeat what they are told—and become upset if they are exposed to any different view. The characteristic human trait is not awareness but conformity . . . Other animals fight for territory or food; but, uniquely in the animal kingdom, human beings fight for their 'beliefs'. . .The reason is that beliefs guide behavior, which has evolutionary importance among human beings. But at a time when our behavior may well lead us to extinction, I see no reason to assume we have any awareness at all. We are stubborn, self-destructive conformists. Any other view of our species is just a self-congratulatory delusion.

Michael Crichton[36]

"*Having an education is one thing, being educated is another.*"

Lee Kuan Yew,
former Prime Minister of Singapore[37]

experience and a delta between intentions and results may appear.

- Your real trading system is the set of feelings you are unwilling to experience.
- In tracking your feelings and in tracking the markets, take whatever comes up and go with it. Trying to force a feeling is like trying to force a market. You might find some joy in the process of allowing feelings and markets to come and go as you experience them.

Why does a trader as successful as Ed Seykota spend so much of his time delving into the subject of feelings? "It is a dominant idea in Western society that we should separate emotion and rationality. Advances in science show that such a separation is not only impossible but also undesirable."[34]

Seykota has known about the "advances in science" for 30 years.

Curiosity Is the Answer, Not Degrees

Can you remember how to experience simple childlike curiosity with no agenda other than simply to know? The curiosity we're talking about is open-ended and enthusiastic. It's the same wide-eyed wonderment that kids have when they take apart their first camera to figure out how it works.

Many traders remain fixated on academic intelligence as their only decision-making tool. They shut themselves off from the emotional side of the equation, a crucial element for success, as William Eckhardt, a longtime trend follower, explains:

"I haven't seen much correlation between good trading and intelligence. Some outstanding traders are quite intelligent, but a few are not. Many outstandingly intelligent people are horrible traders. Average intelligence is enough. Beyond that, emotional makeup is more important."[35]

When it comes to being an outstanding trader, emotional intelligence is just as important as our reasoning ability or IQ. Because we are so conditioned to appearing "book smart," we are often afraid to be curious. We think that by asking questions, we'll be perceived as ignorant, while in truth, by not questioning our world, we get into more trouble. Still others might not fear the question, but instead fear the answer, which might be a piece of new information that requires integration into your life or worse, information that proves you wrong. Open-ended curiosity makes you take a step back and see everything for what it is right now.

For most of their lives, people spend their time listening to someone else feed them information. Then they are judged on how well they can regurgitate that information back to whomever offered it in the first place. When it comes time to taking responsibility for our decision-making, we are constantly waiting for someone else to tell us what to do or checking to see what others are doing. Curiosity has been educated out of us.

For example, "Alan 'Ace' Greenberg, CEO of Bear Stearns, in *Memos from the Chairman* reminds his employees that, 'Our first desire is to promote from within. If somebody with an MBA degree applies for the job, we will certainly not hold it against them, but we are really looking for people with PSD* degrees. They built this firm and there are plenty around because our competition seems to be restricting themselves to MBAs.'"[38]

Greenberg "gets" the need for passion and curiosity, but many would-be traders pursue pleasing others as their ticket to trading success. They have spent their lives delivering the "right" answer to their teachers in order to please them. Eventually they equate pleasing people with being right. Ironically, once they leave the academic world and are out on their own, their need to be right often backfires. Ignoring the opinions and contributions of others in order to be "right" is not particularly "pleasing" behavior:

"One doesn't have to be a student to want to please people or want to be right. I would claim that serious students (and professors) know there is much they don't know, and are less interested in what is right. On the other hand, those that know little often feel the need to be in the right about it. People pleasing is an entirely different dimension, though people that need to be right are usually experienced at ignoring others, and therefore, failing to please them."—Charles Faulkner

Sigmund Freud goes right to heart of the problem:

When teaching children, a good chess teacher devises ways to get students through the pain of losing, since they lose a lot when first learning the game. One teacher describes how there is a "hot corner." Students sit with the teacher at the board and talk chess. They cannot move the pieces physically, but instead must tell the teacher their moves. They must play the game in their heads. In the beginning, the students hate a visit to the "hot corner." However, gradually they discover that they can, in fact, play a game of chess in their head. More important, what seems like difficult mental work requiring deep concentration and focus becomes intuition after a while. By learning how to handle defeat, the young students can learn how to win.[39]

Anyone with average intelligence can learn to trade. This is not rocket science.

William Eckhardt

*PSD stands for: Poor, Smart and a Deep Desire to become rich.

Never call on intuition. It calls on you.[40]

"What a distressing contrast there is between the radiant intelligence of the child and the feeble mentality of the average adult."

As simplistic as it sounds, maintaining childlike wonder and enthusiasm for your world keeps the doors to the mind open. Young children are oblivious to the fact that they are still taking form. Is it possible to disengage your ego, and think of yourself as still evolving?

Commitment to Habitual Success

Simply reading trading philosophies and rules alone is not going to make a person hungry. It's not going to make them want to succeed at trading. They must be committed to winning. But if they don't want to win; if they don't have it in their gut, there's a good chance that they won't win.

A top CEO recently spoke before a Harvard MBA class. After his presentation the students asked questions. One of the questions was, "What should we do?" The CEO replied, "Take the rest of the money you have not spent on tuition and do something else." This isn't to say that people with advanced degrees cannot be successful trend followers, but it does say that relying solely on your degree for success in the markets, or in life, for that matter, is not a wise strategy.

Commitment to Trend Following is the same commitment you would make to learning anything new in life. For example you say, "I'm going to be a trend follower but I don't know much about computer coding and I have to somehow code the rules of Trend Following into my home computer system?" You now have a choice: You can drop the whole idea, teach yourself how to write code, or find someone who can help you to code your trading system. If you're committed, you will solve the problem one way or another and then go on to the next step.

Commitment to Trend Following is similar to a commitment to be an athlete. If you're going to be a fantastic baseball player, you keep pushing and pushing. You never give up. By the time you get to the big leagues, you've got what you want. But the only reason you have those things is because you made the commitment at the outset to be a winner. Everyone wants the big leagues and big money, but are they committed to making it happen with relentless drive? Charles Faulkner sees it a bit differently, as he explained to us:

"I see it more as a matter of choosing between what is in accord with your nature or changing your nature to accord with your dreams. Most people don't recognize this as a choice point. They get praised into a career, 'You're good with people, you should be a sales person' or 'You're good at math, you should be a computer programmer.' Few realize that it is possible to hold their dreams constant and vary their behavior until they are good at what they need to be good at. And usually, there is a bit of both."

If you're going to chase success, the basic principles, the basic psychological requirements are the same, no matter what you do in life. You still have to wake up every day with a deep desire to be successful. Then you have to make it happen. You have to be consistently focused every day. You can't just wake up and say, "Hey, I'm going to give a little bit of effort today and see what happens. If it doesn't work out for me, I can say I tried and complain to my wife or girlfriend." You can't just jump around because the newspaper or some TV analyst says, "Here's some get rich quick scheme or Holy Grail." You must know what you're going to do, be keenly aware of the role human behavior plays, and go make it happen.

We sometimes delude ourselves that we proceed in a rational manner and weight all of the pros and cons of various alternatives. But this is seldom the actual case. Quite often "I decided in favor of X" is no more than "I liked X" . . . We buy the cars we "like," choose the jobs and houses we find "attractive," and then justify these choices by various reasons.[41]

Key Points

- Brett Steenbarger's personality self-assessment is located in the appendix.

- Charles Faulkner: "All of the successful traders I have met are consciously aware that their lives are bigger than their trading. They are very interested in the money and they are very interested in what they get to do to get it. They embrace their pasts, as well as who they are. Whether it's mathematics or music, philosophy or psychology, or baseball, their interests in the world around them help carry them through the market, and equity, changes. Every day, whether they make money or not, they get to do what they want. I hear it really helps with sitting with positions, too."

- Ed Seykota: "To freshen a room, open a window. Works for minds too, and for hearts."

- Ed Seykota: "Sometimes people gamble and lose to cover up some other feelings they wish to avoid experiencing . . . guilt, for example."

- Ed Seykota: "Some like to search, some like to find and some realize they already have it."

The strategies of human reason probably did not develop, in either evolution or any single individual, without the guiding force of the mechanisms of biological regulation, of which emotion and feeling are notable expressions. Moreover, even after reasoning strategies become established in the formative years, their effective deployment probably depends, to a considerable extent, on the continued ability to experience feelings.[42]

We know of "traders" whose public image "looks pristine," but their personal lives, mental health and balance are in such dire straights—they are not capable of any type of real success or achievement. They might get "the numbers," but their problematic mental health keeps them back. Bottom line—they never get to where they want to go. Life becomes one big rationalization (or excuse) for them.

If you try to impose a rigid discipline while teaching a child or a chimp, you are working against the boundless curiosity and need for relaxed play that make learning possible in the first place ... learning cannot be controlled; it is out of control by design. Learning emerges spontaneously, it proceeds in an individualistic and unpredictable way, and it achieves its goal in its own good time. Once triggered, learning will not stop—unless it is hijacked by conditioning."

Roger Fouts
2think.org

- If you want to be a successful trader you must become passionate about the learning process.

- Let the hype, crowd emotion, and "I must be right attitude" be someone else's problem.

- Winners take responsibility. Losers place blame.

- You have to believe from the start that you can do it. It takes courage to do what the majority is not doing.

- Who is John Galt?

- Atul Gawande in 'The Learning Curve' speaks directly to the importance of practice: "There have now been many studies of elite performers—concert violinists, chess grandmasters, professional ice-skaters, mathematicians, and so forth—and the biggest difference researchers find between them and lesser performers is the amount of deliberate practice they've accumulated. Indeed, the most important talent may be the talent for practice itself . . . the most important role that innate factors play may be in a person's willingness to engage in sustained training."

- Personality testing options can be found at www.knowyourtype.com.

Decision-Making

7

"'Would you tell me please which way
I have to go from here?' 'That depends a good deal on where
you want to go,' said the cat."
—Lewis Carroll[1]

"We see heuristics as the way the human mind can take advantage of the structure of information in the environment to arrive at reasonable decisions."
—Gerd Gigerenzer and Peter M. Todd[2]

Trend followers approach their trading decisions in a distinctly different way from most traders. As you may have guessed by now, they make it simple. For example, each day traders attempt to evaluate the relentless onslaught of confusing, contradictory, and overwhelming market information to make trading decisions. There is little or no time for in-depth reflection to fully understand the consequences of their decisions. Although they know the right decisions should be educated and based on factual data, they become frustrated by doing the research they think is required for proper decision-making. Confronted by deadlines and other demands on their time, they either end up paralyzed, so they make no decision, or let someone else decide for them.

Any individual decisions can be badly thought through, and yet be successful, or exceedingly well thought through, but be unsuccessful, because the recognized possibility of failure in fact occurs. But over time, more thoughtful decision-making will lead to better overall results, and more thoughtful decision-making can be encouraged by evaluating decisions on how well they were made rather than on outcome.

Robert Rubin[3]

People who make decisions for a living are coming to realize that in complex or chaotic situations—a battlefield, a trading floor, or today's brutally competitive business environment—intuition usually beats rational analysis. And as science looks closer, it is coming to see that intuition is not a gift but a skill.[6]

Terrence Odean, a researcher in the field of behavioral finance, uses the example of a roulette wheel. He postulates that even if before you play, you knew the results for the last 10,000 spins, what materials the roulette wheel is made of, as well as a hundred other pieces of information, you still wouldn't know what really matters, which is where the ball will land next. Ed Seykota takes Odean's thought a step further:[4]

"While fundamental analysis may help you understand how things work, it does not tell you when, or how much. Also, by the time a fundamental case presents, the move may already be over. Just around the recent high in the Live Cattle market, the fundamental reasons included Chinese Buying, Mad Cow Disease, and The Atkins' Diet."[5]

Trend followers control what they know they can control. They know they can choose a certain level of risk. They know they can measure volatility. They understand the transaction costs associated with trading. But there is still plenty they know they do not know, so in the face of uncertainty, what do they do? They swing the bat. The ability to decide is core to their trading philosophy. Their decision-making skills may seem obvious, but the philosophical framework of their decision-making is critical to understanding how they trade.

If we were to put their style into a baseball analogy we would ask, Do you want to play ball or do you not want to play ball? The pitch is coming across the plate. Decide whether to swing the bat. Know how you will decide in advance. And when the pitch comes— if it's your pitch, swing the bat. Why can't you wait for more information before you swing? Because in an uncertain world, if you wait until the data is clear (or the ball has crossed the plate), you will have missed your pitch.

Occam's Razor

Nature operates in the shortest way possible.
                    Aristotle

Tackling the challenge of making smart decisions in a real and complicated world is hardly new. As far back as the 14th century, when medieval life was as rigidly complex as its cathedrals, philosophers grappled with how to make simple decisions when time was pressing. In any scientific realm, when a new set of data requires the creation of a new theory, many hypotheses are proposed, studied, and rejected. Yet, even when all unfit hypotheses are thrown out, several may remain, in some cases reaching the same end, but having different underlying assumptions. In order to choose among similar theories, scientists sometimes use Occam's razor.

Occam's razor is a principle attributed to the 14th century logician and Franciscan friar William of Occam. The principle states that entities must not be multiplied unnecessarily. In its original Latin form Occam's razor is *"Pluralitas non est ponenda sine neccesitate."* This underlies all scientific modeling and theory building. A common interpretation of the principle is that the simplest of two or more competing theories is preferable, and that an explanation for unknown phenomena must first be attempted in terms of what is already known.[7] Occam's razor does not guarantee that the simplest solution will be correct, but it does focus your priorities.

> *We could still imagine that there is a set of laws that determines events completely for some supernatural being who could observe the present state of the universe without disturbing it. However such models of the universe are not of much interest to us mortals. It seems better to employ the principle known as Occam's razor and cut out all the features of the theory which cannot be observed.*
>
> Stephen Hawking[9]

Fast and Frugal Decision-Making

In the field of cognitive science and economics, it has always been assumed that the best decision-makers have the time and ability to process vast amounts of information. The new field of heuristics explores how to make constructive, positive choices by simplifying the process. Gerd Gigerenzer and Peter Todd's *Simple Heuristics That Make Us Smart* analyzes how we cope with the complexities of our world using the simplest of decision-making tools. Their premise is as follows:

"Fast and frugal heuristics employ a minimum of time, knowledge, and computation to make adaptive choices in real environments."[8]

> *Heuristic: "Serving to discover; using trial and error; teaching by enabling pupil to find things out."*
>
> Oxford Dictionary

For example, a component of fast and frugal heuristics is one-reason decision-making. This sounds remarkably like what trend followers do when faced with a trading decision: "They use only a single piece of information for making a decision—this is their common building block. Therefore, they can also stop their search as soon as the first reason is found that allows a decision to be made."[10]

In other words, whether your decisions are about life in general or trading in particular, your decision-making process doesn't have to be so complex. You can make a quick trading decision on a single piece of information, the price. But can you allow yourself to be that confident in simplicity? Charles Faulkner found that great traders share many character traits with other successful people, such as quick reactions or, said another way, being able to turn a position on a dime.[11]

When we are faced with a decision, going with our first instinct is often the right choice. If we reflect, consider our options and alternatives, or try to second-guess ourselves, we may end up making the wrong decision or the same right decision but only after taking valuable time to get there.

Gigerenzer and Todd explain:

"[T]hat fast and frugal heuristics can guide behavior in challenging domains when the environment is changing rapidly (e.g. in stock market investment), when the environment requires many decisions to be made in a successively dependent fashion. These particular features of social environments can be exploited by heuristics that make rapid decisions rather than gathering and processing information over a long period during which a fleeter-minded competitor could leap forward and gain an edge."[12]

Gigerenzer goes on to make an analogy with catching a baseball:

"Consider how players catch a ball—in baseball, cricket, or soccer. It may seem that they would have to solve complex differential equations in their heads to predict the trajectory of the ball. In fact, players use a simple heuristic. When a ball comes in high, the player fixates the ball and starts running. The heuristic is to adjust the running speed so that the angle of gaze remains constant—that is, the angle between the eye and the ball. The player can ignore all the information necessary to compute the trajectory, such as the ball's initial velocity, distance, and angle, and just focus on one piece of information, the angle of gaze."[13]

The same conclusion was reached by baseball catcher Tim McCarver:

"Before each delivery, the catcher flashes a hand signal to the pitcher indicating the best pitch to throw. Imagine that a strong batter faces a count of three balls and two strikes, with runners on first and third. What should the hurler serve up, a fastball high and inside, a slider low and away, or a change-up over the heart of the plate? By the way, Mark McGwire's up next. Former Major

League catcher Tim McCarver didn't wrack his brain over such quandaries. 'You have to put down a sign quickly,' 'The first one is going to be the right one.' For most baseball decisions, he adds, 'I think you can train yourself to be right quicker than in five seconds.'"[14]

McCarver is talking about bare-bones decision-making. Be quick is his message. The transitioning from fast and frugal decision-making by a baseball player, McCarver, to fast and frugal decision-making by a baseball team owner and trader, John W. Henry, is remarkably smooth. John W. Henry and Co. was the first trading firm to publicly focus on the use of heuristics. In a speech before the New York Mercantile Exchange, Mark Rzepczynski, President of John W. Henry and Co., talked about fast and frugal decision-making:

There are lots of misperceptions that influence how people think about and play chess. Most people believe that great players strategize by thinking far into the future, by thinking 10 or 15 moves ahead. That's just not true. Chess players look only as far into the future as they need to, and that usually means thinking just a few moves ahead. Thinking too far ahead is a waste of time: The information is uncertain. The situation is ambiguous. Chess is about controlling the situation at hand.[16]

"We're a trend follower, we use just price information and volatility in order to make decisions. The reason why we do that is because we don't think that we can predict the future . . . [Further] I can't be an expert in every one of them [markets]. In fact I can't be an expert in any of them, so what I have to do is be able to be expert at being able to move faster when I see information that's important . . . So my way in which I can move faster is to just use the price information that's the aggregation of everyone's expectation . . . What we try to do is extract the appropriate signals as quickly as possible so we can act fast to limit our risk and also create opportunities . . . we're frugal in the senses that we use . . . very simple recognition heuristics. . .the price information itself . . . what could be an example of this? We like to think of those as non-linear models. But it's no different than what some people describe as breakout systems."[15]

Leaving the trees could have been our first mistake. Our minds are suited for solving problems related to our survival, rather than being optimised for investment decisions. We all make mistakes when we make decisions.

James Montier
Global Equity Strategy
Dresdner Kleinwort Wasserstein
Securities Limited

Rzepczynski's simple heuristic for trading decisions? No surprise: It's the price. The truth is that the less traders involve themselves in complicated analysis—the fewer trading decisions they allow themselves to make—the better off they are:

"Many people mistakenly think simple means unsophisticated. However, researchers now suggest that simple methods of decision-making are more successful than their more complicated alternatives. This may seem counter-intuitive, but in a complex world where decisions have to be made with limited information and real-world time constraints, there may not be time to consider all possible alternatives."—Mark Rzepczynski[17]

Sporting events, which are played out step by step in the most public of settings, allow the researchers to determine the precise moment that somebody veers from good sense. The professors say that coaches and managers often go awry when faced with a decision involving an obvious, yet ultimately sensible, risk. They seem to focus too much on the worst-case scenario: the Bonds home run, the game-ending brick, the failed fourth down. Travelers who drive hundreds of miles because they are afraid of a plane crash make the same mistake. "It has to be the case that sound knowledge will win out eventually," Thomas Gilovich, a psychology professor at Cornell, said. "But the path is tortuous and slow."[20]

"People have a tendency to make it too complex. Trend Following inherently is very simple, but nobody wants to believe—especially investors—that something that simple can make money. The reason we have done well is we have been able to stay focused and stay very disciplined. We execute the game plan—that is our real strength."[18] However, not everyone agrees with the science of fast and frugal heuristics as Gigerenzer states:

"One group said this can't be true, that it's all wrong, or it could never be replicated. Among them were financial advisers, who certainly didn't like the results. Another group of people said, This is no surprise. I knew it all along. The stock market's all rumor, recognition, and psychology."[19]

If price is the simple heuristic that trend followers use, then their performance data can be seen as clear evidence of the efficacy in one-reason decision heuristics. That being said, staying exclusively with a simple heuristic such as price is not easy. Traders can't help themselves from trying to improve on their trading. They become impatient, greedy, lazy, or most often bored. And far too many simply like to make decisions even if they only suit their short-term needs and have nothing to do with profit or winning.

For example, let's say you have a signal to buy Microsoft. You buy the stock if it follows your philosophy and rules. You trust your rules and your decision-making. Don't try to make it more complicated than it is. That's not to say that Trend Following is simple. But the decisions that go along with it must be.

The Innovator's Dilemma

Clayton M. Christensen, author of *The Innovator's Dilemma*, understands Trend Following. What Christensen understands, like trend followers, are the concepts of odds and reactions:

"They were looking at the book [*Innovator's Dilemma*] for answers rather than for understanding. They were saying 'tell me what to do' as opposed to 'help me understand so I can decide what to do.'. . .[Wall Street analysts] are theory-free investors. All they can do is react to the numbers. But the numbers they react to are measures of past performance, not future performance. That's why they go in big herds. Wall Street professionals and business consultants have enshrined as a virtue the notion that you should be data-driven. That is at the root of the inability of companies to take action in a timely way."[21]

What Christensen is driving at is that you must be able to make decisions without having all the facts, since you cannot foresee how a changing market will look until the change has taken place and then it's too late. Take for an example an up and down stock like Yahoo! You probably said to yourself, I should have bought here and sold there. But there was no way you could have predicted the future of Yahoo! Instead you must act early before the direction of the trend is obvious. You are in "ready, set, go" mode long before the people who watch CNBC get the idea that the trend is now underway. Those people are the herds Christensen alludes to.

We return to decision-making with another baseball analogy similar to the pitcher/catcher relationship of Tim McCarver's earlier example. Years ago in baseball, the catcher and the pitcher called the pitches. Today you still have a catcher and a pitcher, but the coaches are calling the pitches. Why? So the pitcher can execute exactly what he's told to do. When the typical Major League pitcher gets a signal to throw a curveball, he doesn't stand out there on the mound debating it. He's saying to himself, that's the system we're using. I've got a coach on the sidelines with a computer. He's charted everything. He knows I should throw a curve ball. The only thing I'm going to worry about right now is throwing a curveball to the precise location that I'm supposed to throw it.

Likewise, as a trend follower, you wake up and see the market move enough to cause you to take action. For example, the rule says buy at 20. You do it. You don't debate it. It might feel boring. It might feel like you're not in control. It might feel like there should be something more exciting, more glamorous, more fun to do in which case you might consider a trip to Las Vegas. If you want to win, you execute properly. That means you trade at 20, and you throw the curve when it's called by the pitching coach. What do you want? Fun, excitement, glamour? Or do you want to execute and win?

Charles Faulkner quotes Ed Seykota as saying, "I've made phenomenal amounts of money for very simple decisions but I was willing to make them. Somebody had to." Faulkner then comments, "Others are looking for highly complex ways of interacting with the markets, when most of the time it's only the simple ones that are going to work."[22]

Everything should be made as simple as possible, but not simpler.

Albert Einstein

Process v. Outcome

The decision making process is just that—a process. You can't make decisions based on what you want the outcome to be. Michael

The Greek philosopher Archilochus tells us, the fox knows many things, but the hedgehog knows one great thing. The fox—artful, sly and astute—represents the financial institution that knows many things about complex markets and sophisticated marketing. The hedgehog—whose sharp spines give it almost impregnable armor when it curls into a ball—is the financial institution that knows only one great thing: long-term investment success is based on simplicity.

John C. Bogle

Mauboussin and Kristen Bartholdson of Credit Suisse First Boston present a compelling argument for "process":

"In too many cases, investors dwell solely on outcomes without appropriate consideration of process. The focus on results is to some degree understandable. Results—the bottom line—are what ultimately matter. And results are typically easier to assess and more objective than evaluating processes. But investors often make the critical mistake of assuming that good outcomes are the result of a good process and that bad outcomes imply a bad process. In contrast, the best long-term performers in any probabilistic field—such as investing, sports team management, and pari-mutuel betting—all emphasize process over outcome."[23]

Building on Mauboussin and Bartholdson's observations, Edward Russo and Paul Schoemaker, professors in the field of decision making at the Wharton School, present a simple yet effective tool (Chart 7.1) to map out the process v. outcome conundrum:

		Outcome	
		Good	*Bad*
Process Used to Make the Decision	*Good*	Deserved Success	Bad Break
	Bad	Dumb Luck	Poetic Justice

CHART 7.1: Process v. Outcome[24]

The process versus outcome chart (Chart 7.1) is a simple tool trend followers use every day. Imagine the trading process you used to make a decision is a good one. If your outcome is also good, then you view your trading success as deserved. On the other hand, if you use a good process, but your outcome is bad, you view your failure as a bad break. It's that simple.

Key Points

- Ed Seykota: "Gigerenzer's 'fast and frugal heuristics' is another name for 'rules of thumb.' One pretty good one is: Trade with the Trend."

- Do not equate simplicity with unsophisticated thinking.

- As science looks closer, it is beginning to acknowledge that intuition is not a gift, but a skill. Like any skill, it is something you can learn.

- Occam's razor: If you have two equal solutions to a problem, pick the simplest.

- Fearless decision-makers have a plan and execute it. They don't look back. And along the way if something changes, their plan has flexibility built into it so they can adjust.

- Murray N. Rothbard, of Mises.org, states: ". . . if a formerly good entrepreneur should suddenly make a bad mistake, he will suffer losses proportionately; if a formerly poor entrepreneur makes a good forecast, he will make proportionate gains. The market is no respecter of past laurels, however large. Capital does not 'beget' profit. Only wise entrepreneurial decisions do that."

- "With every effort, I learned a lot. With every mistake and failure, not only mine, but of those around me, I learned what not to do. I also got to study the success of those I did business with as well. I had more than a healthy dose of fear, and an unlimited amount of hope, and more importantly, no limit on time and effort ... The point of all this is that it doesn't matter how many times you fail. It doesn't matter how many times you almost get it right. No one is going to know or care about your failures, and neither should you. All you have to do is learn from them and those around you because ... All that matters in business is that you get it right once. Then everyone can tell you how lucky you are."
Mark Cuban
www.blogmaverick.com

Science of Trading 8

Trend followers approach their trading as a science. They view the world like a physicist:

"The science of nature, or of natural objects; that branch of science which treats of the laws and properties of matter, and the forces acting upon it; especially, that department of natural science which treats of the causes that modify the general properties of bodies; natural philosophy."—*Webster's*[2]

Physics and Trend Following have much in common. They are both grounded in numbers and work off models describing relationships. Physics, like Trend Following, is constantly testing models with real-world applications:

"Managing money, just like a physics experiment, means dealing with numbers and varying quantities. And the connection

If you can't measure it, you probably can't manage it . . . Things you measure tend to improve.

Ed Seykota[3]

189

From error to error, one discovers the entire truth.

Sigmund Freud

goes deeper. Physics is actually about developing general descriptions—mathematical models—of the world around us. The models may describe different types of complexity, such as the movement of molecules in a gas or the dynamics of stars in a galaxy. It turns out that similar models can just as well be applied to analogous complex behavior in the financial markets."[4]

When we use the term "science of trading," we are not referring to engineers and scientists who develop elegant but complex academic models and ultimately, sometimes to their disadvantage, forget to keep things simple. Keeping it simple is hard, because it is hardest to do what is obvious. By no means is this chapter meant to cover the complete subject of the science of trading, but it does offer an overview of the scientific perspective taken by trend followers.

Critical Thinking

It is remarkable that a science which began with the consideration of games of chance should have become the most important object of human knowledge . . . The most important questions of life are, for the most part, really only problems of probability.

Pierre Simon, Marquis de LaPlace[5]

Trend followers, like physicists, approach their world with an open mind. They examine and experiment. Like physicists, they think critically, and they ask smart questions. Their skill at asking objective and focused questions (and then finding the answers) is a key reason why they are great traders. To be successful as a trader, to be successful in life, you need to develop an ability to ask the right questions—smart questions:

1. Questions that come from digging deep to face what is real about the problem, instead of mindlessly going for the easy superficial query.

2. Questions that make clear why they are being asked. We need to be completely honest with ourselves regarding the real reason we want an answer.

3. Questions that are not hypocritical but instead help us discover how we were interpreting the information before we asked the question—in other words, questions that offer us the opportunity to make a mid-course correction.

4. Questions that allow us to face the cold facts about who we are.

5. Questions that allow us to face the reality of where the answer leads us.

6. Questions that allow us to face our subjective take on the world and factor in new objective data.

7. Questions that allow us to see what was relevant in asking them in the first place.

8. Questions that engender important details we might have missed had we not asked them.[6]

When we spoke with Charles Faulkner about the importance of critical questions, he prioritized his favorites:

"I think the questions that are most critical—in both senses of that word—are the ones that question our assumptions, our assumptions of what is or is not a fact or a truth or possible. After this comes questions that assist statistical thinking through. Finally, are those directed to checking logic and consistency, which are important, but only if applied to worthwhile assumptions and viable probabilities."

Trend followers are insatiably curious about what is really going on. They do not avoid asking a question if they're suspicious that they may not like the answer. They do not ask self-serving questions that will reinforce an opinion they might have. They do not ask mindless questions, and they do not accept mindless answers. They are also content to ask questions and live with the fact that there may not be an answer.

"Unfortunately, most students do not ask critical questions. The questions they do ask tend to be superficial and ill-informed because they have not taken ownership of the content. Instead they ask dead-end questions like, 'Is this going to be on the test?' Their questions demonstrate their complete lack of desire to think. They might as well be sitting in silence; their minds on pause and mute. To think critically, we want to stimulate our intellect with questions that lead us to—more questions, of course. We want to undo the damage previous traditional 'rote memorization' schooling has done to our manner of learning. We want to resuscitate minds that are 'dead' with what www.criticalthinking.org calls artificial cogitation, the intellectual equivalent of artificial respiration to make dead minds come to life again."[7]

We hope investors who have asked few questions so far and, as a result, been beaten down by their rote memorization of the mantra "buy-and-hold is good for you" will finally ask the critical questions and scientifically examine all the data for themselves.

Probability theory is the underpinning of the modern world. Current research in both physical and social sciences cannot be understood without it. Today's politics, tomorrow's weather report and next week's satellites depend on it.[8]

Do not believe in anything simply because you have heard it. Do not believe in anything simply because it is spoken and rumored by many. Do not believe in anything simply because it is found written in your religious books. Do not believe in anything merely on the authority of your teachers and elders. Do not believe in traditions because they have been handed down for many generations. But after observation and analysis, when you find that anything agrees with reason and is conducive to the good and benefit of one and all, then accept it and live up to it.

Buddha

Chaos Theory:
Linear v. Nonlinear

Everyone's entitled to their own opinion, but they're not entitled to their own facts.

Donald Rumsfeld,
Secretary of Defense 2003[10]

Chaos Theory dictates the world is not linear. The unexpected happens. Spending your life looking for the perfect prediction is an exercise in futility. The future is unknown no matter how educated your fundamental forecast. Manus J. Donahue III, author of *An Introduction to Chaos Theory and Fractal Geometry*, addresses a chaotic nonlinear world head-on:

"The world of mathematics has been confined to the linear world for centuries. That is to say, mathematicians and physicists have overlooked dynamical systems as random and unpredictable. The only systems that could be understood in the past were those that were believed to be linear, that is to say, systems that follow predictable patterns and arrangements. Linear equations, linear functions, linear algebra, linear programming, and linear accelerators are all areas that have been understood and mastered by the human race. However, the problem arises that we humans do not live in an even remotely linear world; in fact, our world must indeed be categorized as nonlinear; hence, proportion and linearity is scarce. How may one go about pursuing and understanding a nonlinear system in a world that is confined to the easy, logical linearity of everything? This is the question that scientists and mathematicians became burdened with in the 19th Century; hence, a new science and mathematics was derived: chaos theory."[9]

While acceptance of a nonlinear world is a new concept for most, it is not a new proposition for trend followers. The big events described in Chapter 4 are nonlinear events. Trend followers won those events because they expected the unexpected. Lack of linearity, or cause and effect, was not something they feared because their trading models were built for the unexpected. How do they do this? Trend followers are statistical thinkers. Most people avoid statistical thinking, even when it would help them navigate the uncertainty of daily life. Gerd Gigerenzer, who was featured in Chapter 7, is a believer in the power of statistical thinking:

I have no special talents. I am only passionately curious.

Albert Einstein

"At the beginning of the 20th century the father of modern science fiction, Herbert George Wells, said in his writings on politics, 'If we want to have an educated citizenship in a modern technological society, we need to teach them three things: reading, writing, and statistical thinking.' At the beginning of the 21st century, how far have we gotten with this program? In our society, we teach most citizens reading and writing from the time they are children, but not statistical thinking."[11]

Here is a simple example of statistical thinking. Consider a case study regarding baby boys and girls' birth ratio:

"There are two hospitals: in the first one, 120 babies are born every day, in the other, only 12. On average, the ratio of baby boys to baby girls born every day in each hospital is 50/50. However, one day, in one of those hospitals twice as many baby girls were born as baby boys. In which hospital was it more likely to happen? The answer is obvious for a good trader, but as research shows, not so obvious for a lay person: It is much more likely to happen in the small hospital. The reason for this is that technically speaking, the probability of a random deviation of a particular size (from the population mean) decreases with the increase in the sample size."[12]

What do statistics about birth and gender have to do with Trend Following? Take two traders who, on average, win 40 percent of the time with their winners being three times as large as their losers. One has a history of 1,000 trades and the other has a history of 10 trades. Who has a better chance in the next 10 trades to have only 10 percent of their total trades be winners (instead of the typical 40 percent)? The one with the 10-trade history has the better chance. Why? The more trades in a history, the greater probability of adhering to the average. The less trades in a history, the greater probability of deviation from the average.

Consider a friend who receives a stock tip and makes some quick money. He tells everyone. You are impressed and think he must really know his trading. You would be less impressed if you were a statistical thinker because you realize his "population" of tips is extremely small. He could just as easily follow the next stock tip and lose it all. One tip means nothing. The sample is too small.

The difference between these two views is why the great trend followers have grown from one-man shops to hugely successful firms that routinely beat the so-called Wall Street powerhouses. Why did Wall Street sit by and allow John W. Henry or Bill Dunn to enter and then dominate arenas they could, and perhaps should, have controlled? The answer lies in Wall Street's fascination with benchmarks. Wall Street is after average index-like performance while trend followers are after absolute performance.

Standard Deviation measures the uncertainty in a random variable (in this case, investment returns). It measures the degree of variation of returns around the mean (average) return. The higher the volatility of the investment returns, the higher the standard deviation will be.

National Institute of Standards and Technology[13]

Mathematics and science are two different notions, two different disciplines. By its nature, good mathematics is quite intuitive. Experimental science doesn't really work that way. Intuition is important. Making guesses is important. Thinking about the right experiments is important. But it's a little more broad and a little less deep, So the mathematics we use here can be sophisticated. But that's not really the point. We don't use very, very deep stuff. Certain of our statistical approaches can be very sophisticated. I'm not suggesting it's simple. I want a guy who knows enough math so that he can use those tools effectively but has a curiosity about how things work and enough imagination and tenacity to dope it out.

Jim Simons[15]

Large, established Wall Street firms, unlike trend followers, judge their success with measures of central tendency, not absolute return. These large firms view an average measure (mean) and the variation from that average to determine whether they are winning or losing. They are so beholden to the irrational needs of their investors that thinking in terms of Trend Following is not plausible.

In other words, volatility around the mean (standard deviation) is the standard Wall Street definition of risk (Chapters 3 and 4). Wall Street aims for consistency instead of absolute returns and, as a result, Wall Street returns are always average. How do we free ourselves from averages? It is difficult. We are influenced heavily by standard finance theory that revolves almost entirely around the normal distribution. Michael Mauboussin and Kristen Bartholdson explain the unfortunate state of affairs:

"Normal distributions are the bedrock of finance, including the random walk, capital asset pricing, value-at-risk, and Black-Scholes models. Value-at-risk (VaR) models, for example, attempt to quantify how much loss a portfolio may suffer with a given probability. While there are various forms of VaR models, a basic version relies on standard deviation as a measure of risk. Given a normal distribution, it is relatively straightforward to measure standard deviation, and hence risk. However, if price changes are not normally distributed, standard deviation can be a very misleading proxy for risk."[14]

The problem of using standard deviation as a risk measurement can be seen with this example: Two traders with similar standard deviations may show entirely different distribution of returns. One may look like the familiar normal distribution, or bell curve. The other may show statistical characteristics called kurtosis and skewness. In other words, the historical pattern of returns does not resemble a normal distribution.

Luck is largely responsible for my reputation for genius. I don't walk into the office in the morning and say, "Am I smart today?" I walk in and wonder, "Am I lucky today?"

Jim Simons[16]

Trend followers never have and never will produce returns that exhibit a normal distribution. They will never produce consistent average returns that hit benchmarks quarter after quarter. When trend followers hit home runs in the zero-sum game and win huge profits from the likes of Barings Bank and Long Term Capital Management, they are targeting the edges or those fat tails of our non-normally distributed world. Jerry Parker of Chesapeake Capital states this outright:

"The way I describe it is that overlaying Trend Following on top of markets produce a non-normal distribution of trades. And that's sort of our edge—in these outlier trades. I don't know if we have an inherent rate of return, but when you place this Trend Following on top of markets, it can produce this distribution—the world is non-normal."[17]

Jean-Jacques Chenier, like Jerry Parker, believes that the markets are far less linear and efficient than Wall Street does. This is because in, say, a currency market the players are not just playing to win, but might also be hedging, like central banks commonly do. Chenier points out that, as a result, they regularly lose:

"The Bank of Japan will intervene to push the yen lower . . . a commercial bank in Japan will repatriate yen assets overseas just to window dress its balance sheets for the end of the fiscal year. These activities create liquidity but it is inefficient liquidity that can be exploited."[18]

In order to make accurate judgments about Trend Following and better understand Jerry Parker's words, it helps to break down the statistical concepts of skew and kurtosis. Skew, according to Larry Swedroe of Buckingham Asset Management, measures the statistical likelihood of a return in the tail of a distribution being higher or lower that that commonly associated with a normal distribution. For example, a return series of -30%, 5%, 10%, and 15% has a mean of 0%. Only one return is less than 0%, while three are higher; but the one that is negative is much further from the mean (0%) than the positive ones. This is called negative skewness. Negative skewness occurs when the values to the left of (less than) the mean are fewer, but farther from the mean than the values to the right of the mean. Positive skewness occurs when the values to the right of (more than) the mean are fewer, but farther from the mean than the values to the left of the mean.[21]

Trend followers, as you might have guessed, exhibit a positive skew return profile. Kurtosis, on the other hand, measures the degree to which exceptional values, much larger or smaller than the average, occur more frequently (high kurtosis) or less frequently (low kurtosis) than in a normal (bell shaped) distribution. High kurtosis results in exceptional values, called "fat tails." Fat tails indicate a higher percentage of very low and very high returns than would be expected with a normal distribution.[22]

Investment manuals suffer another deficiency, which is that expert (and I use the term advisedly) opinion in the field tends to be cyclical, not cumulative. One would not expect to see a home-improvement volume with the title "The New Reality of Plumbing." But the science of investing, at least as it is propagated by financial writers, undergoes a seeming revolution every couple of thousand points on the Dow.[19]

Two Lessons from the St. Petersburg Paradox. The risk-reducing formulas behind portfolio theory rely on a number of demanding and ultimately unfounded premises. First, they suggest that price changes are statistically independent from one another . . . The second assumption is that price changes are distributed in a pattern that conforms to a standard bell curve. Do financial data neatly conform to such assumptions? Of course, they never do.

Benoit B. Mandelbrot[20]

*Skewness is a measure of
symmetry, or more
precisely, the lack of
symmetry. A distribution,
or data set, is symmetric if
it looks the same to the left
and right of the center
point.*

National Institute of
Standards and Technology[24]

Mark Rzepczynski, President of John W. Henry and Co., gives his firm's view:

"Skew may be either positive or negative and affects distribution symmetry. Positive skew means that there is a higher probability for a significant positive return than for a negative return the same distance from the mean. Skew will measure the direction of surprises. Risk management should minimize the number of negative surprises. Outliers, or extremes in performance not normally associated with a distribution, will clearly affect skewness. The crash of 1987 is usually considered an extreme outlier. For example, a positive outlier will stretch the right hand tail of the distribution. Because JWH's trading methodology eliminates losing positions and holds profitable positions, historically there has been a tendency for positive outliers and a higher chance of positive returns. A negative skew results in a higher probability of a significantly negative event for the same distance from the mean."[23]

As valid as these concepts are, they are usually ignored. Few people use statistical thinking in their trading. They either don't understand or dismiss skew, kurtosis, and upside/downside volatility (Chapter 3). If you avoid these concepts, you will never see the reality that John W. Henry or Bill Dunn see every day—the reality of a nonlinear world.

Compounding

*Kurtosis is a measure of
whether the data are
peaked or flat relative to a
normal distribution. That
is, data sets with high
kurtosis tend to have a
distinct peak near the
mean, decline rather
rapidly, and have heavy
tails. Data sets with low
kurtosis tend to have a flat
top near the mean rather
than a sharp peak. A
uniform distribution would
be the extreme case.*

National Institute of
Standards and Technology[25]

Jim Rogers, who is not a technical trader, but who has made a fortune off trading trends, puts the importance of compounding at the top of his list:

"One of the biggest mistakes most investors make is believing they've always got to be doing something . . . the trick in investing is not to lose money . . . the losses will kill you. They ruin your compounding rate; and compounding is the magic of investing."[26]

You can't get rich overnight, but with compounding you at least have a chance. For example, if you manage to make 50 percent a year in your trading, you can compound an initial $20,000 account to over $616,000 in just seven years. Is 50 percent too unrealistic for you? Do the math again using 25 percent. In other words, compounding is essential. You can be a trend follower, make 25 percent a year, and spend all your profit each year. Or you can trend follow like Bill Dunn and compound your 25 percent a year for 20+ years and become rich.

Here is a hypothetical investment of $20,000 (Chart 8.1):

CHART 8.1: Compounding Example

	30%	40%	50%
Year 1	$26,897	$29,642	$32,641
Year 2	$36,174	$43,933	$53,274
Year 3	$48,650	$65,115	$86,949
Year 4	$65,429	$96,509	$141,909
Year 5	$87,995	$143,039	$231,609
Year 6	$118,344	$212,002	$378,008
Year 7	$159,160	$314,214	$616,944

Compounding is not easy to do in a society forever focused on instant gratification. But once again, if great traders such as Dunn, Seykota, and Henry can live and flourish in a compounded world, then perhaps we can too.

For such a long time we thought that most data must have a normal distribution and therefore that the mean is meaningful. With the perfect vision of hindsight, this is a bit odd. Much of the world around us is not normal. . .The point is that it is so difficult to see the simplest things as they really are. We become so used to our assumptions that we can no longer see them or evidence against them. Instead of challenging our assumptions we spend our time in studying the details, the colors of the threads that we tear from the tapestry of the world. That is why science is hard.[27]

Key Points

- Defining risks in terms of number is crucial. If you can't think in terms of numbers, don't play the game.

- To be successful as a trader and to be successful in life, you need to develop the ability to ask the right questions.

- Trend Following strategies make their money on the edges of the bell curve.

- Act as a devil's advocate. Question assumptions. Check your inferences. Consider the improbable or the unpopular.

- People mistakenly see a "regular" event and think it "rare." They think chance will "correct" a series of "rare" events. They see a "rare" event and think it "regular."

- People tend to regard extremely probable events as certain and extremely improbable events as impossible.

Say goodbye to a nice, steady, equilibrium perspective, says Professor Bak. Equilibrium equals death. Things do not rock along smoothly, change in small increments. Change is catastrophic. We must learn to adapt because we cannot predict.[28]

Holy Grails

9

The single biggest mistake traders make is thinking that trading is "easy." They allow themselves to fall for advertisements promising, "You can get rich by trading" or "Earn all the income you've ever dreamed of" or "Leave your day job forever and live off your trading profits." Wall Street only compounds the problem with analysts constantly screaming "buy" or their nearly fanatical pitching of buy and hold as a legitimate trading strategy.

In "Buy and Hold: A Different Perspective," Richard Rudy writes that man has always sought simple solutions to intricate problems. In response to the messy and often frustrating reality, we often develop "rules of thumb," which we use in our decision-

Another psychological aspect that drives me to use timing techniques on my portfolio is understanding myself well enough to know that I could never sit in a buy and hold strategy for two years during 1973 and 1974, watch my portfolio go down 48% and do nothing, hoping it would come back someday.

Tom Basso

making (these subjective rules of thumb are in no way similar to those described in Chapter 7). Whenever we see evidence that our "rules" are even remotely correct, our sense of security is boosted and our simplistic decision making mechanism is validated. If we are faced with evidence contrary to our "rules," we will quickly rationalize it away. Rudy observes that the average investor's approach to the markets stands as a modern testament to this tendency to oversimplify, at one's own expense.[3]

These simplistic, irrational "security blankets" are often referred to as Holy Grails. Grail legends have their origins in Celtic paganism, but became increasingly more Christian in theme. In medieval times, the Holy Grail was the cup used at the Last Supper of Christ. Holy Grail stories are always filled with mystery and hint at some secret that is never completely revealed. While the Grail itself, unimaginably precious, may be found, only the holiest of holy can experience it, and they can never, ever bring it back. The markets have always overflowed with Holy Grails—those systems, strategies, secret formulas, and interpretations of fundamentals that promise riches to whomever trades with them. Today is no different.

Buy-and-Hold

After the stock market bubble burst in spring 2000, the concept of buy and hold as a trading strategy must have been shown as the failure it is once and for all. Yet, four years later, investors still buy and hold because they are unaware of the alternatives. Investors still obey mantras like:"Buy and hold for the long term." "Stay the course." "Buy the dips." "Never surrender." Buy-and-hold mantras are highly suspect because they never answer the basic questions: Buy how much of what? Buy at what price? Hold for how long? Jerry Parker gives a strong rationale for choosing Trend Following over buy-and-hold:

"Trend Following is like democracy. Sometimes it doesn't look so good but it's better than anything else out there. It's a worse investment now, let's say, than it was in the '70s or '80s. But so what? What other choice do we have? Are we going to buy market breaks? Are we going to rely on buy and hold? Buy and hope, that's what I call it. Are we going to double up when we lose money? Are we going to do all these things that everyone else does? Eventually people will come to understand that Trend Following works in other markets, markets that produce trends."[5]

Consider the NASDAQ market crash of 1973–1974. The NASDAQ reached its high peak in December 1972. It then dropped by nearly 60 percent, hitting rock bottom in September 1974. We did not see the NASDAQ break permanently free of the '73–'74 bear market until April 1980. Buy-and-hold did nothing for investors from December 1972 through March 1980. Investors would have made more money during this period in a 3 percent savings account. History repeated itself with the recent 77 percent drop in the NASDAQ from 2000–2002.

Making matters worse is that a pure buy-and-hold strategy during an extended drop in the market makes the recovery back to break-even difficult (if not impossible) as Richard Rudy explains:

"The 'buy and hold' investor has been led to believe (perhaps by an industry with a powerful conflict of interest) that if he has tremendous patience and discipline and 'stays with it' he will make a good long term return. These investors fully expect that they will make back most, if not all, of recent losses soon enough. They believe that the best place for long-term capital is the stock market and that if they give it 5 or 10 or 20 years they will surely do very well. Such investors need to understand that they can go 5, 10 and 20 years and make no return at all and even lose money."[6]

To compound problems even more, buy-and-hold panders to a kind of market revenge. Investors who bought and lost want their money back. They think, "I lost my money in Sun Microsystems, and I'm going to make my money back in Sun Microsystems come hell or high water." They can neither fathom the concept of sunk costs nor admit that buy-and-hold is a doomed strategy.

You will run out of money before a guru runs out of indicators.

Neal T. Weintraub

There is the old trading parable about fishing and revenge. You are out at the fishing hole. The big one gets away, and you throw your hook back in. Are you only after the one that got away? Of course not, you throw the hook back in to catch a big fish—any big fish. Ed Seykota has always said to catch more fish, go where the fish are. Jonathan Hoenig, of Capitalistpig Hedge Fund LLC, puts the emphasis where it must be:

"I am a trader because my interest isn't in owning stocks per se, but in making money. And while I do trade in stocks (among other investments), I don't have blind faith that stocks will necessarily be higher by the time I'm ready to retire. If history has demonstrated anything, it's that we can't simply put our portfolios on autopilot and expect things to turn out for the best. You can't be a trader when you're right and an investor when you're wrong. That's how you lose."

The King of Buy-and-Hold: Warren Buffett

Warren Buffett is the single biggest proponent of buy-and-hold. Like Sir Galahad, he has achieved his Holy Grail, and we salute his success. But is his strategy right for you? Can you achieve what he has by using it? Below are excerpts from Warren Buffett and Charles Munger's (Berkshire's number-two man) remarks at their annual shareholder meeting for Berkshire Hathaway:[7]

There is little point in exploring the Elliott Wave Theory because it is not a theory at all, but rather the banal observation that a price chart comprises a series of peaks and troughs. Depending on the time scale you use, there can be as many peaks and troughs as you care to imagine.[8]

- "We understand technology products and what they do for people. But we don't understand the economics ten years out— the predictability of it. Is it comprehensible? We do think about it, but we don't get anyplace. We would be skeptical of anyone who says they can. Even my friend Bill Gates would agree."— Warren Buffett

- "If you buy something because it's undervalued, then you have to think about selling it when it approaches your calculation of its intrinsic value. That's hard. But if you buy a few great companies, then you can sit on your $%@. That's a good thing."—Charles Munger

- "We want to buy stocks to hold forever."—Warren Buffett

- "Think about a company with a market cap of $500 billion. To justify paying this price, you would have to earn $50 billion every year until perpetuity, assuming a 10 percent discount rate. And if the business doesn't begin this payout for a year, the figure rises to $55 billion annually, and if you wait three years, $66.5 billion. Think about how many businesses today earn $50 billion, or $40 billion, or $30 billion. It would require a rather extraordinary change in profitability to justify that price."—Warren Buffett

- "We've seen companies with market caps of tens of billions of dollars that are worthless, and seen other companies that trade at 20–25% of their true value. It eventually gets sorted out. But the speculative mania in one area is not creating equivalent discounts elsewhere. We're not finding businesses at half their real value today. Forty-five years ago, I had lots of ideas and no money. Today, I have a lot of money but no ideas."—Warren Buffett

How can the trends (up and down) of Microsoft, Cisco, and Sun be ignored? If you follow trends, you don't need to know anything about tech companies to trade their trends. Your trading technique is designed to ride a trend, so neither company earnings nor value nor any other fundamental data is pertinent to your decision making. Furthermore, when Buffett says, "We want to buy stocks to hold forever," what is he advising? Nothing is forever. Even high-profile companies go bankrupt (Enron, WorldCom, Montgomery Ward, Wang, etc.). Assuming investors were able to accurately determine the value of a company, that alone does not translate to trading the share price of that company for profit. Trading is not about buying into companies. Trading is about making money.

> *SUNW probably has the best near-term outlook of any company I know.*
>
> James Cramer
> September 7, 2000[10]

Buffett Now Trades Derivatives

In a May 6, 2002, interview in *Forbes* with David Dukcevich, Buffett seems to be squarely against trading derivatives:

"'Things are less lucrative in the stock market,' Buffett said, sounding a familiar refrain. 'We have more money than ideas,' he said, adding that 6% to 7% was a fair rate of return in the current environment. The company has more than $37 billion in cash to invest. One place the money certainly won't go is derivatives. 'There's no place with as much potential for phony numbers as derivatives,' he said. Buffett's 78-year-old billionaire vice chairman, Charlie Munger, couldn't resist chiming in. 'To say that derivative accounting is a sewer is an insult to sewage.'"[9]

> *Warren Buffett now admits to trading currencies in 2002 and 2003. Does he buy and hold the Euro and the Yen?*

Sixteen days later, Buffett is singing a new, confusing tune:

"Berkshire Hathaway issues first ever-negative coupon security: Omaha, Nebraska May 22, 2002. Berkshire Hathaway Inc. (NYSE: BRK.A and BRK.B), announced today that it has sold $400 million of a new type of security, named 'SQUARZ,' in a private placement to qualified institutional investors . . . 'Despite the lack of precedent, a negative coupon security seemed possible in the present interest rate environment,' said Warren E. Buffett, Chairman of Berkshire Hathaway. Mr. Buffett added, 'I asked Goldman Sachs to create such an instrument and they responded promptly with the innovative security being announced today.'"[11]

When people say the market is over-valued and there's a bubble, whatever that means, they're talking about just a handful of stocks. Most of these stocks are reasonably priced. There's no reason for them to correct violently anytime in the year 2000.

Larry Wachtel,
Market Analyst,
Prudential Securities
December 23, 1999[14]

If Buffett was being forthright on May 6, 2002, what made him change his mind two weeks later and create an investment instrument so complicated and secretive that not even his press release could explain it? Even more confusing is that Buffett contradicts himself again in 2003, now going against his latest financial creation:

"Derivatives are financial weapons of mass destruction, carrying dangers, while now latent, are potentially lethal. . .We view them as time bombs, both for the parties that deal in them and the economic system."[12]

The Buffett legend of buy-and-hold as his one and only strategy has permeated the public consciousness. When he launches a new derivatives strategy that goes against the legend, either no one notices or those who do notice are reluctant to criticize him in public.

Losers Average Losers

Imagine you are at a car auction hoping to buy a beautiful red '66 Corvette. Imagine the car that is being auctioned before the Corvette is a 1955 Mercedes Gull Wing Coupe that sells for $750,000. The Corvette is up next and the Blue Book price is $35,000. What would you bid? Now imagine the car before yours was a "kit" car replica of the Gull Wing Mercedes that sold for $75,000. What would you pay now? Research has shown that incidental price data can affect what you are willing to pay. We have a tendency to pay more if the preceding price is considerably higher!

Jon C. Sundt
President
Altegris Investments
1st Quarter 2004 Commentary

There's a famous picture of Paul Tudor Jones, the great macro trader first profiled in Jack Schwager's Market Wizards, relaxing in his office. Tacked up on the wall behind him on loose-leaf sheet of paper is the simple phrase in black magic marker, "Losers Average Losers." Jones' wisdom was obviously lost on James K. Glassman, judging from the following excerpt from Glassman's *Washington Post* stock picking column of December 9, 2001:

"If you had Enron in your portfolio and didn't sell it at $90 or even at $10, don't feel embarrassed. As Alfred Harrison, a money manager at Alliance Capital Management Holding LP, which owned a ton of Enron, put it, 'On the surface it had always seemed to be a fairly good growth stock. We bought it all the way down.'"[13]

Glassman and Harrison are both dead wrong. What they call dollar-cost averaging is really averaging a loser (Enron in this example) all the way down. Traders should feel sick if they average losers, not just embarrassed. When you have a losing position, it must tell you something is wrong. As unbelievable as it seems to the novice investor, the longer a market declines, the more likely it is to continue declining. Falling markets must never be viewed as places to buy cheap.

Harrison violated a cardinal rule of trading. In the zero-sum world of trading, if the trend is down, it is not a buying opportunity; it is a selling opportunity; a "time to go short" opportunity. Even worse, as an active money manager for clients, he admitted to averaging losers as a strategy. To top it off, Glassman later adds:

"Could the typical small investor have discovered a year ago that Enron was on the brink of disaster? It's highly unlikely. Still, if you looked for the right thing, you would have never bought Enron in the first place."[15]

Actually, there was a way to spot Enron's problems. The price going from $90 to 50 cents was a pretty clear clue that the brink of disaster was just around the corner. Jesse Livermore learned nearly 80 years ago how to spot losers:

"I have warned against averaging losses. That is a most common practice. Great numbers of people will buy a stock, let us say at 50, and two or three days later if they can buy it at 47 they are seized with the urge to average down by buying another hundred shares, making a price of 48.5 on all. Having bought at 50 and being concerned over a three-point loss on a hundred shares, what rhyme or reason is there in adding another hundred shares and having the double worry when the price hits 44? At that point there would be a $600 loss on the first hundred shares and a $300 loss on the second shares. If one is to apply such an unsound principle, he should keep on averaging by buying two hundred shares at 44, then four hundred at 41, eight hundred at 38, sixteen hundred at 35, thirty-two hundred at 32, sixty-four hundred at 29 and so on. How many speculators could stand such pressure? So, at the risk of repetition and preaching, let me urge you to avoid averaging down.'"

Jan, the bottom line is, before the end of the year, [2000] the NASDAQ and Dow will be at new record highs.

Myron Kandel,
Financial Editor and Anchor
CNNfn/Cofounder, CNN
April 4, 2000[16]

Other traders have seen their once great empires scuttled by averaging losers as well. Julian Robertson ran one of the biggest and profitable hedge funds ever. But things ended badly. On March 30, 2000, CNN excerpted a letter Julian Robertson wrote to Tiger's investors blaming the fund's problems on the rush to cash in on the Internet craze:

If you want a guarantee, buy a toaster.

Clint Eastwood

"As you have heard me say on a number of occasions, the key to Tiger's success over the years has been a steady commitment to buying the best stocks and shorting the worst. In a rational environment, this strategy functions well. But in an irrational market, where earnings and price considerations take a back seat to mouse clicks and momentum, such logic, as we have learned, does not count for much. The result of the demise of value investing and investor withdrawals has been financial erosion, stressful to us all. And there is no real indication that a quick end is in sight."[17]

The story of Tiger resembles a Greek tragedy, where the protagonist is the victim of his own self-pride. Tiger's spiral downward started in the fall of 1998 when a catastrophic trade on dollar-yen cost the fund billions. An ex-Tiger employee was quoted as saying, "There's a certain amount of hubris when you take a position so big you have to be right and so big you can't get out when you're wrong. That was something Julian never would have done when he was younger. That isn't good risk/return analysis."[18]

I am of the belief that the individual out there is actually not throwing money at things that they do not understand, and is actually using the news and using the information out there to make smart investment decisions.

Maria Bartiromo,
Anchor, Reporter,
CNBC
March 2001[19]

The problem with Tiger was its philosophically shaky foundation: "Our mandate is to find the 200 best companies in the world and invest in them, and find the 200 worst companies in the world and go short on them. If the 200 best don't do better than the 200 worst, you probably should go into another business."—Julian Robertson

Assimilating and sifting through vast quantities of information was Robertson's forte. According to one associate, "He can look at a long list of numbers in a financial statement he'd never seen before and say, 'that one is wrong,' and he's right." Although this talent is impressive, being able to read and critique a balance sheet doesn't necessarily translate into knowing when and how much to buy or sell as Richard Donchian pointed out in Chapter 2.

Crash and Panic: Retirement Plans

What do Julian Robertson, the concept of losers average losers, and the dot-com stock crash have in common? The investment bubbles mentioned in Chapter 6. Dot-coms are no different from tulips or tea or land. In 1720, when the south sea bubble was at its height, even the greatest genius of his time, Sir Isaac Newton, got sucked into the hysteria. Investing as if his brilliance in science carried over to his finances, Newton eventually lost £20,000.

While bubbles may appear as short-term blips in economic history, more often the aftermath is long-term, resulting in severe recessions and government intervention that usually makes the situation worse. The collapse of bubbles of the past 400 years— threw each nation into a recession lasting a decade or longer. What lesson can we learn from bubbles? "Human nature continues to be the way it has always been and probably always will be."[20]

Today, investors must do more than simply trust someone else for their financial decision-making or glance at their pension statement once a quarter. They can no longer pretend it's just "retirement" and that their nest egg will go back up. Take a quick view of the Japanese Nikkei 225 stock index (Chart 9.1).

You have to say, "What if?" What if the stocks rally? What if they don't? Like a catcher, you have to wear a helmet.

Jonathan Hoenig,
Portfolio Manager,
Capitalistpig Hedge Fund LLC

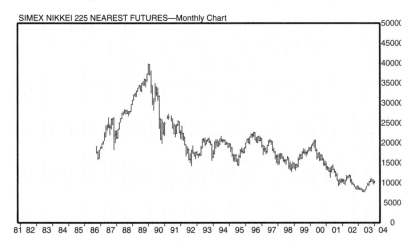

CHART 9.1: Weekly Chart Nikkei 225 1985–2003 *Source:* Barchart.com

The index reached nearly 40,000 in the early 1990s. Now, 13 years later, it hovers around 10,000. Do you think the Japanese still believe in buy-and-hold? Another example reveals a chart (Chart 9.2) of the hot tech stocks of 1968:

CHART 9.2: 1968 Tech Stocks

Company	1968 High	1970 Low	% drop	P/E at High
Fairchild Camera	102.00	18.00	-82	443
Teledyne	72.00	13.00	-82	42
Control Data	163.00	28.00	-83	54
Mohawk Data	111.00	18.00	-84	285
Electronic Data	162.00	24.00	-85	352
Optical Scanning	146.00	16.00	-89	200
Itek	172.00	17.00	-90	71
University Computing	186.00	13.00	-93	118

Who cares what year it is. Bubbles and busts come and go. Unfortunately for investors, financial writers are often too quick to use good metaphors to describe bad predicaments which only further confuses the issue of how to save for retirement:

What makes the Dow at 10,000 particularly noteworthy for us is that it means that the index has to rise a mere 26,000 more points to vindicate the prophecy of those two jokers who achieved 15 seconds of fame when we were in full bubble by predicting it would hit 36,000. We kind of miss them; they were always good for comic relief. Another 500 points and we've a hunch they'll be back peddling the same old moonshine.

Alan Abelson,
Barrons
December 20, 2003[22]

"So now, with your portfolio trashed and Social Security looking insecure, you may be having nightmares about spending your retirement haunting the mac-and-cheese early-bird specials, or about not being able to retire until six years after you've died. With the bull market gone, will the impending retirement of the post-World War II generation be the Boomer Bust?. . .If you work hard, save and adopt more realistic expectations, you can still retire rather than die in the harness. Earning maybe 9 percent on stocks isn't as good as the 20 percent that you might have grown used to. But it's not bad."—Alan Sloan[21]

Alan Sloan is a straight shooter. But, saying 9 percent compounded is not bad compared to 20 percent compounded, ignores the pure math. Imagine the last 25 years and two investments of $1000 each. The first investment generated 9 percent for 25 years, and the second investment generated 20 percent for 25 years.

- $1000 compounded at 9% for 25 years = $8,600.
- $1000 compounded at 20% for 25 years = $95,000.

Here are two examples of the frustration exhibited by not having a compounding plan and using buy-and-hold as your only strategy:

- "What do you do if you find yourself at retirement age without enough to retire on? You keep working."—John Rother, AARP's policy director.
- "I've worked hard all my life and been a responsible citizen and it's not supposed to be threatened at this point."—Gail Hovey, 62, who works for nonprofit groups in Hawaii.

No one wants to see Gail homeless. On the other hand, do we want to live in a society that rewards one group's mistakes with government assistance paid for by a second group who did not make the mistakes? Life must not be contorted into being fair when it isn't. It is fine for us to compound our trading gains, but it's not fine for the government to compound idiocy. Even the top well-paid professionals in charge of pension assets were just buy-and-holders:

"Every major investor in the nation was heavily invested in WorldCom. They were one of the largest corporations in America."—New York State Comptroller[23]

What was their plan? Their plan was the same as the state retirement plans of Michigan, Florida, and California that also lost in WorldCom:

- Michigan (*www.michigan.gov/ors*) reported an unrealized loss of about $116 million on WorldCom.
- Florida's reported an unrealized loss of about $90 million on WorldCom.
- The California Public Employees Retirement System, CalPERS (*www.calpers.ca.gov*), reported an unrealized loss of about $565 million on WorldCom.

Referring to $8.4 million in WorldCom stock now worth only about $492,000: "Until you actually sell it, you haven't lost it."—Robert Leggett, Kentucky Retirement Systems

Thanks Bob. Helluva plan you got there. But, to quote Ed Seykota, didn't everyone ultimately get what they wanted:

"The best measure of your intention is the result you get."[25]

There is no greater source of conflict among researchers and practitioners in capital market theory than the validity of technical analysis. The vast majority of academic research condemns technical analysis as theoretically bankrupt and of no practical value. . .It is certainly understandable why many researchers would oppose technical analysis: the validity of technical analysis calls into question decades of careful theoretical modeling [Capital Asset Pricing Model, Arbitrage Pricing Theory] claiming the markets are efficient and investors are collectively, if not individually, rational.[24]

Wall Street:
Analysis Paralysis

In 2000, there were 28,000 recommendations by brokerage-house analysts. At the start of October 2000, 99.1 percent of those recommendations on U.S. companies were either strong buy, buy, or hold. Just 0.9 percent of the time, analysts said sell. Listening to these analysts for guidance was the public's conscious decision not to think for themselves.

A recent study at Dartmouth College by Kent Womack, observes that brokerage analysts often comment on and recommend companies that their firms have recently taken public. The research shows that stocks recommended by analysts perform more poorly than "buy" recommendations by unaffiliated brokers prior to, at the time of, and subsequent to the recommendation date.

The biggest cause of trouble in the world today is that the stupid people are so sure about things and the intelligent folks are so full of doubts.

Bertrand Russell

However, it seems many ignore the data. Analysts go on TV, and viewers think to themselves, "She sounds bright; she works for JP Morgan or Morgan Stanley, and she's using a lot of financial jargon that I don't understand, so she must know something I don't." She doesn't. The fact that so many analysts told you that you could buy so many stocks in the middle of the dot-com bubble—and were entirely wrong—must be permanent proof that analysts' insight is not the answer. On top of that, the performance of most of Wall Street's advice-givers is closely tied to current market movement anyway. What are you listening for?

Even though there was never any rationale for listening to these analysts, many people did and became angry when the advice proved disastrous. At one point, analyst Jack Grubman became a favorite whipping boy for those investors who refused to accept responsibility for their losses:

We are what we repeatedly do. Excellence, then, is not an act, but a habit.

Aristotle

- "Every time my broker mentions Grubman, I get nauseous."
- "For the past few years, every time I'd call them, they'd say, 'Grubman likes WorldCom' or 'Grubman really likes Global Crossing.' As a result, I now own hundreds of shares of these duds."
- "So now when it comes to investment research, we need to think twice about the veracity of top-rate advice and stock picks from someone earning $20 million a year."
- "Grubman should have warned that this epochal bubble was doomed to burst. After all he was the industry's greatest seer."
- "However unfair it is to blame just Jack Grubman, here's a situation when one person's contribution to wholesale disaster is impossible to overlook."
- "In the late 1990s, telecommunications stocks were explosive. New companies went public, old companies saw spectacular growth, and Grubman never once warned us that this was all a mirage."

No human investigation can be called real science if it cannot be demonstrated mathematically.

Leonardo da Vinci

Does anyone really think Jack Grubman had knowledge that the telecom bubble was about to burst? We are not defending Grubman, but if investors had their life savings tied up in the opinion of one man, they were bound to be in trouble no matter what happened to the stock market. If a stock tanks or an entire sector implodes, who was supposed to warn them? No one was forced to listen to Jack Grubman. Anyone who held Global Crossing or WorldCom all the way down had no one to blame but themselves.

Yet people are still unwilling to take responsibility for their own decisions. Although they may have lost more than half their portfolio in the past few years, they will eagerly accept invitations like this one from a brokerage firm that was publicly caught with its hand in the cookie jar:[26]

"Merrill Lynch cordially invites you to an educational workshop . . . Topics discussed:

- Merrill Lynch Stock Market Forecast for 2002.
- When will the recession end?
- What do I do now?
- What are the factors of a good stock market?
- How did this bear market compare to others?"

Forecasts are financial candy. Forecasts give people who hate the feeling of uncertainty something emotionally soothing.
Thomas Vician, Jr.
Student of Ed Seykota's

If Merrill produced useless forecasts for the last five years, why would they assume anyone would believe their forecast in 2002? Merrill Lynch and other brokerages paid out a $1.4 billion dollar settlement. Why would you even want to trust them now?

Final Thoughts

Will the NASDAQ develop into another bubble anytime soon? No one knows. What you can do is ride trends up and down using a precise set of rules. If you are watching CNBC for prediction of a trend change—you are in trouble, Casey Jones:

Never let the fear of striking out get in your way.
Babe Ruth

Trouble with you is the trouble with me
Got two good eyes but you still don't see
Come round the bend, you know it's the end
The fireman screams and the engine just gleams. . .
—The Grateful Dead[27]

After breaking down a number of wrongheaded trading strategies in which, like Casey Jones, the traders "still don't see," it makes sense to break down the daily strategy of a trend follower. The following chapter looks at what makes a Trend Following trading system work.

The Henry theory—statistically corroborated, of course—is that assets, once in motion, tend to stay in motion without changing direction, and that turns the old saw—buy low, sell high—on its ear.[28]

Enron stock was rated as "Can't Miss" until it became clear that the company was in desperate trouble, at which point analysts lowered the rating to "Sure Thing." Only when Enron went completely under did a few bold analysts demote its stock to the lowest possible Wall Street analyst rating, "Hot Buy."

Dave Barry
February 3, 2002[29]

Key Points

- *Saturday Night Live* "Broker Parody" at *www.turtletrader.com/snl.html.*

- Wall Street works hard to make what they do, which is nothing more than buying and holding, appear complex and sophisticated.

- Why would you be a buy-and-holder when the best in the business don't do it that way?

- Stop your search for "value." Even if you locate value, that alone does not insure your ability to make money in the market.

- The buy-and-hold dream as a retirement solution is toast.

- Stock tips don't work. They are incomplete. They only indicate the buy side of the equation. When do you sell?

- Charlie Wright, Chairman of Fall River Capital, LLC, states: "It took me a long time to figure out that no one really understands why the market does what it does or where it's going. It's a delusion to think that you or any one else can know where the market is going. I have sat through hundreds of hours of seminars in which the presenter made it seem as if he or she had some secret method of divining where the markets were going. Either they were deluded or they were putting us on. Most Elliott Wave practitioners, cycle experts, or Fibonacci time traders will try to predict when the market will move, presumably in the direction they have also predicted. I personally have not been able to figure out how to know when the market is going to move. And you know what? When I tried to predict, I was usually wrong, and I invariably missed the big move I was anticipating, because it wasn't time. It was when I finally concluded that I would never be able to predict when the market will move that I started to be more successful in my trading. My frustration level declined dramatically, and I was at peace knowing that it was OK not to be able to predict or understand the markets."

Part IV

Trading Systems 10

Trend followers have taken their philosophy and reduced it to formulas to guide them in their daily decision-making. These formulas comprise what are commonly called trading systems. There is no limit to the number of different types of trading systems. That being said, most Trend Following systems are similar as they seek to capture the same trends.

Unlike Holy Grails, such as buy-and-hold or subjective fundamentals, trading systems must be quantified with rules that govern your decision-making. Bill Dunn, for example, tells his clients that his trading system has a "programmed risk of a 1% probability of suffering a monthly loss of 20% or more."[2] That's what we mean by quantifying. That's what the pros do. This chapter introduces the concepts that make up a trend follower's trading system.

I think it's much too early to tell. I think all we've learned is what we already knew, is that stocks have become like commodities, regrettably, and they go up to limit and they go down to limit. And we've also known over the years that when they go down, they go down faster than they go up.

Leon Cooperman[3]

Risk, Reward, and Uncertainty

Trend followers understand that life is a balance of risk and reward. If you want the big rewards, take the big risks. If you want average rewards and an average life, take average risks. Charles Sanford, Retired Chairman of Bankers Trust Corporation, gave a commencement address years ago that is as fresh as ever:

"From an early age, we are all conditioned by our families, our schools, and virtually every other shaping force in our society to avoid risk. To take risks is inadvisable; to play it safe is the counsel we are accustomed both to receiving and to passing on. In the conventional wisdom, risk is asymmetrical: it has only one side, the bad side. In my experience—and all I presume to offer you today is observations drawn on my own experience, which is hardly the wisdom of the ages—in my experience, this conventional view of risk is shortsighted and often simply mistaken. My first observation is that successful people understand that risk, properly conceived, is often highly productive rather than something to avoid. They appreciate that risk is an advantage to be used rather than a pitfall to be skirted. Such people understand that taking calculated risks is quite different from being rash. This view of risk is not only unorthodox, it is paradoxical—the first of several paradoxes which I'm going to present to you today. This one might be encapsulated as follows: playing it safe is dangerous. Far more often than you would realize, the real risk in life turns out to be the refusal to take a risk."[4]

Life is fraught with risk. There is no getting away from it. However much we try to control our lives, there are times when we fail. Therefore, we might as well accept that life is a game of chance. If life is a game of chance, to one degree or another, we must be comfortable with assessing odds in the face of risk. We must deal with uncertainty, which is never risk-free—especially with trading and money on the line.

There is no way to avoid making choices, and those choices create risk. Money under a mattress is no good. Buy a house? The house could burn down, or the real estate market could tank. Invest in your company? If the company fails, you lose your employment and your nest egg at the same time. Buy mutual funds? Pray that the empty mantra of "buy and hold" works for you, and that you do not face a bear market at the age of 65.

How do you proceed in the face of all this risk? You begin by accepting the fact that markets do not work on a first come, first served basis. They reward those with the brains, guts, and determination to find opportunity where others have overlooked it; to press on and succeed where others have fallen short and failed.

Think about your finances from a business person's perspective. Every business person is ultimately involved in the business of assessing risk. Putting capital to work in the hopes of making it grow is par for the course. In that sense, all businesses are the same. The right decisions lead to wealth and success; the wrong ones lead to bankruptcy. Here are some issues addressed by a good business plan:

- What is the market opportunity in the market niche?
- What is our solution to the market need?
- How big is the opportunity?
- How do we make money?
- How do we reach the market and sell?
- What is the competition?
- How are we better?
- How will we execute and manage our business?
- What are our risks?
- Why will we succeed?

These same issues are associated with a good trading system. It is important to resolve them in order to assess the risk of a business venture, and it is equally important to resolve them to assess how you are going to trade.

It has been said that the amount of risk we take in life is in direct proportion to how much we want to achieve. If you want to live boldly, you must make bold moves. If your goals are meager and few, they can be reached easily and with less risk of failure, but with greater risk of dissatisfaction once you have achieved them. One of the saddest figures is the person who burns with desire to live, but, to avoid risk, chooses to embrace fear and lives half a life instead. This person is worse off than someone who tries and fails or someone who never had any desire in the first place. Mediocrity condemns itself. The refrain "what if" is a funeral dirge.

[I]f you're trying to reduce the volatility or uncertainty of your portfolio as a whole, then you need more than one security. This seems obvious, but you also need securities which don't go up and down together [reduced correlation] . . . It turns out that you don't need hundreds and hundreds of securities [to be diversified]. Much of the effective diversification comes with 20 or 30 well-selected securities. A number of studies have shown that the number of stocks needed to provide adequate diversification are anywhere from 10 to 30.

Mark S. Rzepczynski
John W. Henry &, Co.[6]

If you study risk, you find there are two kinds, blind risk and calculated risk. The first, blind risk, is suspect. Blind risk is the calling card of laziness, the irrational hope, something for nothing, the cold twist of fate. Blind risk is the pointless gamble, the emotional decision, the sucker play. The man who embraces blind risk demonstrates all the wisdom and intelligence of a drunk stepping into traffic. However, calculated risk has built fortunes, nations, and empires. Calculated risk and bold vision go hand in hand. To use your mind, to see the possibilities, to work things out logically, and then to move forward in strength and confidence is what places man above the animals. Calculated risk lies at the heart of every great achievement and achiever since the dawn of time. Trend followers thrive on calculated risk.

People tend to use discretion or gut feeling to determine the trade size.
David Druz[7]

Trend followers don't worry about what the markets are going to do tomorrow. They don't concern themselves with forecasts, fundamental factors, and technological breakthroughs. They can't undo the past and can't predict the future. Does a 60 percent drop in NASDAQ stocks mean the bull market has finally run its course? Who knows.

Most traders focus only on how to enter and how to exit a market. Many will say, "Hey, I've got a way to beat the markets because this trading system I have, it's right 80 percent of the time. It's only wrong 20 percent of the time." They need to take a step back for a second and say, "Okay. What does 80 percent right mean?" If 80 percent of the time, you don't win much, but 20 percent of the time you lose a lot, your losses can far outweigh your gains even though you're right 80 percent of the time. You must take the magnitude of wins and losses into account.

Lotteries, for example, often reach hundreds of millions or more. And as the jackpot gets bigger, more people buy tickets in the buying feeding frenzy. But as they buy more tickets, the odds of winning do not increase in any appreciable fashion. The ticket buyers still have a better chance of being struck by lightning as they leave the 7-11.

The odds of winning the California Super Lotto Jackpot are 1 in 18 million. If one person purchases 50 Lotto tickets each week, they will win the jackpot about once every 5,000 years. If a car gets 25 miles per gallon, and a gallon of gas is bought for every Lotto ticket bought, there will be enough gas for about 750 round trips to the moon before the jackpot is won. If you know the odds are against you, should you even play?

If your trading system says that you've got a 1 in 30,000 chance of winning, or roughly the same chance as being struck by lightning, you might not want to bet all the money you have on that trade. When you trade, you need to have a mathematical expectation, or "edge," over the course of all of your winners and losers. For example, consider a coin flipping game:

"Imagine for a moment a coin toss game with an unbiased coin. Suppose also that we are offered the opportunity to bet that the next flip will be heads and the payoff will be even money when we win (we received a $1 profit in addition to the return of the wager.) Our mathematical expectation in this example is:

$$(.5) (1) + (.5) (-1) = 0.$$

The mathematical expectation of any bet in any game is computed by multiplying each possible gain or loss by the probability of that gain or loss then adding the two figures. In the preceding example we expect to gain nothing from playing this game. This is known as fair game, one in which a player has no advantage or disadvantage. Now suppose the payoff was changed to 3/2 a gain of $1.50 in addition to our $1 bet—Our expectation would change to:

$$(.5) (1.5) + (.5) (-1) = +.25.$$

Playing this game 100 times would give us a positive expectation of .25."[8]

This is the kind of edge cultivated and honed daily by likes of John W. Henry. It is what we call having a positive mathematical expectation. You might ask, "If everyone knows about expectation, how can I ever find my edge?"

To address that question think about the scene from the movie *A Beautiful Mind*, the biography of mathematician John Nash. Nash and some of his mathematician friends are in a bar when a sexy blonde and four brunettes walk in. Once they've admired the new arrivals, Nash and his friends decide to compete for the blonde. But Nash has reservations, correctly observing that, if everyone goes for the same woman, they will just end up blocking each other out. Worse, they will offend the rest of the women. The only way for everyone to succeed is to ignore the blonde and hit on the brunettes. The scene dramatizes the Nash Equilibrium, his most important contribution to game theory. Nash proved that in any competitive situation—war, chess, even picking up a date at a bar— if the participants are rational, and they know that their opponents

Volatility, risk and profit are closely related. Traders pay close attention to volatility because price changes affect their profits and losses. Periods of high volatility are highly risky to traders. Such periods, however, can also present them with opportunities for great profits.[9]

are rational, there can be only one optimal strategy. That theory won Nash a Nobel Prize in economics and transformed the way we think about competition in both games and the real world. The single problem is that human beings are not rational.[10]

The edge that trend followers exploit to win is the result of a lack of rationality in the majority. If everyone were rational, there would be no edge, and Trend Following would, indeed, require that obituary.

The Five Questions for a Trading System

Answer these five questions and you have the core components of a Trend Following trading system. You are on your way to having your edge:

Sound investment policy is really about intelligent risk management. There is no such thing as a risk free investment. The real issue is not whether you want to take risk, but which risks and how many of them you are willing to accept.

Jim Little and Sol Waksman[11]

1. How does the system determine what market to buy or sell at any time?

2. How does the system determine how much of a market to buy or sell at any time?

3. How does the system determine when you buy or sell a market?

4. How does the system determine when you get out of a losing position?

5. How does the system determine when you get out of a winning position?

While these five questions are seminal to Trend Following, no less critical is your attitude. So don't forget the chapters on human behavior and decision-making as you explore the math. Ask yourself:

"What do you really want? Why are you trading? What are your strengths and weaknesses? Do you have any emotional issues? How disciplined are you? Are you easily convinced? How confident are you in yourself? How confident are you in your system? How much heat can you handle?"—Jason Russell

When we've discussed Trend Following with Ed Seykota and Charles Faulkner, they have both told us that the first thing any person should do before trading is to do a personal inventory by asking these hard questions:

- What is my nature and how well am I suited to trading?
- How much money do I want to make?
- What level of effort am I willing to make to reach my goals?
- What, if any, is my investing/trading experience?
- What resources can I bring to bear?
- What are my strengths and weaknesses?

Answering these questions in advance helps when you are in the middle of the a zero-sum game and the adrenaline is flowing.

If you have a $100,000 account and you're going to risk 5%, you'd have $5,000 to lose. If your examination of the charts shows that the price movement you're willing to risk equals $1,000 per contract, then you can trade five contracts. If you want to risk 10%, then do 10 contracts.

Craig Pauley[12]

What Market Do You Buy or Sell at Any Time?

One of the first decisions any trader makes is what to trade. Will you trade stocks? Currencies? Futures or commodities? What markets will you choose? While some people may focus on limited, market-specific portfolios, such as currencies or bonds, others may structure a more widely diversified portfolio of markets. For example, Bill Dunn's current WMA portfolio (Chart 10.1) trades:

CHART 10.1: Dunn Portfolio Composition/World Monetary Assets Portfolio

U.S. Treasury Bond—CBOT

10-Yr U.S. Treasury Note—CBOT

5-Yr U.S. Treasury Note—CBOT

Eurodollar—CME

Euro Currency—CME

Swiss Franc—CME

Japanese Yen—CME

DAX Index—EUREX

FT-SE 100—LIFFE

Long Gilt (15 Yr)—LIFFE

Short Sterling—LIFFE

Euro Bund—EUREX

Euor BOBL—EUREX

Euribor—LIFFE

CHART 10.1: Dunn Portfolio Composition/World Monetary Assets Portfolio Continued

---

TOPIX Index—TSE

NIKKEI Index—OSAKA

Japanese Bond (10 Yr)—TSE

Australian Bond (3 Yr)—SFE

Australian Bond (10 Yr)—SFE

Crude Oil—NYMEX

Brent Crude Oil—IPE

Natural Gas—NYMEX

Hang Seng Index—HKFE

Bill Dunn and his staff do not have fundamental expertise in all of these markets. They do not have in-depth understanding of each of the companies that comprise the Hang Seng Index. Dunn's expertise is to take these different markets and "make them the same" through price analysis. This particular portfolio of Dunn Capital Management is traded in what the industry commonly calls a reversal system. In other words, Dunn is in all of these markets at all times either long or short. The direct opposite of the reversal system is when a trader is out of a market entirely. Trend followers trade both ways.

When you look at the monthly breakdown of two months of Dunn's performance (Chart 10.2 and Chart 10.3), you see how his losses in one market are offset by winners in another. This is because he never knows which market will be the one to take off with a big trend—hence the need for diversification.

CHART 10.2: Dunn Capital Management May Performance[13]

Non-U.S. interest rates +6.21%

U.S. interest rates +6.76%

Currencies +0.37%

Stock indices -1.85%

Energies -0.18%

CHART 10.3: Dunn Capital Management June Performance[14]

Non-U.S. interest rates -7.21%
U.S. interest rates -1.6%
Currencies -3.14%
Stock indices +2.10%
Energies -0.13%

What if your portfolio had the following composition?

- 37 percent non-U.S. interest rates
- 25 percent U.S. interest rates
- 16 percent major currencies
- 17 percent stock indices
- 5 percent energies
- **100 percent Total**

Is there a perfect portfolio composition? No. This example is the composition of Dunn's World Monetary Assets (WMA) fund. He looks for targets of opportunity to trade worldwide. He is not only focused on the U.S. stock market.

Generally, trend followers trade the same markets. But while larger trend followers may avoid smaller markets, such as pork bellies or wheat, other trend followers may trade currency- or bond-only portfolios. Salem Abraham (profiled in Chapter 2), for example, made a killing off cattle in 2003. Whatever trend followers choose to trade, they must remain open to opportunity when it arrives. Tom Friedman gives a strong argument for sound strategy in a complex world:

"If you can't see the world, and you can't see the interactions that are shaping the world, you surely cannot strategize about the world. And if you are going to deal with a system as complex and brutal as globalization, and prosper within it, you need a strategy for how to choose prosperity for your country or company."[15]

Friedman knows that the real power brokers in today's world are traders, not politicians.

The most important aspect of any trading decision is never the condition of the market, but rather that of your own position. The trick is to be constantly moving toward a position of strength, both within an individual trade and within the marketplace at large. Just like basketball, chess or any other activity that requires focus, you know you're in the "zone" of trading when you start playing for position, not for points.

Jonathan Hoenig,
Portfolio Manager,
Capitalistpig Hedge Fund LLC

How Much of a Market Do You Buy or Sell at Any Time?

There is a random distribution between wins and losses for any given set of variables that defines an edge. In other words, based on the past performance of your edge, you may know that out of the next 20 trades, 12 will be winners and 8 will be losers. What you don't know is the sequence of wins and losses or how much money the market is going to make available on the winning trades. This truth makes trading a probability or numbers game. When you really believe that trading is simply a probability game, concepts like "right" and "wrong" or "win" and "lose" no longer have the same significance. As a result, your expectations will be in harmony with the possibilities.

Mark Douglas
Trading in the Zone

The question investors typically avoid at all costs is the question of money management. Money management is also called risk management, position sizing, or bet sizing, and it is the critical component to Trend Following success as Gibbons Burke of MarketHistory.com observes:

"Money management is like sex: Everyone does it, one way or another, but not many like to talk about it and some do it better than others. When any trader makes a decision to buy or sell (short), they must also decide at that time how many shares or contracts to buy or sell—the order form on every brokerage page has a blank spot where the size of the order is specified. The essence of risk management is making a logical decision about how much to buy or sell when you fill in this blank. This decision determines the risk of the trade. Accept too much risk and you increase the odds that you will go bust; take too little risk and you will not be rewarded in sufficient quantity to beat the transaction costs and the overhead of your efforts. Good money management practice is about finding the sweet spot between these undesirable extremes."[16]

When you look at a trading strategy, you must say to yourself, "I've only got a certain amount of money. What do I need to be concerned about?" If you have $100,000 and you want to trade Microsoft, well, how much of your $100,000 must you trade on Microsoft on your first trade? Must you trade all $100,000? What if you're wrong? What if you're wrong in a big way, and you lose your entire $100,000 on one bet.

How do you determine how much to bet or trade each time? Trend followers all realize you need to make small bet sizes initially. So, if you start at $100,000, and you're going to risk 2 percent, that will be $2,000. You might say to yourself, "Oh my gosh, I've got $100,000, why am I only risking $2,000? I've got $100,000. $2,000 is nothing." But that's not the point. First things first. You can't predict where the trend is going to go. Craig Pauley, another trend follower, presents a view on the initial risk process:

"There are traders who are unwilling to risk more than 1%, but I would find it surprising to hear of any trader who risks more than 5% of assets per trade. Bear in mind that risking too little doesn't give the market the opportunity to allow your profitable trade to occur."[17]

Think about money management as you would about getting into physical shape. Let's say you're a male athlete, and you want to get into great shape. You weigh 185 pounds, and you're six foot one. Well guess what? You can't lift weights six times a day for twelve hours a day for 30 straight days without hurting yourself sometime during those 30 days. There's an optimum amount of lifting that you can do in a day that gets you ahead without setting you back. You want to be at that optimal point just as you want to get to an optimal point with money management. There indeed is just such a number. Ed Seykota describes that optimal point with his concept of "heat":

"Placing a trade with a predetermined stop-loss point can be compared to placing a bet: The more money risked, the larger the bet. Conservative betting produces conservative performance, while bold betting leads to spectacular ruin. A bold trader placing large bets feels pressure—or heat—from the volatility of the portfolio. A hot portfolio keeps more at risk than does a cold one. Portfolio heat seems to be associated with personality preference; bold traders prefer and are able to take more heat, while more conservative traders generally avoid the circumstances that give rise to heat. In portfolio management, we call the distributed bet size the heat of the portfolio. A diversified portfolio risking 2% on each of five instruments has a total heat of 10%, as does a portfolio risking 5% on each of two instruments."[18]

Chauncy DiLaura, a student of Seykota's, adds to the explanation, "There has to be some governor so I don't end up with a whole lot of risk. The size of the bet is small: around 2%." DiLaura learned this method from Ed Seykota, who calls the risk-adjusted equity "core equity" and the risk tolerance percentage "heat." According to Seykota, heat can be turned up or down to suit the trader's pain tolerance—as the heat gets higher, so do the gains, but only up to a point. Past that point, more heat starts to reduce the gain. The trader must be able to select a heat level where he is comfortable.[19]

Also critical is how you handle your capital as it grows or shrinks. Do you trade the same with $100,000 as you would $200,000? What if your $100,000 goes to $75,000?

If you look at the past 30 years, there is only one fundamental investor who has consistently produced huge absolute returns—Warren Buffet. Compare that, however, with countless trend following traders who have outperformed throughout bull and bear market cycles. One of the keys to our success is to have a huge diversification of over 100 financial and commodity markets. A systematic, mechanical approach is the only way to successfully trade so many markets ... every decision ... from market entry, position sizing, stop placement ... must be fully automated.

Christian Baha
CEO Superfund

Trend follower Tom Basso explains that traders usually begin trading small, say with one contract, and as they get more confident, increase to 10 contracts. Eventually they attain a comfort level of 100 or 1000 contracts, where they may stay. Basso counsels against this. He stresses that the goal is to keep things on constant leverage. He points out that his method of calculating the number of contracts to trade is convenient because it keeps him trading the same way even as equity increases.[20]

In limiting risk, people also limit the opportunity for gain. It is common, today, for investors to own six or eight mutual funds, each of which is likely to be invested in hundreds of stocks. This will, they hope, assure that no little bump, no little meltdown, overly upsets their portfolios. But since when was investing about avoiding the bumps?

The Way We Live Now; See a Bubble?
Roger Lowenstein
June 5, 2005

One of the reasons traders have a problem keeping their trading proportional as capital increases is fear. While you may feel comfortable when the math dictates that you trade a certain number of shares or contracts at $50,000, when the math dictates to trade a certain amount at $500,000, you may become risk-averse. So instead of trading the optimal amount at whatever capital you have, you trade less. How can this be avoided? Create an abstract money world. Don't think about what the money can buy, just look at the numbers like you would when playing a board game, like Monopoly® or Risk®.

However, since your capital is always changing, it's critically important to keep your trading consistent. A description of Bill Dunn's trading echoes Basso's view: "Part of Dunn's approach is adjusting trading positions to the amount of equity under management. He says if his portfolio suffers a major drawdown, he adjusts positions to the new equity level. Unfortunately, he says not enough traders follow this rather simple strategy."[21]

If you start with $100,000 and you lose $25,000, you now have $75,000. Make your trading decisions off $75,000, not $100,000. You don't have $100,000 any more. That's Dunn's point. However, Paul Mulvaney, CIO of Mulvaney Capital Management Ltd., felt we were missing a critical final thought on money management:

"Trend Following is implicitly about dynamic rebalancing, which is why I think successful traders appear to be fearless. Many hedge fund methodologies make risk management a separate endeavor. In Trend Following it is part of the internal logic of the investment process."

When Do You Buy or Sell a Market?

When do I buy? When do I sell? These are the questions. Yet there is no reason why the buy/sell process must become a melodrama. Moreover, obsessing over when to buy or sell is not where your energies must be. Needless to say, trend followers apply a method to the buy/sell process.

What are the three best market indicators? In order they are:

1. Price
2. Price
3. Price

When do trend followers enter? Once a trend has begun. As we said in Chapter 1, trend followers have no ability to predict when a trend will start. The only way to know that a trend has started is when it starts to move either up or down. For example, let's say Microsoft is trading between 50 and 55 for six months. All of a sudden Microsoft jumps, or breaks out, to a price level of 63. That type of upward movement from a range is a trigger for trend followers. They say to themselves, "I might not know that Microsoft is going to continue upward, but it's been going sideways for a while, and all of a sudden, the price has jumped to 63. I'm not in this game to try and find bargains or cheap places to buy. I'm in this game to follow trends, and the trend is up." This approach is counter intuitive for the majority. John W. Henry and Company outlines the simplicity:

"As JWH's systems are designed to send a buy or sell signal only when a clear trend develops. By definition we never get in at the beginning of a trend or get out at the top."[22]

If your goal is to ride a trend that starts at 50 and perhaps goes to 100, does it really make a difference whether you got in at 52 or 60 or 70? Even if you got in at 70 and the trend went to 100, you still made a lot, right? Of course if you got in at 52 (and how you think you could predict the bottom we will never know), you made more money than if you got in at 70. There are plenty of traders out there who think, "Oh, I couldn't get in at 52, so I don't get in at all, even if I have the chance to get in at 70." Think about what Richard Dennis has to say:

"Certainly when you have a position with a profit. Anytime the market goes up a reasonable amount—say a strong day's work—after you've put on a position, it's probably worth adding to that position. I wouldn't want to wait for a retracement. That is everyone's favorite technique—to buy something strong that retraces. I don't see any justification in the statistics for that. When beans are at $8.00 and go to $9.00, if the choice is to buy them at $9.00 or buy them if they retrace to $8.80, I'd rather buy them at $9.00. They may never retrace to $8.80. Statistics would show that you make more money buying them and not waiting for a retracement."[23]

Even if they're familiar with Dennis' approach, individuals still focus on entry—a misdirection of energy and focus that Ed Seykota laments: "The entry is a big concern before it happens, a small concern thereafter."[24]

Seykota is saying that once you are in a trade, the entry price isn't important. You have no idea how high the market is going to go, right? You should be concerned about protecting your downside in case the market goes against you as opposed to creating dramas associated with entry. How long can Trend Following trades last? John W. Henry opines:

"Positions held for two to four months are not unusual, and some have been held for more than one year, says a spokesman. Historically, only 30–40% of trades have been profitable."[25]

Remember that only 30–40 percent of trades are typically profitable for trend followers. The words of great baseball player Ted Williams immediately come to mind: "Hitting a baseball, I've said it a thousand times, is the single most difficult thing to do in sport. If Joe Montana or Dan Marino completed three of every ten passes they attempted, they would be ex-professional quarterbacks. If Larry Bird or Magic Johnson made three of every ten shots they took, their coaches would take the basketball away from them."[26]

However analogous it is to baseball, only 40 percent profit in trading is by itself hardly a percentage worth emulating—or is it? The key is to sustain that positive mathematical expectation mentioned earlier in the chapter. But how is that possible with 40 percent winners? Jim Little of trend follower Campbell and Company makes it clear:

"Say, for example, on the 60%, you lose 1% of your capital, but on the 40% winning trades you make 2%. Over longer periods of time, say a year or more, this would net 20% on a broadly diversified program."[27]

In other words, winning and losing trades over time are blended together. Winners make up for small losers. Trend followers' rules to enter and exit are driven by what many call technical indicators. The technical indicator for trend followers is price action. However, most traders remain preoccupied with the hundreds upon hundreds of other indicators that promise "prediction." They discuss and debate which is better—MACD or Bollinger Bands? Which is more profitable—ADX or Williams %R?

Of course the answer is: None of them. Technical indicators are simply small components of an overall trading system and not complete systems. They are like a couple of tools in a toolkit, not the kit itself. A technical indicator accounts for typically 10 percent of the overall trading success of a Trend Following system. When traders say, "I tried Indicator X and found it was worthless" or "I tried Indicator Y and found it useful," they make no sense. These statements imply that an indicator is the actual trading system. By itself, a technical indicator is meaningless.

Since trend followers never know which trend will be their big winner, they accumulate small losses trying to find it. It's like sticking the toothpick in the cake to find out if it's done. They are testing the market to find out if the little trend will grow into a big trend. Hence, you can end up with the 60 percent losing trades that John W. Henry and Jim Little refer to.

I didn't necessarily have system creation as a goal … What I did have as a goal was supplementing my fundamental trading with some technical insights." What resulted was his long-term technical system that he realized worked well for diverse markets, not just grains. He says that moving away from fundamentals made it easier to create something that held true for a variety of markets.

Bernard Drury
Drury Capital
Futures Magazine August 2001

When Do You Get Out of a Losing Position?

The time to think most clearly about why and when to exit is before getting in. In any trading system, the most important thing is to preserve your capital. A sell strategy gives you the opportunity to not only preserve capital, but also to potentially redeploy it to more opportune markets. When do you actually get out of a losing position? Fast! This is a fundamental element of Trend Following. The logic of cutting your losses and then cutting them even more has been around far longer than Trend Following:

"If a speculator is correct half of the time, he is hitting a good average. Even being right 3 or 4 times out of 10 should yield a person a fortune if he has the sense to cut his losses quickly on the ventures where he is wrong."—Bernard Baruch

I learned you are not trading a commodity—you are buying and selling risk. As a technical trader, that's the only way to look at it.

Mark van Stolk[28]

From the beginning of my investigation it became evident that the most direct way to make money and the one most compatible with my strengths, was to be a position trader using computer models to develop the entry and exit points.

Michael J. Clarke
Clarke Capital Management, Inc.

For example, you enter MSFT with a 2 percent stop loss. This means if you lose 2 percent, you exit. Period. Get out. Don't debate it. Look back at the British pound trade in our Bill Dunn profile. The chart (Chart 2.3) shows constant starts and stops. Dunn keeps receiving entry signals and then exit signals. The trend is up, and then it is down. He enters and then exits. Dunn knows he can't predict the direction of the British Pound. He only knows that he has received an entry signal, so he gets on board. Then he receives an exit right after that, so he gets out. Then another entry signal; then exit. Dunn did say he "rides the bucking bronco."

Traders call these back and forth swings whipsaws. Whipsaws are quick ups and downs that go nowhere. Your trade is jerked, or whipsawed, back and forth. Ed Seykota reminded us in Chapter 2 that the only way to avoid whipsaws is to stop trading. This simple, yet blunt, piece of advice demonstrates Seykota's experience. He is saying that whipsaws are part of the game. Live with them. Don't want to live with them? Don't trade.

Before you ever start trading as a trend follower, you already know you will have small losses. You also know that small losses do not go on forever. Big trends invariably show up right about the time you are ready to throw in the towel.

When Do You Get Out of a Winning Position?

You have seen the headline hype: "Use Japanese candlesticks to spot reversals" or "Determine support and resistance" or "Learn proper profit-taking." You can't spot reversals until they happen. There is no way to define the concept of support and resistance, as 100 people could have 100 different definitions. These ideas all try to do the impossible—predict. Tom Basso points out the futility associated with profit objectives:

"A new trader approaches an old trend follower and asks, 'What's your objective on this trade?' The old trend follower replies that his objective is for the position to go to the moon."

Exiting a winning position can be a challenge since you have to be comfortable with letting a trend run as far as it can, crest, and then begin to decline before considering an exit with profits. Say you are up 100 percent in paper profits. If you cash in, those paper profits become real. But the trend is still up. You have just made a big mistake, since you limited yourself in how much you could make. If you are long several positions, there are huge open profits on the table, and the trend is still up—that is not time to get out of your winning position.

Since trend followers do not play the game with the belief that picking tops and bottoms is feasible, they do not set profit targets. Profit targets cap profits. If you have a profit target, you will stop after a set amount of profit. For example, you enter at 100 and before you ever enter you establish that you will exit if the price reaches a 25 percent gain, or 125. The idea of a profit target sounds secure and wise at first blush. But if you have the experience of Ed Seykota or Bill Dunn, you know profit targets are not the way to big wins. If you are riding a trend, you have to let it go as far as it can go. You need to fully exploit the move. You don't want to exit at 125 and watch the trend go to 225.

While profit targets keep you from getting to 225, they also play a damaging role in the overall portfolio of a trend follower. Trend followers need those home runs to pay for all their whipsaw losses. If you are artificially creating a profit target for no other reason than to be comfortable, you may be limiting the potential for those big trends. This, in turn, limits your ability to cover all the small losses you've incurred. If, as a trader, you had used profit targets, how would you have ever been around to win the huge profits from the big events we describe in Chapter 4?

So where in a trend do trend followers earn their profits? They capture the meat, or middle, of a trend. They never get in at the bottom, and they don't get out at the top (Chart 10.4):

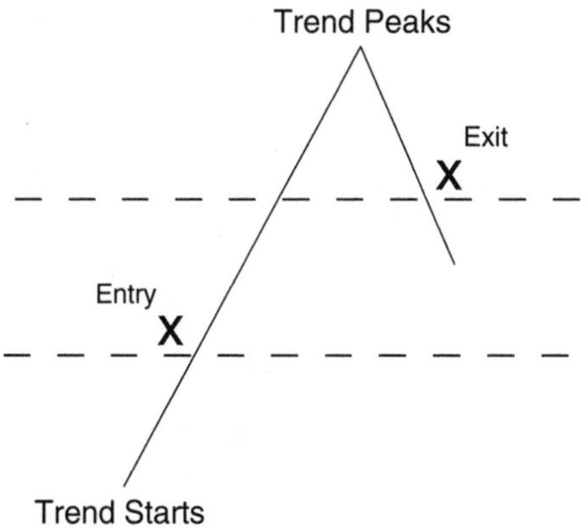

Reason's biological function is to preserve and promote life and to postpone its extinction as long as possible. Thinking and acting are not contrary to nature; they are, rather, the foremost features of man's nature. The most appropriate description of man as differentiated from nonhuman beings is: a being purposively struggling against the forces adverse to his life.

Ludwig Von Mises[29]

CHART 10.4: Trend Following Entry/Exit Example: The Middle

Your Trading System

Evaluating quantitative traders is much more about understanding their research process than looking at the last few years of a track record. The firmest grasp of all the individual, specific risks involved; the most critical and accurate analysis of the inherent underlying assumptions of their research; the knowledge of which statistical measurements are applicable or not; the creation of the purest mathematical descriptions of price structures, moves, and volatility ... these abilities will determine the trader most likely to deliver the highest reward-to-risk in the future.

Mark Abraham
Quantitative Capital Management, L.P.

When you mechanize a system for your personal use, you take all your discretionary judgments and build them into the rules. For example, if you know you are uncomfortable with a high level of risk, you make a rule that sets a tolerable level of risk. If you want to trade a currency-only portfolio, you make that a part of the rules from the beginning. In other words, you hardwire all the different scenarios that you would see in daily trading in advance across your portfolio. If a market rises 100 percent in a day, you have rules that tell you what to do. If a market loses 10 percent, follow your rules. With your trading rules established in advance and put into your system, you can avoid constant discretionary decision-making.

When you are in the heat of the trading battle, your rules for entry or exit or how much to buy must be clear. You cannot afford to think about the rules as the situation unfolds. You must have the precise and unambiguous plan established in advance. It also helps to be on the defensive:

"We approach markets backwards. The first thing we ask is not what can we make, but how much can we lose. We play a defensive game."—Larry Hite[30]

We have an included a sample Trend Following trading system in the appendix from Bob Spear of Trading Recipes software.

Frequently Asked Questions

FAQ #1: How Much Money Do I Need?

Ed Seykota was once asked how much money someone should have before starting to trade. He responded: "Good money management is equity invariant. I'd ask a trader who thinks he needs a certain amount before he can trade exactly what amount he would need to stop trading." His point is that there is no dollar amount too little or too big that allows you to sit back and assume that your starting capital alone is some secret key to success.

There are numerous factors related to the correct amount of starting capital, not least of which is a trader's own personal discipline and ability to stick with it. Anyone who promises a magic number of how much is needed to win is not truthful. No one can guarantee you profits. But what if you have unlimited resources? That should be to your advantage, right? However, unlimited starting capital can be a benefit or a strike against you. Jaromir Jagr, the famous hockey player, and William Eckahrdt, Richard Dennis' longtime partner, obviously have contradicting views on how much is enough starting capital. Jagr sounds like a riverboat gambler:

"Jaromir Jagr does not do moderation. This is a man who doesn't just play the stock market but romps through it; last year, published reports estimated he took a hit [loss] of anywhere from $8 million to $20 million in the dot.com market. He doesn't just have a girlfriend who is pretty and bright; he has a girlfriend who is a former Miss Slovakia and a second-year law student."[31]

Jagr might be a great hockey player, but his trading approach is leading him straight to the poor house. Backed by the millions he made playing hockey, Jagr is exactly the type of trader William Eckhardt avoided.

"I know of a few multimillionaires who started trading with inherited wealth. In each case, they lost it all because they didn't feel the pain when they were losing. In those formative first years of trading, they felt they could afford to lose. You're much better off going into the market on a shoestring, feeling that you can't afford to lose. I'd rather bet on somebody starting out with a few thousand dollars than on somebody who came in with millions."[32]

The peripheral mishigas, your attitude, wardrobe, education and expertise mean nothing to the market. From old-timer to first-timer, it will chew up a doctorate just as easily as a drug addict . . . in the markets and indeed in life, success starts with realizing that one's opinion means nothing. The market will move as life will move, perfectly unpredictable and with the best laid plans going horribly awry. We can't control the market just as we can't control the future. So the winners are simply those best-positioned to benefit from a future not yet seen.

Jonathon Hoenig
Portfolio Manager,
Capitalistpig Hedge Fund LLC

FAQ #2: Is Trend Following for Stocks?

One of the great myths regarding Trend Following is that it does not apply to stocks. Trends in stocks are no different than trends in currencies, commodities, or futures. Chesapeake Capital, Jerry Parker's Trend Following firm, for example, has adapted its system to stock trading for both performance and client reasons. Parker says his system works well with stocks, particularly stocks in outlier moves that are in single industries. He adds:

"Our expertise [is] in systematic Trend Following, or model development. So maybe we trend follow with Chinese porcelain. Maybe we trend follow with gold and silver, or stock futures, or whatever the client needs. We're trading these great systems, and testing, and making sure what we do has worked in the past. And being disciplined, and unemotional, and applying our methods to the futures markets. But limiting our trading to this one group of

Robert Hormats, the vice-chairman of Goldman Sachs International, observed that to understand and explain globalization it is useful to think of yourself as an intellectual nomad. In the world of the nomad, there is no carefully defined turf.

Thomas Friedman[38]

markets. We need to look at the investment world globally and communicate our expertise of systematic trading."[33]

Bruce Terry, President of Weston Capital Investment Services and a disciple of Richard Donchian, dismisses out of hand the idea that Trend Following is not for stocks:

"Originally in the 1950s, technical models came out of studying stocks. Commodity Trading Advisors (CTAs) applied these to futures. In the late 1970s and early 1980s, stocks were quiet and futures markets took off. That is how the CTA market started. It has come full circle. People are beginning to apply these models to stocks once again."[34]

Finally, we are reminded by the opening line of a 1979 article from Managed Account Reports:

"Trading stocks and commodity futures by means of trend following techniques is an art with a long history."[35]

FAQ #3: Can You Offer Insight on Computers and Curve-Fitting?

Larry Hite, a prominent trend follower, once said that a computer can't get up on the wrong side of the bed in the morning, which is why he relied on computers for decision-making:

"If your boyfriend or girlfriend breaks up with you, you'll feel one way; if you get engaged, you'll feel another way."[36]

Hite went on to say he would much rather have one real smart guy working on a lone Macintosh than a team of well-paid timekeepers with an army of supercomputers. At the same time, however, Hite was adamant that the real key to using computers successfully was the thinking that went into the computer code. When someone asked why even go the computer route if people power was so important. Hite responded:

"[B]ecause it works—it's countable and replicable. I'm a great fan of the scientific method. And the other things are not scientific. If I give you the algorithms, you should be able to get the same results I did. That to me means a great deal."[37]

However, there are challenges that go along with PC-based testing. Computer technology can be easily used to over optimize or curve-fit a trading system and produce a system that looks good—

on paper. By testing thousands of possibilities, anyone can create a system that works in theory as Barbara Dixon warned:

"When designing a system, I believe it's important to construct a set of rules which fit more like a mitten than like a glove. On the one hand, markets move in trends, but on the other hand, past results are not necessarily indicative of future performance. If you design a set of rules which fit the curve of your test data too perfectly, you run an enormous risk that it will fizzle under different future conditions."[39]

A robust trading system, one that is not curve-fit, must ideally trade all markets at all times in all conditions. Trend Following parameters, or rules, should work across a range of values. System parameters that work over a range of values are considered robust. If the parameters of a system are slightly changed and the performance adjusts drastically, beware. For example, if a system works great at 20, but does not work at 19 or 21, the system is not robust. On the other hand, if your system parameter is 50 and it also works at 40 or 60, your system is much more robust (and reliable).

David Druz, a student of Ed Seykota, has long championed robustness. He dismisses the trades of short-term traders, who fight for quick hitting arbitrage style profits, as noise. Traders who focus on short-term trading often miss the longer-term trends—those areas where long-term trend followers wait patiently for their opportunities. In order to "wait" as Druz describes, you need complete faith in your trading system. It comes from your own experience of the system through testing and practice. However, you are in serious trouble if all you think you need is the latest hardware and software to succeed at trading. Barbara Dixon, once again makes it clear:

"Contemporary databases, software, and hardware allow system developers to test thousands of ideas almost instantaneously. I caution these people about the perils of curve fitting. I urge them to remember that one of their primary goals is to achieve discipline which will enable them to earn profits. With so many great tools it's easy to change or modify a system and to develop indicators rather than rules, but is it always wise."[40]

It is difficult today to *not* get caught up in the hype of computer programs for trading. You can go out and spend several thousand

Whales only get harpooned when they come to the surface, and turtles can only move forward when they stick their neck out, but investors face risk no matter what they do.

Charles A. Jaffe

*I heard this story and I
think it's true. Anyway, it's
a pretty good story. It's
about how the Air Force
trains pilots. When a
trainee made a good
landing, he would be
praised. When a trainee
made a bad landing, he
would be ridiculed. Well,
it was perfectly clear to the
general that the first
approach was lousy and
the second approach was
good. He had statistics
demonstrating that when
you praised a pilot who
made a perfect landing, his
next landing was not likely
to be as good. Whereas, if
you berated a pilot who
made a bad landing, his
next landing was likely to
be much better. However,
if you think about it, it
doesn't matter what you
do, because landings are
most likely to be average.
If a pilot had an
exceptional landing, his
next landing was likely to
be average. If he had a
poor landing, his next
landing was likely to be
average, also. By slicing
the data and only looking
at what follows good
landings and praise, you
only see part of the picture.
You must consider how
data was selected before
you can draw conclusions.*

James Simons
The Greenwich Roundtable
June 17, 1999

dollars to purchase fancy charting software that makes you feel like you are the president and sole trader of your own hedge fund. What were trend followers doing before they had PCs? When describing his early trading successes, John W. Henry made clear the key was philosophy, not technology:

"In those days, there were no personal computers beyond the Apple. There were few, if any, flexible software packages available. These machines, far from being the ubiquitous tool seen everywhere in the world of finance and the world at large today, were the province of computer nerds . . . I set out to design a system for trading commodities. But things changed quickly and radically as soon as I started trading. My trading program, however, did not change at all. As I said, it hasn't changed even to this day."[41]

One of Henry's employees years earlier elaborated: "Originally all of our testing was done mechanically with pencil and graph that turned into lotus spreadsheets, which was still used extensively in a lot of our day to day work. With the advent of some of these new modeling systems like system writer, day trader and some of the other things, we've been able to model some of our systems on these products. Mostly just to back test what we already knew, that Trend Following works."[42]

Tom Basso's experience is also noteworthy: "You'll find that the more you're computerized, the more markets you'll be able to handle. Computers leverage your time if you know how to use them."[43]

Richard Donchian's timeless observations should likewise embarrass overly excited day traders, or at least give them pause:

"If you trade on a definite trend-following loss limiting-method, you can [trade] without taking a great deal of time from your regular business day. Since action is taken only when certain evidence is registered, you can spend a minute or two per [market] in the evening checking up on whether action-taking evidence is apparent, and then in one telephone call in the morning place or change any orders in accord with what is indicated. [Furthermore] a definite method, which at all times includes precise criteria for closing out one's losing trades promptly, avoids . . . emotionally unnerving indecision."

Of course to reach the "minute or two" Donchian refers to takes preparation time. We are not minimizing the work and effort needed to succeed, but we are quoting him as great insight and motivation. Once you have tested your system and are satisfied enough with the results to begin trading, your work is not done. The system results must be periodically compared to actual results to ensure that your testing closely reflects what is happening in real time. It is also helpful to keep a journal to record how well you are sticking to the processes of executing your system.

The obvious is always least understood.

Prince Klemens von Metternich

FAQ #4: What Are the Limitations with Day Trading?

When you trade more or with higher frequency, the profit that you can earn per trade decreases, while your transaction costs will stay the same. This is not a winning strategy. Yet there are traders who still believe that short-term trading is less risky. Short-term trading, by definition, is no less risky, as evidenced by the catastrophic consequences for Victor Niederhoffer and LTCM. Do some short-term traders excel? Yes. Think about who you are competing with when you are trading short term. Professional short-term traders, such as Kenneth Griffin of Citadel Investments, have hundreds of staffers working as a team 24/7. And even though Griffin has an exceptional track record, you have to wonder if he views the world as a normal distribution as well.

Day trading is emotional anesthesia—the frenetic pace works well to keep people preoccupied from feelings they do not wish to experience.

Thomas Vician, Jr.
Student of Ed Seykota's

Unfortunately, the flaws in day trading are often invisible to those who must know better. Sumner Redstone, CEO of Viacom, was interviewed recently and talked of constantly watching Viacom's stock price, hour after hour, day after day. While Redstone is a brilliant entrepreneur, having built one of the great media companies of our time, his obsession with following his company's share price is not prudent. Redstone may feel his company is undervalued, but staring at the screen will not boost the share price.

FAQ #5: What Is a Good Example of the Wrong Way to View a Trade?

This chapter ends with a mini–case study about a prominent player in the Chicago futures markets. Leo Melamed is the Chairman Emeritus and senior policy advisor to the Chicago Mercantile Exchange. He is recognized as the founder of financial futures. At the close of 1999, he was named (by the former editor of the *Chicago Tribune*) to the top ten important Chicagoans in business of the 20th century. Yet with all this tremendous experience, he is not a trend follower, as evidenced by these excerpts from his book:

"The Hunt silver debacle also provided the setting for my worst trade. My company partner George Fawcett and I had become bullish on silver beginning in June 1978, when it was trading around $5.00 an ounce level.

"We were right in the market, and silver prices moved higher. In September 1979, silver reached the high price of $15.00 an ounce, and the profit we were each carrying was substantial. George and I had never before made that kind of money, it was truly a killing. How much higher would silver go?

"Wasn't it time to take the profit?

"Large profits, as I learned, were even more difficult to handle than large losses. I had a very good friend . . . with special expertise in the precious metals markets.

". . . Since he knew I was long silver, I ventured to ask him his opinion. 'Well, Leo,' he responded, 'you have done very well with your silver position and I really can't predict how much higher silver will go. But I'll tell you this, at $15.00 it is very expensive. On the basis of historical values, silver just doesn't warrant much higher prices.'

"I never doubted that he gave me his honest and best opinion. I transmitted this information to George and we decided that if nothing happened by the end of the week, we would liquidate our positions and take our profits.

"That's exactly what we did. This was in late October 1979. So why was this my worst trade when in fact it was the biggest profit I had ever made up to that time? Because, within 30 days after we got out of our position, the Hunt silver corner took hold. It did not stop going higher until it hit $50.00 an ounce in January 1980. George and I had been long silver for nearly two years, and had we stayed with our position for just another 30 days, we would have been forced to take a huge profit. We both vowed never to calculate how many millions we left on the table."—Leo Melamed[44]

If we critique how Leo Melamed traded from a Trend Following point of view, we can see why his 1979 silver trade was his "worst

...it is important to understand that in trading, as in real life, risk is an integral part of the process and one that deserves great respect. To earn a considerable return, one must take a comparable risk. It is essential, therefore, to have accurate measures of both risk and reward.

Alejandro Knoepffler
Cipher Investment Management

Life shrinks or expands in proportion to one's courage.

Anais Nin

trade." To begin with, he had no predefined entry criteria. He never gives a reason why he and his partner were bullish on silver in 1978, nor does he explain why he entered the silver market other than because it was trading at such a low price ($5.00). When the price of silver started to increase, he attempted to find out how high it would go, which, as all trend followers know, is impossible. However, since he had no clearly defined exit rationale, he was uncertain when to get out, unlike trend followers, who know how they will handle their profits before they ever enter a trade. Without a strategy, Melamed fell back on conventional trading wisdom that buying higher highs is wrong. Melamed used fundamentals to determine that the price of silver would not continue to increase and set a profit target to get out of the trade. By having a profit target, instead of an exit plan, Melamed lost out on millions of dollars of profit.

What is the lesson learned? Rob Romaine, a long-time trend follower, notes:

"The value of a disciplined trading approach is that it allows you to design your strategy during nonstressful times. Then, when the markets are tough, you need only to execute your plan rather than being forced to face difficult decisions under pressure when you are most likely to make mistakes."

"The computer model tells us when to get in and when to get out," he says. "The computer understands what the price is telling us about the trend of the market." What does the software look at, exactly? "Volatility, price behavior. How much does it change every day? We're trying to use as much data as we can get to interpret potential future price." Successful positions remain in place for about six months; Ken Tropin's programs bail out of unsuccessful trades after a month. "All of the systems are designed to risk modest amounts of capital and to stay with winners as long as possible."

Ken Tropin: Programmed to Succeed
Institutional Investor; June 2003

Key Points

- Trend followers are right for the trend and wrong at each end.
- Ed Seykota: "A system should support and reflect the attitude of a trader."
- Ed Seykota: "There is no best system any more than there is a best car. There might however be a best car for you."
- Ed Seykota: "If you can't afford to lose, you can't afford to trade."
- Concentrate on the process, not the results.
- Money is only a means of keeping score.
- Taking losses should be easy. You should have them quantified before ever entering the market.
- Trust your trade. If you can't trust it, don't trade.

- The exact turning point, the top or bottom, can't be known until it is over and a matter of record.
- Once you take your signals and enter, trading becomes a waiting game. Wait to see what happens next.
- The more volatile the market, the less you want to risk. The less volatile the market, the more you want to risk.
- Big trends make big profits.
- Ken Tropin of Graham Capital, a very successful trend follower, offered at a Greenwich Roundtable: "In order for a system to be successful, it has to be what I call robust. Robust means that I can test that system in a market I designed it around. Say I'm using it in the treasury bonds, and then if I switch that market and I try that system in the Euro, it still works. And if I change its parameters, it still works. And if I switch it over to corn— something totally different than treasury bonds—it still works. And if I look at some data that was out of sample from what I designed it around, it still works. Then I have something that might be interesting and have a chance of living in the future. Because the nature of data is it changes a little all the time. And so the key to success in systems trading is to have what I call a loose fitting suit. I can't have a suit that's so tight and perfectly proportioned to me that if I gain two pounds, it won't fit the data anymore."

Conclusion

11

"Trends come and go. Trend followers do too.
Some stay longer than others."
—Ed Seykota[1]

In *Absolute Returns*, Alexander Ineichen stresses that trading is a game. There are no rules for the game except the constant of change. But, it is crucial that you avoid becoming the "game." He outlines three types of players:

- Those who know they are in the game.
- Those who don't know they are in the game.
- Those who don't know they are in the game and have become the game.[2]

If, within a half of an hour of playing poker, you don't know who the patsy is, you are the patsy. In this book, we met those traders who didn't know they were in the game and therefore became the game in the big events of LTCM and Barings. We met those traders and investors who did not know they were in the game pursuing

Larry Hite described his conversation with a friend who couldn't understand his absolute adherence to a mechanical trading system. His friend asked, "Larry, how can you trade the way you do? Isn't it boring?" Larry replied, "I don't trade for excitement; I trade to win."

Holy Grails. Lastly we met the trend followers, who know they are in a game and bring an edge to the table every time they play. If you know trading is a game and you want to be a part of it, you have stark choices.

Slow Acceptance

In case you're concerned that this book will create a whole new generation of trend followers and their impact in the markets will negatively affect the frequency, direction, and intensity of trends (as well as your ability to make money), take note from trend follower Keith Campbell:

"We are trend followers, not trend generators. At the beginning or end of a major trend we may provide a little bump or a minor goose, but it will be an extremely superficial, temporary effect . . ."[3]

Campbell is correct. Trend followers don't generate trends. Recall Larry Harris' point in Chapter 3: Traders play the zero-sum game for many reasons. Not all play to win. However, trend followers do play the zero-sum game to win and win big. This attitude causes many people to feel intimidated or defensive. For Trend Following to lose its effectiveness, these intimidated, defensive minded people would have to make dramatic changes in their behavior:

- **People would no longer buy and hold:** People believing in fundamental analysis (the vast majority of market participants) would have to switch how they trade. They would need to cease buy-and-hold approaches and start trading as trend followers.
- **People would start trading long and short:** Most people do not trade short because of fear, ignorance, or laziness. They trade long only.
- **People would force mutual fund changes:** Most mutual funds are buy-and-holders. The mutual fund industry would need to change their basic investing style.
- **People would embrace money management:** Most traders don't think about how much to buy or how much to sell. They only worry about when to buy and rarely think about when to sell.

- **People would disengage their emotions and egos from trading:** As long as there are human beings involved in the process, there will be excessive reactions and trends to exploit.

However, the majority of investors are still more comfortable with the status quo. Sustaining the focus, self-discipline, and recognition of reality is too demanding. They would rather simply watch CNBC or chat at Motley Fool than learn how to trade correctly.

Blame Game

Trend followers are sometimes accused of throwing the markets into disarray. Whenever a stock tanks, bubble bursts or a scandal hits, winning traders catch blame. The blame is *never* affixed to the little old lady in Omaha who thought Drugstore.com would replace WalMart, and consequently lost her life savings gambling on dot-coms. No one wants to take responsibility for their own losses, and who better to target than the winners when "life isn't fair." Here are misconceptions that purportedly make trend followers the "bad guys":

- **They trade derivatives:** The vast majority of Trend Following trading is on regulated exchanges. We can all trade there. If we can all trade there, why are trend followers singled out?

- **They use leverage:** No one thinks it's odd that residential real estate is built on a foundation whereby you only have to put 10 percent down. Great traders use the tools at their disposal, one of which is leverage.

- **They cause worldwide panics:** Trend followers do not generate trends or worldwide panics, they react to them.

- **They don't invest. They just trade:** The markets are for trading, not for investing. The markets reward winners, not losers.

- **Long Term Capital Management (LTCM) proved even the best traders will fail:** LTCM proved that bad traders fail. Trend Following did not fail as proved in Chapter 4.[6]

Trend followers are strongly condemned for making money on the downside as well:

"The broad application of these principles globally in markets all around the world, Chinese porcelain, gold, silver, markets that exist, that don't exist today, markets that others are making lots of money in that we're not trading. We will eventually start broadening out and realizing that Trend Following is a great way to trade. What other way can you trade and get a handle on risk?"

Jerry Parker[5]

Future shock [is] the shattering stress and disorientation that we induce in individuals by subjecting them to too much change in too short a time.

Alvin Toffler

"The hedge fund industry has always been an easy target for the press whenever the public is looking for someone to blame for volatile markets. After Soros and the Sterling crisis, LTCM and the liquidity crisis, the press have singled out 'The Short Sellers'. . . Perception or reality, many will now picture hedge funds as bad boys, or 'boys having a bit of fun' . . . Making money in downside markets is portrayed as obscene and to blame for additional turbulence. The hedge fund industry is not about 'bad boys' manipulating the market and gambling; it is about specific trading skills practiced by highly experienced managers who are rewarded on performance alone."[7]

Most battles are won before they are ever fought.
General George S. Patton

The attitude that "making money in down markets" is "obscene" is in itself obscene. The market has rules. You can go long or you can go short. All players know the rules.

Understand the Game

The Sharpe ratio appears at first blush to reward returns (good) and penalize risks (bad). Upon closer inspection, things are not so simple. The standard deviation takes into account the distance of each return from the mean, positive or negative. By this token, large positive returns increase the perception of risk as though they could as easily be negative, which for a dynamic investment strategy may not be the case. Large positive returns are penalized and therefore the removal of the highest returns from the distribution can increase the Sharpe ratio: a case of 'reductio ad absurdum' for Sharpe ratio as a universal measure of quality.
David Harding
Winton Capital
www.hedgefundsreview.com

Whether you want to trade for yourself, or place money with a trend follower, or manage money for clients, or you are an established trend follower with clients, trading for other people presents challenges both trader and client must deal with. Jerry Parker, for one, thinks trend followers could do better at explaining their skill set:

"I think another mistake we made was defining ourselves as managed futures, where we immediately limit our universe. Is our expertise in that, or is our expertise in systematic Trend Following, or model development. So maybe we trend follow with Chinese porcelain. Maybe we trend follow with gold and silver, or stock futures, or whatever the client needs. We need to look at the investment world globally and communicate our expertise of systematic trading . . . People look at systematic and computerized trading with too much skepticism. But a day will come when people will see that systematic Trend Following is one of the best ways to limit risk, and create a portfolio that has some reasonable expectation of making money . . . I think we've miscommunicated to our clients what our expertise really is."[8]

In an unpredictable world, Trend Following is your best tool to manage risk and, ultimately, uncertainty. While that is true, it doesn't make it easy to teach. Richard Dennis, for example, had some difficult times during his career and, as a result, has become the poster boy for any perceived failures of Trend Following. However, to dismiss Trend Following based on Dennis' managed money attempts alone discounts the performance data of Dunn, Parker, Campbell, Henry, and other trend followers over the past 30 years. Dennis was not hesitant about his lessons:

"I certainly learned customers have a lower appetite for risk than I might . . . and that is probably incorporated into my risk appetite today. It's easier to trade for one's self than it is to trade for other people."[9]

Decrease Leverage; Decrease Return

Richard Dennis' students were originally instructed to make as much money as possible. They had no restrictions except to shoot for home runs. They were absolute return traders while under Dennis' guidance. However, later on, when they went out on their own to manage money for clients, some changed how they traded. Many of them accepted clients who demanded less leverage and ultimately less return. As a result, their performance records have been far less impressive than old pro trend followers.

Traders like Dunn, Henry, Parker, and Seykota know that in order to win big profits, the manager and client must be aligned. Bill Dunn is adamant about aligning himself with his clients:

"Now there is of course the possibility of turning down the leverage and trading more capital, but with less leverage. That works fine if the client will go along with you and you're charging management fees because you're charging management fees on the capital and then incentive fees on the profit. Dunn Capital Management does not charge any management fees to any of its clients. So we care about the numbers that are generated."[11]

You might feel safe with watered down Trend Following from a low-risk, low-reward standpoint, but the true way to win is through Dunn's approach of higher risk, higher reward. And when you are Bill Dunn and you shoot for higher risk, higher reward, you're less inclined to worry about management fees from your clients, since your incentive fees on an absolute return basis can be fantastic paydays. The key is for the client and the manager to be in concert:

Everyone wants to invest when you're at new highs and making 50 percent a year. Everyone says they want to get in at a 10 percent drawdown or a 20 percent, or whatever and no one ever does it. I just want to point that out that right now, here is another chance to do just that—buy us at historical lows—and very few people are thinking in those terms. They want to buy the lows, but never seem to.

Richard Dennis[10]

Some turtles won. Some were dismal failures. There were reasons for this.

For example, today is in the middle of June and there is a lot of talk about the weather, the grain situation, and whether it rains or snows or is dry. I have no idea. It's not the kind of thing I deal with. I don't have any way to use information like that. I don't think anyone else really does either . . . If I think it is going to rain, perhaps it's an indication of how I should dress for the day, but little else.[12]

"Managers often say that they are managing to long-term objectives but act to meet short-term objectives of clients who have not spent the time understanding what Trend Following means to them. As much as the managers, industry and regulators try to educate and illustrate, the ultimate responsibility lies in the hands of the client."—Jason Russell

Of course, you might opt to trade as a trend follower for your own account, and never hire a Bill Dunn or Ed Seykota. In that instance, you can pay fees to yourself for a job well done.

Fortune Favors the Bold

Trend Following is not easy. Like any entrepreneurial endeavor, it demands you be responsible for yourself as Charles Faulkner emphasized to us:

"Trend trading, and even trading in general, isn't for everyone. As too few people check out what the day-to-day life of a trader is like, and trend trading specifically, I strongly recommend they find out before making a life changing commitment."

Optimism means expecting the best, but confidence means knowing how to handle the worst.

Max Gunther[13]

What does "life changing commitment" involve? You commit to not wanting to be right all of the time. Most people have to be right. They want other people to know they're right. They don't want the success. They don't want to win. They don't want money. They just want to be right. The winners, on the other hand, just want to win.

You also commit to patience and faith in a system that is not structured on quarterly performance. You work hard to gain experience. Great experience leads to great intuition. You commit to thinking for the long term and not feeling insecure if you don't have a steady earnings stream. You might have one year where you are down 10 percent. The following year you might be down 15 percent. The next year you might be up 115 percent. If you quit at the end of the second year, you will never get to the third year. That's the reality.

Although this may seem a paradox, all exact science is dominated by the idea of approximation.

Bertrand Russell[14]

As a trend follower, you commit to a choice: Trade yourself, or let a Trend Following trader trade for you. There are pros and cons to both and you won't find them out until you get in the game.

Afterword

"If you can find someone who is really open to seeing anything,
then you have found the raw ingredient of a good trader, and I
saw that in Bruce right away."
—Michael Marcus on Bruce Kovner

Bill Miller and Legg Mason

*Success and happiness—
the conditions needed to
thrive on this earth--are
reflections of the choices
we make.*

Brett N. Steenbarger

The first edition of *Trend Following* hit the streets in April 2004. Almost immediately, the book made a splash landing in the top 500 of all books available at Amazon.com. Soon the success of the book brought me in contact with an assortment of even more Wall Street pros.

Late that same summer, Richard Cripps, the Chief Market Strategist at Legg Mason, wrote a review of *Trend Following*. Following his review, he invited me to their Baltimore headquarters for lunch with his colleague, Timothy McCann. We had a great conversation regarding my book and the Legg Mason Equity Compass, a systematic trading model for stocks. After our conversation, Richard escorted me up a flight of stairs to a nondescript door. I had no idea where I was headed. Upon entering the room, I was surprised to find it filled with what I could only guess were young investment banking associates listening to a speaker who stood before them at a podium. Michael Mauboussin, Legg Mason's Chief Investment Strategist, smiled and motioned for me to sit down. I quickly recognized that the speaker was Bill Miller, the renowned fund manager of the $20 billion dollar Legg Mason Value Trust. Bill Miller has beaten the S&P 500 Index for 14 straight years.

Miller continued to speak for a few more minutes, and then introduced me to the audience and invited me to the podium. Until that moment, I had no idea I would be asked to speak. For the next hour, Miller, from one side of the room, and Mauboussin, from the other side, alternately peppered me with questions about trend following, risk management, and technical analysis. As I continued to field questions, I realized that the audience was primarily fundamentally trained, but very curious and open to hearing about new ideas and concepts.

After the presentation, I thanked Miller for the opportunity to make my case. I asked him how he found out about my book. He said: "I read a lot. I surf Amazon.com for all types of books. I came across yours, bought it, liked it, and told all my people at Legg Mason that they should read it."

At that moment, I knew *Trend Following* was catching on in a big way. Forget sales—I knew that if the book's message had struck a chord with Bill Miller, I was on to something.

Market Wizard Larry Hite

The same curiosity that would ultimately produce *Trend Following* motivated me to seek out and interview even more traders in person. And during the first five months of 2005, I interviewed, either in their offices or homes, many of the world's greatest traders, collectively managing over $10 billion USD.

Not long after meeting Bill Miller, I had the opportunity to sit down with Larry Hite at his home in Manhattan and his office on Park Avenue. In the 1990s, Larry was instrumental in transforming a sleepy, 200-year-old London-based sugar-trading firm known as ED & F Man into The Man Group, now the largest hedge fund manager in the world with over $42 billion USD under management. The fundamental driver of Man's growth was the application of a risk-management concept developed by Larry that he calls Asymmetrical Leverage (ASL). For The Man Group, Hite devised a "guaranteed fund" that offered investors above-market rates of return while setting aside a portion of the money in zero-coupon bonds to protect the principle.

Most of the Ivy League guys I know are so used to being 'right' they get very uncomfortable dealing with uncertainty—when there is no right answer. Their ego often makes them so afraid of being 'wrong', that they're unable to make good bets. They aren't comfortable with the idea of risk, because they don't know how to assess it or measure it. [They have been] taught to absorb knowledge, not what to do with it.

Larry Hite
Hite Capital

Chatting in Larry's living room, grabbing some sushi at one of his favorite spots, and talking about the joys of entrepreneurship was a blast. But it was later in his office, as Larry stood at the chalkboard explaining some of the basic concepts of Asymmetrical Leverage, that I really 'got' Larry.

He described efforts to predict the exact dimensions of a market's movement as futile. Then he asked me, "What is the value of perfect knowledge?" "What if we knew the ending prices at the end of the year across a portfolio of markets?" And that was when he told me about the experiment: "In an attempt to answer these questions, we went to our databases and looked up the prices on December 31st of a given year. We asked ourselves, 'With this knowledge, how much leverage could we have used to get the maximum advantage at the beginning of that same year on January 1st?' We found that even with perfect foresight of the ending price, we could not sustain more than 3 to 1 leverage because we could not predict the path it took to get there."

Luckily I knew where Larry was going, but I am sure he stumps most people with this particular story. The big lesson from Larry, however, involves "bets." Larry provided me with an excerpt from a speech of his that really struck a chord:

"Life is nothing more than a series of bets, and bets are really nothing more than questions and their answers. There is no real difference between, 'Should I take another hit on this Blackjack hand?' and 'Should I get out of the way of that speeding and wildly careening bus?' Each shares two universal truths: a set of probabilities of potential outcomes and the singular outcome that takes place. Everyday we place hundreds if not thousands of bets— large and small, some seemingly well considered and others made without a second thought. The vast majority of the latter, life's little gambles made without any thought, might certainly be trivial. 'Should I tie my shoes?' seems to offer no big risk, nor any big reward. While others, such as the aforementioned 'speeding and wildly careening bus,' would seem to have greater impact on our lives. However, if deciding not to tie your shoes that morning causes you to trip and fall down in the middle of the road when you finally decide to fold your hand and give that careening bus plenty of leeway, well then, in hindsight the trivial has suddenly become paramount."

Our response to this environment has to be disciplined. If disagreement of opinions lead to trends, we need to maintain our positions. Similarly, we must be willing to close or change positions without ambiguity if called for. Risk management is especially opportune at this time. Will Rogers summed it up succinctly: "Even if you are on the right track, you'll get run over if you just sit there."

Mark S. Rzepczynski
President, John W. Henry & Company

To this day, I can't figure out why thinking in terms of probabilities is so hard for most people. But then again, not many of them have access to such a down-to-earth teacher as Larry Hite.

Inefficient Markets

As every author knows, especially first-time unknown authors writing about relatively obscure subjects such as trend following trading, you spend a significant amount of your time on the road promoting your book. Since I fit the definition of "first-time unknown author" to a tee, that's exactly what I did, with no idea whether *Trend Following* would sell ten or ten thousand copies. To my delight, the book has sold tens of thousands of copies and is being translated into a surprising number of languages. But as a result of the book's success, I soon found myself point man for confusion about the strategy and performance of trend following style traders. With each forecast of doom, usually in the form of book review, column, and/or interview, I tried to "set the record straight."

I'd usually start by addressing the assumption that generates much of the confusion in the first place—the efficient market hypothesis. The hypothesis essentially says that you can't find an edge to beat the market, and simply sticking with a benchmark or index is the best path to take for profit. Proponents of the efficient market hypothesis argue that because markets are efficient and prices fully reflect all information, traders who consistently outperform the market do so out of luck, not skill. Of course, in the real world, markets are both efficient and inefficient, some more than others. In the real world, there are traders who do beat the market by a wide margin, and many of them are trend followers.

But great trend trading does not translate into only up years. 2004 and 2005 have showed both the typical trend following drawdown and the typical trend following recovery.

What accounts for the patience, discipline, and commitment to long-term success as a trend follower? It may ultimately be about making a profit, but it is also an understanding and keen appreciation for the scientific method. Just as scientists start with a hypothesis, trend followers start with a certain view of the world. Their divergent view sees the world in trends. Facing the reality of any and all market environments head on is the philosophical foundation of trend following. Yet if the approach is that simple (and profitable), then why does trend following continue to confuse bright and market-wise people?

A recent email from a skeptic confessed that, "...*the consistent volatility [and drawdown] of [trend following] makes it an untenable strategy, at least for me.*"

Trend following is, indeed, untenable for those who cannot stand the feelings of being in a drawdown or dealing with volatility. Trend followers believe that if you attempt to avoid volatility and drawdown, you will avoid large profits as well, a mindset that can be threatening to those who feel safest when they think they are pursuing supposedly low-risk trading methods. In my interviews with many of the great traders, we wondered why so many criticize trend following for drawdowns (which they typically recover from rather quickly), but seemingly ignore stock market drawdowns. This focus on trend following drawdowns may account for *The Financial Times*' Philip Coggan's tentative review of my book in December 2004:

"It is possible that momentum-based strategies might work. Academic studies have suggested some success in the short term, although mean reversion occurs over longer periods."

"It is *possible* that momentum-based strategies *might* work"? Don't the results of John W. Henry, David Harding, Jerry Parker, Larry Hite, George Crapple, Ken Tropin, Salem Abraham, Dinesh Desai, Paul Rabar, Louis Bacon, Bruce Kovner, and Bill Dunn to name just a few—count for something? I'll trust the actual trading results of these men over "academic studies" and "suggestions" any day. You cannot argue with hard data—even though I know many people who do. To quell the naysayers, myself and a close associate, Justin Vandergrift, have added performance reports on 20+ trend-following trading programs to Appendix B, "Performance Guide," of this expanded version. The month-by-month data should be an "aha" moment for everyone. You say you want the big money? Are you prepared to deal with the reality of what the performance data shows?

Take, for example, the following commentary from trend follower Salem Abraham's May 2005 letter to his investors:

Hendrik Houthakker, a prominent Harvard economist, ran a test on trend following...he ran it on one contract. I believe it was wheat. Well some years it made money, some years it didn't make money. Houthakker... didn't try to trend follow across the board [just one market]. He came to the conclusion that trend following did not work.

Larry Hite
Hite Capital

I get the same sort of value from these books [Trend Following] as I do from studying the Keech cult, supernatural operators such as Uri Geller and horoscope readers.

Victor Niederhoffer
See page 136 for more on Niederhoffer.

I decided almost 20 years ago, that rather than become an expert trend follower, I could better leverage my time by becoming an expert at identifying other trend followers. The decision has been very rewarding. Having placed over a billion dollars with trend followers over the years, I have become increasingly convinced that the level of passion, discipline, intelligence and hard work to become a long term success at trend following is enormous.

Jon C. Sundt
President
Altegris Investments

"Our research allows us to select trades that put the odds in our favor. However, it takes time to prove that the odds truly are in our favor. The statistics below demonstrate this truth:

Percentage of time we make money in any day: 54%

Percentage of time we make money in any month: 56%

Percentage of time we make money in any 3 months: 64%

Percentage of time we make money in any 6 months: 77%

Percentage of time we make money in any 12 months: 92%

Percentage of time we make money in any 24 months: 100%

We do not have a crystal ball, so we do not know when this current losing period will end. However, we can look in the rear view mirror and see that when we experienced periods like this before, not only did we survive, but we thrived."

At the end of the day, you could argue that trading is all about drawdown and recovery. Those are the facts of life as great trend following traders demonstrate repeatedly. Do we wish the roller coaster rides were smoother? Perhaps, but you have to deal with the real world, and the real world is uncertain and volatile.

Trend Following Confusion Reigns

My interviews with the great traders also confirmed what I have always believed, and repeatedly say, to be the primary reason people are confused about trend following. Their confusion is linked directly to a trading and investing culture familiar and therefore comfortable with only one approach to the markets: fundamental analysis. Fundamental traders and investors think the only way to beat the market is to gather all of the information you can find. They want news, they want CNBC, they want Jim Cramer, they want crop reports, they want OPEC rumors, they want Greenspan's shoe size—they believe all of this extraneous information will help them to make profitable trading decisions. Trend followers, on the other hand, who are technical traders by nature, say enough! The market price is the best source of information about the market direction because the market price is the aggregate vote of everyone. Think about it—what else can you really believe in besides the market price?

It may help to clear up some of the confusion about trend following by examining the viewpoints of some trend following critics. When Peter Deoteris at Welling@Weeden reviewed *Trend Following*, he diminished the trend following community by mistakenly referring to John W. Henry and Ed Seykota as "a couple of commodities traders." The universe of trend-following traders is hardly a party of two composed of Ed Seykota and John W. Henry alone. There are many successful trend followers, and the majority of them trade stocks, currencies, bonds, and commodities. And what is the implication of the word "commodity"? Too many people associate the term "commodity" as "risky," but forget that *all* trading methods are risky. The trick is to understand the risk in any trading approach and to know what to do with it on a daily basis.

Deoteris also perpetuates the myth that trend followers attempt to forecast significant market events:

"…there clearly is a strong element of revisionist history at work here…looking back and using subsequent events to justify various traders' positions. When those positions were established, however, they were based on logic and assumed risks that were often entirely different."

As any reader of *Trend Following* now knows, trend followers take trading positions with no knowledge that an event or crisis will occur. They take their positions as markets move. With price leading the way, they follow along. The fact that these particular small, initial price trends lead to big trends that lead to big events is not something anyone could predict.

Another source of confusion stems from trend following's reliance on reactive technical analysis. For example, one form of technical analysis attempts to "read" charts to divine the market direction. The second form of technical analysis, practiced by trend followers, is based on reacting to market movements whenever they occur. Although I make this distinction clear in Chapter 1 of *Trend Following*, I still find myself explaining the difference to bewildered investors and traders. Trend followers are perfectly happy to accept the fact that their method of price analysis never allows them to enter at the exact bottom or exit at the exact top of a trend.

However, this particular concept is hard to fathom for many market players. For example, in the winter of 2004, when Citigroup fired their entire technical analysis group as a cost-cutting measure

The market serves a valuable function in our economy not often talked about: It provides an efficient mechanism for transferring precious capital from those who are ill-equipped to steward its growth to those who are adept. A variety of market participants provide this service up and down the food chain. The financial markets are voluntary arrangements. No one is compelled to purchase a piece of trading software. No guns are involved in herding investors into seminars. Advisory letters are sent to those who willingly subscribe to them, and may be cancelled at will. Investors who avail themselves of these services without exercising due diligence and taking responsibility for their own actions are the true dangerous lot— they are a danger to themselves. They blame others for their bad decisions and misfortunes; they delude themselves about the true nature of their problem, so the solution remains ever beyond their ken.

Gibbons Burke
MarketHistory.com

and replaced it with more fundamental analysis, media coverage jumped all over the idea that technical analysis was dead. Immediately I started receiving emails asking if trend following was now dead (see page 112 for a reminder).

The real question with the Citigroup firings is not why they were replacing technical with fundamental analysis, but what kind of technical analysis were they using in the first place. It certainly wasn't the price-based analysis used by trend followers. Yet the only conclusion most people drew from Citigroup's actions was that technical analysis had been thoroughly discredited.

Media response to events such as the Citigroup firings are encouraged by financial "experts" whose reputations hinge on making pronouncements about the market. James Altucher, a disciple of Victor Niederhoffer and, these days, a popular financial writer, recently posted an article on trend following. The article elicited an abundance of feedback. One trend follower wrote me saying:

"John W. Henry and his peers advertise the riskiness of their investments on their sleeve, while some of the mean reversion hedge fund boys spend sleepless nights hoping no one ever figures out how much risk they are really taking. Most of those guys won't even admit to themselves how much risk they are taking!"

But what about supposed "lower-risk" strategies such as PIPEs or arcane forms of arbitrage? Trend follower Jake Carriker emailed me this observation:

"What a novel way to avoid being in a drawdown: trade an instrument that is so illiquid that there is no market for it except under special circumstances. That makes it a lot more convenient to pretend that there is very little risk. If I get to make up my own price quote for an instrument on every day between my buy and sell points, then I can create an infinite Sharpe ratio as long as I sell it for more than I buy it. The only case where I ever have to face up to the big risks I really take is if the asset goes to a level that forces me to liquidate at a big loss. In that case, my strategy does not appear quite so risk free."

As I accumulated reader feedback, it became clear that some people believed I hadn't accentuated the drawdowns of trend followers enough. Yet I am very clear on pages 95–100. There are no free lunches. You can make money, and you can lose money. To get

I mean look at the concept of price targets. Someone, analyst, mutual fund manager, whoever will come on and say, "I have a price target for this stock of XXX—which is up 30pct from here." I see it getting there over the next 6 months. Yeah right. When someone tells me they know where a stock is going, I can only laugh and ask them why they haven't mortgaged the house and put it all in the stock. Of course I know the answer. They don't want to put their money in the stock; they want YOU to put YOUR money in the stock so the price of the stock they own goes up. Get long and get loud. Why can't we just admit they are pitching a stock and treat it like a trinket on QVC?

Mark Cuban
www.blogmaverick.com

the big gains—there will be periods of pain and drawdown. No risk, no return. But how often do you hear about the Nasdaq being in a −60% drawdown five years after the bubble burst?

If further proof was needed, it occurred a few months ago. I had picked up the phone and called a top trend follower. His firm no longer reports their performance data, but they continue to trade billions. I had never talked with this man before, and he is not mentioned in this book. At first, he was uneasy talking with me. "How did you find me?" "Why are you calling?" But he had a good sense of humor, even though he quickly said that he did not want to be quoted on the record. We talked for 45 minutes.

His insights:

- He backed that many more Long Term Capital Managements are ready to implode. He said to look at the numbers of the arbitrage guys. He pointed out that for the last four years, the arbitrage ("stat arb., convertible arb., etc.") guys are using more and more leverage to generate less and less return ("too much gearing"). He added, "They think they have found the Key to Rebecca and they have not found anything."

- He acknowledged that his billion dollar plus fund was on the other side of LTCM's losses in the zero-sum game: "We were the other side...they were an accident waiting to happen...now seven years later, the risks for these types of strategies are just as great."

- Wall Street investment banks only want 35-year-old traders. You get to be 50, and they don't want you. What's his point here? Wall Street ignores experience like Richard Donchian trading into his nineties. I know great trend followers ranging in age from 30 to 70.

If you have the good fortune to make some money in this world, you will always have detractors. John W. Henry, the owner of the Red Sox baseball team and one of the best trend followers ever, is no exception. Spring 2005 has seen the catcalls for John's head in some investment circles. Why is this? You have a choice of answers: John's success or his critic's ignorance. It's probably both. And for those who think Henry's trading prowess has diminished, check out his approximate +9% return for May 2005 and for good measure his +9% for June 2005.

Hedge Fund Hype

In June of 2005, Reuters was still misinterpreting trend followers' relationship with the soaring price of oil:

"SINGAPORE, June 20 (Reuters)—Oil prices soared to a new record high over $59 a barrel on Monday, extending last week's surge as a threat against Western consulates in OPEC member Nigeria jolted traders already worried about tight supplies. Oil prices climbed more than 9 percent, or nearly $5, last week,

I met with a near billion-dollar hedge fund in their Texas office in Spring 2005. Funded primarily from the principals' personal wealth (they hit it big with one of the top technology firms of all-time), their firm was seeking insights into trend following. They want to invest with trend following traders, but they are having a hard time wrapping their arms around a strategy (trend following) not rooted in fundamentals. The three executives I met with were more comfortable with a trader who traded one market alone. They liked the idea that a trader might be able to fundamentally know everything he could about that one market. They liked the idea of that type of skill compared to trend following skill. The trend following skill of reducing all markets to the common denominator of price just did not connect with them. This group is very bright and they are doing extreme due diligence on trend following trading. Unlike some who dismiss trend following, these folks will get it since they are willing to learn something new.

drawing additional buying interest from trend-following hedge funds as they surpassed the previous early April high."

Besides sowing confusion about trend followers *pushing* the oil market to $60, Reuters demonstrated the media's proclivity for the next "new" thing by combining the words "trend following" with "hedge funds." I am absolutely certain that the phrase "hedge fund" is hot. Even if they aren't sure what a hedge fund is or does, the word seems to be de rigueur for those journalists searching for the next sound bite.

Perhaps we have reached the point where the use of the phrase "hedge fund" is more confusing than helpful. Consider this quote from *Futures Magazine*: *"Hedge fund should be renamed, perhaps to 'anything-but-hedge' funds."* People who run hedge funds do not make money by hedging. They make money by speculating. They take risk and hopefully reward will follow. There are untold numbers of different hedge fund trading strategies.

But then, how *do* you categorize trend followers? Many of them are regulated by the United States federal government and labeled by the Commodity Futures Trading Commission (CFTC) as Commodity Trading Advisors (CTAs). But the term CTA is a misnomer. CTA doesn't come close to accurately describing trend following traders who take positions in stocks, bonds, currencies, and energies. Have a conversation with trend follower Bill Dunn about being called a CTA and he will say he is a fund manager. "Fund manager." Now there's a descriptor that accurately reflects what these traders do. I suggest we dispense with "hedge funds," "commodity trading advisors," and other arcane academics terms. Let's just call people who trade money for clients "fund managers" while keeping in mind that there are different trading strategies for different fund managers.

But even if we agree on what to call a hedge fund, the mainstream press still insists on "blaming" fund managers for all that is "bad." Consider the following excerpt that reinforces the "odious hedge fund fear":

"Long Term Capital Management wasn't the first hedge fund to get itself into serious strife but it's the one that is always recalled whenever the market turns choppy. A choppy market is one that doesn't seem to make sense and is hungry for direction. The uncertainty it produces invariably causes traders, investors, analysts, and everyone else in the money game to start worrying about a downturn. When that happens, people want a bad guy to blame for the doom that might be ahead. Nowadays, when there's no obvious candidate, suspicion tends to fall on hedge funds. Run by outrageously paid managers, these vast pools of exclusive private capital are used for highly leveraged investments and are a major component of today's market. But because hedge funds are largely unregulated and not subject to disclosure rules that apply in other sectors of the market, much of what they do remains a mystery. In unsettled times this makes people nervous."[1]

Great traders don't sit around during so-called choppy periods looking for someone to "blame." Great traders accept responsibility and aim to control what they can control. You can't control the timing of choppy or trending markets, but you better know how to handle either situation. You can't eliminate uncertainty, but you better have an idea of how you will deal with it. Very little of what great traders "do" is a mystery, but if you accept blindly the constant sound bites and "blame the other guy" language of the Wall Street press corps, I can imagine it might be very hard to get "it."

Final Thoughts

A friend of mine in the hedge fund world, approached me this spring about attending an investment conference in La Jolla, California, co-sponsored by Altegris Investments, Inc. Tom had just accepted an invitation to join Altegris. Altegris has placed over $1 billion of client assets with various fund managers of futures trading programs, commodity pools, and hedge funds, including significant placements with trend followers. Upon my arrival at the conference, Tom introduced me to the President and CEO of Altegris, Jon Sundt. Jon's presentation at the conference hit home. He postulated:

"Can a great trader have great skill and no opportunity to make money? Can a bad trader have no skill and tons of opportunity to make money? The answer is yes to both questions. Luck is at play in the short-term for most traders. There will always be "some guy" with a great one-year return, but the sustained edge appears only over time."

When you strip away all the noise, we see that long term price movements, bull and bear markets, are a function of fear and greed. These human emotions, reacting to shifts and imbalances of supply and demand...will always exist. Superfund employs a disciplined, systematic approach and profits from investor emotion by harnessing clear price trends. Human emotion does not impact the positions we take or the open risk that we allow in our trades...

Christian Baha
CEO Superfund

Now, there's one thing that you men will be able to say when you get back home, and you may thank God for it. Thirty years from now when you're sitting around your fireside with your grandson on your knee, and he asks you, What did you do in the great World War Two? You won't have to say, "Well, I shoveled shit in Louisiana." Alright now, you sons of bitches, you know how I feel. I will be proud to lead you wonderful guys into battle anytime, anywhere. That's all.

General George S. Patton, Jr.
3rd Army Speech — May 31, 1944

What's Jon's big picture point? He wants you to think about what happens when the bad trader with no skill finally finds himself with no opportunity. If you don't want to embrace his wisdom, you will eventually feel the pain in your trading account.

There will always be critics, and there will always be cheerleaders. I, however, find solace in the performance numbers. And trend following performance numbers are the real story. No matter how many people agree or disagree with the content of this book, the performance numbers paint a picture you either accept or reject—it's your choice.

Introduction to Appendices

The following appendices are not just "extra" material. They are not just research notes. Each appendix adds additional value and clarification to the main book text. A careful consideration of all eight appendices will provide even greater trend following education.

Appendix A: Fidelity Wealth-Lab Pro™: A great tool for testing trend following trading systems. Jose Cruset, Volker Knapp, and Dion Kurczek add real value with their example systems and software screen shots.

Appendix B: Performance Guide: Historical performance data from professional trend followers provides concrete results not just theory. Thanks to Justin Vandergrift for all of his efforts on this appendix.

Appendix C: Short-Term Trading: Short-term trading is hard, but not impossible. Market Wizards Jim Simons and Toby Crabel do win as short term traders, but Ed Seykota offers good insight on the difficulty for the average guy.

Appendix D: Personality Traits of Successful Traders: Understanding the role of personality and temperament in great trading can be critical.

Mean reversion works almost all the time and then it stops and you are kind of out of business. So the market is always reverting to the mean except when it doesn't and then we [trend followers] are on board this big huge trend and these people lose a lot of money. There are two competing philosophies [trend following v. mean reversion]...then every eight years you [mean reversion] are out of business because when it doesn't revert to the mean your philosophy loses...mean reversion is somewhat uninformed.

Jerry Parker
Chesapeake Capital
Futures Industry
Association Presentation

Appendix E: Trend Following Models: Paul Mulvaney of Mulvaney Capital Management presents a useful visual model for trend following trading.

Appendix F: Trading Systems Example from Trading Recipes: Bob Spear of Trading Recipes software presents a sample trend following trading system.

Appendix G: Modern Portfolio and Managed Futures.

Appendix H: Critical Questions for Trading Systems: Understand critical questions that must be answered to have a successful trend following trading system.

Fidelity
Wealth-Lab Pro™

A

All trend following systems in this appendix have been developed and tested with Wealth-Lab Developer. These basic principles are universal to all presented systems:

- Detect major trends by measuring the price changes.
- Profitable trades are not exited until the trend changes ("let the profits run").
- Unprofitable trades are exited at a predefined stop-loss point ("cut the losers short").
- Money management (position sizing) is based on the maximum risk we are willing to take; i.e., the maximum amount we accept to lose in a single position.

Several basic concepts exist to define a trend. The most common ones are as follows:

- Moving averages.
- Donchian channels (high/low breakouts).
- Bollinger Bands (standard deviation breakouts).

Source of Charts in this Appendix A: Fidelity Investments. © 2005 FMR Corp. All Rights Reserved

The statements and opinions expressed in this book are those of the author. Fidelity Investments is not responsible for the accuracy or completeness of any statements or data contained in this book. Fidelity Investments has not examined, nor does it endorse, any trading strategy discussed in this publication

Misunderstanding of probability may be the greatest of all impediments to scientific literacy.

Stephen Jay Gould

Data

All systems in our example systems use daily price information. Each day has the following: open, high, low, and close. Neither volume nor intraday information is used. The systems were tested on this portfolio:

Sector	Market
Currencies	British Pound
	Japanese Yen
	Swiss Franc
	Euro
Energies	Crude Oil
	Natural Gas
Metals	Gold (Commex)
	Silver (Commex)
Grains	Corn
	Soybean Oil
	Wheat, KC
Softs	Coffee
	Cotton #2
	Sugar #11
Financials	S&P 500
	Nasdaq 100
	T-Note, 5yr
	T-Bonds
Meats	Live Cattle
	Live Hogs

Total: 20 Markets

This portfolio was chosen for its lack of correlation and because the markets are very liquid. We used 15 years (1/1/1990–12/31/2004) of continuous ratio-back-adjusted data from Pinnacle Corp. Ratio-back-adjusted data simplifies the back-testing process by merging contract data from different delivery months into one continuous data stream. Price differences in adjacent contracts resulting from carrying charges and interests are taken into account by adjusting backward data (usually past data is lifted up, except for fixed income where it is lowered). This data is good for back-testing trading systems as it provides one single price stream for each contract. Although this approach makes back-testing comfortable, we should bear in mind that this is a simplification of the reality. These facts have to be considered:

- Back-adjusted data merges adjacent contracts but does not take rollover-trades into account. Rollover-trades account for slippage and commission like all other trades. Depending on the contract, between 4 and 12 rollover trades occur within a year.

- By doing the back-adjusting process, past data of a contract is raised either by adding (or subtracting) a fixed value or by applying a multiplier to all values that are older than the rollover date. This eliminates the gaps from one contract to another. But it also inflates past data, resulting sometimes in incorrect simulation results. The farther back the data goes, the higher the differences between real prices and back-adjusted prices. Example: Corn traded in the last 30 years in a range between 110 and 513; today it trades around 200. Back-adjusted data shows corn today at a price of 200 as well, but it shows corn 30 years ago trading at prices of above 4000! When calculating position size, this fact has to be taken into account.

- When rolling from one contract to the next during the back-adjusting process, different data providers use different rules for the exact timing when to switch. When analyzing back-adjusted data, you should find out the process the data provider follows when switching from one contract to the next in order to see if this rollover rule matches your own rollover process in real-life trading.

Thus, results based on back-adjusted data cannot reflect reality 100%. However, they still can provide a good indication about whether a certain trading strategy is profitable or not. Results presented here should therefore be seen as a good start and working ground for further investigation. To get the most realistic results, you should use systems that excel on non-adjusted data using proper rollover procedures to simulate reality as close as possible.

Position Sizing

The starting equity for all of our simulations is 1 M USD. The initial position size is based on the maximum amount of risk we are willing to take for each position. All simulations have an initial risk of 2%; i.e., if the market goes against us, we will lose a maximum of 2% of our equity. To determine the position size, we have to take the stop-price of our system into account. We assume the worst case—that the stop will be hit and that there will be slippage on each trade. In this case, we have to calculate the maximum number of contracts resulting in a loss that is smaller than 2% of our current equity. The result is the position size for this trade. So, we can be sure that on each trade, only 2% of our equity is at risk (except in situations in which there are large overnight gaps and we have to exit on the next open). In cases in which the stop is very close to the entry price, this position size would result in very high positions. In these cases, large overnight gaps would produce higher losses than 2%. To avoid this risk, we additionally restrict the exposure of each position to 10% of our current equity.

Commission and Slippage

In our simulations, we also deducted $20 roundturn commission for each contract and four ticks of slippage. This makes our simulations more realistic.

Stability Tests

When developing trading systems, it is important to make sure a system is robust enough to withstand ongoing changes in market behavior. Whenever we find an edge in the market, we assume our rules will persist, but we also know that the market will never behave exactly in the future as it did in the past. Systems that rely too much on past data and past occurrences are likely to fail in the future.

Out-of-Sample Data   A good test as to whether a system will work in different market conditions involves running a simulation on completely different (i.e., out-of-sample) data than it was designed for. Before risking money, you should test any system in various markets and other time periods to verify its robustness. We will use the following out-of-sample portfolio to validate our system's stability:

Sector	Market
Currencies	Australian Dollar
	Canadian Dollar
	Mexican Peso
Energies	Heating Oil
	Unleaded Gas
Metals	Copper
	Platinum
Grains	Soybeans
	Rough Rice
	Oats
Softs	Cocoa
	Lumber
	Orange Juice
Financials	Dow Jones
	Nikkei Index
	T-Note, 2yr
	T-Note 10yr
	Eurodollars
Meats	Feeder Cattle
	Pork Bellies
Total: 20 Markets	

Testing Various Parameter Values   Whenever a system uses certain input-parameters (such as number of days), you should test whether the performance differs if parameters are changed. Certain parameter combinations might work well in the past but not in the future. So, in our simulations, we present simulation results of various different input parameters to prove robustness.

Monte Carlo Simulation   We also recommend a Monte Carlo simulation of all trades. During this process, all of our generated trades will be scrambled as if they occurred at different times and in a different order. So, you get a new and different equity curve that might have different drawdown and performance values. The add-on product

Monte Carlo Lab for Wealth Lab Developer helps in doing this test in running a simulation several hundred times in order to analyze the robustness of a system. This simulation assures that the result you get in a normal simulation is not the result of luck but of a certain edge the system has in the market. If after a Monte Carlo simulation your system still provides good performance numbers, the chance of having found a robust strategy is much higher.

The Systems

Concept: Moving Averages

Moving averages are the most common technical indicators in use today. They exist in various forms: The Simple Moving Average (SMA) is simply the average price over the specified period. The average is called "Moving" because it is plotted on the chart bar by bar, forming a line that moves along the chart as the average value changes. Whereas a Simple Moving Average (SMA) calculates a straight average of the data, the Weighted Moving Average (WMA) and the Exponential Moving Average (EMA) apply more weight to the more recent data. The most weight is placed on the most recent data point. Because of the way it's calculated, a WMA and an EMA will follow prices more closely than a corresponding SMA. However, results differ not very much. We therefore use only the SMA in our systems.

Although moving averages are widely used, they can be problematic because they usually lag in their trend-detection—they only detect a trend after it has been established. Entering a trend at this point means giving away a big part of the possible profit. However, trend followers accept this as part of the process and part of the risk of possibly making big money.

Fast SMA Crossover Slow SMA 100-50   Our first system uses two different Simple Moving Averages (SMAs), a fast one that follows the short-term trend and a slow one that reflects the long-term trend. Our system uses a fast-moving average out of the last 50 days and a slow one using 100 days. A typical chart would look like the one in Figure A.1.

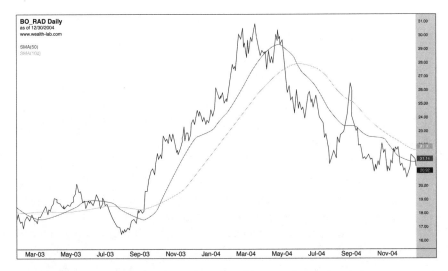

FIGURE A.1 Soybean Oil: 50-day SMA (dotted line) and 100-day SMA (solid line)

Notice how the fast SMA (dotted line) reacts faster to price changes than the slow SMA (solid line). As soon as the fast SMA line crosses over the slow SMA line, the market is about to change its long-term trend direction, and thus this crossover will be used as a market entry signal. The system we present here will identify and enter as soon as the fast SMA crosses over the slow SMA.

Rules:

- Go Long the next day at Market (on the Open) as soon as the fast SMA (of 50 periods) crosses over the slow SMA (of 100 periods).

- Exit Long and Go Short the next day at Market as soon as the fast SMA (of 50 periods) crosses under the slow SMA (of 100 periods).

- Set a stop loss of four times the ATR (Average True Range) of 10 days.

We use a stop loss to control our risk and to avoid more than a 2% loss of our equity.

The Average True Range of our system is calculated by applying the moving average of a specified period to the True Range. The True Range takes 'gaps' into account, which can occur between the previous close and the open. The True Range is always a positive number and is defined to be the greatest of the following for each period:

- The distance from today's high to today's low.
- The distance from yesterday's close to today's high.
- The distance from yesterday's close to today's low.

Position sizing:

2% based on initial stop loss (based on four times the 10-day-ATR).

Example trade:

Figure A.2 shows some example trades in the S&P. The up arrows show long entries (and short exits), the down arrows short entries (and long exits) and the triangles stop loss exits. This system experiences whipsaws in sideways markets (like from November 01 until March 02) and excels at long trends, like the bear trend from April 02 until December 02. It usually never buys at the lowest price and never sells at the highest price—very typical of any trend following system.

FIGURE A.2 Example trades in the S&P show whipsaws in sideways markets and large gains in trending markets.

Results:

The portfolio equity curve (Figure A.3) shows a steady increase until the beginning of 2001 with very little drawdowns. Then, volatility in the portfolio equity curve increases and the system experiences a maximum drawdown of 47%. However, the annualized profit of almost 19.6% makes this system very attractive for someone who is willing to withstand deep drawdown phases.

Less than 40% of this system's trades are profitable. On average, each of these trades makes 14.0% profit, enough to withstand the 60% unprofitable trades whose average loss is 5.9%. Long trades for this system seem to be more profitable than short trades.

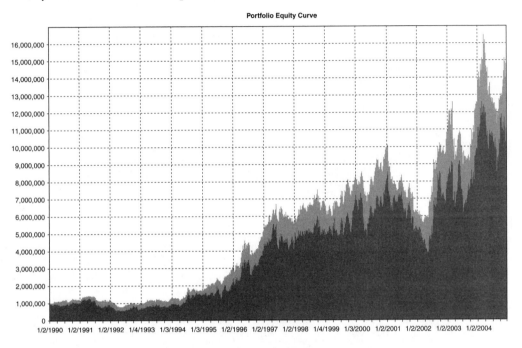

FIGURE A.3 Portfolio equity curve.

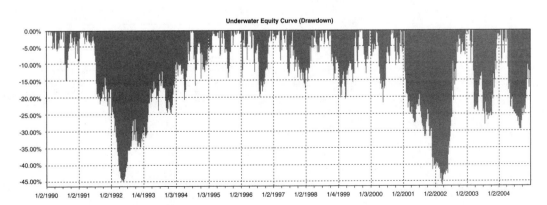

FIGURE A.4 Drawdown curve.

Performance results:

	Long + Short	Long Only	Short Only
Starting Capital	$1,000,000.00	$1,000,000.00	$1,000,000.00
Ending Capital	$14,651,969.00	$13,372,551.00	$2,279,417.75
Net Profit	$13,651,969.00	$12,372,551.00	$1,279,417.75
Net Profit %	1,365.20%	1,237.26%	127.94%
Annualized Gain %	19.59%	18.86%	5.64%
Exposure	21.61%	22.14%	11.97%
Number of Trades	515	368	147
Avg Profit/Loss	$26,508.68	$33,621.06	$8,703.52
Avg Profit/Loss %	1.78%	2.46%	0.10%
Avg Bars Held	84.18	83.64	85.52
Winning Trades	199	145	54
Winning %	38.64%	39.40%	36.73%
Gross Profit	$39,654,793.64	$30,758,031.33	$8,896,762.30
Avg Profit	$199,270.32	$212,124.35	$164,754.86
Avg Profit %	13.95%	15.16%	10.71%
Avg Bars Held	148.22	148.58	147.24
Max Consecutive	8	9	7
Losing Trades	316	223	93
Losing %	61.36%	60.60%	63.27%
Gross Loss	$-26,002,824.58	$-18,385,480.10	$-7,617,344.48
Avg Loss	$-82,287.42	$-82,446.10	$-81,906.93
Avg Loss %	-5.88%	-5.80%	-6.06%
Avg Bars Held	43.85	41.42	49.69
Max Consecutive	12	12	10
Max Drawdown	$-5,631,295.00	$-5,325,782.00	$-3,470,406.25
Max Drawdown %	-46.96%	-75.77%	-60.36%
Max Drawdown Date	8/25/2004	8/27/2004	11/3/2004

Wealth-Lab Score	48.08	20.65	18.70
Profit Factor	1.53	1.67	1.17
Recovery Factor	2.42	2.32	0.37
Payoff Ratio	2.37	2.61	1.77
Sharpe Ratio	0.83	0.68	0.34
Ulcer Index	18.00	23.87	25.97
Wealth-Lab Error Term	16.87	17.45	25.67
Wealth-Lab Reward Ratio	1.16	1.08	0.22
Luck Coefficient	12.43	11.44	6.38
Pessimistic Rate of Return	1.32	1.46	0.80
Equity Drop Ratio	0.25	0.32	0.98

Stability Test: Different Lookback Periods for Moving Averages Initially, we used 50 and 100 as parameters for the SMA-periods. But we also ran several simulations where we used different parameters in order to prove our system's robustness. Although it is possible to design a system in Wealth Lab Developer using the best parameter for each market, we believe this would lead us into a curve-fitting-trap. If you search for (and later apply) the best parameter for each market, the system might not be robust enough in the future and might likely produce no profit.

Our simulation has been run for each parameter combination, and the annualized profit has been painted in Figure A.5. The different shading represents different annualized profit ratios (percent profit per year). The vertical axis shows values for the fast SMA. The horizontal axis shows the difference between the fast and the slow SMA. So, for example, the point at (50, 50) represents a simulation result using 50 as parameter for the fast SMA and 100 for the slow SMA.

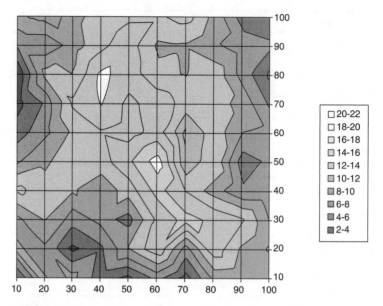

FIGURE A.5 Graph showing system profit (% p.a.) for different SMA-combinations.

The graphic shows optimum values in the center of the chart. Combinations of 40–60 for the fast SMA and 100–120 for the slow SMA provide the best results in backtesting.

Our optimum combination of (50, 60; i.e., SMAs of 50 and 110) is surrounded by parameter combinations with results of more than 12% p.a. So, this parameter combination is a good choice because slight changes in the market behavior still provide good results.

SMA Crossover Weekly   We also decided to test if a weekly bar system works. So, instead of computing our moving average points every day, we will use weekly SMAs, which are calculated using the closing price of each week instead of the closing price of each day. So, there will be a possible crossover only once a week (Friday evening) and therefore new orders have to be submitted to the broker only once a week (Monday morning). This makes trading such a system much easier. According to the initial system with SMA parameters of 50 and 100 days, we will now use the weekly counterpart—i.e., 10 and 20 weeks of lookback periods.

However, with our initial risk setting of 2%, we are getting a low margin to equity ratio (exposure) of only 8.2%. Therefore, we allow an exception here and execute this test with 3% risk stop. All other parameters remain the same.

Rules:

- Go Long the next day at Market (on the Open) as soon as the fast SMA (of 10 weeks) crosses over the slow SMA (of 20 weeks).
- Exit Long and Go Short the next day at Market as soon as the fast SMA (of 10 weeks) crosses under the slow SMA (of 20 weeks).
- Set a stoploss of four times the ATR (Average True Range*) of 10 weeks.

Position sizing:

3% based on initial stop loss (based on four times the 10-week-ATR).

Example trade:

Figure A.6 shows example trades in Crude Oil. During 2003, our system experiences nasty whipsaws in trendless periods. But at the end of 2003, the system enters a long trade all the way until the end of 2004. Even though it enters when the trend is seemingly established and perhaps exhausted, it still catches 16 full points of profit.

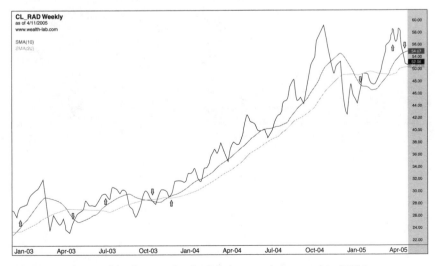

FIGURE A.6 The weekly chart in Crude Oil shows a long trend in 2004 which the system is able to catch.

Results:

Our portfolio equity curve (Figure A.7) has a similar shape as our daily system. However, it does not show the same (high) performance nor the same (high) drawdown. Still, the annualized gain of over 11% is acceptable, especially taking the low number of trades into account (400 in 15 years). Maximum drawdown is 38.6%, which is also lower than our daily system. Also note in the drawdown graph (Figure A.8) that most drawdowns are below 10%, whereas in the daily system (Figure A.4) most are between 10% and 20%. Again, this system shows a low number of profitable trades (40%) with a high profit per trade of almost 15%. Exposure (12.4%) is still much lower than our daily system (21.6%) and therefore, increasing the position size (money management) even further could be considered in order to possibly improve our profits.

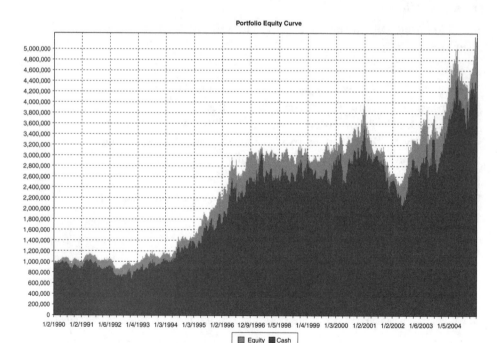

FIGURE A.7 Portfolio equity curve.

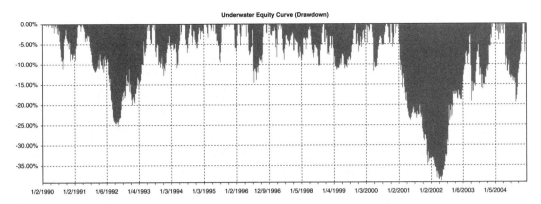

FIGURE A.8 Drawdown curve.

Performance results:

	Long + Short	Long Only	Short Only
Starting Capital	$1,000,000.00	$1,000,000.00	$1,000,000.00
Ending Capital	$5,080,527.63	$4,701,566.13	$1,378,961.63
Net Profit	$4,080,527.63	$3,701,566.13	$378,961.63
Net Profit %	408.05%	370.16%	37.90%
Annualized Gain %	11.45%	10.87%	2.17%
Exposure	12.43%	12.50%	1.41%
Number of Trades	400	380	20
Avg Profit/Loss	$10,201.32	$9,740.96	$18,948.08
Avg Profit/Loss %	2.26%	2.21%	3.29%
Avg Bars Held	19.41	19.21	23.15
Winning Trades	161	153	8
Winning %	40.25%	40.26%	40.00%
Gross Profit	$10,118,227.49	$9,555,140.84	$563,086.65
Avg Profit	$62,846.13	$62,451.90	$70,385.83
Avg Profit %	14.91%	14.86%	15.85%
Avg Bars Held	31.42	31.37	32.50
Max Consecutive	7	8	3

Long + Short	Long Only	Short Only	
Losing Trades	239	227	12
Losing %	59.75%	59.74%	60.00%
Gross Loss	$-6,042,733.17	$-5,858,608.18	$-184,124.99
Avg Loss	$-25,283.40	$-25,808.85	$-15,343.75
Avg Loss %	-6.26%	-6.32%	-5.08%
Avg Bars Held	11.32	11.02	16.92
Max Consecutive	14	14	4
Max Drawdown	$-1,517,648.25	$-1,507,480.38	$-174,799.88
Max Drawdown %	-38.60%	-42.18%	-12.03%
Max Drawdown Date	4/8/2002	4/8/2002	3/29/2004
Wealth-Lab Score	56.56	50.32	135.19
Profit Factor	1.67	1.63	3.06
Recovery Factor	2.69	2.46	2.17
Payoff Ratio	2.38	2.35	3.12
Sharpe Ratio	0.73	0.67	0.36
Ulcer Index	12.13	13.96	6.24
Wealth-Lab Error Term	11.59	11.64	5.26
Wealth-Lab Reward Ratio	0.99	0.93	0.41
Luck Coefficient	12.03	12.07	2.46
Pessimistic Rate of Return	1.39	1.37	1.04
Equity Drop Ratio	0.45	0.52	0.56

Trend with Pattern Entry The following system combines trend following and countertrend concepts. It is called Trend with Pattern Entry (TPE) and was first introduced by Dion Kurczek and Volker Knapp in *Active Trader Magazine* in April 2003. The system's premise is that prices above the SMA indicate a bull trend and prices below the SMA indicate a bear trend. Additionally, the system waits for a short-term countertrend reaction to enter the market. If prices are above the SMA, the system waits for three consecutive down-days to enter long the next day. Consequently, if the price is below the SMA, the system waits for three consecutive up-days to enter short the next day. The exit rule uses a trailing stop, which is four times the ATR of 10 days apart from the current close. The trailing stop will be adjusted if the price moves into our favor but remains if the price moves against us.

Rules:

- Go Long the next day at Market if the price is below the 100-day SMA and the Closing price increased during the last three days.

- Exit Long at Stop if the price reaches the trailing stop, which will be computed by subtracting four times the ATR of 10 days from the current closing price.

- Go Short the next day at Market if the price is above the 100-day SMA and the Closing price decreased during the last three days.

- Exit Short at Stop if the price reaches the trailing stop, which will be computed by adding four times the ATR of 10 days to the current closing price.

Position sizing:

2% based on initial stop loss (based on four times the 10-day-ATR).

Example trade:

Figure A.9 shows an example trade in the S&P. The thick line shows the 100-day SMA. The system enters at the end of October 2000 when the market experiences a strong up-move three times in a row while still below the SMA. The system goes short and exits as soon as the price crosses the trailing stop, which is represented by the small dots in the chart. The trailing stop will be calculated every day and, as this is an example of a short trade, it is adjusted downward but never upward.

FIGURE A.9 The short trade catches almost 200 points in the S&P and exits when the trailing stop is hit after six months.

Results:

Our equity curve grows nicely (Figure A.10) until the beginning of 2002. Then, we are hit with a nasty drawdown of 49%. And if we examine our drawdown curve (Figure A.11), we see several drawdowns over 20%. However, the system is able to recover quickly from these drawdowns—a sign of a good trend following system. Although it experiences drawdowns, the system's annualized profit is still 21.8%. As we can see from the performance result table, we have almost the same number of short and long trades, but the short trades are on average losing trades whereas the long trades are profitable.

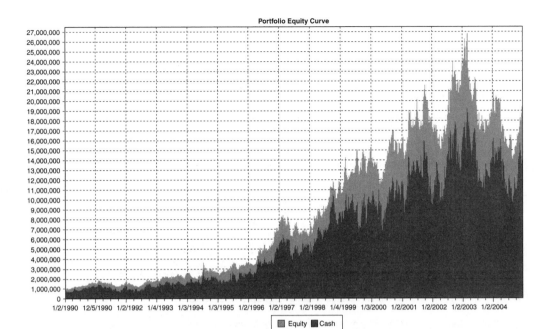

FIGURE A.10 Portfolio equity curve.

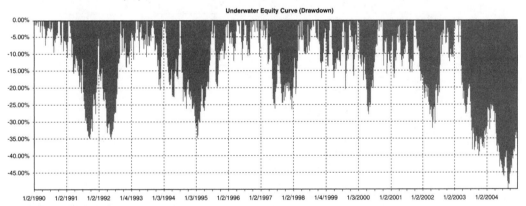

FIGURE A.11 Drawdown curve.

Performance results:

	Long + Short	Long Only	Short Only
Starting Capital	$1,000,000.00	$1,000,000.00	$1,000,000.00
Ending Capital	$19,207,066.00	$21,856,120.00	$-1,649,053.63
Net Profit	$18,207,066.00	$20,856,120.00	$-2,649,053.63
Net Profit %	1,820.71%	2,085.61%	-264.91%
Annualized Gain %	21.77%	22.82%	0.00%
Exposure	28.09%	20.93%	32.33%
Number of Trades	1,243	626	617
Avg Profit/Loss	$14,647.68	$33,316.49	$-4,293.44
Avg Profit/Loss %	0.69%	1.16%	0.21%
Avg Bars Held	40.30	40.39	40.20
Winning Trades	497	258	239
Winning %	39.98%	41.21%	38.74%
Gross Profit	$116,910,604.93	$66,666,494.66	$50,244,110.27
Avg Profit	$235,232.61	$258,397.27	$210,226.40
Avg Profit %	8.18%	8.73%	7.60%
Avg Bars Held	65.58	63.44	67.90
Max Consecutive	8	7	8
Losing Trades	746	368	378
Losing %	60.02%	58.79%	61.26%
Gross Loss	$-98,703,539.32	$-45,810,375.61	$-52,893,163.72
Avg Loss	$-132,310.37	$-124,484.72	$-139,929.00
Avg Loss %	-4.31%	-4.15%	-4.45%
Avg Bars Held	23.45	24.24	22.69
Max Consecutive	16	11	13
Max Drawdown	$-13,438,228.00	$-7,595,336.00	$-18,730,228.00
Max Drawdown %	-49.06%	-76.64%	-113.27%
Max Drawdown Date	9/1/2004	4/16/2002	5/27/2004

Wealth-Lab Score	39.47	25.48	0.00
Profit Factor	1.18	1.46	0.95
Recovery Factor	1.35	2.75	0.14
Payoff Ratio	1.90	2.10	1.71
Sharpe Ratio	0.75	0.68	0.36
Ulcer Index	17.93	20.86	50.01
Wealth-Lab Error Term	12.37	14.16	184.14
Wealth-Lab Reward Ratio	1.76	1.61	0.00
Luck Coefficient	14.45	13.55	7.09
Pessimistic Rate of Return	1.17	1.31	0.96
Equity Drop Ratio	0.22	0.30	0.00

Impact of Money Management   As a general rule, when trying to define the optimum position size, you should focus more on the losing part of a trade than on the winning part. "Control your risk; the returns will take care of themselves" is well-known advice among the great traders. Our position size should be small enough to withstand long drawdown periods, but also high enough to provide us with enough profit.

The results for our first system (SMA Crossover using 50 and 100 days as parameters) using different risk-parameters and concentrating only on the drawdown, is best illustrated by the underwater equity curve (Figures A.12 to A.16).

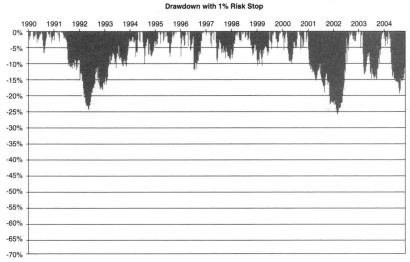

FIGURE A.12 Drawdown with 1% risk stop.

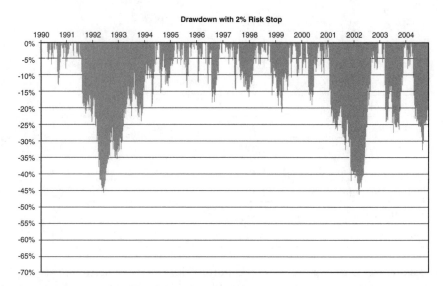

FIGURE A.13 Drawdown with 2% risk stop.

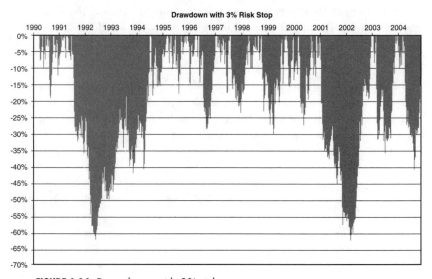

FIGURE A.14 Drawdown with 3% risk stop.

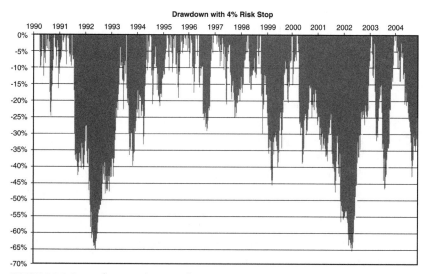

FIGURE A.15 Drawdown with 4% risk stop.

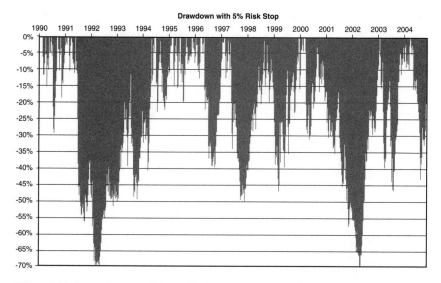

FIGURE A.16 Drawdown with 5% risk stop.

The higher our risk stop parameter, the higher the maximum drawdown and the larger the time until a new equity high is reached. Remember, when using only 1% risk stop, most drawdown peaks are below 10%, whereas at a risk stop parameter of 5%, most are between 20% and 30% with two occurrences where they reach 70%. Trading a system every day that loses up to 70% of its capital before recovering is a difficult task for just about anyone. And of course, it is a completely different issue to experience and accept real money losses compared to analyzing drawdowns backtesting a system hypothetically.

SMA Crossover Pyramiding   Pyramiding techniques are designed to get you into a market a second time at a later stage following the original entry of the first position. The idea is that there is a higher probability that a trend exists and that it will persist—so take advantage and add to your position. Our system takes the first position with the same rules mentioned previously and takes a second position after the first trade has become profitable by a certain percentage. All other parameters, as well as our position sizing rules, remain the same. In case of an exit, the system will exit all positions at the same time.

Rules:

- Go Long the next day at Market (on the Open) as soon as the fast SMA (of 50 periods) crosses over the slow SMA (of 100 periods).
- Enter one additional long position next day at Market as soon as the price increases 1% from the entry price.
- Exit Long and Go Short the next day at Market as soon as the fast SMA (of 50 periods) crosses under the slow SMA (of 100 periods).
- Enter one additional short position next day at Market as soon as the price decreases 1% from the entry price.
- Set a stop loss of four times the ATR (Average True Range) of 10 days.

Position sizing:

2% based on initial stop loss (based on four times the 10-day-ATR).

Example trade:

Figure A.17 shows some example trades in British Pounds. At the end of October 2003, the system detects a crossover from the fast SMA over the slow SMA. It enters long at a price of 162. It waits for a 1% gain, which occurs in November 2003. Then, the system opens a second long position at a price of 164. Both positions are closed in May 2004 when an opposite crossover occurs.

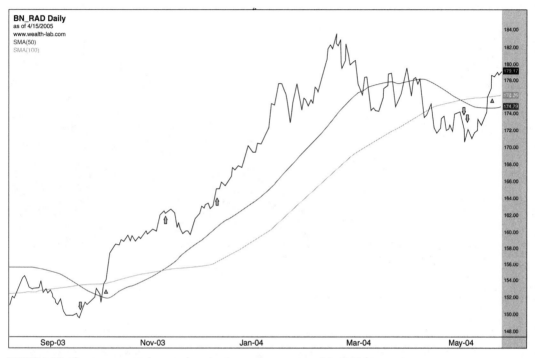

FIGURE A.17 The system catches and scales into a long uptrend in British Pounds which lasts six months.

Results:

Applying an additional system rule improves our system performance considerably. Our system's performance is boosted 25%. However, the portfolio equity curve (Figure A.18) shows much higher volatility. The maximum drawdown (see Figure A.19) increases to (an unsustainable) 64%, which is reached twice during the simulation period. Furthermore, when comparing the results with the figures from the original system (without pyramiding), we must take into account that higher profit has been achieved due to higher exposure (risk).

As a result of our simulation, we can conclude that applying appropriate pyramiding rules to an already profitable system can help increase performance considerably.

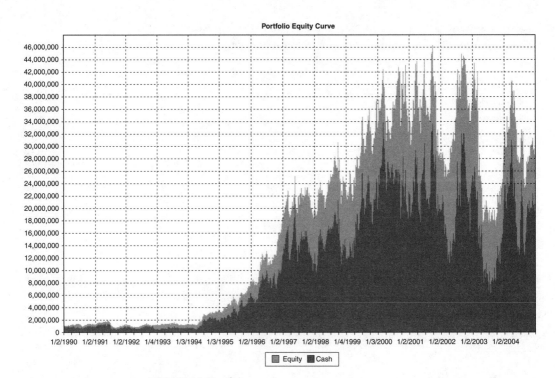

FIGURE A.18 Portfolio equity curve.

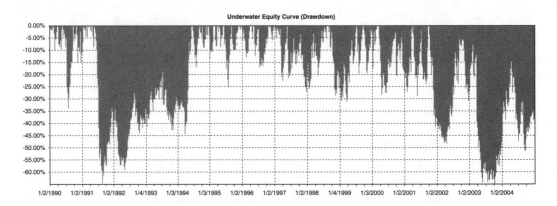

FIGURE A.19 Drawdown curve.

Performance results:

	Long + Short	Long Only	Short Only
Starting Capital	$1,000,000.00	$1,000,000.00	$1,000,000.00
Ending Capital	$28,508,580.00	$14,571,771.00	$14,936,809.00
Net Profit	$27,508,580.00	$13,571,771.00	$13,936,809.00
Net Profit %	2,750.86%	1,357.18%	1,393.68%
Annualized Gain %	25.02%	19.55%	19.74%
Exposure	35.55%	40.44%	28.37%
Number of Trades	1,028	505	523
Avg Profit/Loss	$26,759.32	$26,874.79	$26,647.82
Avg Profit/Loss %	1.39%	2.45%	0.36%
Avg Bars Held	78.94	83.48	74.55
Winning Trades	359	198	161
Winning %	34.92%	39.21%	30.78%
Gross Profit	$212,883,447.74	$100,225,367.85	$112,658,079.90
Avg Profit	$592,990.11	$506,188.73	$699,739.63
Avg Profit %	14.48%	15.03%	13.81%
Avg Bars Held	152.28	150.85	154.04
Max Consecutive	11	9	7
Losing Trades	669	307	362
Losing %	65.08%	60.79%	69.22%
Gross Loss	$-185,374,870.05	$-86,653,597.35	$-98,721,272.70
Avg Loss	$-277,092.48	$-282,259.27	$-272,710.70
Avg Loss %	-5.63%	-5.66%	-5.61%
Avg Bars Held	39.58	40.03	39.20
Max Consecutive	18	18	21
Max Drawdown	$-30,615,356.00	$-30,390,216.00	$-25,157,492.00
Max Drawdown %	-64.28%	-120.49%	-117.91%
Max Drawdown Date	7/17/2003	3/31/2004	12/31/2004

	Long + Short	Long Only	Short Only
Wealth-Lab Score	25.13	-9.90	-12.46
Profit Factor	1.15	1.16	1.14
Recovery Factor	0.90	0.45	0.55
Payoff Ratio	2.57	2.66	2.46
Sharpe Ratio	0.74	0.38	0.48
Ulcer Index	27.15	43.82	40.93
Wealth-Lab Error Term	31.89	102.95	47.63
Wealth-Lab Reward Ratio	0.78	0.19	0.41
Luck Coefficient	11.97	11.53	4.34
Pessimistic Rate of Return	1.26	1.51	0.96
Equity Drop Ratio	0.29	0.00	0.00

Stability Test: Different Parameter Combinations As with our original system, we want to test our parameter stability in the SMA Crossover pyramiding system. Accordingly, we ran various simulations across different parameters (lookback days) for our moving averages. Figure A.20 shows the results. The different shadings represent different annualized profits (% p.a.). Again, the vertical axis represents the fast SMA and the horizontal axis the difference between the fast and the slow SMA.

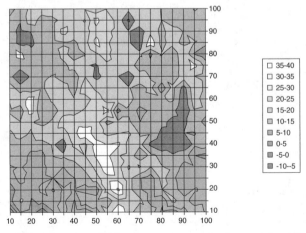

FIGURE A.20 Graph showing system profit (% p.a.) for different SMA combinations.

The global maximum (light area) can be found for combinations of 30–40 days for the fast SMA and 80–100 days for the slow SMA. These combinations achieve profits of over 35% p.a. However, when applying these parameters for your own trading, you may very well achieve lower profits.

Concept: Donchian Channel

The Donchian channel indicator was created by Richard Donchian and is composed of a higher and a lower band concept. The higher band indicates the highest high of the past 'n' days and the lower band indicates the lowest low of 'n' days.

Technical trading theory postulates that a crossover of these psychologically important lines is the result of a change in the market's opinion, and thus a continuation of the initial movement could possibly be expected.

Many trend following systems are based around this seemingly simple concept. A breakout (and entry) signal occurs when the price crosses over a band. When the opposite band is crossed, the position is reversed. A variation uses two different bands, one with a long lookback period (and therefore a wider range) used for entries and one with a short lookback period (with a smaller range) used for exits.

Donchian Channel Breakout 100 Our next system uses a Donchian channel of 100 days. It enters the market as soon as it breaks out of a price range. Figure A.21 shows a typical S&P chart:

FIGURE A.21 The S&P together with its Donchian channel of 100 days.

You can see in this chart that the Donchian channel increases its height along with price volatility. For example, during August 2002, the distance from the higher band to the lower band was almost 400 points, whereas in July 2004 the distance was less than 100 points. This helps us avoid entries in caused by "noise"—which might produce false signals—instead of possibly real trend changes.

Rules:

- Go Long/Short at Stop as soon as the price crosses the upper/lower Donchian band of 100 days.
- Exit and reverse position as soon as the opposite Donchian band is crossed.
- Use four times ATR of 10 days as the parameter for the maximum risk to calculate the position size.

Position sizing:

2% based on initial stop loss (based on four times the 10-day-ATR).

Example trade:

Figure A.22 shows example trades in the Nasdaq 100. Our system caught the long downtrend in June of 2000. It entered short and held the position until November 2002 when it then switched to a long position. When the system entered the market in June 2000, the Nasdaq had already lost almost 2,000 points from its peak. However, our system still caught 2,500 points when it exited its short position in November 2002. Of course, trend following systems never get in at the exact bottom and never get out at the exact top. But as we can see in this example, they are able to catch the main move or "meat" of big trends.

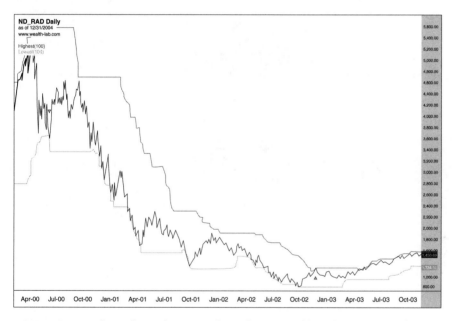

FIGURE A.22 Donchian channel system takes advantage of long bear trend in the Nasdaq.

Results:

Our portfolio equity curve (Figure A.23) shows a nice increase over the entire simulation period with only a few valleys short in duration. The annualized profit reaches 21.2%. Most drawdowns (Figure A.24) are below a generally acceptable 15%. The maximum drawdown of 32.7% is reached only once. Overall, this system shows noteworthy performance over the simulation period and may have the making of good long term trading future in the real world.

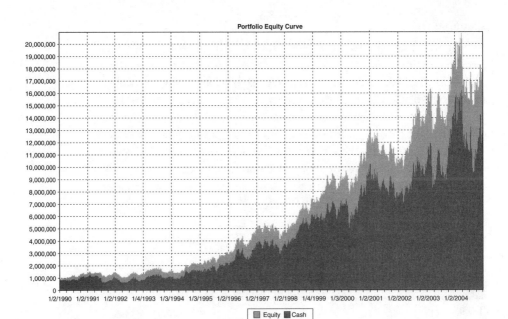

FIGURE A.23 Portfolio equity curve.

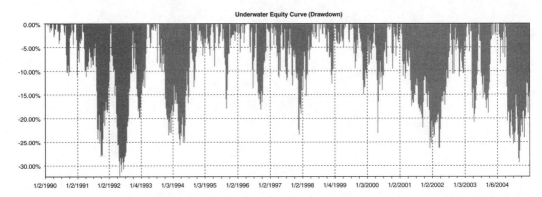

FIGURE A.24 Drawdown curve.

Performance results:

	Long + Short	Long Only	Short Only
Starting Capital	$1,000,000.00	$1,000,000.00	$1,000,000.00
Ending Capital	$17,986,668.00	$19,171,986.00	$-185,319.63
Net Profit	$16,986,668.00	$18,171,986.00	$-1,185,319.63
Net Profit %	1,698.67%	1,817.20%	-118.53%
Annualized Gain %	21.24%	21.75%	0.00%
Exposure	26.25%	20.61%	26.92%

Number of Trades	409	206	203
Avg Profit/Loss	$41,532.20	$88,213.52	$-5,839.01
Avg Profit/Loss %	2.32%	4.18%	0.43%
Avg Bars Held	171.06	172.86	169.22
Winning Trades	161	93	68
Winning %	39.36%	45.15%	33.50%
Gross Profit	$48,632,918.02	$31,222,964.54	$17,409,953.48
Avg Profit	$302,067.81	$335,730.80	$256,028.73
Avg Profit %	19.98%	20.06%	19.87%
Avg Bars Held	289.81	268.23	319.34
Max Consecutive	6	6	4
Losing Trades	248	113	135
Losing %	60.64%	54.85%	66.50%
Gross Loss	$-31,646,251.76	$-13,050,978.50	$-18,595,273.26
Avg Loss	$-127,605.85	$-115,495.38	$-137,742.76
Avg Loss %	-9.15%	-8.90%	-9.36%
Avg Bars Held	93.96	94.38	93.61
Max Consecutive	11	9	22
Max Drawdown	$-6,305,069.00	$-5,858,167.00	$-9,604,234.00
Max Drawdown %	-32.74%	-65.73%	-105.67%
Max Drawdown Date	9/2/2004	8/26/2004	12/31/2004
Wealth-Lab Score	54.42	36.17	0.00
Profit Factor	1.54	2.39	0.94
Recovery Factor	2.69	3.10	0.12
Payoff Ratio	2.18	2.25	2.12
Sharpe Ratio	0.88	0.84	0.05
Ulcer Index	12.09	18.44	37.45
Wealth-Lab Error Term	9.14	11.74	47.87

	Long + Short	Long Only	Short Only
Wealth-Lab Reward Ratio	2.32	1.85	0.00
Luck Coefficient	6.49	6.47	3.47
Pessimistic Rate of Return	1.23	1.52	0.87
Equity Drop Ratio	0.23	0.26	0.00

Stability Test: Out-of-Sample Simulation   We will run our system on the out-of-sample portfolio to test its stability across various markets. All other parameters remain the same.

Results:

The simulation on out-of-sample data showed very similar performance to the in-sample test. The annualized profit is 21.5% (compared to 21.2%) with maximum drawdowns of 33.7% (compared to 32.7%), which occurred twice during the simulation. The portfolio equity curve (Figure A.25) shows a smooth increase over almost the entire simulation period. And most drawdowns persist only for a short time, as can be seen in Figure A.26.

This stability test showed that our system performs well across a variety of markets and is likely to show good performance into the future. However, there can always be more testing to validate our system's robustness.

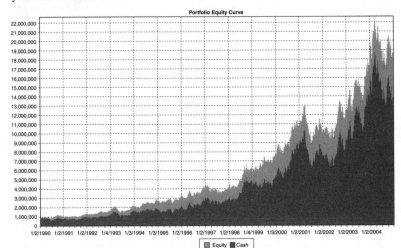

FIGURE A.25 Portfolio equity curve.

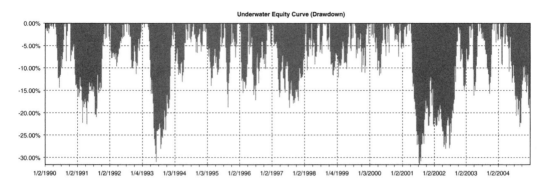

FIGURE A.26 Drawdown curve.

Performance results:

	Long + Short	Long Only	Short Only
Starting Capital	$1,000,000.00	$1,000,000.00	$1,000,000.00
Ending Capital	$18,659,290.00	$23,326,314.00	$-3,667,022.00
Net Profit	$17,659,290.00	$22,326,314.00	$-4,667,022.00
Net Profit %	1,765.93%	2,232.63%	-466.70%
Annualized Gain %	21.53%	23.35%	0.00%
Exposure	26.19%	19.26%	30.79%
Number of Trades	386	190	196
Avg Profit/Loss	$45,749.46	$117,506.92	$-23,811.34
Avg Profit/Loss %	2.22%	4.37%	0.14%
Avg Bars Held	173.59	176.01	171.26
Winning Trades	153	77	76
Winning %	39.64%	40.53%	38.78%
Gross Profit	$48,136,018.19	$34,384,462.21	$13,751,555.98
Avg Profit	$314,614.50	$446,551.46	$180,941.53
Avg Profit %	19.76%	22.92%	16.55%
Avg Bars Held	300.67	296.25	305.16
Max Consecutive	6	6	7

	Long + Short	Long Only	Short Only
Losing Trades	233	113	120
Losing %	60.36%	59.47%	61.22%
Gross Loss	$-30,476,726.10	$-12,058,148.59	$-18,418,577.51
Avg Loss	$-130,801.40	$-106,709.28	$-153,488.15
Avg Loss %	-9.29%	-8.27%	-10.25%
Avg Bars Held	90.15	94.07	86.45
Max Consecutive	10	9	19
Max Drawdown	$-5,675,776.00	$-3,379,750.00	$-10,980,358.00
Max Drawdown %	-33.75%	-32.03%	-150.14%
Max Drawdown Date	8/31/2004	6/9/2004	12/31/2004
Wealth-Lab Score	54.48	82.40	0.00
Profit Factor	1.58	2.85	0.75
Recovery Factor	3.11	6.61	0.43
Payoff Ratio	2.13	2.77	1.61
Sharpe Ratio	0.93	0.96	0.35
Ulcer Index	11.63	12.32	40.88
Wealth-Lab Error Term	5.41	11.40	140.00
Wealth-Lab Reward Ratio	3.98	2.05	0.00
Luck Coefficient	5.40	4.65	3.86
Pessimistic Rate of Return	1.20	1.53	0.83
Equity Drop Ratio	0.21	0.19	0.00

Summary

The following table summarizes the profit and drawdown results from all of our systems.

System	Annualized Profit	Max. Drawdown
Fast SMA Crossover Slow SMA 100-50	3.95%	46.96%
SMA Crossover Weekly	11.45%	38.60%
Trend with Pattern Entry	21.77%	49.06%
SMA Crossover Pyramiding	25.02%	64.28%
Donchian Channel Breakout 100	21.24%	32.74%

Conclusion

The aim of this appendix was to introduce the idea of using software to test your trading ideas. It is very important to prove the stability of your trend following trading system rules before risking real money. Furthermore, you should be aware that all simulations we have presented herein are based on past data. Performance from the past is never a guarantee of future results. However, by running as many stability tests as possible, you can reduce the probability of failure in the future and build your confidence along the way. And yes, this is exactly the process the great trend followers undertake with their trading, too. Now roll up your sleeves and do some homework!

Source of Charts in this Appendix A: Fidelity Investments. © 2005 FMR Corp. All Rights Reserved

The statements and opinions expressed in this book are those of the author. Fidelity Investments is not responsible for the accuracy or completeness of any statements or data contained in this book. Fidelity Investments has not examined, nor does it endorse, any trading strategy discussed in this publication.

Buy and hold is far from the sure thing it's made out to be. It works in bull markets. It works if you invest in dribs and drabs, catching the ups and downs along the way. It works in mild bear markets, when declines are quickly reversed. It may work if you've got 20 years to wait for stock to recover from a half-off sale. Otherwise, it's risky. It's risky when you're holding stocks you bought at extravagant prices. It's extremely risky when your retirement depends on a positive result and you're planning to take up golf in a decade or less.

John Rothchild

If you do your homework and remain rational and responsible, you can invest in commodities with perhaps less risk than playing the stock market. You don't need me to emphasize that investing in anything is a risky business. But let me point out something that you might not have realized: There has been more volatility in the Nasdaq in recent years than in any commodities index. Cisco, Yahoo!, and even Microsoft have been much more volatile than soybeans, sugar, or metals. Compared with the risk record of most tech stocks, commodities look safe enough to be part of any organization's "widows and orphans fund."

Jim Rogers
Hot Commodities

Additional information about the Wealth-Lab software product and various indicators mentioned in this appendix can be found here:

Wealth-Lab Developer:
www.wealth-lab.com

Trend Strength A Indicator:
http://www.wealth-lab.com/cgi-bin/WealthLab.DLL/libraryview?item=396

Trend Strength C Indicator:

http://www.wealth-lab.com/cgi-bin/WealthLab.DLL/libraryview?item=394

Trend Strength Demo Script:

http://www.wealth-lab.com/cgi-bin/WealthLab.DLL/editsystem?id=39161

Performance Guide
Trend Following Historical Performance Data

B

Appendix B contains historical performance data from professional trend followers so that you can see the concrete results for yourself. We had planned to include this data in the first release of the book, but editors thought it would be too much information. As you might have guessed, some readers questioned whether the performance numbers we gave were real, which made us realize how important it was to add the performance data back in for this edition. If you have questions about any trader or track record that we mentioned feel free to contact me at www.michaelcovel.com. A big thank you to Justin Vandergrift for all of his research efforts on this appendix.

Much of what happens in history comes from 'Black Swan dynamics', very large, sudden, and totally unpredictable 'outliers'...Our track record in predicting those events is dismal; yet by some mechanism called the hindsight bias we think that we understand them...Why are we so bad at understanding this type of uncertainty? It is now the scientific consensus that our risk-avoidance mechanism is not mediated by the cognitive modules of our brain, but rather by the emotional ones. This may have made us fit for the Pleistocene era. "Our risk machinery is designed to run away from tigers; it is not designed for the information-laden modern world."

Nassim Nicholas Taleb
Learning to Expect the Unexpected
Edge.org

Abraham Trading Company

Annual Performance Breakdown

	Yearly Statistics		
Year	Return	Drawdown	Assets
2005	-16.62 %	-23.35 %	$175,900,000
2004	15.38 %	-12.25 %	$210,300,000
2003	74.66 %	-14.71 %	$33,400,000
2002	21.51 %	-11.81 %	$11,000,000
2001	19.16 %	-14.11 %	$7,700,000
2000	14.49 %	-17.00 %	$5,900,000
1999	4.76 %	-15.17 %	$5,400,000
1998	4.39 %	-14.34 %	$20,700,000
1997	10.88 %	-12.05 %	$63,200,000
1996	-0.42 %	-19.69 %	$107,000,000
1995	6.12 %	-21.02 %	$122,200,000
1994	24.22 %	-10.99 %	$73,400,000
1993	34.29 %	-10.50 %	$38,200,000
1992	-10.50 %	-26.55 %	$22,500,000
1991	24.39 %	-27.01 %	$27,100,000
1990	89.95 %	-7.90 %	$8,900,000
1989	17.81 %	-31.96 %	$700,000
1988	142.04 %	-22.12 %	$200,000

Month by Month Returns

						Month by Month Returns						
Year	Jan	Feb	Mar	Apr	May	Jun	Jul	Aug	Sep	Oct	Nov	Dec
1988	4.17	-2.59	-8.78	-12.35	32.34	71.99	-2.82	3.45	-1.98	8.01	17.83	4.51
1989	-8.05	-12.64	13.91	-20.08	38.65	-4.40	16.08	-13.84	-7.75	-14.40	10.30	39.52
1990	3.65	1.81	9.45	12.90	-7.90	2.49	20.08	18.54	8.57	-0.36	0.31	-0.09
1991	-15.94	1.30	2.43	-13.70	2.94	2.11	-1.52	-6.33	11.61	16.61	-2.09	33.75
1992	-12.60	-6.00	-5.47	0.31	-5.71	6.58	16.52	1.92	-0.34	-3.31	4.65	-4.54
1993	-4.21	6.10	4.57	9.24	4.88	-1.22	6.60	-5.28	1.16	-6.59	3.71	12.83
1994	-1.45	-4.16	2.87	-8.39	15.01	1.47	0.98	-7.38	5.05	5.43	14.24	1.06
1995	-7.91	1.24	6.63	4.73	8.22	0.11	-8.75	-5.34	-1.84	-6.67	-0.19	19.11
1996	-6.85	-13.78	9.66	14.27	-9.41	1.52	-6.30	-3.34	6.03	16.84	2.45	-6.41
1997	5.28	9.15	-1.50	-5.16	-1.32	0.38	4.11	-8.08	4.95	-5.37	2.10	7.46
1998	-0.90	4.09	-4.45	-4.45	2.61	-2.34	-0.83	23.24	-3.33	-11.39	0.94	4.67
1999	-11.56	13.35	-9.43	7.52	-6.09	-0.68	-0.83	3.12	0.99	-9.57	13.64	8.41
2000	8.02	-9.05	-4.16	5.48	-2.58	-2.19	-5.26	11.76	-4.53	9.51	8.58	-0.18
2001	2.28	2.99	15.17	-10.20	5.13	4.47	-2.85	4.89	9.28	4.13	-13.68	-0.50
2002	-1.73	1.33	-6.62	4.99	1.51	7.75	-3.97	9.86	3.29	-10.19	-1.80	18.41
2003	24.18	13.18	-4.73	2.02	5.59	-7.06	-4.86	-3.54	7.02	22.09	-0.03	8.69
2004	0.47	8.38	0.88	-6.22	2.53	1.37	6.74	-12.25	7.84	4.32	2.79	-0.51
2005	-5.48	-8.95	-1.00	-10.04	1.93							

Performance Summary

Performance Breakdown	
Total Months:	209
Number of Winning Months:	116
Percent Winning Months:	55.50 %
Average Winning Month:	8.62 %
Maximum Winning Month:	71.99 %
Number of Losing Months:	93
Percent Losing Months:	44.50 %
Average Losing Month:	-5.83 %
Maximum Losing Month:	-20.08 %
Average Win Month/Average Lose Month:	1.48

Charts

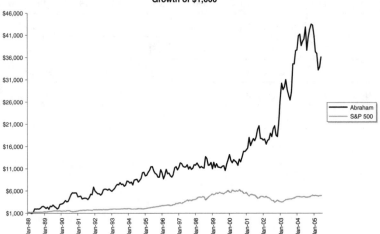

Abraham Trading Company Diversified Compared to the S&P 500
Growth of $1,000

Beach Capital Management Ltd—Discretionary

Annual Performance Breakdown

Yearly Statistics			
Year	Return	Drawdown	Assets
2005	-14.88 %	-19.01 %	$686,000,000
2004	0.36 %	-22.11 %	$1,277,200,000
2003	37.52 %	-10.90 %	$1,018,600,000
2002	19.89 %	-10.18 %	$476,000,000
2001	12.71 %	-7.55 %	$380,400,000
2000	11.15 %	-8.12 %	$368,900,000
1999	31.42 %	-3.55 %	$207,600,000
1998	47.51 %	-1.76 %	$106,800,000
1997	6.06 %	-6.03 %	$36,300,000
1996	7.70 %	-8.75 %	$20,500,000
1995	14.21 %	-3.22 %	$8,600,000
1994	22.32 %	-3.01 %	$3,700,000
1993	40.27 %	-2.78 %	$2,500,000
1992	-4.74 %	-20.76 %	$2,500,000
1991	21.37 %	-6.60 %	$2,500,000
1990	10.94 %	-11.90 %	$2,500,000
1989	8.64 %	-2.47 %	$2,500,000

Month by Month Returns

Month by Month Returns												
Year	Jan	Feb	Mar	Apr	May	Jun	Jul	Aug	Sep	Oct	Nov	Dec
1989	- -	- -	- -	- -	- -	0.22	-1.16	-1.33	2.58	0.82	4.20	3.14
1990	4.17	-4.71	0.94	3.54	-9.71	-2.03	4.45	0.75	14.26	-4.47	2.54	2.64
1991	-2.21	-4.49	6.42	-0.05	6.03	6.77	-3.50	1.51	5.33	3.40	-1.38	2.57
1992	-5.63	-5.76	-5.09	-4.21	-2.00	3.38	-1.42	6.93	1.46	4.87	4.92	-1.18
1993	2.15	-1.33	1.91	1.06	2.31	3.64	6.39	8.50	4.46	-2.78	4.83	3.70
1994	1.88	8.79	5.00	0.00	0.00	5.57	-0.27	-2.75	0.79	0.36	0.03	1.45
1995	2.07	-3.22	4.40	0.95	-0.88	0.31	-0.68	3.57	3.49	0.41	-0.04	3.26
1996	-0.17	-0.32	-0.44	7.33	-4.28	-3.16	-1.56	0.03	3.02	8.08	2.10	-2.39
1997	3.04	0.88	-1.49	-0.21	-0.10	-1.42	5.20	-6.03	1.66	-1.53	4.34	2.07
1998	3.90	2.11	8.37	0.25	7.48	2.52	0.13	7.49	0.58	1.64	-1.76	7.45
1999	-2.57	7.68	-3.55	4.23	0.65	6.45	2.14	1.01	-0.27	0.22	7.74	4.68
2000	3.89	1.16	-4.04	0.89	-0.94	-3.73	-0.48	3.86	-0.60	1.35	2.04	7.81
2001	0.06	1.58	6.82	-5.50	0.69	-0.03	-2.67	-0.14	13.53	1.57	-5.22	2.74
2002	-0.41	-6.99	1.09	-4.08	5.63	9.83	7.83	2.03	5.11	-6.01	-2.70	8.79
2003	7.85	3.59	-5.85	3.31	14.40	-4.04	-3.96	-3.32	3.52	9.04	-0.37	10.40
2004	2.92	9.68	-2.58	-9.21	-1.40	-5.67	-0.32	-5.05	5.00	1.32	7.73	-1.12
2005	-9.53	5.92	-2.41	-10.62	-3.11							

Performance Summary

Performance Breakdown	
Total Months:	192
Number of Winning Months:	116
Percent Winning Months:	60.42 %
Average Winning Month:	4.02 %
Maximum Winning Month:	14.40 %
Number of Losing Months:	74

Performance Breakdown	
Percent Losing Months:	38.54 %
Average Losing Month:	-2.91 %
Maximum Losing Month:	-10.62 %
Average Win Month/Average Lose Month:	1.38

Charts

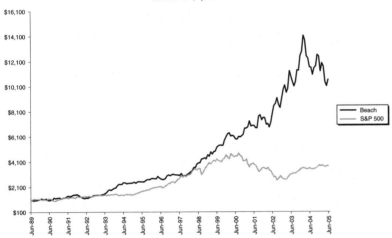

Beach Capital - Discretionary Program
Growth of $1,000

Campbell & Company, Inc. — Financial Metals & Energy — Large Program

Annual Performance Breakdown

Yearly Statistics			
Year	Return	Drawdown	Assets
2005	8.58 %	-3.23 %	$9,499,600,000
2004	6.96 %	-12.98 %	$8,472,100,000
2003	20.41 %	-5.29 %	$5,411,500,000
2002	16.39 %	-8.09 %	$3,246,500,000
2001	6.21 %	-9.62 %	$2,480,600,000
2000	14.32 %	-4.12 %	$2,020,400,000
1999	6.81 %	-4.83 %	$1,421,800,000
1998	20.07 %	-5.88 %	$1,140,500,000
1997	18.75 %	-7.57 %	$764,000,000
1996	35.96 %	-5.63 %	$462,700,000
1995	19.46 %	-4.91 %	$304,100,000
1994	-16.76 %	-16.76 %	$344,200,000
1993	4.68 %	-14.59 %	$485,600,000
1992	13.47 %	-10.52 %	$339,800,000
1991	31.12 %	-9.35 %	$195,700,000
1990	35.24 %	-11.50 %	$125,700,000
1989	42.23 %	-11.58 %	$30,700,000
1988	7.96 %	-6.90 %	$21,400,000
1987	64.38 %	-13.91 %	$100,000
1986	-30.45 %	-41.92 %	$200,000
1985	33.05 %	-14.51 %	$900,000
1984	26.96 %	-5.50 %	$1,200,000
1983	-10.34 %	-10.34 %	$900,000

Month by Month Returns

Month by Month Returns

Year	Jan	Feb	Mar	Apr	May	Jun	Jul	Aug	Sep	Oct	Nov	Dec
1983	- -	- -	- -	-0.40	0.18	-3.71	3.27	-1.47	0.83	-4.18	-1.93	-3.21
1984	1.27	2.12	2.44	0.09	9.78	-5.50	6.86	-1.34	8.32	2.79	-3.12	1.49
1985	3.63	11.59	0.74	5.97	2.92	-2.18	5.48	-3.63	-11.29	3.95	10.45	3.40
1986	-6.28	17.84	6.48	-7.87	5.01	-17.68	5.21	7.61	-17.22	-11.74	-11.84	1.84
1987	33.71	3.23	13.51	15.39	-4.17	-3.21	9.80	-1.12	2.71	-13.45	-0.53	2.11
1988	-0.08	2.39	-1.88	-5.12	1.63	8.29	-0.68	-0.22	4.80	-0.06	-0.35	-0.42
1989	7.90	-1.99	10.74	1.94	13.72	1.88	0.55	-0.81	-4.27	-6.88	2.46	12.88
1990	3.00	0.59	3.37	4.62	-11.50	8.29	10.04	12.30	2.59	1.25	-1.35	-0.54
1991	-7.89	-1.59	20.41	-1.87	2.81	1.49	-7.96	3.79	6.07	0.63	-2.03	17.45
1992	-5.54	-3.58	1.05	-2.78	1.14	10.66	10.40	4.99	-2.17	-4.67	6.26	-1.36
1993	-0.71	13.74	-5.79	2.99	2.81	2.55	5.55	-4.33	-4.83	-6.19	0.59	-0.08
1994	-4.67	-6.81	7.00	-1.77	-2.78	5.24	-4.36	-3.79	6.91	0.36	-7.02	-5.08
1995	-4.53	5.85	9.58	2.08	0.88	-0.90	-4.05	5.83	-3.47	1.20	-0.24	6.82
1996	5.46	-5.63	5.62	3.49	-1.71	1.29	0.01	1.78	2.47	12.06	12.22	-4.29
1997	5.26	2.26	-2.08	-3.84	-1.84	2.23	9.27	-5.14	4.23	2.39	0.57	4.95
1998	3.25	-2.38	4.95	-5.88	4.34	2.04	-3.68	9.23	2.97	4.41	-0.50	0.64
1999	-4.83	1.45	0.87	5.60	-3.25	4.63	-0.15	1.22	1.75	-4.25	0.53	3.64
2000	3.70	-0.35	-1.96	-1.86	2.74	1.96	-1.72	3.08	-3.23	3.19	5.98	2.38
2001	-1.09	0.71	6.97	-8.09	1.23	-1.71	1.45	2.10	6.94	4.97	-9.62	3.72
2002	-0.71	-1.98	-1.60	-4.03	4.12	7.73	7.64	3.61	3.90	-4.75	-1.31	3.65
2003	7.75	2.09	7.71	-4.38	2.77	-0.77	-4.56	2.42	-1.37	2.84	0.79	4.29
2004	2.36	10.79	0.94	-6.67	-0.54	-3.14	-0.61	-1.10	-1.54	2.41	4.04	0.78
2005	-2.15	-1.10	0.12	0.50	5.00							

Performance Summary

Performance Breakdown	
Total Months:	266
Number of Winning Months:	156
Percent Winning Months:	58.65 %
Average Winning Month:	4.88 %
Maximum Winning Month:	33.71 %
Number of Losing Months:	110
Percent Losing Months:	41.35 %
Average Losing Month:	-3.70 %
Maximum Losing Month:	-17.68 %
Average Win Month/Average Lose Month:	1.32

Charts

Campbell and Company Financial and Metals (Large)
Growth of $1,000

Chesapeake Capital Corporation — Diversified Program

Annual Performance Breakdown

Year	Return	Drawdown	Assets
		Yearly Statistics	
2005	-5.78 %	-8.89 %	$1,327,800,000
2004	4.84 %	-16.12 %	$1,347,100,000
2003	23.08 %	-11.11 %	$1,124,500,000
2002	11.07 %	-4.75 %	$862,100,000
2001	-7.98 %	-15.15 %	$806,900,000
2000	5.23 %	-11.66 %	$842,300,000
1999	3.30 %	-12.59 %	$887,800,000
1998	16.31 %	-5.40 %	$1,097,700,000
1997	9.94 %	-7.88 %	$1,096,700,000
1996	15.05 %	-7.64 %	$971,500,000
1995	14.09 %	-7.48 %	$896,500,000
1994	15.87 %	-8.52 %	$549,700,000
1993	61.82 %	-2.69 %	$330,300,000
1992	1.81 %	-16.62 %	$149,700,000
1991	12.51 %	-8.58 %	$122,600,000
1990	43.12 %	-4.61 %	$41,800,000
1989	28.30 %	-20.58 %	$15,500,000
1988	48.91 %	-19.05 %	$6,200,000

Month by Month Returns

Month by Month Returns

Year	Jan	Feb	Mar	Apr	May	Jun	Jul	Aug	Sep	Oct	Nov	Dec
1988	- -	-2.63	-6.89	-10.71	6.93	32.42	-9.41	6.85	2.03	10.65	11.06	7.04
1989	4.93	-5.42	6.64	-8.82	22.38	-8.28	11.66	-11.75	-2.82	-7.40	3.90	28.56
1990	0.49	3.37	8.62	4.37	-4.61	1.77	6.25	15.15	0.60	1.86	-0.25	0.11
1991	-1.29	4.84	2.32	-2.80	0.27	-1.25	-1.75	-3.32	4.39	4.21	-4.68	12.08
1992	-10.98	-2.86	0.53	-0.44	-3.66	6.52	12.96	3.16	-6.78	5.21	2.27	-1.93
1993	0.42	15.99	5.86	7.38	0.40	0.98	9.49	5.88	-2.63	-0.06	1.03	5.77
1994	-3.33	-4.88	0.09	-0.60	9.06	7.02	-1.70	-2.98	3.49	1.97	4.83	2.86
1995	-3.23	-4.39	8.60	1.45	6.84	0.88	-3.09	-2.66	0.20	-1.11	1.76	9.18
1996	1.69	-4.26	0.28	10.16	-3.04	3.27	-7.64	0.57	6.47	5.92	6.57	-4.30
1997	1.86	5.48	-1.24	-2.41	-2.28	1.44	6.24	-7.88	5.06	-2.34	1.70	4.88
1998	-1.29	6.06	3.65	-2.16	3.62	-0.67	3.03	7.27	-0.59	-3.21	-1.68	1.80
1999	-2.76	1.90	-2.65	8.42	-8.71	3.57	-4.80	3.37	1.98	-7.88	4.16	8.49
2000	-0.87	0.92	1.88	-3.80	0.63	-0.99	-3.71	3.90	-7.30	-0.62	7.42	8.80
2001	-0.43	3.75	4.98	-7.50	-1.43	0.16	-3.06	-3.40	7.15	5.01	-10.09	-1.92
2002	-2.11	-1.79	2.43	-3.27	2.26	4.19	2.84	2.55	3.81	-2.63	-1.58	4.31
2003	6.52	3.61	-8.76	0.29	5.35	-5.65	-1.85	2.42	-2.78	15.48	1.91	6.61
2004	1.63	5.05	-2.70	-6.05	-0.50	-2.90	-1.86	-3.23	3.50	2.32	8.89	1.53
2005	-3.82	0.46	-0.92	-3.62	-1.25							

Performance Summary

Performance Breakdown

Total Months:	208
Number of Winning Months:	120
Percent Winning Months:	57.69 %
Average Winning Month:	5.16 %
Maximum Winning Month:	32.42 %
Number of Losing Months:	88

Performance Breakdown	
Percent Losing Months:	42.31 %
Average Losing Month:	-3.70 %
Maximum Losing Month:	-11.75 %
Average Win Month/Average Lose Month:	1.39

Charts

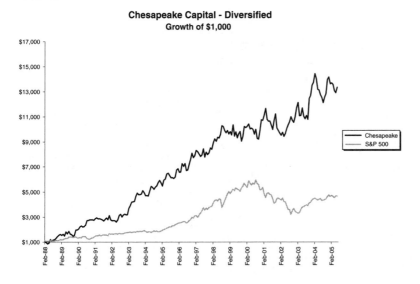

Chesapeake Capital - Diversified
Growth of $1,000

Clarke Capital Management, Inc. — Millennium Program

Annual Performance Breakdown

Yearly Statistics			
Year	Return	Drawdown	Assets
2005	0.24 %	-8.38 %	$169,900,000
2004	11.19 %	-7.81 %	$196,200,000
2003	39.23 %	-18.09 %	$219,100,000
2002	34.30 %	-12.99 %	$48,300,000

Yearly Statistics			
Year	**Return**	**Drawdown**	**Assets**
2001	2.89 %	-9.07 %	$73,000,000
2000	42.73 %	-3.84 %	$37,200,000
1999	5.86 %	-5.79 %	$21,300,000
1998	37.26 %	-21.31 %	$17,200,000

Month by Month Returns

Month by Month Returns												
Year	**Jan**	**Feb**	**Mar**	**Apr**	**May**	**Jun**	**Jul**	**Aug**	**Sep**	**Oct**	**Nov**	**Dec**
1998	0.29	-6.94	-3.17	-12.67	16.89	-7.02	4.13	30.61	16.26	-6.90	4.82	3.71
1999	-1.30	1.07	-0.07	3.28	-5.61	4.13	4.80	-0.09	0.84	-5.79	5.26	-0.09
2000	2.74	0.60	-2.52	1.01	5.73	3.07	-2.58	5.12	-2.18	-1.70	12.31	16.37
2001	2.49	0.88	8.83	-7.15	2.06	-4.04	1.38	-0.02	0.06	5.74	-5.85	-0.41
2002	-2.35	-4.09	-1.22	-5.95	1.64	13.01	10.08	7.71	1.76	-5.43	-4.06	22.75
2003	9.49	15.75	-18.09	3.91	25.02	-10.04	-3.30	1.84	3.38	8.08	-3.50	8.08
2004	-4.11	5.62	2.24	-5.33	5.91	-6.43	5.60	-6.70	10.09	1.95	9.00	-5.04
2005	-5.08	-3.48	2.53	-1.74	8.27	0.31						

Performance Summary

Performance Breakdown	
Total Months:	90
Number of Winning Months:	52
Percent Winning Months:	57.78 %
Average Winning Month:	6.70 %
Maximum Winning Month:	30.61 %
Number of Losing Months:	38
Percent Losing Months:	42.22 %
Average Losing Month:	-4.53 %
Maximum Losing Month:	-18.09 %
Average Win Month/Average Lose Month:	1.48

Charts

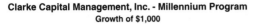

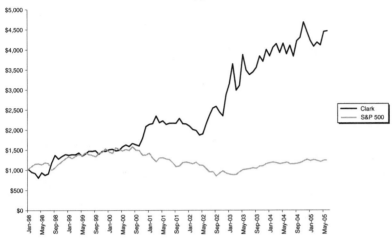

Clarke Capital Management, Inc. - Millennium Program
Growth of $1,000

Drury Capital, Inc. — Diversified Trend Following Program

Annual Performance Breakdown

Yearly Statistics			
Year	Return	Drawdown	Assets
2005	-17.30 %	-17.30 %	$416,600,000
2004	7.27 %	-19.08 %	$565,900,000
2003	25.77 %	-12.77 %	$347,800,000
2002	5.55 %	-14.83 %	$139,700,000
2001	20.62 %	-9.34 %	$134,200,000
2000	15.80 %	-6.76 %	$74,100,000
1999	10.46 %	-10.07 %	$57,700,000
1998	47.21 %	-7.82 %	$34,400,000
1997	30.42 %	-13.12 %	$2,400,000

Month by Month Returns

Year	Jan	Feb	Mar	Apr	May	Jun	Jul	Aug	Sep	Oct	Nov	Dec
1997	- -	- -	- -	- -	-4.57	14.98	12.49	-2.12	-2.08	-9.35	17.34	3.64
1998	7.84	6.11	6.60	-5.46	7.78	2.20	-1.38	19.34	-5.22	-2.74	4.25	2.46
1999	0.06	6.05	-2.82	4.46	-5.56	-0.36	-4.43	8.54	-3.59	-1.24	5.20	4.88
2000	-5.58	0.35	-1.59	11.91	1.14	-4.41	1.49	4.92	-1.70	3.26	6.33	-0.12
2001	-6.20	4.95	15.48	-4.19	2.41	4.97	-3.66	2.03	6.23	3.82	-9.34	4.82
2002	0.52	-1.32	-2.05	-3.68	-5.13	11.62	4.82	3.75	4.35	-9.42	-5.97	10.19
2003	7.76	6.94	-6.32	-4.10	9.42	-6.35	-4.41	-0.87	4.17	13.80	-1.03	6.64
2004	2.45	11.09	2.33	-6.97	-6.06	-1.21	-0.45	-5.85	7.78	-1.13	7.20	-0.36
2005	-2.34	-4.57	0.27	-5.56	-4.06							

Performance Summary

Performance Breakdown	
Total Months:	97
Number of Winning Months:	51
Percent Winning Months:	52.58 %
Average Winning Month:	6.34 %
Maximum Winning Month:	19.34 %
Number of Losing Months:	46
Percent Losing Months:	47.42 %
Average Losing Month:	-3.85 %
Maximum Losing Month:	-9.42 %
Average Win Month/Average Lose Month:	1.65

Charts

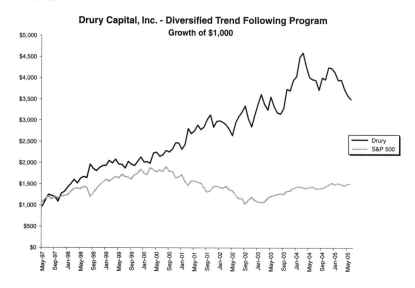

Drury Capital, Inc. - Diversified Trend Following Program
Growth of $1,000

DUNN Capital Management, Inc. —
Targets of Opportunity System

Annual Performance Breakdown

Yearly Statistics			
Year	Return	Drawdown	Assets
2005	-3.64 %	-13.36 %	$467,000,000
2004	11.47 %	-22.51 %	$493,300,000
2003	-12.94 %	-29.13 %	$405,500,000
2002	42.68 %	-24.16 %	$420,300,000
2001	1.67 %	-27.51 %	$261,000,000
2000	39.04 %	-17.25 %	$262,800,000
1999	-19.72 %	-19.72 %	$166,900,000
1998	24.10 %	-13.41 %	$192,800,000
1997	21.46 %	-25.15 %	$150,400,000
1996	36.74 %	-20.23 %	$125,000,000

Yearly Statistics			
Year	Return	Drawdown	Assets
1995	37.96 %	-10.71 %	$88,300,000
1994	-25.09 %	-29.85 %	$76,200,000
1993	19.69 %	-10.03 %	$89,900,000
1992	39.92 %	-18.15 %	$23,600,000
1991	76.14 %	-17.13 %	$16,000,000
1990	44.44 %	-9.64 %	$700,000
1989	3.64 %	-25.36 %	$400,000

Month by Month Returns

Month by Month Returns											
Year	Jan	Feb	Mar	Apr	May	Jun	Jul	Aug	Sep	Oct	Nov	Dec
1989	- -	- -	- -	- -	19.58	1.68	3.45	-13.86	-4.88	-8.91	7.14	3.04
1990	5.59	0.44	14.67	2.59	4.02	5.40	16.86	-2.60	-0.71	1.98	0.41	-8.75
1991	0.13	5.44	33.17	-11.56	-6.30	13.10	-3.53	-8.18	9.44	1.01	3.00	32.53
1992	-15.10	-3.59	0.98	3.29	2.46	12.92	25.07	13.09	-0.10	-1.38	0.03	1.62
1993	-2.20	17.61	1.39	5.90	4.91	-5.07	1.68	-1.07	1.05	-1.41	-5.43	2.68
1994	-7.10	1.10	13.70	-1.42	-3.29	3.33	-4.56	-10.40	-2.41	3.90	-4.52	-13.99
1995	-7.60	9.87	22.70	1.32	0.97	-6.11	-4.29	2.97	-3.50	2.84	16.14	1.51
1996	27.41	-20.12	8.68	13.86	2.01	-9.98	0.67	-11.98	6.71	17.49	16.19	-8.40
1997	18.00	5.86	7.75	-15.92	-10.33	-0.72	33.60	-16.15	5.03	0.46	0.14	1.85
1998	-0.13	-0.37	2.58	-13.41	3.00	-1.01	-1.08	9.48	12.90	7.78	-1.01	5.57
1999	-17.06	12.25	3.33	0.71	-0.87	-0.05	-6.60	-4.76	5.20	-9.05	2.10	-3.76
2000	-0.45	-1.62	3.91	-10.23	-1.79	-5.33	-0.86	5.65	-1.77	5.10	15.20	31.41
2001	3.25	3.73	5.75	-16.16	2.00	-10.32	-5.48	20.97	12.13	14.44	-23.33	4.05
2002	-1.88	-5.55	-4.50	-1.08	-4.56	4.70	22.24	19.78	11.80	17.37	-19.70	5.71
2003	8.41	13.31	-17.87	-1.58	13.04	-11.15	1.80	5.08	-8.55	-5.70	-4.25	-1.17
2004	-0.25	14.46	1.63	-10.83	-2.57	-4.44	-6.66	6.48	-1.20	12.61	11.86	-6.45
2005	-4.25	-6.08	-2.44	-1.25	11.24							

Performance Summary

Performance Breakdown	
Total Months:	193
Number of Winning Months:	106
Percent Winning Months:	54.92 %
Average Winning Month:	8.49 %
Maximum Winning Month:	33.60 %
Number of Losing Months:	87
Percent Losing Months:	45.08 %
Average Losing Month:	-6.18 %
Maximum Losing Month:	-23.33 %
Average Win Month/Average Lose Month:	1.37

Charts

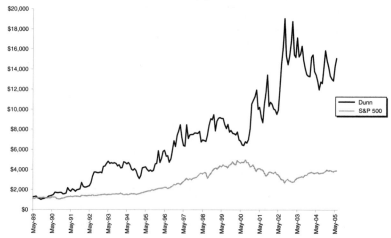

DUNN Capital Management, Inc. - Targets of Opportunity System
Growth of $1,000

DUNN Capital Management, Inc. — World Monetary Assets

Annual Performance Breakdown

Yearly Statistics			
Year	Return	Drawdown	Assets
2005	-17.54 %	-27.04 %	$542,900,000
2004	-16.69 %	-36.86 %	$703,500,000
2003	-13.40 %	-28.86 %	$630,800,000
2002	54.05 %	-23.41 %	$586,700,000
2001	1.12 %	-23.52 %	$759,500,000
2000	13.07 %	-41.46 %	$1,066,200,000
1999	13.33 %	-13.18 %	$909,300,000
1998	13.73 %	-18.03 %	$790,600,000
1997	44.60 %	-11.97 %	$857,300,000
1996	58.19 %	-17.44 %	$566,400,000
1995	98.66 %	-6.52 %	$342,500,000
1994	-19.32 %	-35.08 %	$178,000,000
1993	60.25 %	-5.02 %	$177,300,000
1992	-21.78 %	-25.45 %	$118,800,000
1991	16.91 %	-14.93 %	$196,000,000
1990	51.57 %	-11.23 %	$150,000,000
1989	30.54 %	-28.63 %	$34,900,000
1988	-18.71 %	-22.66 %	$15,500,000
1987	72.14 %	-7.18 %	$8,900,000
1986	3.56 %	-26.85 %	$3,700,000
1985	-21.69 %	-49.76 %	$4,200,000
1984	5.09 %	-10.95 %	$500,000

Month by Month Returns

Month by Month Returns

Year	Jan	Feb	Mar	Apr	May	Jun	Jul	Aug	Sep	Oct	Nov	Dec
1984	- -	- -	- -	- -	- -	- -	- -	- -	- -	- -	-10.95	18.01
1985	6.23	10.03	-7.25	-13.09	21.66	-6.79	-8.36	-13.48	-30.68	6.69	13.61	10.02
1986	-1.50	24.55	11.93	-5.59	-5.98	-13.98	-4.20	12.45	0.64	-2.79	-6.18	-0.11
1987	8.81	-1.75	7.18	31.63	-2.69	-4.61	5.97	-2.98	5.50	-5.59	17.76	1.96
1988	0.73	4.34	-6.55	-2.47	3.88	-0.56	-1.83	-2.65	1.98	1.92	-0.72	-16.70
1989	21.10	-4.23	9.30	6.09	20.02	3.21	8.15	-13.02	-1.56	-16.65	7.34	-5.42
1990	23.45	5.35	6.11	6.80	-11.23	3.99	1.37	2.07	3.76	-0.40	5.44	-1.19
1991	-7.05	-4.51	10.30	-4.49	-4.99	-0.46	-2.54	9.93	9.23	-14.93	1.20	31.22
1992	-14.53	-0.90	4.04	-15.10	-0.36	13.04	11.43	9.18	-8.23	-5.42	-4.30	-8.15
1993	2.90	13.99	-3.28	12.37	3.76	0.58	7.41	8.42	-5.02	1.59	1.03	6.10
1994	-1.71	-5.34	14.90	6.97	5.21	3.29	-13.38	-17.67	-4.68	-1.02	0.74	-4.22
1995	0.49	13.71	24.41	3.80	-2.60	-3.59	0.63	18.46	-6.52	10.82	11.16	4.44
1996	15.78	-13.33	9.55	9.17	-1.18	0.60	-12.40	-5.20	12.55	20.28	26.94	-7.09
1997	17.83	-0.15	2.21	-6.47	-5.88	10.38	16.84	-10.21	6.45	-0.64	9.82	1.55
1998	4.25	-5.30	3.99	-11.05	-4.76	-0.38	-1.37	27.51	16.18	3.79	-13.72	0.32
1999	-13.18	3.91	4.22	4.09	7.63	9.61	0.52	5.77	3.60	-7.01	1.35	-5.44
2000	6.85	-2.94	-17.34	-12.36	-7.59	-3.95	0.56	3.29	-9.70	9.12	28.04	29.39
2001	7.72	0.55	6.26	-8.96	-0.91	-8.31	0.09	6.47	1.13	20.74	-23.52	6.73
2002	3.03	-8.07	2.39	-5.71	5.41	24.24	14.82	10.50	9.10	-12.27	-12.70	21.34
2003	6.94	13.83	-22.44	1.57	9.45	-8.07	-4.75	16.70	-7.63	-4.23	-4.45	-4.47
2004	-2.86	8.38	-2.90	-18.35	-6.84	-9.86	-5.16	9.29	1.58	7.93	5.32	-0.69
2005	-4.09	-6.72	-4.04	-15.01	13.02							

Performance Summary

Performance Breakdown

Total Months:	247
Number of Winning Months:	134
Percent Winning Months:	54.25 %
Average Winning Month:	9.00 %
Maximum Winning Month:	31.63 %
Number of Losing Months:	113
Percent Losing Months:	45.75 %
Average Losing Month:	-6.99 %
Maximum Losing Month:	-30.68 %
Average Win Month/Average Lose Month:	1.29

Charts

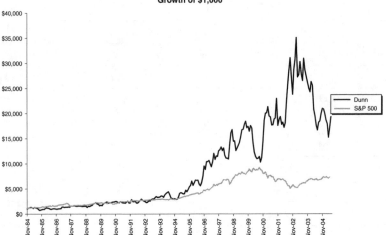

DUNN Capital Management, Inc. - World Monetary Asset
Growth of $1,000

Eckhardt Trading Company—Standard Program

Annual Performance Breakdown

Yearly Statistics			
Year	Return	Drawdown	Assets
2005	5.33 %	-3.90 %	$468,900,000
2004	4.49 %	-10.98 %	$453,700,000
2003	15.01 %	-2.45 %	$411,700,000
2002	11.07 %	-5.49 %	$340,600,000
2001	5.34 %	-4.65 %	$312,900,000
2000	17.94 %	-7.11 %	$271,000,000
1999	-4.54 %	-10.83 %	$255,500,000
1998	27.10 %	-8.20 %	$310,000,000
1997	46.01 %	-6.19 %	$244,500,000
1996	47.94 %	-17.05 %	$98,800,000
1995	47.33 %	-21.43 %	$63,600,000
1994	-11.69 %	-18.87 %	$56,800,000
1993	57.95 %	-8.28 %	$72,100,000
1992	-7.26 %	-27.11 %	$16,900,000
1991	38.22 %	-1.00 %	$7,900,000

Month by Month Returns

Month by Month Returns											
Year	Jan	Feb	Mar	Apr	May	Jun	Jul	Aug	Sep	Oct	Nov	Dec
1991	- -	- -	- -	- -	- -	- -	- -	-1.00	6.64	0.25	2.09	27.92
1992	-15.27	-7.56	-5.70	2.22	-3.45	9.35	11.43	7.51	-1.18	-4.35	7.70	-4.60
1993	-1.38	9.63	-8.28	9.41	3.81	12.13	9.41	4.85	-6.67	1.74	4.90	9.45
1994	-18.30	-0.70	10.58	2.17	5.05	1.66	-0.10	-8.59	13.36	-10.50	8.74	-10.45
1995	-1.39	8.85	14.13	3.21	20.13	-1.32	-10.31	-3.27	-2.80	-5.58	9.24	13.01

Month by Month Returns

Year	Jan	Feb	Mar	Apr	May	Jun	Jul	Aug	Sep	Oct	Nov	Dec
1996	8.72	-5.40	2.60	17.48	-9.28	-3.32	-4.28	-1.20	17.55	16.24	11.43	-5.51
1997	12.66	6.91	6.60	1.24	1.89	5.39	9.18	-4.11	6.51	-0.41	-3.54	-2.35
1998	4.77	2.48	-3.20	-5.17	1.89	1.57	-1.59	25.28	0.18	0.39	-0.15	0.65
1999	1.49	5.12	-6.18	-2.59	-2.43	1.43	5.18	-5.62	3.31	-2.86	0.04	-0.73
2000	-2.14	-0.61	-1.94	-0.29	1.88	-1.45	-2.71	0.43	1.48	0.83	12.30	10.02
2001	1.63	-1.07	0.40	-0.48	3.40	-3.28	-1.42	5.87	-3.28	5.58	-2.36	0.76
2002	2.69	-4.55	-0.99	3.92	-0.68	2.59	2.24	-0.34	-1.01	-1.90	-1.40	10.79
2003	1.56	7.26	-0.58	0.31	4.78	-0.80	-1.55	0.44	0.15	-0.70	0.86	2.69
2004	-2.22	4.28	-0.75	-4.37	0.04	-3.65	-2.69	4.40	0.86	5.96	4.38	-1.16
2005	-3.42	0.19	1.28	-1.84	6.10							

Performance Summary

Performance Breakdown	
Total Months:	166
Number of Winning Months:	92
Percent Winning Months:	55.42 %
Average Winning Month:	5.88 %
Maximum Winning Month:	27.92 %
Number of Losing Months:	74
Percent Losing Months:	44.58 %
Average Losing Month:	-3.49 %
Maximum Losing Month:	-18.30 %
Average Win Month/Average Lose Month:	1.68

Charts

Eckhardt Trading Company - Standard Program
Growth of $1,000

Eclipse Capital Management, Inc. — Global Monetary Program

Annual Performance Breakdown

Yearly Statistics			
Year	**Return**	**Drawdown**	**Assets**
2005	-12.00 %	-14.19 %	$421,500,000
2004	-10.75 %	-17.73 %	$493,100,000
2003	20.19 %	-4.20 %	$379,300,000
2002	17.68 %	-12.31 %	$286,900,000
2001	-5.08 %	-11.03 %	$264,300,000
2000	4.50 %	-20.54 %	$387,500,000
1999	12.31 %	-5.08 %	$504,000,000
1998	5.05 %	-16.51 %	$355,500,000
1997	15.91 %	-4.93 %	$300,600,000
1996	30.67 %	-2.19 %	$62,400,000

Yearly Statistics			
Year	Return	Drawdown	Assets
1995	20.23 %	-2.34 %	$42,700,000
1994	-11.36 %	-22.35 %	$52,800,000
1993	30.36 %	-2.11 %	$63,600,000
1992	12.96 %	-12.06 %	$35,600,000
1991	69.76 %	-15.92 %	$11,500,000
1990	-12.45 %	-18.78 %	$900,000

Month by Month Returns

Month by Month Returns											
Year	Jan	Feb	Mar	Apr	May	Jun	Jul	Aug	Sep	Oct	Nov	Dec
1990	- -	- -	- -	- -	- -	- -	- -	-2.16	-2.62	-14.75	9.01	-1.12
1991	1.15	8.01	23.70	-3.29	-13.06	12.41	8.99	-0.51	3.23	-0.96	2.50	16.96
1992	-6.77	-5.38	5.51	-5.29	-0.24	11.74	16.56	8.13	-10.27	1.88	2.33	-2.50
1993	4.23	9.34	-2.11	1.42	-1.02	3.03	3.09	0.81	3.61	2.06	-0.03	2.84
1994	1.34	3.00	6.09	-3.43	-2.91	0.28	-11.70	-5.12	-1.42	0.90	4.50	-2.24
1995	-2.28	1.19	4.52	0.84	8.09	-2.34	1.04	6.80	-0.57	0.34	2.16	-0.64
1996	5.45	-0.07	-0.30	5.58	1.96	0.11	0.58	3.04	2.77	3.51	7.03	-2.19
1997	2.07	-0.41	1.67	-4.93	4.01	0.34	8.80	-2.21	5.00	-0.77	-1.63	3.66
1998	1.66	-3.12	-0.63	-10.67	2.81	-2.19	-3.46	13.15	6.02	1.78	-2.33	3.79
1999	-2.57	3.27	2.92	4.64	0.44	3.12	2.35	1.49	1.50	-4.30	-0.45	-0.37
2000	0.87	-6.10	3.29	-4.25	4.53	-3.28	-6.56	-1.57	-7.34	-0.70	14.25	14.12
2001	0.63	-1.43	2.63	-7.35	-0.29	1.56	-3.72	0.38	5.97	6.01	-11.03	2.88
2002	0.42	-0.79	-0.29	0.52	0.37	11.33	4.08	3.22	4.73	-9.00	-3.64	6.90
2003	7.79	5.16	-3.63	1.27	7.44	-2.68	-1.22	-0.15	0.44	-0.63	0.52	5.01
2004	-0.99	4.46	-0.36	-11.32	0.20	-1.42	-5.74	1.12	2.90	0.24	0.13	0.43
2005	-4.95	-1.62	-4.75	-1.53	-2.16							

Performance Summary

Performance Breakdown	
Total Months:	178
Number of Winning Months:	102
Percent Winning Months:	57.30 %
Average Winning Month:	4.25 %
Maximum Winning Month:	23.70 %
Number of Losing Months:	76
Percent Losing Months:	42.70 %
Average Losing Month:	-3.39 %
Maximum Losing Month:	-14.75 %
Average Win Month/Average Lose Month:	1.25

Charts

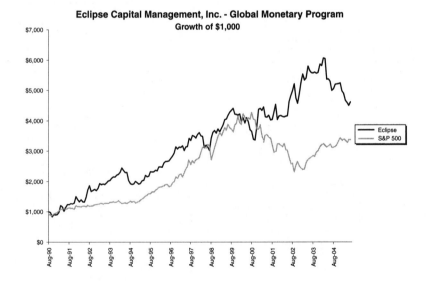

Hawksbill Capital Management—
Global Diversified Program

Annual Performance Breakdown

Yearly Statistics			
Year	Return	Drawdown	Assets
2005	-0.01 %	-12.09 %	$33,700,000
2004	-8.84 %	-20.14 %	$34,200,000
2003	27.59 %	-15.81 %	$33,200,000
2002	36.37 %	-17.49 %	$24,700,000
2001	22.76 %	-17.44 %	$19,100,000
2000	24.76 %	-26.67 %	$21,100,000
1999	-24.55 %	-33.05 %	$19,700,000
1998	43.72 %	-33.95 %	$33,200,000
1997	73.51 %	-16.63 %	$28,100,000
1996	-27.10 %	-34.38 %	$18,200,000
1995	-7.86 %	-28.65 %	$95,200,000
1994	11.48 %	-22.57 %	$131,400,000
1993	114.26 %	-9.39 %	$106,900,000
1992	17.24 %	-35.12 %	$33,800,000
1991	-29.92 %	-56.19 %	$32,400,000
1990	252.61 %	-12.76 %	$35,600,000
1989	56.45 %	-43.75 %	$1,900,000
1988	12.05 %	-7.40 %	$900,000

Month by Month Returns

Month by Month Returns

Year	Jan	Feb	Mar	Apr	May	Jun	Jul	Aug	Sep	Oct	Nov	Dec
1988	- -	- -	- -	- -	- -	- -	- -	- -	- -	- -	-7.40	21.00
1989	-19.40	-14.20	20.26	-8.01	51.65	3.69	-10.28	-21.02	0.06	-20.66	33.40	73.30
1990	0.90	19.65	12.83	30.52	-10.10	11.64	34.75	21.87	37.93	-1.23	-5.54	-6.49
1991	-40.07	-7.14	13.52	-12.86	-9.17	12.43	-14.19	-9.18	9.69	-5.87	0.42	54.28
1992	-22.18	-13.61	6.67	-6.82	-2.91	18.10	11.18	13.20	20.40	5.90	2.08	-6.59
1993	3.03	11.01	4.24	30.97	4.87	10.80	15.30	5.42	-6.13	2.65	-5.96	7.22
1994	-17.64	0.63	19.56	-6.11	17.96	24.00	-7.12	-16.63	22.37	-17.58	21.50	-13.67
1995	-28.65	2.14	11.08	-4.42	8.78	-2.38	-11.32	14.48	-2.63	-8.72	0.76	23.34
1996	-2.76	-7.18	-13.47	10.43	-9.07	-3.30	-8.80	-5.12	8.12	27.74	9.13	-26.29
1997	10.73	10.71	13.78	-10.38	6.86	-1.47	26.07	-16.63	6.84	1.30	0.95	14.80
1998	14.31	-0.84	-6.65	-19.50	-1.66	-3.86	-6.24	80.29	5.48	-8.16	0.92	7.99
1999	-3.47	7.25	4.74	1.56	-5.55	6.11	-7.05	-8.89	-6.54	-15.41	7.26	-4.81
2000	4.71	-1.46	-4.68	-9.80	5.11	-4.80	-13.50	14.61	-8.51	-3.43	15.01	39.51
2001	2.91	-3.53	2.25	-16.21	-0.11	0.14	11.41	15.06	10.39	11.09	-7.12	-1.18
2002	-4.97	-13.18	17.07	-8.14	9.06	15.04	17.03	3.45	4.78	-7.95	-4.47	9.82
2003	3.52	5.48	-15.81	5.05	17.28	4.28	1.52	2.06	4.34	-1.19	-8.54	10.57
2004	1.30	6.15	-0.87	-8.66	-2.01	-5.86	-4.39	3.95	-3.28	1.48	8.20	-3.84
2005	-8.83	15.63	-2.10	-10.20	7.10							

Performance Summary

Performance Breakdown	
Total Months:	199
Number of Winning Months:	107
Percent Winning Months:	53.77 %
Average Winning Month:	13.02 %
Maximum Winning Month:	80.29 %
Number of Losing Months:	92
Percent Losing Months:	46.23 %
Average Losing Month:	-8.87 %
Maximum Losing Month:	-40.07 %
Average Win Month/Average Lose Month:	1.47

Charts

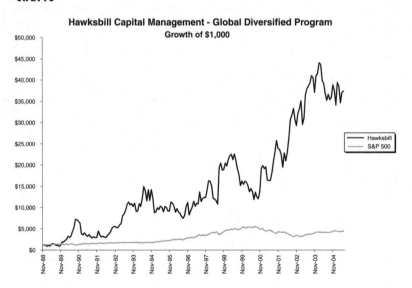

Hyman Beck & Company, Inc. — Global Portfolio

Annual Performance Breakdown

Yearly Statistics			
Year	Return	Drawdown	Assets
2005	-13.82 %	-15.77 %	$311,800,000
2004	-4.75 %	-29.27 %	$361,300,000
2003	10.98 %	-11.95 %	$332,000,000
2002	21.36 %	-14.47 %	$275,000,000
2001	20.46 %	-12.73 %	$204,700,000
2000	-10.48 %	-25.39 %	$172,500,000
1999	0.81 %	-6.91 %	$330,200,000
1998	16.84 %	-8.45 %	$254,000,000
1997	24.38 %	-2.99 %	$203,600,000
1996	10.83 %	-10.14 %	$132,600,000
1995	29.12 %	-7.60 %	$117,300,000
1994	3.79 %	-11.12 %	$82,200,000
1993	14.63 %	-4.95 %	$64,400,000
1992	22.56 %	-10.93 %	$22,500,000
1991	36.31 %	-1.95 %	$6,000,000

Month by Month Returns

Month by Month Returns											
Year	Jan	Feb	Mar	Apr	May	Jun	Jul	Aug	Sep	Oct	Nov	Dec
1991	- -	- -	- -	-0.29	1.80	1.29	-0.86	1.52	6.32	-1.95	6.07	19.13
1992	-7.45	-3.44	3.15	-3.38	2.51	13.10	18.27	6.40	-6.68	3.39	-0.37	-1.88
1993	-3.97	8.65	2.10	5.65	4.55	-4.95	5.00	0.51	-0.80	-0.63	-2.78	1.34
1994	-0.45	-7.45	12.48	-2.17	4.22	5.14	-4.30	-4.40	-2.85	4.72	3.43	-2.95
1995	-6.35	9.02	18.71	6.22	6.34	-1.12	-1.68	-1.80	-2.16	-1.08	1.27	0.80

Month by Month Returns

Year	Jan	Feb	Mar	Apr	May	Jun	Jul	Aug	Sep	Oct	Nov	Dec
1996	3.97	-8.23	-1.21	2.39	-3.20	1.38	1.80	-1.15	4.36	11.17	9.79	-8.71
1997	8.76	1.69	-0.23	-2.77	0.20	1.79	10.78	-2.78	2.13	-1.06	1.65	2.75
1998	-0.15	-0.41	-0.08	-3.56	3.23	-2.28	-2.01	13.70	7.19	-2.94	-5.68	10.56
1999	-3.48	1.67	-1.00	3.83	-3.63	3.41	-0.14	1.22	2.14	-6.91	0.48	3.85
2000	-1.75	-8.39	-5.07	1.65	-4.68	-5.27	-2.02	1.67	-4.50	0.93	3.84	14.49
2001	3.57	4.27	10.24	-8.86	3.44	-4.59	-1.45	7.90	13.37	6.93	-11.44	-1.46
2002	-2.81	-1.45	-4.19	-6.80	5.11	13.18	7.69	1.23	4.48	-3.17	-0.88	9.11
2003	6.90	2.19	-3.98	-0.10	7.09	-1.69	-2.13	-2.03	-6.59	6.22	0.13	5.60
2004	-0.90	5.54	-6.03	-10.28	-5.63	-2.97	-5.01	-3.55	2.69	8.30	12.81	2.63
2005	-7.10	-0.59	-2.45	-6.50	1.50							

Performance Summary

Performance Breakdown

Total Months:	170
Number of Winning Months:	86
Percent Winning Months:	50.59 %
Average Winning Month:	5.51 %
Maximum Winning Month:	19.13 %
Number of Losing Months:	84
Percent Losing Months:	49.41 %
Average Losing Month:	-3.41 %
Maximum Losing Month:	-11.44 %
Average Win Month/Average Lose Month:	1.62

Charts

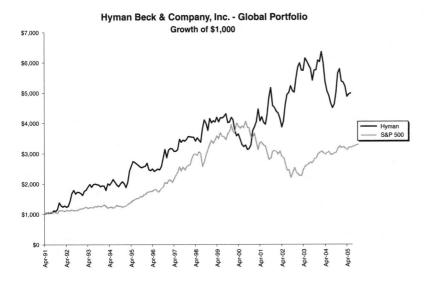

Hyman Beck & Company, Inc. - Global Portfolio
Growth of $1,000

John W. Henry & Company, Inc. — Financial & Metals Program

Annual Performance Breakdown

Yearly Statistics			
Year	Return	Drawdown	Assets
2005	-15.24 %	-21.95 %	$427,000,000
2004	6.01 %	-33.33 %	$498,000,000
2003	19.41 %	-11.35 %	$357,000,000
2002	45.05 %	-14.27 %	$256,000,000
2001	7.15 %	-17.83 %	$251,000,000
2000	13.04 %	-25.88 %	$366,000,000
1999	-18.69 %	-23.90 %	$713,900,000
1998	7.21 %	-18.30 %	$1,119,300,000
1997	15.26 %	-13.53 %	$1,324,700,000
1996	29.67 %	-5.53 %	$1,182,700,000

Yearly Statistics			
Year	Return	Drawdown	Assets
1995	38.52 %	-4.04 %	$842,600,000
1994	-5.32 %	-14.31 %	$657,100,000
1993	46.85 %	-1.98 %	$709,500,000
1992	-10.89 %	-39.53 %	$457,400,000
1991	61.88 %	-15.45 %	$619,200,000
1990	83.60 %	-22.73 %	$274,600,000
1989	34.62 %	-37.17 %	$69,200,000
1988	4.02 %	-20.31 %	$36,800,000
1987	252.42 %	-27.59 %	$15,200,000
1986	61.55 %	-19.88 %	$1,200,000
1985	20.66 %	-34.68 %	$200,000
1984	9.93 %	-3.16 %	$100,000

Month by Month Returns

Month by Month Returns												
Year	Jan	Feb	Mar	Apr	May	Jun	Jul	Aug	Sep	Oct	Nov	Dec
1984	- -	- -	- -	- -	- -	- -	- -	- -	- -	1.61	-3.16	11.72
1985	6.62	17.71	-9.28	-7.77	-7.69	-1.75	41.26	-10.12	-27.32	6.37	26.63	1.93
1986	4.79	21.87	-6.30	3.67	-17.52	17.57	24.95	9.42	-0.23	2.56	-3.56	-0.46
1987	33.01	12.10	34.24	18.23	-7.16	-10.69	12.25	-14.61	-8.89	28.02	32.54	21.21
1988	-12.56	9.77	-2.30	-15.02	0.28	44.19	5.47	6.89	-8.09	2.50	5.18	-19.19
1989	31.69	-8.66	8.51	3.17	37.03	-6.63	4.43	-8.17	-14.92	-17.53	21.63	-4.53
1990	27.98	19.50	11.40	2.41	-22.73	6.91	12.16	11.16	8.32	-5.01	3.09	-3.68
1991	-2.28	3.80	4.46	-0.79	-0.32	-1.29	-13.39	4.78	25.80	-7.74	6.62	39.37
1992	-18.03	-13.53	2.98	-12.17	-5.68	21.90	25.46	10.18	-5.23	-4.50	-0.80	-2.59
1993	3.34	13.89	-0.30	9.34	3.35	0.12	9.69	-0.78	0.22	-1.10	-0.33	2.88
1994	-2.93	-0.55	7.21	0.89	1.29	4.47	-6.11	-4.12	1.49	1.65	-4.38	-3.51
1995	-3.76	15.67	15.35	6.10	1.24	-1.66	-2.33	2.08	-2.13	0.31	2.64	1.65

Year	Jan	Feb	Mar	Apr	May	Jun	Jul	Aug	Sep	Oct	Nov	Dec
1996	5.99	-5.53	0.66	2.28	-1.74	2.25	-1.13	-0.76	3.22	14.33	10.95	-2.55
1997	4.41	-2.23	-0.69	-2.85	-8.33	4.15	15.75	-3.65	2.20	2.02	2.48	2.86
1998	-3.50	-3.98	-1.56	-7.93	3.18	-4.84	-0.92	17.50	15.26	-3.78	-7.50	8.87
1999	-4.84	0.90	-2.56	1.63	5.89	6.12	-2.30	-3.15	-7.01	-8.12	-3.18	-2.78
2000	-3.59	-6.20	-2.28	2.51	-2.06	-8.97	-1.74	-0.43	-6.20	9.39	13.33	23.02
2001	3.34	2.53	12.84	-8.30	1.01	-4.14	-4.44	8.47	5.41	4.64	-17.83	7.44
2002	-0.81	-6.00	-5.45	-1.04	11.01	28.33	11.25	3.59	7.39	-8.53	-6.28	10.01
2003	11.38	4.51	-3.48	1.85	9.11	-4.96	-3.36	2.52	-3.86	0.65	-2.71	7.89
2004	1.66	6.53	-6.50	-10.73	-5.52	-5.45	-10.59	5.08	0.51	14.07	18.72	2.66
2005	-9.48	-6.74	-5.90	-1.75	8.60							

Performance Summary

Performance Breakdown	
Total Months:	248
Number of Winning Months:	132
Percent Winning Months:	53.23 %
Average Winning Month:	9.99 %
Maximum Winning Month:	44.19 %
Number of Losing Months:	116
Percent Losing Months:	46.77 %
Average Losing Month:	-5.87 %
Maximum Losing Month:	-27.32 %
Average Win Month/Average Lose Month:	1.70

Charts

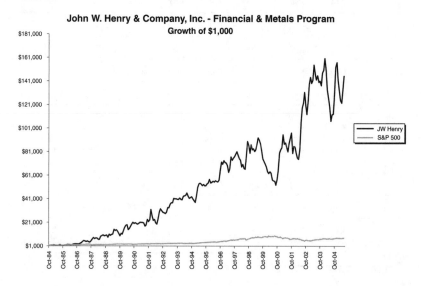

John W. Henry & Company, Inc. - Financial & Metals Program
Growth of $1,000

John W. Henry & Company, Inc. — Strategic Allocation

Annual Performance Breakdown

Yearly Statistics			
Year	Return	Drawdown	Assets
2005	-19.44 %	-26.79 %	$1,744,000,000
2004	13.71 %	-30.73 %	$1,959,000,000
2003	8.36 %	-21.79 %	$1,141,000,000
2002	30.88 %	-13.82 %	$690,000,000
2001	-1.09 %	-17.28 %	$589,000,000
2000	20.36 %	-16.05 %	$522,000,000
1999	-1.46 %	-11.64 %	$531,700,000
1998	16.97 %	-7.69 %	$502,000,000
1997	13.32 %	-3.75 %	$ 0
1996	25.46 %	-1.38 %	$ 0

Month by Month Returns

Year	Jan	Feb	Mar	Apr	May	Jun	Jul	Aug	Sep	Oct	Nov	Dec
1996	- -	- -	- -	- -	- -	- -	-0.84	0.16	6.41	11.50	7.96	-1.38
1997	3.87	0.05	0.45	-0.61	-2.90	0.41	7.55	-3.17	-0.60	2.79	1.34	3.89
1998	-1.41	-0.33	1.02	-3.28	4.31	-1.39	-0.89	9.81	7.82	0.78	-7.69	8.50
1999	-2.56	2.99	-0.87	4.65	0.26	4.10	-2.59	0.43	-2.06	-7.78	2.46	0.17
2000	1.45	1.36	-4.08	-1.22	-0.88	-3.80	-3.52	3.62	-7.05	5.66	13.19	16.57
2001	-0.58	-0.57	11.38	-9.37	2.70	-4.66	-4.10	6.06	3.11	4.20	-14.70	8.60
2002	-0.74	-3.40	-5.53	1.29	8.70	20.81	7.43	3.50	6.65	-7.77	-6.56	6.29
2003	14.61	7.82	-6.65	2.78	5.47	-8.88	-0.62	4.16	-9.39	-8.49	1.46	9.20
2004	3.94	9.42	-5.53	-10.34	-5.75	-10.99	-2.23	-0.29	10.46	20.06	11.58	-2.46
2005	-13.93	-4.76	0.10	-10.78	10.04							

Performance Summary

Performance Breakdown	
Total Months:	107
Number of Winning Months:	58
Percent Winning Months:	54.21 %
Average Winning Month:	5.82 %
Maximum Winning Month:	20.81 %
Number of Losing Months:	49
Percent Losing Months:	45.79 %
Average Losing Month:	-4.49 %
Maximum Losing Month:	-14.70 %
Average Win Month/Average Lose Month:	1.30

Charts

John W. Henry & Company, Inc. - Strategic Allocation
Growth of $1,000

Mark J. Walsh & Company—Standard Program

Annual Performance Breakdown

Yearly Statistics			
Year	**Return**	**Drawdown**	**Assets**
2005	-5.92 %	-9.52 %	$86,800,000
2004	19.37 %	-12.20 %	$67,000,000
2003	11.32 %	-12.40 %	$34,200,000
2002	46.46 %	-12.31 %	$27,000,000
2001	-4.88 %	-15.72 %	$21,500,000
2000	37.91 %	-4.98 %	$20,600,000
1999	-17.41 %	-26.69 %	$16,900,000
1998	40.24 %	-17.44 %	$13,100,000
1997	23.02 %	-25.62 %	$5,400,000
1996	24.70 %	-19.09 %	$3,600,000
1995	55.98 %	-36.16 %	$7,400,000

Year	Return	Drawdown	Assets
1994	-25.33 %	-43.04 %	$25,100,000
1993	74.93 %	-16.29 %	$39,600,000
1992	-25.74 %	-27.93 %	$23,600,000
1991	8.62 %	-21.87 %	$38,000,000
1990	122.92 %	-20.60 %	$2,700,000
1989	19.30 %	-38.51 %	$1,500,000
1988	24.28 %	-41.29 %	$300,000
1987	142.92 %	-17.33 %	$900,000
1986	20.21 %	-28.35 %	$600,000
1985	22.04 %	-3.57 %	$300,000

Month by Month Returns

Month by Month Returns

Year	Jan	Feb	Mar	Apr	May	Jun	Jul	Aug	Sep	Oct	Nov	Dec
1985	- -	- -	- -	- -	- -	- -	- -	- -	-2.00	-1.60	13.40	11.60
1986	-6.10	31.20	9.00	11.10	-8.40	5.10	6.70	2.40	-22.70	-1.70	-5.70	6.90
1987	15.70	-3.90	9.30	44.30	14.50	-0.20	10.10	-7.90	2.70	-12.60	22.30	8.90
1988	-5.30	-4.80	-14.20	-24.10	7.30	68.60	-10.70	-14.10	2.70	21.70	8.10	12.90
1989	5.10	-0.20	15.10	-9.00	26.30	2.00	4.80	-27.40	3.80	-18.40	1.00	29.50
1990	-1.40	6.10	13.90	23.40	-20.60	3.80	23.90	36.80	8.80	3.20	1.00	-4.30
1991	-8.60	-1.50	8.60	-10.00	-7.40	6.90	-10.30	2.10	5.60	-2.20	1.10	30.40
1992	-7.30	-6.30	-9.40	-4.20	-4.40	8.20	13.60	2.60	-14.10	-4.20	1.10	-1.80
1993	-5.23	11.04	4.59	24.38	7.76	0.38	6.73	-13.28	-0.85	-2.64	11.65	18.42
1994	-20.22	8.00	9.98	-5.36	7.00	-7.85	-12.90	-8.53	1.54	-20.37	25.83	4.18
1995	-16.41	16.96	32.33	6.57	15.79	-2.25	-15.50	-5.55	-3.08	-15.57	6.63	43.53
1996	5.37	-9.36	2.11	19.51	-13.66	0.94	-6.17	-1.06	10.22	18.63	13.31	-10.74
1997	10.30	13.73	10.61	-10.70	-2.58	3.75	14.20	-18.67	3.87	-11.95	5.52	9.59
1998	5.61	4.64	-7.14	-11.09	2.82	3.43	-2.73	40.83	12.85	-1.81	0.58	-5.33
1999	-2.96	16.10	-7.88	0.88	-2.25	-1.75	0.87	-8.04	7.03	-16.21	1.80	-3.01

Month by Month Returns

Year	Jan	Feb	Mar	Apr	May	Jun	Jul	Aug	Sep	Oct	Nov	Dec
2000	0.92	-3.34	1.83	1.12	5.23	2.56	-2.19	5.03	-4.66	-0.34	6.10	22.84
2001	0.88	-3.67	12.14	-8.69	-4.52	-3.24	-0.09	7.19	7.06	3.76	-9.61	-3.78
2002	-6.57	-3.63	3.16	-3.49	10.10	16.98	12.46	1.42	8.19	-9.70	-2.89	17.23
2003	5.66	4.35	-12.40	1.77	9.74	-4.18	-0.06	0.40	7.12	1.79	-4.94	3.56
2004	5.85	8.19	4.09	-6.87	-0.41	-5.33	3.20	-0.47	2.12	4.85	8.81	-4.70
2005	-8.13	6.73	-3.61	-4.27								

Performance Summary

Performance Breakdown	
Total Months:	236
Number of Winning Months:	133
Percent Winning Months:	56.36 %
Average Winning Month:	10.24 %
Maximum Winning Month:	68.60 %
Number of Losing Months:	103
Percent Losing Months:	43.64 %
Average Losing Month:	-7.33 %
Maximum Losing Month:	-27.40 %
Average Win Month/Average Lose Month:	1.40

Charts

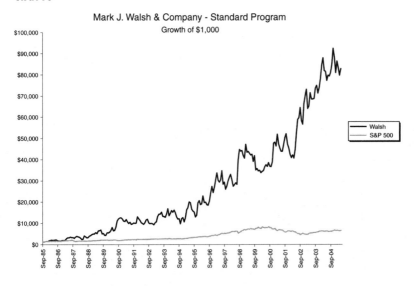

Mark J. Walsh & Company - Standard Program
Growth of $1,000

Millburn Ridgefield Corporation — Diversified Program

Annual Performance Breakdown

Yearly Statistics			
Year	Return	Drawdown	Assets
2005	-5.65 %	-11.73 %	$723,600,000
2004	-2.66 %	-22.19 %	$783,600,000
2003	1.56 %	-12.81 %	$625,400,000
2002	24.55 %	-11.87 %	$299,900,000
2001	-5.80 %	-14.44 %	$288,900,000
2000	12.70 %	-13.14 %	$344,200,000
1999	-1.99 %	-13.56 %	$404,200,000
1998	7.11 %	-8.86 %	$479,800,000
1997	12.68 %	-9.76 %	$328,900,000
1996	17.33 %	-11.58 %	$174,000,000
1995	32.76 %	-3.09 %	$140,800,000

Yearly Statistics			
Year	Return	Drawdown	Assets
1994	11.78 %	-8.92 %	$99,800,000
1993	10.88 %	-8.06 %	$111,100,000
1992	17.30 %	-11.06 %	$102,600,000
1991	4.44 %	-10.87 %	$93,600,000
1990	53.01 %	-5.66 %	$109,800,000
1989	-0.94 %	-28.13 %	$189,300,000
1988	2.70 %	-12.52 %	$249,700,000
1987	35.80 %	-14.86 %	$277,500,000
1986	-19.36 %	-33.47 %	$226,400,000
1985	22.50 %	-16.98 %	$340,600,000
1984	21.72 %	-14.10 %	$215,300,000
1983	-9.44 %	-14.79 %	$207,800,000
1982	29.35 %	-11.00 %	$279,400,000
1981	38.50 %	-10.72 %	$201,700,000
1980	64.38 %	-4.09 %	$121,000,000
1979	58.38 %	-2.45 %	$54,400,000
1978	18.64 %	-18.82 %	$25,900,000
1977	3.72 %	-13.60 %	$5,400,000

Month by Month Returns

Month by Month Returns												
Year	Jan	Feb	Mar	Apr	May	Jun	Jul	Aug	Sep	Oct	Nov	Dec
1977	- -	-1.07	2.27	6.23	-7.51	1.21	6.84	-4.37	-9.65	4.80	-3.62	10.57
1978	6.33	3.91	13.76	-17.86	12.78	-2.57	8.54	0.59	5.34	12.01	-14.17	-5.42
1979	-2.45	5.52	0.66	6.82	4.45	7.41	-1.76	1.82	14.84	-0.74	5.42	6.11
1980	20.82	3.81	8.62	-2.97	5.25	3.44	1.18	-2.32	-1.81	7.59	3.75	5.44
1981	11.39	10.40	-8.62	9.48	7.43	9.74	6.96	-0.15	-3.60	-4.79	8.24	-10.00
1982	4.77	8.68	9.14	-1.38	-0.82	8.99	-11.00	3.32	7.66	-4.04	-2.57	5.49

Year	Jan	Feb	Mar	Apr	May	Jun	Jul	Aug	Sep	Oct	Nov	Dec
1983	6.28	-1.29	-2.12	-0.42	1.13	-6.95	-1.11	5.57	-2.05	2.25	-7.08	-3.13
1984	5.03	0.05	1.08	2.45	4.76	-6.11	19.22	-9.05	4.14	-2.80	-6.69	11.04
1985	5.69	7.69	-4.65	-2.12	-4.52	-2.12	14.68	-2.75	-14.63	9.15	12.43	5.61
1986	3.84	14.91	1.59	-7.05	-2.74	-9.34	5.98	7.22	-18.35	-6.21	-5.36	-1.44
1987	14.52	0.16	3.34	10.29	-3.59	-3.63	1.12	-3.72	-5.88	1.66	9.67	9.44
1988	-8.23	1.30	-4.11	-1.87	6.09	17.89	-9.26	-0.47	0.67	1.64	6.11	-4.27
1989	3.18	-4.67	7.53	-1.51	17.04	-8.11	-3.62	-8.53	-2.74	-8.78	4.74	7.93
1990	4.13	4.21	2.99	2.40	-5.66	3.51	16.05	3.39	2.67	7.65	3.00	0.24
1991	-5.32	1.40	2.60	-0.09	-1.13	1.63	-4.02	-6.09	0.91	-0.30	0.10	16.35
1992	-8.53	-1.34	-0.72	-0.73	0.90	14.25	8.87	7.56	-0.19	-3.95	2.66	-0.73
1993	-2.69	5.78	-0.70	5.76	-1.79	-2.54	5.11	-8.06	1.09	-0.70	1.33	9.02
1994	-7.56	-1.47	7.67	-2.27	4.63	5.80	-3.00	-5.26	3.68	3.02	4.76	2.46
1995	-3.09	6.81	16.85	4.64	-1.10	0.99	-2.48	1.43	-1.84	0.06	0.19	7.90
1996	7.43	-11.05	0.80	5.72	-6.72	3.91	1.37	-1.88	2.79	10.64	3.96	1.08
1997	8.14	5.72	-2.83	-3.01	1.50	0.52	8.15	-8.52	1.20	-2.22	-0.31	5.02
1998	2.87	-2.71	1.14	-7.38	4.04	2.32	-4.96	6.94	5.53	-1.84	-0.75	2.71
1999	-4.01	3.08	1.21	5.51	-3.34	5.80	-3.82	1.17	0.73	-11.81	2.19	2.68
2000	1.99	-1.73	-4.55	0.67	-1.94	-4.43	-1.85	3.23	-2.77	4.50	6.02	14.41
2001	0.62	-1.54	9.12	-5.39	1.89	-2.24	-5.38	3.26	-2.85	4.20	-8.21	1.85
2002	1.88	-4.31	1.05	-3.26	6.01	13.44	6.06	1.55	6.62	-8.06	-4.14	7.38
2003	4.28	6.91	-9.34	-0.07	10.74	-4.10	1.95	2.05	-0.96	-8.93	-3.11	4.14
2004	1.27	4.01	-1.59	-8.75	-2.48	-4.23	-4.89	-2.45	0.85	6.73	9.46	0.80
2005	-3.63	-0.04	-3.52	-5.02	2.23							

Performance Summary

Performance Breakdown	
Total Months:	340
Number of Winning Months:	195
Percent Winning Months:	57.35 %
Average Winning Month:	5.48 %
Maximum Winning Month:	20.82 %
Number of Losing Months:	145
Percent Losing Months:	42.65 %
Average Losing Month:	-4.31 %
Maximum Losing Month:	-18.35 %
Average Win Month/Average Lose Month:	1.27

Charts

Millburn Ridgefield Corporation - Diversified Program
Growth of $1,000

Rabar Market Research, Inc. — Diversified

Annual Performance Breakdown

Yearly Statistics			
Year	Return	Drawdown	Assets
2005	-6.44 %	-10.30 %	$628,400,000
2004	-2.81 %	-24.33 %	$719,600,000
2003	23.93 %	-10.40 %	$303,300,000
2002	24.57 %	-8.33 %	$142,900,000
2001	0.77 %	-9.36 %	$122,700,000
2000	1.79 %	-12.32 %	$175,700,000
1999	-9.27 %	-16.25 %	$244,000,000
1998	24.29 %	-7.65 %	$208,800,000
1997	11.39 %	-9.06 %	$183,500,000
1996	0.66 %	-12.89 %	$205,700,000
1995	12.57 %	-29.82 %	$300,200,000
1994	33.91 %	-15.90 %	$155,700,000
1993	49.55 %	-13.39 %	$115,600,000
1992	-4.45 %	-17.14 %	$56,500,000
1991	-5.69 %	-24.91 %	$89,200,000
1990	122.51 %	-13.61 %	$61,100,000
1989	10.00 %	-27.77 %	$20,500,000
1988	90.34 %	-17.83 %	$2,600,000
1987	78.20 %	-24.88 %	$ 0
1986	125.85 %	-24.75 %	$2,100,000
1985	91.72 %	-28.20 %	$2,000,000

Month by Month Returns

Year	Jan	Feb	Mar	Apr	May	Jun	Jul	Aug	Sep	Oct	Nov	Dec
Month by Month Returns												
1985	-0.70	10.80	-9.00	-21.10	25.60	-15.40	79.30	-0.70	-4.10	11.20	16.00	3.70
1986	13.30	108.10	22.80	-13.50	-4.40	-9.00	13.60	10.30	-9.20	-10.10	-1.70	3.10
1987	13.30	-16.00	13.00	106.40	-5.80	-5.40	11.10	-8.70	5.20	-21.00	1.20	5.60
1988	1.00	9.90	-8.70	-10.00	4.00	56.90	0.80	1.60	2.70	1.60	8.70	10.10
1989	-0.77	-3.57	13.82	-0.18	13.76	-2.61	-2.84	-13.76	2.69	-13.81	5.24	17.01
1990	1.89	7.76	12.16	16.71	-13.61	9.50	16.06	21.80	10.40	4.87	2.51	-2.45
1991	-7.43	-7.75	2.26	-5.58	-1.17	3.32	-8.12	-2.93	2.43	0.66	-0.27	22.14
1992	-12.26	-3.31	0.57	-2.13	-0.77	5.47	12.93	7.70	-7.12	-0.69	1.45	-3.93
1993	-0.12	14.17	0.22	10.89	3.45	-1.28	14.75	-3.89	-4.10	-6.03	5.63	10.07
1994	-10.51	-6.02	19.43	2.47	11.40	18.00	-4.31	-4.42	3.35	-4.17	10.65	-1.25
1995	-9.45	14.00	15.25	5.84	8.91	-2.45	-9.28	-8.66	-9.11	-4.48	2.42	14.20
1996	-0.13	-9.52	-1.49	3.33	-3.45	1.54	-2.13	-1.30	3.75	10.75	5.95	-5.08
1997	5.37	5.07	-0.64	-6.41	-2.10	-0.11	14.84	-7.75	3.11	-3.33	0.51	4.24
1998	2.28	1.55	0.00	-6.43	4.17	2.12	1.16	19.37	6.10	-4.05	-3.75	1.60
1999	-1.90	3.70	-4.30	3.30	-6.90	0.00	-2.90	-0.40	0.10	-6.00	2.10	4.30
2000	-0.70	0.20	-2.10	-5.30	-0.10	-3.70	-1.20	4.70	-1.80	0.40	5.60	6.50
2001	1.50	0.30	4.80	-4.60	-2.00	-1.80	0.60	-1.60	2.00	6.40	-8.10	4.20
2002	-0.70	-4.00	2.30	-6.00	6.80	11.40	7.90	3.20	3.50	-3.50	-2.10	4.90
2003	3.40	5.20	-10.40	4.20	10.80	-2.60	-0.40	0.00	1.30	4.00	-1.50	9.40
2004	2.70	8.30	-1.20	-13.10	-3.80	-4.60	-2.10	-1.90	0.90	3.10	11.90	-0.80
2005	-6.40	5.20	-3.80	-5.30	4.30							

Performance Summary

Performance Breakdown	
Total Months:	245
Number of Winning Months:	130
Percent Winning Months:	53.06 %
Average Winning Month:	9.49 %
Maximum Winning Month:	108.10 %
Number of Losing Months:	112
Percent Losing Months:	45.71 %
Average Losing Month:	-5.07 %
Maximum Losing Month:	-21.10 %
Average Win Month/Average Lose Month:	1.87

Charts

Rabar Market Research, Inc. - Diversified
Growth of $1,000

Saxon Investment Corporation—Aggressive Diversified Program

Annual Performance Breakdown

Yearly Statistics			
Year	Return	Drawdown	Assets
2005	-10.84 %	-13.13 %	$44,000,000
2004	4.93 %	-20.93 %	$59,000,000
2003	88.84 %	-11.59 %	$36,000,000
2002	9.31 %	-27.80 %	$16,500,000
2001	14.39 %	-11.17 %	$10,100,000
2000	40.18 %	-11.50 %	$9,000,000
1999	24.53 %	-16.15 %	$6,100,000
1998	26.31 %	-20.11 %	$5,000,000
1997	6.56 %	-27.96 %	$4,600,000
1996	18.26 %	-35.97 %	$5,000,000
1995	-46.04 %	-58.19 %	$4,900,000
1994	142.60 %	-41.21 %	$3,600,000
1993	39.54 %	0.00 %	$1,000,000

Month by Month Returns

Month by Month Returns												
Year	Jan	Feb	Mar	Apr	May	Jun	Jul	Aug	Sep	Oct	Nov	Dec
1993	- -	- -	- -	- -	- -	- -	- -	- -	- -	- -	9.47	27.47
1994	-16.98	-22.70	11.59	-17.90	41.14	37.85	17.52	-11.67	13.99	22.30	15.43	26.96
1995	-25.79	-8.54	38.90	7.36	-13.59	3.70	-34.45	-19.52	-6.98	-4.91	6.80	19.39
1996	-5.59	-13.44	-21.65	44.99	-30.54	11.65	-0.40	0.97	30.63	37.01	10.66	-17.53
1997	6.83	19.29	12.09	-8.24	-7.10	4.23	10.49	-23.15	19.32	-16.04	-4.69	3.56
1998	1.30	-4.55	-3.27	-7.84	-0.05	-6.06	0.77	47.13	12.24	2.19	-5.56	-2.82
1999	4.35	-1.37	-3.48	9.50	-16.15	3.96	-0.92	23.01	7.23	-5.87	5.91	0.80
2000	-0.26	8.01	0.68	-7.50	7.09	2.50	1.67	3.34	-1.24	-10.39	16.46	17.55

Year	Jan	Feb	Mar	Apr	May	Jun	Jul	Aug	Sep	Oct	Nov	Dec
2001	-3.61	-1.52	-2.87	-3.20	-0.42	4.91	8.71	-2.68	1.29	19.21	-11.17	8.11
2002	-4.32	-8.51	7.89	-15.01	14.39	16.58	10.60	1.50	12.61	-9.14	-20.54	11.89
2003	15.22	3.87	-11.59	8.85	19.12	-3.69	1.43	1.20	12.04	21.16	-8.70	12.34
2004	3.13	8.56	4.44	-10.36	0.06	-6.29	-5.93	0.63	4.11	-0.77	10.99	-1.64
2005	-5.93	-1.69	3.85	-9.55	6.54							

Performance Summary

Performance Breakdown	
Total Months:	139
Number of Winning Months:	78
Percent Winning Months:	56.12 %
Average Winning Month:	12.08 %
Maximum Winning Month:	47.13 %
Number of Losing Months:	61
Percent Losing Months:	43.88 %
Average Losing Month:	-9.15 %
Maximum Losing Month:	-34.45 %
Average Win Month/Average Lose Month:	1.32

Charts

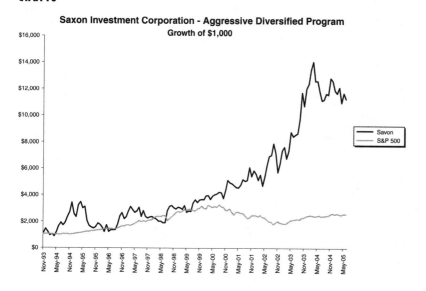

Saxon Investment Corporation - Aggressive Diversified Program
Growth of $1,000

Sunrise Capital Partners LLC — Expanded Diversified

Annual Performance Breakdown

	Yearly Statistics		
Year	Return	Drawdown	Assets
2005	-8.73 %	-8.70 %	$1,521,000,000
2004	5.98 %	-13.90 %	$1,821,100,000
2003	17.44 %	-9.41 %	$1,246,900,000
2002	14.49 %	-8.61 %	$708,000,000
2001	13.62 %	-10.33 %	$528,300,000
2000	8.22 %	-10.91 %	$372,200,000
1999	4.44 %	-5.27 %	$367,600,000
1998	25.84 %	-5.68 %	$290,200,000
1997	20.69 %	-5.92 %	$30,600,000
1996	19.34 %	-5.80 %	$12,900,000
1995	11.53 %	-9.32 %	$8,100,000

Month by Month Returns

Year	Jan	Feb	Mar	Apr	May	Jun	Jul	Aug	Sep	Oct	Nov	Dec
1995	-8.46	4.71	19.10	2.45	-3.77	-0.74	-1.94	-0.44	-2.67	0.75	-0.84	5.17
1996	0.54	-5.80	4.53	9.28	0.11	-0.56	-0.77	-0.49	0.93	6.85	1.29	2.73
1997	4.56	8.59	1.48	-0.46	4.39	-2.86	5.95	-3.32	-1.53	-1.18	1.82	2.25
1998	1.37	3.28	2.66	1.59	2.65	3.34	-0.61	9.54	3.21	-1.02	-4.71	2.51
1999	-0.88	5.14	-1.44	4.18	-1.20	2.18	-1.53	-0.13	0.42	-4.08	4.36	-2.20
2000	3.78	-3.31	-1.51	-4.65	-1.43	-0.46	0.43	3.91	-1.28	0.07	6.16	6.95
2001	1.67	3.74	7.27	-6.25	3.27	-1.27	-1.63	2.49	7.36	6.25	-10.33	1.88
2002	-2.52	-2.83	0.30	0.94	4.26	8.59	1.59	0.66	6.06	-3.74	-5.06	6.39
2003	9.16	4.62	-6.15	0.09	5.24	-3.66	-1.71	0.18	-3.40	5.98	-1.08	8.28
2004	0.98	7.70	2.40	-4.80	-1.30	-2.80	-1.60	-4.20	0.70	3.40	4.90	1.20
2005	-6.10	-0.10	-0.60	-1.40	-0.40							

Performance Summary

Performance Breakdown	
Total Months:	125
Number of Winning Months:	70
Percent Winning Months:	56.00 %
Average Winning Month:	3.90 %
Maximum Winning Month:	19.10 %
Number of Losing Months:	55
Percent Losing Months:	44.00 %
Average Losing Month:	-2.53 %
Maximum Losing Month:	-10.33 %
Average Win Month/Average Lose Month:	1.54

Charts

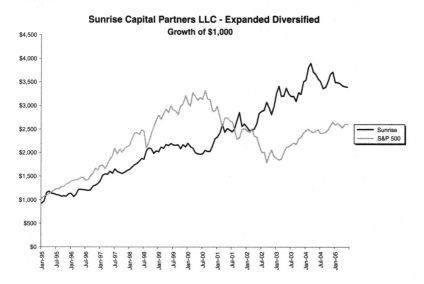

Transtrend B.V. — Diversified Trend Program — Enhanced Risk (USD)

Annual Performance Breakdown

	Yearly Statistics		
Year	Return	Drawdown	Assets
2005	1.70 %	-4.35 %	$1,318,000,000
2004	12.82 %	-9.41 %	$1,299,000,000
2003	8.48 %	-6.78 %	$831,000,000
2002	26.26 %	-4.38 %	$207,000,000
2001	26.36 %	-3.12 %	$59,000,000
2000	12.40 %	-4.82 %	$10,900,000
1999	-2.21 %	-8.59 %	$32,000,000
1998	21.95 %	-5.46 %	$56,300,000
1997	37.93 %	-8.58 %	$7,300,000
1996	31.68 %	-7.10 %	$2,600,000
1995	29.09 %	-6.29 %	$2,400,000

Month by Month Returns

Year	Jan	Feb	Mar	Apr	May	Jun	Jul	Aug	Sep	Oct	Nov	Dec
1995	-6.16	9.57	10.15	2.16	6.49	3.63	-3.70	-0.58	1.75	-3.81	2.07	5.70
1996	5.38	-6.65	-0.48	8.59	-4.40	-0.30	3.88	7.26	7.51	10.37	1.46	-3.12
1997	9.64	5.12	-2.17	-4.07	-0.62	0.20	19.27	1.02	1.87	-8.58	5.72	7.95
1998	0.25	0.21	2.79	-5.43	3.55	1.36	-4.75	19.57	1.93	0.86	-1.06	2.70
1999	-3.86	1.22	-2.77	3.11	-3.10	4.51	1.95	-2.51	0.63	-6.82	1.84	4.29
2000	1.55	-1.99	-2.29	0.14	2.52	-2.44	-0.77	1.81	0.62	2.54	5.97	4.47
2001	0.72	0.60	6.75	-1.48	1.29	-1.36	4.72	2.37	7.82	1.07	-3.12	4.86
2002	-1.17	-0.69	2.00	-0.99	2.34	8.41	5.97	2.78	3.44	-2.72	-1.71	6.58

Year	Jan	Feb	Mar	Apr	May	Jun	Jul	Aug	Sep	Oct	Nov	Dec
2003	5.18	4.03	-5.04	3.77	5.81	-2.45	-2.36	-0.09	-2.04	2.48	-0.69	0.22
2004	2.08	4.95	-2.18	-3.17	-0.31	-2.35	-1.34	-0.42	1.63	3.20	8.97	1.71
2005	-4.35	2.74	2.03	-3.48	1.03	4.02						

Performance Summary

Performance Breakdown	
Total Months:	126
Number of Winning Months:	79
Percent Winning Months:	62.70 %
Average Winning Month:	4.09 %
Maximum Winning Month:	19.57 %
Number of Losing Months:	47
Percent Losing Months:	37.30 %
Average Losing Month:	-2.68 %
Maximum Losing Month:	-8.58 %
Average Win Month/Average Lose Month:	1.52

Charts

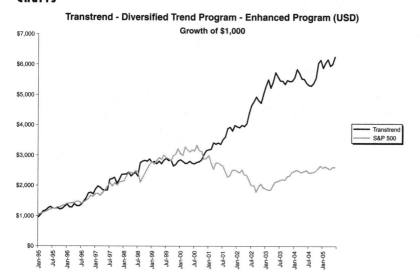

Transtrend - Diversified Trend Program - Enhanced Program (USD)
Growth of $1,000

Winton Capital Management Ltd — Diversified Trading Program

Annual Performance Breakdown

Yearly Statistics			
Year	Return	Drawdown	Assets
2005	10.75 %	-5.16 %	$2,705,000,000
2004	20.31 %	-11.72 %	$1,497,600,000
2003	25.52 %	-11.14 %	$321,200,000
2002	12.86 %	-16.29 %	$208,000,000
2001	5.56 %	-11.28 %	$276,800,000
2000	9.72 %	-13.87 %	$147,400,000
1999	13.24 %	-14.73 %	$113,400,000
1998	53.26 %	-5.65 %	$16,200,000
1997	3.68 %	-12.97 %	$1,900,000

Month by Month Returns

Year	Jan	Feb	Mar	Apr	May	Jun	Jul	Aug	Sep	Oct	Nov	Dec
1997	- -	- -	- -	- -	- -	- -	- -	- -	- -	-12.97	9.96	8.34
1998	1.50	3.27	8.02	-1.48	8.53	3.23	1.35	11.06	4.52	-5.65	1.18	9.19
1999	-1.51	3.55	-4.24	10.09	-8.58	5.31	-1.93	-3.64	-0.16	-6.13	13.12	9.20
2000	-3.66	1.75	-3.13	1.53	-0.50	-1.28	-4.33	2.82	-7.54	2.50	7.10	16.04
2001	4.58	0.57	7.48	-5.23	-3.32	-2.95	0.72	0.02	4.48	12.45	-7.56	-4.02
2002	-10.81	-6.14	11.44	-4.66	-3.80	7.32	4.79	5.48	7.42	-7.76	-1.09	13.46
2003	5.30	11.95	-11.14	2.07	10.18	-5.85	-1.15	0.69	0.71	5.46	-2.68	10.00
2004	2.65	11.93	-0.50	-8.27	-0.16	-3.12	0.88	2.64	4.78	3.37	6.38	-0.58
2005	-5.16	5.72	4.70	-4.03	6.62							

Performance Summary

Performance Breakdown	
Total Months:	92
Number of Winning Months:	54
Percent Winning Months:	58.70 %
Average Winning Month:	5.91 %
Maximum Winning Month:	16.04 %
Number of Losing Months:	38
Percent Losing Months:	41.30 %
Average Losing Month:	-4.39 %
Maximum Losing Month:	-12.97 %
Average Win Month/Average Lose Month:	1.35

Charts

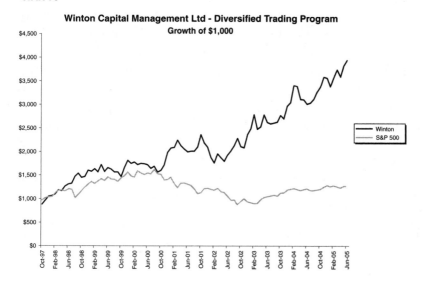

Winton Capital Management Ltd - Diversified Trading Program
Growth of $1,000

Risk Disclaimer

THE RISK OF LOSS IN TRADING COMMODITIES CAN BE SUBSTANTIAL. YOU SHOULD THEREFORE CAREFULLY CONSIDER WHETHER SUCH TRADING IS SUITABLE FOR YOU IN LIGHT OF YOUR FINANCIAL CONDITION.

THE HIGH DEGREE OF LEVERAGE THAT IS OFTEN OBTAINABLE IN COMMODITY TRADING CAN WORK AGAINST YOU AS WELL AS FOR YOU. THE USE OF LEVERAGE CAN LEAD TO LARGE LOSSES AS WELL AS GAINS. IN SOME CASES, MANAGED COMMODITY ACCOUNTS ARE SUBJECT TO SUBSTANTIAL CHARGES FOR MANAGEMENT AND ADVISORY FEES.

IT MAY BE NECESSARY FOR THOSE ACCOUNTS THAT ARE SUBJECT TO THESE CHARGES TO MAKE SUBSTANTIAL TRADING PROFITS TO AVOID DEPLETION OR EXHAUSTION OF THEIR ASSETS. THE DISCLOSURE DOCUMENT FOR ANY PRODUCT YOU PURCHASE WILL CONTAIN A COMPLETE DESCRIPTION OF THE PRINCIPAL RISK FACTORS AND EACH FEE TO BE CHARGED TO YOUR ACCOUNT BY THE COMMODITY TRADING ADVISOR ("CTA"). THE REGULATIONS OF THE COMMODITY FUTURES TRADING COMMISSION ("CFTC") REQUIRE THAT PROSPECTIVE CLIENTS OF A CTA RECEIVE A DISCLOSURE DOCUMENT AT OR PRIOR TO THE TIME AN ADVISORY AGREEMENT IS DELIVERED AND THAT CERTAIN RISK FACTORS BE HIGHLIGHTED. THIS DOCUMENT SHOULD BE READILY ACCESSIBLE FROM THE CTA OR THROUGH THE PLACEMENT FIRM THROUGH WHICH YOU BUY ANY PRODUCT.

THIS BRIEF STATEMENT CANNOT DISCLOSE ALL OF THE RISKS AND OTHER SIGNIFICANT ASPECTS OF THE COMMODITY MARKETS. THEREFORE, YOU SHOULD READ THE DISCLOSURE DOCUMENT AND STUDY IT CAREFULLY TO DETERMINE WHETHER SUCH TRADING IS APPROPRIATE FOR YOU IN LIGHT OF YOUR FINANCIAL CONDITION. THE CFTC DOES NOT PASS UPON THE MERITS OF PARTICIPATING IN ANY TRADING PROGRAM, NOR ON THE ADEQUACY OR ACCURACY OF ANY DISCLOSURE DOCUMENT. OTHER DISCLOSURE STATEMENTS ARE REQUIRED TO BE PROVIDED TO YOU BEFORE A COMMODITY ACCOUNT MAY BE OPENED FOR YOU.

Short-Term
Trading

C

Ed Seykota was recently asked at Seykota.com:

"I am new to trend following and wish to ask you what your favorite chart is for determining a given market's trend? Daily, weekly, yearly, hourly?"

Ed responded:

"Hmmm.....your list seems to lack scaling options for minute, second, and millisecond. If you want to go for the really high-frequency stuff, you might try trading visible light, in the range of one cycle per 10–15 seconds. Trading gamma rays, at around one cycle per 10–20 seconds, requires a lot of expensive instrumentation, whereas you can trade visible light 'by eye.' I don't know of even one short-term trader, however, who claims to show a profit at these frequencies. In general, higher-frequency trading succumbs to declining profit potential against non-declining transaction costs. You might consider trading a chart with a long enough time scale that transaction costs are a minor factor—something like a daily price chart, going back a year or two."

I agree with Ed's pithy wisdom, but he is not saying short-term is impossible. There do exist shorter-term systematic traders who have done quite well (Toby Crabel and Jim Simons, for example).

He's barely rated a mention in the nation's most important newspapers, but pay close attention to what Institutional Investor wrote about him..."Jim Simons [President of Renaissance Technologies and operator of the Medallion Fund] may very well be the best money manager on earth."

Long Island Business News

They would agree with Ed that their style is hard. The shorter you go, the more you need great execution, fantastic data, and multiple systems. To be a great shorter-term mechanical trader is a different animal than trend following, but it is a style that a select few have mastered.

Personality Traits of Successful Traders

D

We are grateful for the following contribution from Brett Steenbarger:

In my book *The Psychology of Trading*, I referred to personality traits that tend to distinguish successful traders from less successful ones. Several of these traits are also likely to influence the degree of success traders are likely to have in adopting a Trend Following approach to trading. Below are several self-assessment questions that might be useful in determining whether you'll face particularly great challenges in riding market trends. Please write down "yes" or "no" answers to each of the 12 questions before reading further:

1. When something goes against you in the market, do you often find yourself venting your frustration?

2. Do you enjoy (or as a child did you enjoy) roller coasters or other thrill rides?

3. Do you often find yourself procrastinating over work?

4. Do you consider yourself moody—sometimes rather up, sometimes rather down?

5. Would you generally prefer going out and partying with friends rather than staying at home with a good book or movie?

Luck is a dividend of sweat. The more you sweat, the luckier you get.

Ray Kroc
Founder of McDonalds

6. Do you often find yourself apologizing to others because you forgot to do something you were supposed to do?

7. Are you generally high-strung, tense, or stressed?

8. If given the choice at a buffet, would you prefer to try exotic foods you've never heard of rather than familiar dishes?

9. When you have a task that needs to be done around the house, do you tend to take a quick and dirty approach, rather than a meticulous, painstaking approach?

10. After a losing trade, do you often feel guilty or get down on yourself?

11. Have you experimented with or regularly used two or more recreational drugs (other than alcohol) in your life?

12. Are you often late for appointments or for social plans you've made?

If you indicated "yes" to most or all of questions 1, 4, 7, and 10, you most likely score high on a trait called "neuroticism." Neuroticism is the tendency toward negative emotional experience, and it shows up as anger, anxiety, or depression.

If you responded "yes" to most or all of questions 2, 5, 8 and 11, you probably score high on a trait called "openness to experience." Openness reflects a tendency toward sensation seeking and risk-taking.

If you answered "yes" to most or all of questions 3, 6, 9, and 12, you potentially score low on a trait called "conscientiousness." Conscientiousness measures the degree to which an individual is oriented toward duty, responsibility, and dependability.

Other things being equal, the ideal personality pattern for Trend Following is one of high conscientiousness, low neuroticism, and low openness. A good trend-follower will stick with rules and systems (conscientious), won't impulsively enter or exit trades on the whim of emotion (neuroticism), and will trade for profits, not stimulation (low openness). In my experience, some of the best systems traders are among the least flashy people. They are meticulous and conscientious about their research and execution, and they don't let their emotions or needs pull them from their discipline.

Conversely, individuals who are high risk-takers and who crave novelty, stimulation, and action often take impulsive and imprudent risks. Very frequently, the neurotic emotions kick in after a series of losing high-risk trades. Such individuals are trading for excitement and self-validation, not just profits. Even if they are given a tested, profitable trading system, they will not be able to follow it faithfully.

System traders often focus their research and energy on defining the optimal parameters for a system's profitability. Equally important is finding a trading strategy that meshes with one's personality. Traders who are relatively risk-averse may trade shorter time frames and/or smaller positions than those who are risk-tolerant. Traders with a higher need for novelty and stimulation may benefit from trading a greater number of stocks and/or markets rather than focusing on a relative few. Are some personalities simply unsuited for trading? I would say yes, just as some personalities are not cut out to be fighter pilots or surgeons. It is difficult to imagine a trader enjoying ongoing success without the capacity for disciplined risk-taking.

Personality testing options can be found at www.knowyourtype.com. Myers-Briggs testing can be useful for all traders from beginner to advanced.

It is not at all unusual to find that a trader is losing with a Trend Following approach because he or she is acting out unmet personality needs in the market. One of the best trading strategies one can employ is to find adequate outlets for attention/affection, achievement, self-esteem, emotional well being, and excitement outside of trading. Sometimes traders I talk with try to impress me by explaining that trading is their entire life. They do not realize that their very "passion" and "obsession" with the markets are likely to sabotage them, imposing undue pressures and interference. If you have a trading system and you faithfully execute that system, trading should be reasonably boring and routine. Better to enjoy roller coasters outside of market hours than ride them with your equity curve!

Brett N. Steenbarger, Ph.D. is Associate Professor of Psychiatry and Behavioral Sciences at SUNY Upstate Medical University in Syracuse, NY. He is also an active trader and writes occasional feature articles on market psychology for MSN's Money site (www.moneycentral.com). Many of Dr. Steenbarger's articles and trading strategies are archived on his website, www.brettsteenbarger.com.

Trend Following Models

E

Paul Mulvaney, CIO of Mulvaney Capital Management Ltd., provided the following visual models of Trend Following:

Man can learn nothing unless he proceeds from the known to the unknown.

Claude Bernard

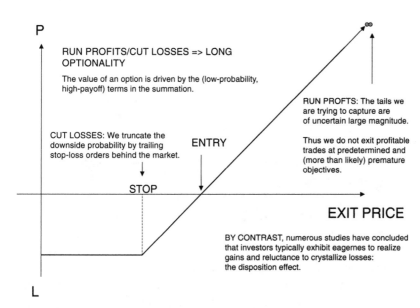

CHART E.1: How Classic Trend Following Models Generate Payout. *Source: Mulvaney Capital Management Ltd.*

According to Mulvaney, the "hockey stick'" diagram (E.1) depicts how classic Trend Following models generate payouts analogous to long options positions. We know from options theory that the value of an option is dominated by the low probability/large magnitude events. The diagonal line slopes upward to infinity. Trend followers do not predict the extent of price changes but seek to capture large outsize moves over significant periods of time. The horizontal line represents the truncation of risk by stop placement,and can be likened to paying a finite premium for an option.

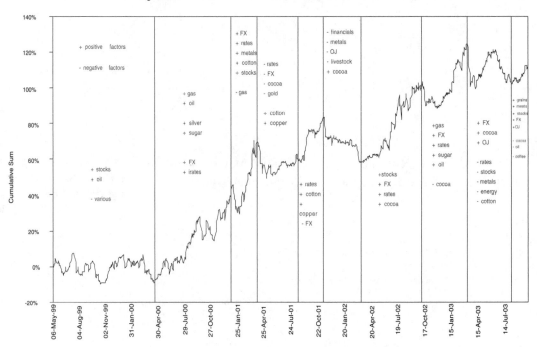

CHART E.2: The Typical Trend Follower's Portfolio Is Well Diversified. *Source: Mulvaney Capital Management Ltd.*

Mulvaney notes that Trend Following does not rely on a uni-directional, single-market position as buy-and-hold stock investing does. A single Trend Following model has multiple sources of return, morphing itself into whatever and wherever the market is. As you can see from the Mulvaney Capital Management P&L chart above, (E.2) the typical trend follower's portfolio is well diversified, allowing it to profit from the tendency of markets to trend at different times.

Mulvaney concludes:

"Two lessons derive from the empirical data. Price changes in financial and commodity markets are approximately uncorrelated over time and thus are not predictable. This is the Martingale property: the best estimate of tomorrow's price is today's price. This is absolutely not saying that profitable systems cannot be designed, just that mean returns cannot be estimated, in a strict econometric sense. This observation underpins a 'run profits' strategy. By contrast, systematic profit-taking at calculated objectives is a form of mean estimation and is untenable. On the other hand, the volatility of financial and commodity markets changes over time and exhibits autocorrelation. Returns of like magnitude tend to be clustered over time. Volatility tends to come in waves, so that financial markets are characterised by tranquil and volatile periods. Large price changes tend to be followed by large changes and small changes by small changes, but of either sign. As a result, predictive models for volatility can be derived. In modelling terms, this means we do estimate the volatility of returns, detecting nascent trends when price changes exceed previous volatility estimates and a tail starts to form."—Paul Mulvaney, CIO of Mulvaney Capital Management Ltd.

The vertical thinker says: "I know what I am looking for." The lateral thinker says: "I am looking but I won't know what I am looking for until I have found it."

Edward de Bono

Trading System Example from Trading Recipes

F

"Part of back-testing is to determine position sizing and risk management strategies that fit within your drawdown tolerance envelope."
—Ed Seykota[1]

In this appendix, we'll see how a trader might construct a simple, mechanical Trend Following system on Trading Recipes Portfolio Engineering Software.

Grow your own dope— plant an economist.

Graffiti seen at London School of Economics

We'll start with a broad look at the system's trading ideas, which echo many of the ideas discussed in this book. We'll construct a hypothetical portfolio and run a backtest up to a certain point in time. Then, we'll examine in detail how the software enters, sizes, and manages a trade. Afterwards, we'll run our backtest to the end of our data and examine the results without and with money management.

Please note that we provide this information to illustrate a concept; we do not necessarily recommend that anyone trade this system, nor do we offer it as trading advice.

System Background Information

Our sample Trend Following system enters on a 89-day price breakout and exits on a 13-day price breakdown, bets 2 percent of equity on every trade, and implements a mechanism to ensure that we don't risk too much. This system is run over a small portfolio of futures markets. Portfolio selection is a critical element of trading performance, but we did not put the portfolio used here under a microscope.

Chart F.1 shows the markets included in the sample portfolio:

CHART F.1: Markets Included in Sample Portfolio

Sector	Market	Symbol	Exchange
Currencies	British Pound	BP	CME (day)
	Canadian Dollar	CD	CME (day)
	Japanese Yen	JY	CME (day)
	Swiss Franc	SF	CME (day)
	U.S. Dollar Index	DX	NYBT
Energies	Crude Oil	CL	NYMEX
	Heating Oil	HO	NYMEX
	Natural Gas	NG	NYMEX
	Unleaded Gas	HU	NYMEX
Grains	Corn	C_	CBT (day)
	Soybean Oil	BO	CBT (day)
	Wheat – KC	KW	KCBT
Softs	Coffee	KC	NYBT
	Cotton	CT	NYBT
	Sugar #11	SB	NYBT

Our test comprises in-sample data only; we do not verify our in-sample results with out-of-sample data. Before risking real money in the market, you'd be prudent to test several samples.

System Details

Before we review portfolio-level performance, we'll examine the code used in Trading Recipes to generate entry and exit signals and to size positions (money management). Please note that words in ALL CAPS represent elements from Trading Recipes's programming language, whereas words following an apostrophe are explanatory comments.

Each day, we'll calculate the following values:

```
SYSTEM = 1                               'unique ID # for this system
COL1 = ATR[15]                        '15-day avg true range of current market
MANAGER[1] = COL1[1] * POINTVALUE      'dollar value of that volatility
COL2 = MAX[H,89,1] + TICK[1]            '89-day breakout for long entry
COL3 = MIN[L,13,1] - TICK[1]            '13-day breakdown for long exit
COL4 = MIN[L,89,1] - TICK[1]            '89-day breakout for short entry
COL5 = MAX[H,13,1] + TICK[1]            '13-day breakdown for short exit
```

As it processes each day of each market, our system will search for a breakout to enter a trade (long or short):

```
BUYSTOP = COL2                                     'long entry stop
SELLSTOP = COL4                                    'short entry stop
```

If an entry signal is generated, the system will execute position sizing rules to determine how many contracts (futures) or shares (equities) to trade.

In the rules below, you can see that we are risking 2 percent of our equity on each trade. However, we trade conservatively in that we trade *the lesser quantity of contracts* as calculated by 2% divided by new risk (defined as the dollar value of the absolute value of [entry – stop]) or 2% divided by twice the dollar value of 15-day average volatility.

```
STARTUPCASH = 1000000                          'start with $1 million
STARTDATE = 19910101                       '10-year in-sample dataset
ENDATE = 20001231
MEMORY[1] = (TOTALEQUITY * .02) / NEWRISK
                             'risk 2% of equity / dollar risk on trade
MEMORY[2] = (TOTALEQUITY * .02) / (MANAGER[1] * 2)
                      'risk 2% of equity / dollar value of volatility
IF MEMORY[1] < MEMORY[2] THEN MEMORY[2] = MEMORY[1]
                                'put lesser of two values into MEM2
IF MEMORY[2] > 100 THEN MEMORY[2] = 100        'don't trade too large
NEWCONTRACTS = MEMORY[2]             'use value of MEM2 to size position
```

Once in a trade, our Trend Following system will search for a breakdown to exit a trade (long or short):

```
SELLSTOP = COL3                                    'long exit stop

BUYSTOP = COL5                                     'short exit stop
```

A Canadian Dollar Trade

Let's follow a Canadian Dollar trade to see exactly how our Trend Following system enters, sizes, and exits a trade.

On December 14, 1994, the Canadian Dollar hit an 89-day low (as represented by the line in the midst of the price bars) intraday. Because our Trend Following system had a sellstop "on the floor," the order was filled and the system went short. (See Chart F.2.)

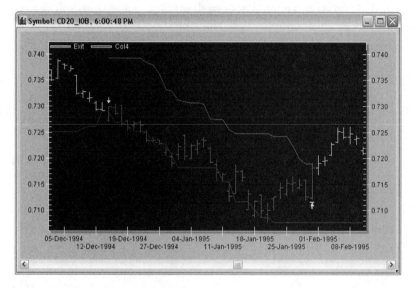

CHART F.2: Short Entry 12-Dec-1994.

It indicates the trailing stop (a 13-day high) via the line above the price bars. While in a trade, Trading Recipes compares daily data to that line. If a day's price range touches that line, as it does on 31-Jan-1995, then the exit stop is hit and a buy order is generated to cover the short.

How was the position sized? Let's review our sizing rules in the context of the equity level when the entry signal was generated.

After our portfolio was marked-to-market at the close on 13-Dec-1994, we had $2,205,963 in equity. As it sizes the Canadian Dollar entry, our system calculates the following values (please note that a 1.0 move in the Canadian Dollar is worth $100,000 per our data setup):

```
MEMORY[1] = (TOTALEQUITY * .02) / NEWRISK
Where TOTALEQUITY = $2,205,963
     TOTALEQUITY * .02 = $44,119.26
     NEWRISK = ABS(.7273 - .7392) * $100,000 = $1190
Thus  MEMORY[1] = $44,119.26 / $1190 = 37.0750084


MEMORY[2] = (TOTALEQUITY * .02) / (MANAGER[1] * 2)
Where TOTALEQUITY = $2,205,963
     TOTALEQUITY * .02 = $44,119.26
     MANAGER[1] = .0023 * $100,000 = $230
     MANAGER[1] * 2 = $460
Thus  MEMORY[2] = $44,119.26 / $460 = 95.91143478


IF MEMORY[1] < MEMORY[2] THEN MEMORY[2] = MEMORY[1]
Where MEMORY[1] is indeed < MEMORY[2], so MEMORY[2] = 37.0750084


IF MEMORY[2] > 100 THEN MEMORY[2] = 100
Where the condition evaluates to false


NEWCONTRACTS = MEMORY[2]
Where Trading Recipes rounds down and sizes the position at 37 contracts
```

By taking the smaller of two possible position sizes, this example illustrates clearly one of the maxims of Trend Following: Bet conservatively so that you might live to see another day.

System Performance

We can use some of Trading Recipes's analysis tools to see how our Trend Following system performed over the entire portfolio. The portfolio summary provides a wealth of useful information. Chart F.3 shows the statistics for our 10-year in-sample test over 15 markets. Note that, for the sake of simplicity, commission and slippage costs (which can be very significant) were not factored into the backtest.

CHART F.3: 10-Year In-Sample Test

Initial Balance	1,000,000	$ Won	13,774,599
Net Win Loss	5,732,456	$ Lost	8,770,406
Ending Equity	6,732,456	Incentive + Fees	0
ROI	573.25%	Other Credits	3,143
Compound Annual ROI	21.02%	Other Debits	0
Max Drawdown %	23.05%		
Max Drawdown % Date	19931101	Long Wins	113
Longest Drawdown in Years	0.28	Long Losses	150
Longest Drawdown Start Date	19920901	Short Wins	132
Longest Drawdown End Date	19940506	Short Losses	181
MAR Ratio	0.91	Long $ Won	8,030,086
Sharpe Ratio	1.02	Long $ Lost	4,104,701
Return Retracement Ratio	2.88	Short $ Won	5,744,513
Sterling Ratio	0.68	Short $ Lost	4,665,705
Std. Dev. Daily % Returns	1.23%	Largest Winning Trade	480,563
Average Expectation Value	20.33	Largest Losing Trade	141,900
Expectation	32.79%	Average Winning Trade	56,223
DU Area / DD Area	1.21	Average Losing Trade	26,497
Percent New Highs	6.61%	Max Consecutive Wins	8
		Max Consecutive Losses	15
Trades	576	Days Winning	1,350
Trades Rejected	85	Days Losing	1,176
Wins	245		
Losses	331	Number of Margin Calls	0
Percent Wins	42.53%	$ Largest Margin Call	0
Avg $Win to Avg $Loss	2.12		
Average Days in Winning Trade	37	Size Adjustments	0
Average Days in Losing Trade	15	Size Adjusted Items	0
Start Date	19910102		
End Date	20001231	Total Slippage + Commission	0
Max Items Held	588	PSR run time (H:M:S)	0:00:03
Total Items Traded	18,879		

To see how our equity curve looked in relationship to our drawdown, we can chart the logarithmic equity curve (Chart F.4). Note that through 1992 and 1993, the curve failed to gain traction, as it was hampered by large drawdowns—drawdowns that proved to be historic. But in mid-1994, the system hit its stride, and the equity curve began a nice trajectory upward.

The search for truth is more precious than its possession.

Albert Einstein[2]

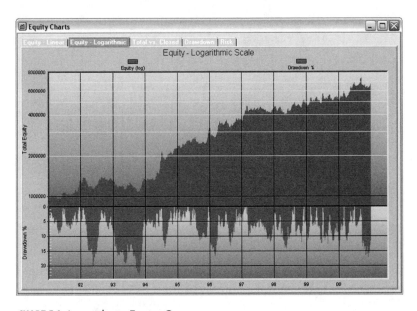

CHART F.4: Logarithmic Equity Curve

To see how our system performs in rolling, annual blocks of time, we can chart the 12-month rolling returns (Chart F.5). Note how frequently these rolling returns result in positive gains—an excellent sign of robustness.

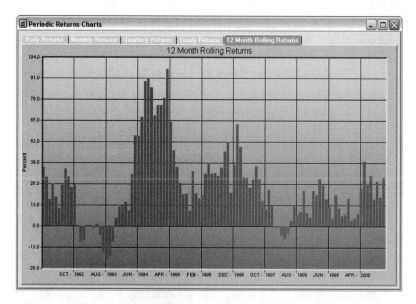

CHART F.5: Twelve-Month Rolling Returns

Summary

In this appendix, we presented a simple Trend Following system in the context of a portfolio, discussed the rules and calculations in detail, and examined the results via table and charts. This is the type of process all trend followers go through in their trading.

Bob Spear is the creator of Trading Recipes software. For more information about Trading Recipes, see www.tradingrecipes.com *and* www.mechanicasoftware.com.

Modern Portfolio Theory and Managed Futures

G

Earlier, we mentioned that Jerry Parker does it a little differently. Parker, like many other traders, pursues a strategy for clients based on Modern Portfolio Theory. What do we mean?

All trend followers have an extremely low to zero correlation with traditional investments, such as the S&P stock index. The case can be made that beyond achieving absolute returns, Trend Following also provides additional diversification to traditional portfolios.

This concept is called Modern Portfolio Theory (MPT). A traditional portfolio is typically 60 percent stocks and 40 percent bonds. What Modern Portfolio Theory demonstrates is that you could add a noncorrelated asset like a Trend Following investment to the portfolio and actually increase return and potentially reduce "risk." Millburn Ridgefield, one of the oldest trend followers, explains this concept further:

"The Millburn Diversified Portfolio has a 10 percent allocation which has historically exhibited superior performance characteristics coupled with an almost zero correlation of monthly returns to those of traditional investments. If an investor had invested 10 percent of his or her portfolio in the Millburn Diversified Portfolio from February 1977 through August 2003 he or

In mathematics you don't understand things. You just get used to them.

Johann von Neumann

she would have increased the return on his or her traditional portfolio by 73 basis points (a 6.2 percent increase) and decreased risk (as measured by standard deviation) by 0.26 of a percent (an 8.2 percent decrease)."[1]

What Are Managed Futures?

Jim Hamer, a successful trend follower and a student of Ed Seykota's, offered insight into the concept of managed futures:

"Like most investors, you are probably familiar with and have invested in traditional investment classes—stocks, bonds, mutual funds, CDs and money market funds. These are the backbone of most portfolios. Yet, if there was an investment that could potentially lower the volatility of your portfolio and increase your return over time (with commensurate risk), wouldn't you want that investment to be part of your overall portfolio mix? Well, there is such an investment . . . managed futures:

"What are managed futures?. . . Commodity Trading Advisors (CTA) or Commodity Pool Operators (CPO) are experienced, professional money managers . . . who manage investor's assets using investments in the commodities and futures markets just as a stock mutual fund manager would invest his clients assets in a variety of different stocks.

"Managed futures investments are best used as long term vehicles with a potential for aggressive growth. They are meant to be a piece of the portfolio pie and not the whole pie itself. Their true benefit is found when properly mixed with other traditional assets such as mutual funds, bonds, stocks, money market funds, and CDs.

"Academic studies (such as those conducted by former Harvard University professor Dr. John Lintner) have concluded that managed futures investments can provide significant portfolio diversification benefits due to their historically non-correlated relationship to stock and bonds.

"Real diversification should include some asset classes with low correlation to each other. Managed futures statistically fit this description and may provide qualified investors with the benefit of reducing overall portfolio volatility and increasing overall returns."—Jim Hamer, President, Hamer Trading Inc.[2]

How should skeptics be addressed? Jerry M. Harris, Senior Vice President and Principal, Welton Investment Corporation offers:

Inspiration comes slowly and quietly.

Brenda Ueland

"Regrettably, when considering managed futures, many people approach the situation with what I call the 'hole in the donut' syndrome. Just think for a minute how many people you know who view their lives in terms of 'what they don't have' rather than from the perspective of 'what they do have.' These types of folks go through life focusing on the hole of a donut rather than the donut itself. Why should someone look at the hole of a donut? There is nothing there! Going through life like this is, in general, rather unproductive and wasteful. And so it is, at times, with investors considering managed futures who tend to focus on a series of perceived negatives of this alternative asset class rather than the real benefits. In general, such perceived negatives are things they have either experienced through an unrepresentative sample in the distant past, heard from a friend, or perhaps been warned about by their mother. I'm sure you know them: The 'D' and 'L' factors— 'Managed futures? It's too risky—after all they include derivatives and use leverage.' If you are an investor considering managed futures as an alternative investment, remember, don't focus on the hole in the donut. Instead of asking 'Why managed futures?' you should, I believe, more appropriately ask 'Why not?'"[3]

Additional information on Modern Portfolio Theory can be found at our Web site, *www.trendfollowing.com*.

Critical Questions for Trading Systems

There are many questions you should ask about your trading system. Here are a few:

1. What have been the largest actual and simulated drawdowns you have experienced on a daily basis? What was the maximal loss in equity, simulated and actual, in a single day?

2. What is the maximal number of consecutive losing months the system has sustained?

3. How often do drawdowns occur?

4. Are drawdowns typically short-lived, or do they develop gradually?

5. On the average, how long does it take to recover all the losses incurred during a drawdown? What is the longest it has taken to complete a recovery?

6. Is the risk of each trade calculated? If so, what variables are included when making the calculation, and is the procedure accomplished by the computer or "by hand?"

7. How is overall risk controlled?

On the Cuban Revolution:
Michael: I saw an interesting thing happen today. A rebel was being arrested by the military police, and rather than be taken alive, he exploded a grenade he had hidden in his jacket. He killed himself, and he took a captain of the command with him.
Random Observer: Those rebels you know they're crazy.
Michael: Maybe so but it occurred to me—the soldiers are paid to fight. The rebels aren't.
Hyman Roth: What does that tell you?
Michael: They could win.[3]

8. Are there circumstances under which all trading could be halted in order to avoid further losses? If so, what are they? If not, why not?

9. Are there markets in which the system consistently performed poorly? If so, why does it not work well in those markets?

10. Does the system adapt quickly or slowly to changes in the volatility of markets?

11. Does the system have any way to minimize losses caused by whipsawing in the markets?

12. Does the system permit discontinuation of trading when equity falls to a prespecified point and call for resumption of trading when market conditions seem to warrant?

13. On what principles are stops established?

14. How much does portfolio diversification reduce risk in the trading system?[2]

Resources

The companion web site for *Trend Following* is:

www.trendfollowing.com

You will find information on seminars and educational course offerings online at our Web site. Additionally you will find our recommended and continually updated reading list as well.

Educational Web sites for Trend Followers are:

www.turtletrader.com
www.michaelcovel.com

There are many who find a good alibi far more attractive than an achievement. For an achievement does not settle anything permanently. We still have to prove our worth anew each day: we have to prove that we are as good today as we were yesterday. But when we have a valid alibi for not achieving anything we are fixed, so to speak, for life.

Eric Hoffer

Endnotes

Preface

1. Recruitment ad for Shackleton's Antarctic Expedition. *The Times*, London, 1913. Believed to have been posted in the personals section.

2. Van K. Tharp, *Trade Your Way to Financial Freedom*. New York: McGraw-Hill, 1999.

Chapter 1

1. See *www.mises.org*.

2. Robert Koppel, *The Intuitive Trader*, John Wiley and Sons, Inc., 1996, 88.

3. Ludwig von Mises, *Human Action: A Treatise on Economics*. 4th revised ed. Irvington-on-Hudson, NY: The Foundation for Economic Education, Inc., 1996, printed 1998. First published 1949.

4. Jack Schwager, *Market Wizards: Interviews with Top Traders*. Harper Collins, 1993.

5. Ludwig von Mises, *Human Action: A Treatise on Economics*. 4th revised ed. Irvington-on-Hudson, NY: The Foundation for Economic Education, Inc., 1996, printed 1998. First published 1949.

6. Barclay Trading Group, Ltd. *Barclay Managed Futures Report*. Vol. 3, No. 3 (Third quarter 1992), 3.

7. Allison Colter. Dow Jones. July 13, 2001.

8. *Trading System Review*, Futures Industry Association Conference, November 2, 1994.

9. Jack Schwager, *Getting Started in Technical Analysis*. John Wiley & Sons, 1999.

10. The History of rhe Motley Fool. Fool.com, November 4, 2003. See *www.fool.com*.

11. The State of the Industry. *Managed Account Reports, Inc*. June, 2000.

12. John Allen Paulos. *A Mathematician Plays the Stock Market*. Basic Books, 2003, 47.

13. Quantitative Strategy: Does Technical Analysis Work? Equity Research, Credit Suisse First Boston. September 25, 2002.

14. Daniel P. Collins in *Futures*, October 2003.

15. Disclosure Document. John W. Henry & Company, Inc. August 22, 2003.

6. Disclosure Document. John W. Henry & Company, Inc. August 22, 2003.

17. Carla Cavaletti, Top Traders Ride 1996 Trends. *Futures*. (March 1997), 68.

18. Jack Schwager, *Getting Started in Technical Analysis*. John Wiley & Sons, 1999.

19. Ginger Szala, Abraham Trading: Trend Following Earns Texas Sized Profits. *Futures* (March 1995), 61.

20. Desmond MacRae, Valuing trend-followers' returns. *Managed Account Reports*, Inc. No. 242 (April 1999), 12.

21. Speech given to financial consultants on November 17, 2000. See *www.jwh.com*.

22. Presentation in Geneva, Switzerland on September 15, 1998.

23. *Futures*. Vol.22, No.12 (November 1993), 98.

24. *AIMA Newsletter*, June 2001. Alternative Investment Management Association.

25. Morton S. Baratz, *The Investor's Guide to Futures Money Management*. Columbia MD: Futures Publishing Group, 1984

26. Guest Article, 249. *Managed Account Reports* (November 1999), 9.

27. Speech given to financial consultants on November 17, 2000. See *www.jwh.com*.

28. From Upstairs/Downstairs Seminar with Tom Baldwin. Futures Industry Association, 1994.

29. Performance Review, February 1999. John W Henry & Company, Inc.

30. Tass Twenty Traders Talk. Held June 29, 1996 at the Montreal Ritz Carlton Hotel in Montreal, Canada.

31. Jack Schwager, *Market Wizards: Interviews with Top Traders*. New York: Harper Business, 1989.

32. Riva Atlas, Macro, Macro Man. *Institutional Investor Magazine*. 1996.

33. Trend Following: Performance, Risk and Correlation Characteristics. White Paper. Graham Capital Management.

34. Trend Following: Performance, Risk and Correlation Characteristics. White Paper. Graham Capital Management.

35. Trends in Currency Markets: Which Way the $? *AIMA Newsletter*, June 2002. Alternative Investment Management Association.

36. The Trading Tribe at Seykota.com. See *www.seykota.com/tribe/*.

37. Mary Greenebaum, Funds: The New Way to Play Commodities. *Fortune*, November 19, 1979.

38. Brett N. Steenbarger, *The Psychology of Trading*. John Wiley and Sons, 2002, 316–.317.

39. Brenda Ueland, *How to Write*. 10th ed. Graywolf Press, 1997. First published 1938.

40. Bruce Cleland, Campbell and Co. Futures (March, 2004), 72.

41. David Whitford, *Why Owning the Boston Red Sox Is Like Running a Successful Hedgefund*. Fortune Small Business (October 25, 2003).

42. The Whizkid of Futures Trading. *Business Week* (December 6, 1982), 102.

43. Anonymous "Super Trader" in Van Tharp, Two Contrasting Super Traders.

Chapter 2

1. Jim Rogers, *Investment Biker*. New York: Random House, 1994.

2. Thomas Friedman, *The Lexus and the Olive Tree*. New York: Farrar, Straus and Giroux, 1999.

3. Daniel P. Collins, Seeding Tomorrow's Top Traders; Managed Money; Dunn Capital Management Provides Help to Commodity Trading Advisor Start-ups. *Futures*, No. 6, Vol. 32, 67, (May 1, 2003) ISSN: 0746-2468.

4. In J. R. Newman (ed.) *The World of Mathematics*. New York: Simon and Schuster, 1956.

5. Jim Collins, *Good to Great*, New York: HarperBusiness, 2001.

6. Robert Koppel, *The Intuitive Trader*. John Wiley and Sons, Inc., 1996, 74.

7. The Reason Foundation. See *www.reason.org*.

8. Daniel P. Collins, Seeding Tomorrow's Top Traders; Managed Money; Dunn Capital Management Provides Help to Commodity Trading Advisor Start-ups. *Futures*, No. 6, Vol. 32, 67, (May 1, 2003) ISSN: 0746-2468.

9. Tricycle Asset Management, part of the Market Wizards Tour. Held on May 15, 2003 in Saskatoon, Saskatchewan.

10. Tricycle Asset Management, part of the Market Wizards Tour. Held on May 15, 2003 in Saskatoon, Saskatchewan.

11. Tricycle Asset Management, part of the Market Wizards Tour. Held on May 15, 2003 in Saskatoon, Saskatchewan.

12. Amy Rosenbaum, 1990s Highs and Lows: Invasions, Persuasions and Volatility. *Futures*, Vol. 19, No. 14 (December, 1990), 54.

13. Andrew Osterland, For Commodity Funds, It Was as Good as It Gets. *Business Week* (September 14, 1998).

14. Jack Reerink, Dunn: Slow Reversal Pays Off. *Futures*, Vol. 25, No. 3 (March 1996).

15. Mike Mosser, Learning from Legends. *Futures*, Vol. 29, No. 2 (Feb. 2000).

16. How Managed Money Became a Major Area of the Industry; Futures Market. *Futures*, Vol. 21, No. 9 (July 1992), 52.

17. Daniel P. Collins, Bob Pardo: Perfecting a Model. *Futures*, Vol. 31, No.13 (October 2002), 90.

18. Denise G. Shekerjian, *Uncommon Genius*. New York: Penguin Books, 1990.

19. Mary Ann Burns, Industry Icons Assess the Managed Futures Business. *Futures Industry Association* (May/June 2003).

20. Jack Reerink, Dunn: Slow Reversal Pays Off. *Futures*, Vol. 25, No. 3 (March 1996).

21. Carla Cavaletti, Comeback Kids: Managing Drawdowns According to Commodity Trading Advisors. *Futures* Vol. 27, No. 1 (January, 1998), 68.

22. Excerpt from Dunn Capital Management Monthly Commentary for February 2003.

23. Barclay Trading Group, Ltd. *Barclay Managed Futures Report*. Vol. 3, No. 3 (Third quarter 1992), 2.

24. A Conversation with William Lipschutz and Daniel Dunn. Tricycle Asset Management Webcast Conference.

25. Monster.com Ad.

26. Disclosure Document. Dunn Capital Management.

27. Ginger Szala, John W. Henry: Long-term Perspective. *Futures* (1987).

28. Pallavi Gogoi, Placing Bets in a Volatile World. *BusinessWeek* (Sep 30, 2002).

29. Presentation in Geneva, Switzerland on September 15, 1998.

30. Lois Peltz, *The New Investment Superstars*. New York: John Wiley & Sons, Inc., 2001.

31. Mary Ann Burns, Industry Icons Assess the Managed Futures Business. *Futures Industry Association* (May/June 2003).

32. Mark S. Rzepczynski, John W. Henry & Co. Year in Review, December 2000

33. Oliver Conway, Cover story about John W. Henry & Company, Inc. *Managed Derivatives* (May 1996).

34. W.H. Auden and L. Kronenberger (eds.). *The Viking Book of Aphorisms*. New York: Viking Press, 1966.

35. Michael Peltz, John W. Henry's Bid to Manage the Future. *Institutional Investor* (August 1996).

36. Ginger Szala, John W. Henry: Long-term Perspective. *Futures* (1987).

37. Lois Peltz, *The New Investment Superstars*. New York: John Wiley & Sons, Inc., 2001.

38. Speech given to financial consultants on November 17, 2000. See *www.jwh.com*.

39. Lois Peltz, *The New Investment Superstars*. New York: John Wiley & Sons, Inc., 2001.

40. 2002 Year in Review. John W. Henry & Company, Inc.

41. Futures Industry Association Conference Seminar. Trading System Review, November 2, 1994.

42. John W. Henry, Morgan Stanley Dean Witter Achieve Conference. Naples, Florida, November 17, 2000

43. Presentation in Geneva, Switzerland on September 15, 1998.

44. Presentation in Geneva, Switzerland on September 15, 1998.

45. Presentation in Geneva, Switzerland on September 15, 1998.

46. FIA Research Division Dinner held in New York City on April 20, 1995.

47. Jack Schwager, *The Market Wizards*. New York: HarperBusiness, 1989, 172.

48. The Trading Tribe at Seykota.com. See *www.seyokota.com/tribe/*.

49. Email to *TurtleTrader.com*.

50. Daniel P. Collins, Long-term Technical Trend-following Method for Managed Futures Programs. *Futures*, Vol 30, No. 14 (November, 2001). 22.

51. The Trading Tribe at Seykota.com. See *www.seyokota.com/tribe/*.

52. Thom Hartle, ed., Ed Seykota of Technical Tools. Technical Analysis of *Stocks & Commodities*, Vol. 10, No. 8, (August 1992)328–331. (Used with permission; *www.traders.com*).

53. Van K. Tharp, *Trade Your Way to Financial Freedom*. New York: McGraw-Hill, 1999.

54. Thom Hartle, ed., Ed Seykota of Technical Tools. Technical Analysis of *Stocks & Commodities*, Vol. 10, No. 8, (August 1992) 328–331. (Used with permission; *www.traders.com*).

55. Thom Hartle, ed., Ed Seykota of Technical Tools. Technical Analysis of *Stocks & Commodities*, Vol. 10, No. 8, (August 1992) 328–331. (Used with permission; *www.traders.com*).

56. Thom Hartle, ed., Ed Seykota of Technical Tools. Technical Analysis of *Stocks & Commodities*, Vol. 10, No. 8, (August 1992) 328–331. (Used with permission; *www.traders.com*).

57. Shawn Tully, Princeton's Rich Commodity Scholars. *Fortune* (February 9, 1981), 94.

58. Jack Reerink, Hot New CTAs of 1995. *Futures*, Vol 24., No. 11 (October, 1995), 78.

59. The Trading Tribe at Seykota.com. See *www.seyokota.com/tribe/*.

60. *http://sysdyn.clexchange.org/sd-intro/home.html*.

61. Kelly, J. L., Jr., A New Interpretation of Information Rate. *Bell System Technical Journal* (July 1956), 917–926.

62. The Trading Tribe at Seykota.com. See *www.seyokota.com/tribe/*.

63. Jack Reerink, The Power of Leverage. *Futures*, Vol. 24, No. 4 (April 1995), 59.

64. Gibbons Burke, How to Tell a Market by Its Covers: Financial Market Predictions Based on Magazine Covers. *Futures*, Vol. 22, No. 4 (April 1993), 30.

65. Your Trading Edge. See *http://www.yte.com.au*.

66. Joe Niedzielski, Wild Market Swings Take Toll on Commodity Trading Advisers. *Dow Jones Newswires*, April 25, 2000.

67. H. Weyl, Mathematics and the Laws of Nature. In I. Gordon and S. Sorkin (eds.) *The Armchair Science Reader*. New York: Simon and Schuster, 1959.

68. Darrell R. Jobman, How Managed Money Became a Major Area of the Industry. *Futures* Vol. 21, No. 9 (July 1992), 52.

69. Futures Industry Association Conference Excerpt. Campbell and Company.

70. Mary Ann Burns, Industry Icons Assess the Managed Futures Business *Futures Industry Association* (May/June 2003).

71. Value of Adding Managed Futures. Marketing Documents. Campbell and Company.

72. 2003 Disclosure Document. Campbell and Company.

73. Desmond McRae, 31 year Track Record of 18.1%. *Managed Account Reports: Extracting Inherent Value from Managed Futures* (March 2003).

74. Barclay Trading Group, Ltd. *Barclay Managed Futures Report*. Vol. 2, No. 3 (Third quarter 1991), 2.

75. The Futures and Industry Association's Future and Options Expo '98. Held at the Sheraton Chicago Towers & Hotel in Chicago, Ill., on October 14–16, 1998.

76. The Futures and Industry Association's Future and Options Expo '98. Held at the Sheraton Chicago Towers & Hotel in Chicago, Ill., on October 14–16, 1998.

77. The Futures and Industry Association's Future and Options Expo '98. Held at the Sheraton Chicago Towers & Hotel in Chicago, Ill., on October 14–16, 1998.

78. The Futures and Industry Association's Future and Options Expo '98. Held at the Sheraton Chicago Towers & Hotel in Chicago, Ill., on October 14–16, 1998.

79. The Futures and Industry Association's Future and Options Expo '98. Held at the Sheraton Chicago Towers & Hotel in Chicago, Ill., on October 14–16, 1998.

80. Chuck Epstein, The World According to J. Parker. *Managed Account Reports* (November 1998).

81. Barclay Trading Group, Ltd. *Barclay Managed Futures Report*. Vol. 2, No. 3 (Third quarter 1991), 7.

82. Barclay Trading Group, Ltd. *Barclay Managed Futures Report*. Vol. 2, No. 3 (Third quarter 1991), 2.

83. Simon Romero, A Homespun Hedge Fund, Tucked Away in Texas. *New York Times*, December 28, 2003, Business, 1.

84. *Futures* (March 1995).

85. Simon Romero, A Homespun Hedge Fund, Tucked Away in Texas, *New York Times*, December 28, 2003, Business, 1.

86. See *www.abrahamtrading.com*.

87. Ayn Rand, *The Fountainhead*. New York: Bobbs-Merrill Company, 1943.

88. Simon Romero, A Homespun Hedge Fund, Tucked Away in Texas, *New York Times*, December 28, 2003, Business, 1.

89. Jack Schwager, *Market Wizards: Interviews with Top Traders*, New York: New York Institute of Finance, 1989.

90. Stanley W. Angrist, Commodities: Winning Commodity Traders May Be Made, Not Born. *The Wall Street Journal*, September 5, 1989.

91. Greg Burns, Rich Dennis: A Gunslinger No More. *Business Week* (April 7, 1997).

92. Susan Abbott, Richard Dennis: Turning a Summer Job into a Legend. *Futures* (September 1983), 58.

93. Susan Abbott, Richard Dennis: Turning a Summer Job into a Legend. *Futures* (September 1983), 59.

94. Susan Abbott, Richard Dennis: Turning a Summer Job into a Legend. *Futures* (September 1983), 57.

95. Susan Abbott, Richard Dennis: Turning a Summer Job into a Legend. *Futures* (September 1983), 58.

96. Paul Rabar, Managed Money: Capitalizing on the Trends of 1990, *Futures* Vol. 20, No. 3 (March 1991).

97. Jack Schwager, *Market Wizards: Interviews with Top Traders*, New York: New York Institute of Finance, 1989.

98. Barbara Dixon, Richard Donchian: Managed Futures Innovator and Mentor. *Futures Industry Association*.

99. William Baldwin, Rugs to Riches (Section: The Money Men), *Forbes*, (March 1, 1982).

100. Barbara Dixon, Richard Donchian: Managed Futures Innovator and Mentor. *Futures Industry Association*.

101. Barbara Dixon, Richard Donchian: Managed Futures Innovator and Mentor. *Futures Industry Association*.

102. Barbara Dixon, Richard Donchian: Managed Futures Innovator and Mentor. *Futures Industry Association*.

103. William Baldwin, Rugs to Riches (Section: The Money Men), *Forbes*, (March 1, 1982).

104. Barbara Dixon, Richard Donchian: Managed Futures Innovator and Mentor. *Futures Industry Association*.

105. William Baldwin, Rugs to Riches (Section: The Money Men), *Forbes*, (March 1, 1982).

106. Futures Industry Association Review: Interview: Money Managers. See *www.fiafii.org*.

107. Barbara S. Dixon—Discretionary Accounts. *Managed Account Reports*. Report No. 20, No. 14, 5.

108. Barbara S. Dixon—Discretionary Accounts. *Managed Account Reports*. Report No. 20, No. 14, 5.

109. Edwin Lefevre. *Reminiscences of a Stock Operator*. New York: George H. Doran Company, 1923.

110. Andrew Leckey, Dabble, Don't Dive, in Futures. *Chicago Tribune* Oct. 2, 1986, C1.

111. Dickson G. Watts, *Speculation as a Fine Art*. Reprint. Fraser Publishing Co., 1997.

Chapter 3

1. Sir Arthur Conan Doyle, "A Scandal in Bohemia" in *The Adventures of Sherlock Holmes*. New York: A. L. Burt, 1892.

2. Alexander M. Ineichen, *Absolute Returns*. New York, John Wiley and Sons, 2003, 19.

3. Disclosure Document. John W. Henry & Company, Inc., August 22, 2003.

4. BMFR. Barclay Trading Group (First Quarter 2003).

5. International Traders Research Star Ranking System Explanation. See *http://managedfutures.com*.

6. Ludwig von Mises, *Human Action: A Treatise on Economics*. 4th revised ed. Irvington-on-Hudson, NY: The Foundation for Economic Education, Inc., 1996, printed 1998. First published 1949.

7. Larry Harris, *Trading and Exchanges: Market Microstructure for Practioners*. New York: Oxford University Press, 2003.

8. David Greising, How Managed Funds Managed to Do So Poorly. *Business Week*, No. 3294 (Nov. 23, 1992), 112.

9. Daniel P. Collins, The Return of Long-term Trend Following. *Futures*, Vol. 32, No. 4 (March 2003), 68–73.

10. Desmond McRae, Top Traders. *Managed Derivatives* (May 1996).

11. Trend Following: Performance, Risk and Correlation Characteristics. White Paper, Graham Capital Management.

12. Larry Harris, *Trading and Exchanges: Market Microstructure for Practioners*. New York: Oxford University Press, 2003.

13. Ben Warwick, The Holy Grail of Managed Futures (cover story). *Managed Account Reports* (MAR), No. 267 (May, 2001), 1.

14. The Trading Tribe at Seykota.com. See *www.seyokota.com/tribe/*.

15. Definition from the Institutional Advisory Services Group (IASG). See *www.iasg.com*.

16. Laurie Kaplan, Turning Turtles into Traders. *Managed Derivatives* (May 1996).

17. Marketing Materials. Dunn Capital Management, Inc.

18. Carla Cavaletti, Comeback Kids; Managing Drawdowns According to Commodity Trading Advisors, *Futures*, Vol. 27, No. 1 (January 1998), 68.

19. Michael Peltz, John W. Henry's Bid to Manage the Future. *Institutional Investor* (August 1996).

20. D. Harding, G. Nakou and A. Nejjar, "The Pros and Cons of Drawdown as a Statistical Measure of Risk for Investments." *AIMA Journal*, April 2003, 16-17.

21. Carla Cavaletti, Comeback Kids: Managing Drawdowns According to Commodity Trading Advisors *Futures*, Vol. 27, No. 1 (January 1998), 68.

22. *The Value of a Long-Term Perspective*. Marketing Document. John W. Henry and Company, Inc. October 1999.

23. Carla Cavaletti, Comeback Kids: Managing Drawdowns According to Commodity Trading Advisors. *Futures*, Vol. 27, No. 1 (January 1998), 68.

24. Thomas F. Basso, When to Allocate to a CTA?—Buy Them on Sale.

25. New Fans for Managed Futures. *Euromoney Institutional Investor PLC* (February 1, 2003), 45.

26. InvestorWords.com. See *http://investorwords.com*.

27. Julius A. Staniewicz, Learning to Love Non-Correlation. Investor Support. John W. Henry and Company, Inc.

28. Ginger Szala, Tom Shanks: Former "Turtle" Winning Race the Hard Way. *Futures*, Vol. 20, No. 2 (Jan. 15, 1991), 78.

29. Carla Cavaletti, Turtles on the Move. *Futures Magazine*, Vol. 27 (June 1998), 79.

30. Laurie Kaplan, Turning Turtles into Traders. *Managed Derivatives* (May 1996).

31. Larry Harris, *Trading and Exchanges: Market Microstructure for Practioners*. New York: Oxford University Press, 2003.

32. Larry Harris, The Winners and Losers of the Zero-Sum Game: The Origins of Trading Profits, Price Efficiency and Market Liquidity. Draft 0.911, May 7, 1993.

33. Larry Harris, The Winners and Losers of the Zero-Sum Game: The Origins of Trading Profits, Price Efficiency and Market Liquidity. Draft 0.911, May 7, 1993.

34. Larry Harris, The Winners and Losers of the Zero-Sum Game: The Origins of Trading Profits, Price Efficiency and Market Liquidity. Draft 0.911, May 7, 1993.

35. Danny Hakim, Huge Losses Move Soros to Revamp Empire. *The New York Times*. May 1, 2000.

36. Enoch Cheng. "Of Markets and Morality . . ." *Café Bagola* weblog, August 27, 2002. See *http://bagola.blogspot.com/ 2002_08_25_bagola_archive.html*.

37. Ayn Rand, "Philosophical Detection," *Philosophy: Who Needs It?* Edited by Leonard Peiikoff. Indianapolis: Bobbs-Merrill, 1998.

38. Written Testimony Submitted for the Record of Lawrence Parks, Executive Director, The Foundation for the Advancement of Monetary Education. Before the Subcommittee on Capital Markets, Securities, and GSE's; House Committee on Banking and Financial Services, United States House of Representatives. Hearing on Hedge Funds, March 3, 1999.

39. Danny Hakim, Huge Losses Move Soros to Revamp Empire. *The New York Times*. May 1, 2000.

40. Danny Hakim, Huge Losses Move Soros to Revamp Empire. *The New York Times*. May 1, 2000.

41. In re Merrill Lynch & Co. Inc. Research Reports Securities Litigation, 02 MDL 1484. Ruling by Federal Judge Milton Pollack dismissing class-action claims brought against Merrill Lynch & Co. and its former analyst Henry Blodgett.

42. Gregory J. Millman, The Chief Executive (Jan.–Feb. 2003).

43. Bill Dries, Futures (August, 1995), 78.

Chapter 4

1. Nassim Taleb, *Fooled by Randomness*. New York: Texere, 2001.

2. Herb Greeenberg, Answering the Question—Who Wins From Derivatives Losers. *The San Francisco Chronicle*, March 20, 1995, D1.

3. Herb Greeenberg, Answering the Question—Who Wins From Derivatives Losers. *The San Francisco Chronicle*, March 20, 1995, D1.

4. Alexander M. Ineichen, *Absolute Returns*. New York: John Wiley and Sons, 2003, 416.

5. Michael J. Mauboussin and Kristen Bartholdson, Integrating the Outliers: Two Lessons from the St. Petersburg Paradox. *The Consilient Observer*. Vol. 2, No. 2 (Credit Suisse First Boston, Jan. 28, 2003).

6. Jason Russell. See *www.jrussellcapital.com*.

7. Trend Following: Performance, Risk and Correlation Characteristics. White Paper, Graham Capital Management.

8. Thomas S. Y. Ho and Sang Bin Lee, *The Oxford Guide to Financial Modeling*. Oxford University Press, 2004, 559.

9. Ginger Szala, Barings Abyss. *Futures*, Vol. 24, No. 5 (May 1995), 68.

10. John W. Henry & Company, Inc., 1998 Corporate Brochure. See *www.jwh.com*.

11. Mark S. Rzepczynski, President, John W. Henry and Co., Presentation. See *www.jwh.com*.

12. Erin E. Arvedlund, Swinging for the Fences: John W. Henry's Managed Futures Funds Are Striking Out. *Barrons* (Dec. 4, 2000).

13. Speech given to financial consultants on November 17, 2000. See *www.jwh.com*.

14. Erin E. Arvedlund, Whiplash! Commodity-Trading Advisers Post Sharp Gains *Barrons* (Jan. 15, 2001).

15. Fast Finish Makes 2000 a Winner. *Managed Account Reports*, No. 263 (January 2001).

16. Speech given to financial consultants on November 17, 2000. See *www.jwh.com*.

17. Pallavi Gogoi, Placing Bets in a Volatile World. *Businessweek* (Sep. 30, 2002).

18. Email to *TurtleTrader.com*.

19. Barclay Managed Futures Report. Barclay Trading Group (Fourth Quarter 2002).

20. Larry Swedroe, Buckingham Asset Management. See: *http://www.bamstl.com/*.

21. The Trading Tribe at Seykota.com. See *www.seyokota.com/tribe/*.

22. Paul Barr, Trending Markets Lead to Profit: September 11 example will go in case studies. *Money Management World* (Sept. 25, 2001).

23. Trillion Dollar Bet. *Nova*, No. 2075. Airdate: Feb. 8, 2000.

24. Broadcast Transcript, Trillion Dollar Bet. *Nova*, No. 2075. Airdate: Feb. 8, 2000.

25. Kevin Dowd, Too Big to Fail? Long-Term Capital Management and the Federal Reserve. Cato Institute Briefing Paper, No. 52 (September 23, 1999).

26. Roger Lowenstein, *When Genius Failed*. New York: Random House, 2000, 34.

27. Roger Lowenstein, *When Genius Failed*. New York: Random House, 2000, 69.

28. Roger Lowenstein, *When Genius Failed*. New York: Random House, 2000, 69.

29. Clay Harris and Wiliam Hall, Top-Tier Departures Expected at UBS. *Financial Times: London Edition* (October 2, 1998), 26.

30. Organization for Economic Cooperation and Development, The LTCM crisis and its Consequences for Banks and Banking Supervision, June 1999.

31. The Futures and Industry Association's Future and Options Expo '98, Held at the Sheraton Chicago Towers & Hotel in Chicago, Ill. on October 14–16 1998.

32. Presentation in Geneva, Switzerland on September 15, 1998.

33. Broadcast Transcript, Trillion Dollar Bet. *Nova*, No. 2075. Airdate: Feb. 8, 2000.

34. See *www.pbs.org*.

35. Roger Lowenstein, *When Genius Failed*. New York: Random House, 2000, 71.

36. Andrew Osterland, For Commodity Funds, It Was as Good as it Gets. *Businessweek* (Sep. 14, 1998).

37. John W. Meriwether, Letter to Investors, September 1998.

38. Broadcast Transcript, Trillion Dollar Bet. *Nova*, No. 2075. Airdate: Feb. 8, 2000.

39. Bruce Cleland, Campbell and Co., The State of the Industry. *Managed Account Reports*, Inc. (June, 2000).

40. Robert Lenzner, Archimedes on Wall Street. *Forbes* (October 19, 1998).

41. Kevin Dowd, Too Big to Fail? Long-Term Capital Management and the Federal Reserve. Cato Institute Briefing Paper, No. 52 (September 23, 1999).

42. Malcolm Gladwell, *The New Yorker*, April 22 & 29, 2002.

43. G. K. Chesterton, "The Point of a Pin" in *The Scandal of Father Brown*. London, Cassell and Company, 1935.

44. Philip W. Anderson, "Some Thoughts About Distribution in Economics," in W. B. Arthur, S. N. Durlaf, and D.A. Lane, eds. *The Economy as an Evolving Complex System II*. Reading, MA: Addison-Wesley, 1997, 566.

45. Dan Colarusso, Gray Monday's First Casualty: Famed Soros Confidant Victor Niederhoffer. *TheStreet.com* (Oct. 29, 1997).

46. Mark Etzkorn. Bill Dunn and Pierre Tullier: The Long Run (Trader Profile). *Futures*, Vol. 26, No. 2 (Feb. 1997).

47. David Henry, *USA Today*, October 30, 1997.

48. *http://www.thestreet.com/funds/fwfeatures/626822.html*.

49. Source: *Barclay Managed Futures Report*.

50. Mark Etzkorn, Bill Dunn and Pierre Tullier: The Long Run (Trader Profile). *Futures*, Vol. 26, No. 2 (Feb. 1997).

51. Source: *The Stark Report* (Second Quarter 1997).

52. Greg Burns, Whatever Voodoo He Uses, It Works: Trader Victor Niederhoffer Is as Eccentric as He is Contrarian. *Businessweek* (Feb. 10, 1997).

53. Greg Burns, Whatever Voodoo He Uses, It Works: Trader Victor Niederhoffer Is as Eccentric as He is Contrarian. *Businessweek* (Feb. 10, 1997).

54. George Soros. *Soros on Soros*. New York: John Wiley & Sons, 1995.

55. Victor Niederhoffer and Laurel Kenner, Why the Trend Is Not Your Friend. *The Speculator: MSN Money* (May 2, 2002). See *moneycentral.msn.com*.

56. Victor Niederhoffer and Laurel Kenner, *Practical Speculation*. Hoboken, NJ: John Wiley and Sons, Inc., 2003, 74.

57. Victor Niederhoffer and Laurel Kenner, *Practical Speculation*. Hoboken, NJ: John Wiley and Sons, Inc., 2003, 2.

58. Victor Niederhoffer, *The Education of a Speculator*. New York: John Wiley & Sons, 1997.

59. Greg Burns, Whatever Voodoo He Uses, It Works: Trader Victor Niederhoffer Is as Eccentric as He Is Contrarian. *Businessweek* (Feb. 10, 1997).

60. Malcolm Gladwell, *The New Yorker*, April 22 & 29, 2002.

61. Report of the Inspectors of Barings Futures (Singapore) PTE, Ltd.

62. Source: IFCI International Financial Risk Institute.

63. Mark Hawley, Dean Witter Managed Futures, Futures Industry Association Dinner, New York City, April 20, 1995.

64. Presentation in Geneva, Switzerland on September 15, 1998.

65. Sharon Reier, Easy to Beat Up, Hard to Kill. *The International Herald Tribune* (March 23, 2002). See *www.iht.com*.

66. Ed Krapels, Re-examining the Metallgesellschaft Affair and its Implication for Oil Traders. *Special Report Oil & Gas Journal* (March 26, 2001).

67. Ed Krapels, Re-examining the Metallgesellschaft Affair and its Implication for Oil Traders. *Special Report Oil & Gas Journal* (March 26, 2001).

68. John Digenan, Dan Felson, Robert Kelly, and Ann Wiemert, Metallgesellschaft AG: A Case Study. *The Journal of Research and Ideas on Financial Markets and Trading*, Stuart School of Business, Illinois Institute of Technology.

69. Lewis Carroll, *Through the Looking Glass*, 1872.

70. The Value of a JWH Investment as a Portfolio Diversifier. Marketing Materials. John W. Henry and Company, September 1998.

71. Marketing Materials. John W. Henry and Company, September 1998.

72. Barclay Trading Group, Ltd., Technical vs. Fundamental: How Do Traders Differ? *Barclay Managed Futures Report*, Vol. 2, No. 3 (2000).

73. Sir Arthur Conan Doyle, *The Sign of Four*. London and New York: Pitman and Sons, 1890.

74. Christopher L. Culp, *Media Nomics* (April, 1995), 4.

75. The Coming Storm, *The Economist* (February 17, 2004), see *www.economist.com/buttonwood*.

76. Emanuel Derman, *The Journal of Derivatives* (Winter, 2000), 64.

77. Frederic Townsend, *Futures* (December, 2000), 75.

78. Another Two Bites the Dust. *Derivative Strategies* (May 16, 1994), 7.

Chapter 5

1. Michael J. Mauboussin and Kristen Bartholdson, The Babe Ruth Effect: Frequency versus Magnitude *The Consilient Observer*. Vol. 1, No. 2 (Credit Suisse First Boston, January 29, 2002).

2. Michael Lewis, *Moneyball: The Art of Winning an Unfair Game*. New York: W.W. Norton and Company, 2003.

3. Michael Lewis, *Moneyball: The Art of Winning an Unfair Game*. New York: W.W. Norton and Company, 2003.

4. Michael Lewis, *Moneyball: The Art of Winning an Unfair Game*. New York: W.W. Norton and Company, 2003.

5. The Trading Tribe at Seykota.com. See *www.seyokota.com/tribe/*.

6. Earnshaw Cook, *Percentage Baseball*. Baltimore: Waverly Press, 1964.

7. Rob Neyer, A New Kind of Baseball Owner. *ESPN.com*, August 15, 2002.

8. Richard Driehaus, Unconventional Wisdom in the Investment Process. Speech given in 1994.

9. John Dorschner, Boca Raton, Fla.-Based Firm Is a Standout in Futures. *The Miami Herald*, January 27, 2001.

10. Greg Burns, Former 'Turtle' Turns Caution into an Asset. *Chicago Sun-Times*, May 29, 1989, 33.

11. Rob Neyer, Examining the Art of Evaluating: Q&A with Michael Lewis. *ESPN.com*, May 13, 2003.

12. Michael Lewis, *Moneyball: The Art of Winning an Unfair Game*. New York: W.W. Norton and Company, 2003.

13. James Surowiecki, The Buffett of Baseball. *The New Yorker* (Sept. 23, 2002).

14. Rob Neyer, Red Sox Hire James in Advisory Capacity. *ESPN.com*, Nov. 7, 2002.

15. Bill James, Red Sox Hire. *Baseball Abstract*. *USA Today*, Nov. 15, 2002.

16. James Surowiecki, The Buffett of Baseball. *The New Yorker* (Sept. 23, 2002).

17. Ben McGrath, The Professor of Baseball. *The New Yorker* (July 14, 2003), 38.

18. John W. Henry, quoted in *The New York Times*, Sept. 26, 2002.

19. Rob Neyer, Red Sox Hire James in Advisory Capacity. *ESPN.com*, Nov. 7, 2002.

20. Jon Birger, Baseball by the Numbers. *Money* (April, 2003), 110.

21. Jon Birger, Baseball by the Numbers. *Money* (April, 2003), 110.

22. Jon Birger, Baseball by the Numbers. *Money* (April, 2003), 110.

23. Thomas Boswell, Evaluation by Numbers Is Beginning to Add Up. *Washington Post*, May 29, 2003, D01.

24. Jon Birger, Baseball by the Numbers. *Money* (April, 2003), 110.

25. Rob Neyer, Red Sox Hire James in Advisory Capacity. *ESPN.com*, Nov. 7, 2002.

26. Eric Perlmutter, Little Not Big Enough for Sox. *The Brown Daily Herald*, October 29, 2003.

27. Michael Lewis, Out of Their Tree. *Sports Illustrated* Vol. 100 No. 9 (March 1, 2004), 7.

28. Stephen Jay Gould, *Triumph and Tragedy in Mudville: A Lifelong Passion for Baseball*. New York: W.W. Norton and Company, 2003, 176–177.

29. Stephen Jay Gould, *Triumph and Tragedy in Mudville: A Lifelong Passion for Baseball*. New York: W.W. Norton and Company, 2003, 176–177.

30. Jeff Merron, The Worst Sports Moves of 2003. *Espn.com*.

31. In H. Eves, *Mathematical Circles Squared*. Boston: Prindle, Weber and Schmidt, 1972.

Chapter 6

1. *Financial Trader*, Vol. 1, No. 7 (Sept./Oct. 1994), 26.2.

2. Jason Russell, Hedgehogcapital.com. See *www.hedgehogcapital.com*.

3. Gerard Jackson, *Brookesnews.com*, April 21, 2003.

4. Jason Zweig, Do You Sabotage Yourself? *Business 2.0* (May 2001).

5. David Dreman, *Contrarian Investment Strategies*. New York: Simon & Schuster; 1998.

6. Lao Tsu, Verse XXXIII, *Tao Te Ching*.

7. Steven Pearlstein, The New Thinking about Money Is That Your Irrationality Is Predictable. *The Washington Post*, Jan 27, 2002, H01.

8. Daniel Goleman, What Makes a Leader? *Harvard Business Review*, 1998.

9. Harris Collingwood, The Sink or Swim Economy. *The New York Times*, June 8, 2003.

10. Jack D. Schwager, *The New Market Wizards*. New York: HarperBusiness, 1992.

11. Ayn Rand, *Atlas Shrugged*. New York: Random House, 1957.

12. *Animal House*. Universal Pictures, 1978. Written by Harold Ramis, Douglas Kenney, and Chris Miller.

13. Daneen Skube, Self Knowledge Keys. *The Seattle Times*, 2002.

14. *Futures*, Vol. 22, No. 12. (November 1993), 98.

15. Alexis de Tocqueville, *Democracy in America*. New York: G. Dearborn and Co., 1838.

16. Daniel Goleman, *Emotional Intelligence*. New York: Bantam, 1995.

17. Daniel Goleman, "What Makes a Leader?" *Harvard Business Review*, 1998.

18. Daniel Goleman, "What Makes a Leader?" *Harvard Business Review*, 1998.

19. Ayn Rand, *Atlas Shrugged*. New York: Random House, 1957.

20. Denise G. Shekerjian, *Uncommon Genius*. New York: Penguin Books, 1990.

21. Daniel Goleman, "What Makes a Leader?" *Harvard Business Review*, 1998.

22. Tom Girard, The Wizards Cast a Spell, *Financial Trader*, No. 4 (July 1995).

23. Gustave Le Bon, *The Crowd: A Study of the Popular Mind*. London: T.F. Unwin, 1925.

24. Ayn Rand, *Atlas Shrugged*. New York: Random House, 1957.

25. Tom Girard, The Wizards Cast a Spell, *Financial Trader*, No. 4 (July 1995).

26. Tom Girard, The Wizards Cast a Spell, *Financial Trader*, No. 4 (July 1995).

27. Jack D. Schwager, *The New Market Wizards*. New York: HarperBusiness, 1992, 416.

28. The Trading Tribe at Seykota.com. See *www.seykota.com/tribe/*.

29. Ludwig Von Mises, *Human Action*. New Haven, CT: Yale University Press, 1963.

30. Jack Schwager, *Getting Started in Technical Analysis*. New York: John Wiley & Sons, 1999.

31. Robert Koppel, *The Intuitive Trader*. New York: John Wiley and Sons, Inc, 1996, 74.

32. David Nusbaum, Mind Games; Trading Behavior. *Futures*, Vol. 23, No. 6 (June 1994), 60.

33. Michelle Conlin, *Businessweek* (Jun. 30, 2003).

34. Michael J. Mauboussin and Kristen Bartholdson, All Systems Go: Emotion and Intuition in Decision-Making. *The Consilient Observer*, Vol. 3, No. 2 (January 27, 2004).

35. Jack D. Schwager, *The New Market Wizards*. New York: HarperBusiness, 1992.

36. Michael Crichton, *The Lost World*. New York: Knopf, 1995.

37. Educated in England, Lee Kuan Yew led Singapore to independence and served as its first prime minister. He was regularly re-elected from 1959 until he stepped down in 1990. Under his guidance, Singapore became a financial and industrial powerhouse, despite a lack of abundant natural resources.

38. Alan Greenberg, *Memos from the Chairman*. New York: Workman Publishing, 1996.

39. Anna Muoio, All The Right Moves—If You See a Good Idea, Look for a Better One. *Fast Company*, No. 24 (May 1999), 192.

40. Jason Russell. See *www.jrussellcapital.com*.

41. Robert B. Zajonc, Feeling and Thinking: Preferences Need No Inferences, *American Psychologist*, 35, 1980, 151–175.

42. Antonio R. Damasio, *Descartes' Error: Emotion, Reason, and the Human Brain*. (New York: Avon Books, 1994), xii.

Chapter 7

1. Lewis Carroll, *Alice's Adventures in Wonderland*. 1865.

2. Gerd Gigerenzer and Peter M. Todd, *Simple Heuristics That Make Us Smart*. New York: Oxford University Press, 1999, 28.

3. Robert Rubin, Harvard Commencement Address before the graduating class of 2001. See *www.commencement.harvard. edu/2001/rubin.html*.

4. Carla Fried, The Problem with Your Investment Approach. *Business 2.0* (November 2003), 146.

5. *Seykota.com*.

6. Thomas A. Stewart, How to Think With Your Gut, *Business 2.0* (November 2002). See *http://www.business20.com/articles/mag/print/ 0,1643,44584,FF.html*.

7. See *www.2think.org*.

8. Gerd Gigerenzer and Peter M. Todd, *Simple Heuristics That Make Us Smart*. New York: Oxford University Press, 1999, 14.

9. Stephen Hawking, *A Brief History of Time*. New York: Bantam Books, 1988.

10. Gerd Gigerenzer and Peter M. Todd, *Simple Heuristics That Make Us Smart*. New York: Oxford University Press, 1999, 358.

11. *Futures*, Vol.22, No.12 (November 1993), 98.

12. Gerd Gigerenzer and Peter M. Todd, *Simple Heuristics That Make Us Smart*. New York: Oxford University Press, 1999, 361.

13. Gerd Gigerenzer, Smart Heuristics. Edge Foundation, Inc., March 31, 2003. See *www.edge.org*.

14. Bruce Bower, For Sweet Decisions, Mix a Dash of Knowledge with a Cup of Ignorance. *Science News*, Vol. 155, No. 22 (May 29, 1999). See *www.sciencenews.org*.

15. Presentation before the New York Mercantile Exchange.

16. Anna Muoio, All The Right Moves—If You See a Good Idea, Look for a Better One. *Fast Company*, No. 24 (May 1999), 192.

17. Market Commentary. John W. Henry and Company.

18. Daniel P. Collins, Building a Stronger Fort (Trader Profile: Yves Balcer and Sanjiv Kumar). *Futures*, Vol. 21, No. 6 (May 1, 2003), 82.

19. Gerd Gigerenzer, Smart Heuristics. Edge Foundation, Inc., March 31, 2003. See *www.edge.org*.

20. David Leonhardt, Caution Is Costly, Scholars Say. *The New York Times,* July 30, 2003.

21. Clayton M. Christensen, *The Innovator's Dilemma*. Boston: Harvard Business School Press, 1997.

22. Tom Girard, The Wizards Cast a Spell, *Financial Trader*, No. 4 (July 1995).

23. Michael J. Mauboussin and Kristen Bartholdson, Be the House: Process and Outcome in Investing. *The Consilient Observer*, Vol. 2, No. 19 (Credit Suisse First Boston, Oct. 7, 2003).

24. J. Edward Russo and Paul J. H. Schoemaker, *Winning Decisions*. New York: Doubleday, 2002.

Chapter 8

1. Thomas Harris, *The Silence of the Lambs*. New York: St. Martin's Press, 1988.

2. Definition of physics taken from *Webster's Revised Unabridged Dictionary*. Springfield, MA: G.C. Merriam, 1913.

3. The Trading Tribe at Seykota.com. See *www.seyokota.com/tribe/*.

4. Jessica James and Neil Johnson, Physics and Finance. *Visions: Briefing Papers for Policy Makers*. Institute of Physics and IOP Publishing Ltd., 1999–2000.

5. Pierre Simon, Marquis de LaPlace, *Theorie Analytique des Probabilites*, 1812.

6. See *www.criticalthinking.org*.

7. See *www.criticalthinking.org*.

8. Darrell Huff, *How to Take a Chance*. New York: W.W. Norton and Company, 1959.

9. Manus J. Donahue III, An Introduction to Chaos Theory and Fractal Geometry, 1997. See *www.duke.edu/~mjd/chaos/chaosh.html*.

10. Donald Rumsfeld, Secretary of Defense, 2003. *Washington Post* Editorial 2003.

11. Gerd Gigerenzer, Smart Heuristics. Edge Foundation, Inc., March 31, 2003. See *www.edge.org*.

12. Elementary Concepts in Statistics. See *http://statsoftinc.com/textbook/stathome.html*.

13. National Institute of Standards and Technology. See *www.itl.nist.gov*.

14. Michael J. Mauboussin and Kristen Bartholdson, A Tail of Two Worlds, Fat Tails and Investing. *The Consilient Observer*, Vol. 1, No. 7 (Credit Suisse First Boston, Apr. 9, 2002).

15. Lux, Ha, The Secret World of Jim Simons. *Institutional Investor*, Vol. 34, No. 11 (November 1, 2000), 38.

16. Lux, Ha, The Secret World of Jim Simons. *Institutional Investor*, Vol. 34, No. 11 (November 1, 2000), 38.

17. Jerry Parker, The State of the Industry. *Managed Account Reports, Inc.* (June, 2000).

18. Daniel P. Collins, Chenier: Systematizing What Works (Trader Profile). *Futures*, Vol. 32, No. 9 (July 1, 2003), 86.

19. Roger Lowenstein, *Wall Street Journal*, June 13, 2003.

20. Benoit B. Mandelbrot, A Multifractal Walk Down Wall Street. *Scientific American*, Vol. 280, No. 2 (Feb. 1999), 70–73.

21. Larry Swedroe, Buckingham Asset Management. See *http://www.bamstl.com/*.

22. Larry Swedroe, Buckingham Asset Management. See *http://www.bamstl.com/*.

23. Mark Rzepczynski, Ph.D., Return Distribution Properties of JWH Investment Programs, Stock and Bond Indices, and Hedge Funds. John W. Henry and Co., No. V, June 2000.

24. National Institute of Standards and Technology. See *www.itl.nist.gov*.

25. National Institute of Standards and Technology. See *www.itl.nist.gov*.

26. Jim Rogers, *Investment Biker*. New York: Random House, 1994.

27. Larry S. Liebovitch, Two Lessons from Fractals and Chaos. *Complexity*, Vol. 5, No. 4 (2000), 34–43.

28. The Paula Gordon Show. See *http://www.paulagordon.com/shows/bak/*.

Chapter 9

1. Of Pimps, Punters and Equities. *The Economist* (March 24, 2001).

2. *Crossfire*. CNN (Dec. 21, 1999).

3. Richard Rudy, Buy and Hold: A Different Perspective. *Barclay Managed Futures Research* (Fourth quarter 2001).

4. Buy it now! For a fine keepsake of the internet boom! Review of *Dow 36000* by James Glassman, Amazon.com., November 7, 2001.

5. Jerry Parker, The State of the Industry. *Managed Account Reports, Inc.* (June, 2000).

6. Richard Rudy, Buy and Hold: A Different Perspective. *Barclay Managed Futures Research* (Fourth quarter 2001).

7. *http://www.fool.com/boringport/2000/boringport000501.htm.*

8. William R. Gallacher, *Winner Take All*. New York: McGraw-Hill, 1994.

9. David Dukcevich. *Forbes* (May 6, 2002).

10. James Cramer, Host, CNBC, Kudlow and Cramer. Yahoo! Chat, September 7, 2000.

11. News Release. Berkshire Hathaway, Inc. May 22, 2002.

12. *Washington Post*, March 6, 2003, E01.

13. James K. Glassman, *Washington Post*, Dec. 9, 2001.

14. *Moneyline*. CNN (Dec. 23, 1999).

15. James K. Glassman, *Washington Post*, Feb, 17, 2002.

16. *Street Sweep*. CNN (Apr. 4, 2000).

17. Jennifer Karchmer, Tiger Management Closes: Julian Robertson Plans to Return Money to Shareholders after Losses in Value Stocks. *CNNfn*, March 30, 2000: 6:59 p.m. EST.

18. Aaron L. Task, Requiem for a Heavyweight. *TheStreet.com.*

19. *Larry King Live. CNN* (March 2001).

20. Edward Clendaniel, After the Sizzle Comes the Fizzle. *Forbes.com*, Mar. 25, 2002.

21. Allan Sloan, *Washington Post*, Mar. 26, 2002, E01.

22. Alan Abelson, Up and Down Wall Street. *Barrons*, Monday, December 15, 2003.

23. See *http://www.charlotte.com/mld/observer/business/3560508.htm.*

24. David Rode and Satu Parikh, An Evolutionary Approach to Technical Trading and Capital Market Efficiency. The Wharton School, University of Pennsylvania, May 1, 1995.

25. The Trading Tribe at Seykota.com. See *www.seykota.com.*

26. See *http://www.turtletrader.com/images/merrill.gif* to view this direct mail marketing flyer.

27. Jerry Garcia and Robert Hunter, "Casey Jones." Originally appears on The Grateful Dead, *Workingman's Dead,* 1970.

28. David Whitford, Why Owning the Boston Red Sox Is Like Running a Successful Hedge Fund. *Fortune Small Business* (October 25, 2003).

29. Dave Barry. February 3, 2002.

Chapter 10

1. The Trading Tribe at Seykota.com. See *www.seykota.com.*

2. Marketing Materials. Dunn Capital Management, Inc.

3. Leon G. Cooperman, CNBC Interview with Ron Insana. Leon G. Cooperman founded Omega Advisors, Inc., a $3.5 billion hedge fund based in New York City. Prior to starting Omega, Mr. Cooperman spent 25 years at Goldman, Sachs & Co., where he was a General Partner, and Chairman & Chief Executive Officer of Goldman's Asset Management division. Mr. Cooperman received his MBA from Columbia University and his undergraduate degree from Hunter College.

4. Commencement address given before the graduating class of 1989, University of Georgia, June 17, 1989.

5. Gibbons Burke, Managing Your Money. *Active Trader* (July 2000).

6. Mark Rzepczynski, Portfolio Diversification: Investors Just Don't Seem to Have Enough. *JWH Journal*.

7. Jack Reerink, The Power of Leverage, *Futures*, Vol. 24, No. 4 (April 1995).

8. Edward O. Thorp, *The Mathematics of Gambling*. Hollywood CA, 1984.

9. Larry Harris, *Trading and Exchanges: Market Microstructure for Practioners*. New York: Oxford University Press, 2003.

10. Going Once, Going Twice. *Discover* (August 2002), 23.

11. Jim Little, Sol Waksman, A Perspective on Risk. *Barclay Managed Futures Report*.

12. Craig Pauley, How to Become a CTA. Based on Chicago Mercantile Exchange Seminars, 1992–1994. June 1994.

13. Monthly Commentary. Dunn Capital Management, Inc.

14. Monthly Commentary. Dunn Capital Management, Inc.

15. Thomas L. Friedman, *The Lexus and The Olive Tree*. New York: Farrar, Straus, Giroux, 1999.

16. Gibbons Burke, Managing Your Money. *Active Trader* (July 2000).

17. Craig Pauley, How to Become a CTA. Based on Chicago Mercantile Exchange Seminars, 1992–1994. June 1994.

18. Ed Seykota and Dave Druz, Determining Optimal Risk. *Technical Analysis of Stocks and Commodities Magazine*, Vol. 11, No. 3, March 1993. 122–124. See *www.traders.com*. Used with permission.

19. Gibbons Burke, Gain Without Pain: Money Management in Action. *Futures*, Vol. 21, No. 14 (December 1992), 36.

20. Tom Basso, How to Become a CTA. Based on Chicago Mercantile Exchange Seminars, 1992–1994. June 1994.

21. Carla Cavaletti, Comeback Kids: Managing Drawdowns According to Commodity Trading Advisors. *Futures*, Vol. 27, No. 1 (January, 1998), 68.

22. Michael Peltz, John W. Henry's Bid to Manage the Future. *Institutional Investor* (August 1996).

23. InterMarket, *The Worldwide Futures and Options Report*. Chicago: InterMarket Publishing Group, July 1984.

24. The Trading Tribe at Seykota.com. See *www.seykota.com*.

25. Oliver Conway, Cover story about John W. Henry & Company, Inc. *Managed Derivatives* (May 1996).

26. Ted Williams, *The Science of Hitting*. New York: Simon & Schuster, 1986, 7.

27. Desmond McRae, 31 Year Track Record of 18.1%. *Managed Account Reports: Extracting Inherent Value from Managed Futures* (March 2003).

28. Daniel Colton, Trading the Pain Threshold (Trader Profile: Mark van Stolk). *Futures*. Nov. 2003, 98.

29. Ludwig von Mises, *Human Action: A Treatise on Economics*. 4th revised ed. Irvington-on-Hudson, NY: The Foundation for Economic Education, Inc., 1996, printed 1998. First published 1949.

30. Ellyn E. Spragins, Gary Weiss, and Stuart Weiss, Contrarians. *Business Week*, The Best of 1986 (Dec. 29, 1986), 74.

31. *Washington Post*, Dec. 9, 2001.

32. Jack D. Schwager, *The New Market Wizards*. New York: HarperBusiness, 1992.

33. Jerry Parker, The State of the Industry. *Managed Account Reports, Inc.* (June, 2000).

34. Bruce Terry, *Managed Account Reports* (September 2001).

35. Morton Baratz, Do Trend Followers Distort Futures Prices? *Managed Account Reports*, No. 43, 9.

36. Sharon Schwartzman, Computers Keep Funds in Mint Condition: A Major Money Manager Combines the Scientific Approach with Human Ingenuity, *Wall Street Computer Review*, Vol. 8, No. 6 (March 1991), 13.

37. Sharon Schwartzman, Computers Keep Funds in Mint Condition: A Major Money Manager Combines the Scientific Approach with Human Ingenuity. *Wall Street Computer Review*, Vol. 8, No. 6 (March 1991), 13.

38. Thomas L Friedman, *The Lexus and the Olive Tree*. New York: Farrar, Straus, Giroux, 1999.

39. Barclay Trading Group, Ltd., *Barclay Managed Futures Report*, Vol. 4, No. 1 (First quarter 1993), 3.

40. Barclay Trading Group, Ltd., *Barclay Managed Futures Report*, Vol. 4, No. 1 (First quarter 1993), 10.

41. Presentation in Geneva, Switzerland on September 15, 1998.

42. Trading System Review. Futures Industry Association Conference Seminar on November 2, 1994.

43. Tom Basso, How to Become a CTA. Based on Chicago Mercantile Exchange Seminars, 1992–1994. June 1994.

44. Leo Melamed, *Escape to the Futures*. New York: John Wiley and Sons, 1996.

Chapter 11

1. The Trading Tribe at Seykota.com. See *www.seykota.com*.

2. Alexander M. Ineichen, *Absolute Returns*. New York: John Wiley and Sons, 2003, 64.

3. Keith Campbell, Campbell & Co., *Managed Account Reports*.

4. Carla Cavaletti, Turtles on the Move, *Futures*, Vol. 27, No. 6 (June 1998), 77.

5. Jerry Parker, The State of the Industry. *Managed Account Reports, Inc.* (June, 2000).

6. Thomas Scheeweis, Dealing with Myths of Hedge Fund Investment. *The Journal of Alternative Investments* (Winter 1998).

7. Who's to Blame Next? *Asterias Info-Invest*, Editoral. London, Asterias, Ltd.

8. Jerry Parker, The State of the Industry. *Managed Account Reports, Inc.* (June, 2000).

9. Carla Cavaletti, Comeback Kids: Managing Drawdowns According to Commodity Trading Advisors. *Futures* Vol. 27, No. 1 (January, 1998), p. 68.

10. Richard Dennis, The State of the Industry. *Managed Account Reports, Inc.* (June, 2000).

11. Bill Dunn, MAR's Mid Year Conference on Alternative Investment Strategies held June 22–24, 1999.

12. Van Tharp's Interview with Two Super Traders.

13. Max Gunther, *The Zurich Axioms*. New York: New American Library, 1985.

14. W.H. Auden and L. Kronenberger (eds.), *The Viking Book of Aphorisms*. New York: Viking Press, 1966.

Afterword

1. David Nelson, "Hedge Funds 'to Blame'." *The Australian*, May 30, 2005.

Appendix F

1. The Trading Tribe at Seykota.com. See *www.seykota.com/tribe/*.

2. *The American Mathematical Monthly*, Vol. 100, No. 3.

Appendix G

1. See *www.millburncorp.com*.
2. See *www.jimhamer.com*.
3. Jerry M. Harris, Considering Managed Futures? Don't Focus on the Hole in the Donut. Managed Funds Association, October 1999.

Appendix H

1. In J. R. Newman (ed.), *The World of Mathematics*. New York: Simon and Schuster, 1956.
2. Morton S. Baratz, *The Investor's Guide to Futures Money Management*. Columbia, MD: Futures Publishing Group, 1984, 78–79.
3. Mario Puzo, *The Godfather*. New York: Putnam, 1969 (also screenplay with Francis Ford Coppola, 1972, Paramount Pictures).

About the Author

1. Denise G. Shekerjian, *Uncommon Genius*. New York: Penguin Books, 1990.

Bibliography

Abbott, Susan. Turning a Summer Job into a Legend. *Futures*, Vol. 12, No. 9 (Sept. 1983): 57–59.

Amin, Gaurav. S., and Kat, Harry M. Who Should Buy Hedge Funds? The Effects of Including Hedge Funds in Portfolios of Stocks and Bonds. ISMA Centre for Education and Research in Securites Markets. Working Paper Series (2002).

Angrist, Stanley W. Sensible *Speculation in Commodities or How to Profit in the Bellies, Bushels and Bales Markets*. New York: Simon and Schuster, 1972.

Aronson, Mark. Learning from a Legend. *Trading Advisor Review* (June 1997).

Baratz, Morton S. *The Investor's Guide to Futures Money Management*. Columbia, MD: Futures Publishing Group, 1984.

Barber, Brad and Terrance Odean. Trading Is Hazardous to Your Wealth: The Common Stock Investment Performance of Individual Investors. *Journal of Finance*, Vol. LV, No. 2 (April 2000): 773–806.

Basso, Thomas F. When to Allocate to a CTA? Buy Them on Sale (1997).

Basso, Thomas F. The Driving Force Behind Profits in the Managed Futures Industry. Trendstat Capital Management, Inc. (1998).

Basso, Thomas F. Some Leverage Is Good, Too Much Is Dangerous. Trendstat Capital Management, Inc. (March 1999).

Basso, Thomas F.,Study of Time Spent in Trending and Sideways Markets. Trendstat Capital Management, Inc. (1999).

Bernstein, Peter L. *Against The Gods: The Remarkable Story of Risk*. Canada: John Wiley & Sons, Inc., 1996.

Bogle, John. C. *Common Sense on Mutual Funds*. New York: John Wiley & Sons, Inc., 1999

Borish, Peter. Managed Money. *Futures* Vol. 27, No. 3 (March 1998).

Brealey, Richard and Stewart C. Myers. *Principles of Corporate Finance*, Fifth Edition. New York: Irwin McGraw Hill, 1996.

Brooks, Chris, and Harry M. Kat, The Statistical Properties of Hedge Fund Index Returns and Their Implications for Investors. *Journal of Alternative Investment*, 5 (2002): 26–44.

Brorsen, B.W. and S.H. Irwin. Futures Funds and Price Volatility. *Review of Futures Markets* 6 (1987): 119–135.

Burke, Gibbons. Your Money. *Active Trader* (July 2002): 68–73.

Burns, Greg. A Gunslinger No More. *Businessweek* (April 7, 1997): 64–72.

Canoles, W. Bruce, Sarahelen R. Thompson, Scott H. Irwin, and Virginia G. France. An Analysis of the Profiles and Motivations of Habitual Commodity Speculators. Working Paper 97-01, Office for Futures and Options Research, University of Illinois, Champagne-Urbana (1997).

Cavaletti, Carla. 1997's Home Run Hitters. *Futures*, Vol. 27, No. 3, (March 1998).

Chandler, Beverly. *Managed Futures*. England: John Wiley & Sons, 1994.

Chang, E.C. and B. Schachter. Interday Variations in Volume, Variance and Participation of Large Speculators. Working Paper, Commodity Futures Trading Commission, 1993.

Christensen, Clayton M. *The Innovator's Dilemma: When New Technologies Cause Great Firms to Fail*. Boston: Harvard Business School Press, 1997.

Christensen, Clayton M. and Matt Verlinden, Disruption, Disintegration, and the Dissipation of Differentiability. Harvard Business School Working Paper, 2000.

Clendaniel, Edward. Bubble Troubles. *Forbes* (March 25, 2002).

Collins, James C. and Jerry I. Porras. *Built to Last: Successful Habits of Visionary Companies*. New York: HarperBusiness, 1994.

Collins, Jim. *Good to Great*. New York: HarperBusiness, 2001.

Commodity Futures Trading Commission, Division of Economic Analysis. Survey of Pool Operators in Futures Markets with an Analysis of Interday Position Changes. Washington, D.C., 1991.

de Tocqueville, Alexis. *Democracy in America*. New York: Vintage Books, 1959.

Diz, Fernando. How do CTAs' Return Distribution Characteristics Affect Their Likelihood of Survival? *Journal of Alternative Investments*, Vol. 2, No. 2 (Fall 1999): 37–41.

Douglas, Mark. *The Disciplined Trader: Developing Winning Attitudes*. New York: New York Institute of Finance, 1990.

Eales, J.S., B.K. Engel, R.J. Hauser, and S.R. Thompson. Grain Price Expectations of Illinois Farmers and Grain Merchandisers. *American Journal of Agricultural Economics*, 72 (1990): 701–708.

Ecke, Robert. Allocation to Discretionary CTAs Grow as Market Stalls. *Barclay Trading Group Roundtable*, Vol. 9, No. 3. (Third quarter, 1998).

Eckhardt, William. The c-Test. *Stocks and Commodities*. Vol. 12, No. 5 (1994): 218–221.

Edwards, Franklin R., and Mustafa Onur Caglayan. Hedge Fund and Commodity Fund Investment Styles in Bull and Bear Markets. *Journal of Portfolio Management*, 27 (2001): 97–108

Ellis, Charles D. *Winning the Loser's Game*, Third ed. New York: McGraw Hill, 1998.

Energy Traders on the Verge of Extinction. *Barclay Trading Group Roundtable*, Vol. 8, No. 3 (Third quarter, 1997).

Epstein, Richard A. The *Theory of Gambling and Statistical Logic*. San Diego, CA: Academic Press, Inc., 1995.

Feynman, Richard P., as told to Ralph Leighton. *"What Do You Care What Other People Think?" Further Adventures of a Curious Character*. New York: W.W. Norton & Company, 1988.

Fabozzi, Frank J., Francis Gupta, and Harry M. Markowitz. The Legacy of Modern Portfolio Theory. Institutional Investor, Inc., 2002.

Fleckenstein, Bill. The Long and Short of Short-Selling (Sept. 2002). See *http://moneycentral.msn.com*.

Forrester, Jay W. *Principles of Systems*. Cambridge, MA: Wright-Allen Press, Inc., 1968.

Forrester, Jay W. System Dynamics and the Lessons of 35 Years, in *The Systemic Basis of Policy Making in the 1990s*, Kenyon B. De Greene, ed., 1991.

Friedman, Thomas L. *The Lexus and the Olive Tree*. New York: Farrar, Straus, Giroux, 1999.

Fung, William, and Hsieh, David A. Asset-Based Hedge-Fund Styles and Portfolio Diversification, *Financial Analyst Journal* (September 2001).

Fung, William, and Hsieh, David A. Hedge-Fund Benchmarks: Information Content and Biases, *Financial Analyst Journal* (2002).

Fung William and David A. Hsieh. Pricing Trend Following Trading Strategies: Theory and Empirical Evidence (1998).

Fung, William, and David A.Hsieh. The Risk in Hedge Fund Strategies: Theory and Evidence from Fixed Income Funds. *Journal of Fixed Income*, 14 (2002).

Gadsden, Stephen. Managed the Future. *The MoneyLetter*, Vol. 25, No. 20 (Oct. 2001).

Gallacher, William R. *Winner Take All*. New York: McGraw-Hill, 1994.

Gann, W.D. *How to Make Profits Trading in Commodities*. Pomeroy: Library of Gann Publishing Co. Inc., 1951.

Garber, Peter M. *Famous First Bubbles: The Fundamentals of Early Manias*. Cambridge, MA: MIT Press, 2000.

Gardner, B.L. Futures Prices in Supply Analysis. *American Journal of Agricultural Economics*, 58 (1976), 81–84.

Gary, Loren. The Right Kind of Failure. *Harvard Management Update*.

Gigerenzer, Gerd and Peter M. Todd. *Simple Heuristics That Make Us Smart*. Oxford: Oxford University Press, 1999.

Gilovich, Thomas, Robert Valone, and Amos Tversky. The Hot Hand in Basketball: On the Misperception of Random Sequences. *Cognitive Psychology*, 17 (1985), 295–314.

Ginyard, Johan. Position-sizing Effects on Trader Performance: An Experimental Analysis. Uppsala University, Department of Psychology, 2001.

Goldbaum, David. Technical Analysis, Price Trends, and Bubbles.

Gould, Stephen Jay. *Full House*. New York: Three Rivers Press, 1996.

Gould, Stephen Jay. The Streak of Streaks. *The New York Times Review of Books* (Aug. 18, 1988). See *www.nybooks.com/articles/4337*.

Grof, Stanisslav. *The Adventure of Self-Discovery: Dimensions of Consciousness and New Perspectives in Psychotherapy and Inner Exploration*. Albany: State University of New York, Press, 1988.

Hakim, Danny. Hedging Learned at the Family Farm. *The New York Times*, July 26, 2002.

Harlow, Charles V. D.B.A. and Michael D. Kinsman, Ph.D, CPA. The Electronic Day Trader & Ruin. *The Graziadio Business Report* (Fall 1999).

Harris, Larry. *Trading and Exchanges*. New York: Oxford University Press, 2003.

Harris, Lawrence. The Winners and Losers of the Zero-Sum Game: The Origins of Trading Profits, Price Efficiency and Market Liquidity. University of Southern California (1993)

Haun, Bruce. Rebalancing Portfolios Lowers Volatility and Stabilizes Returns. B. Edward Haun & Company (June 1994).

Irwin, Scott H. and Satoko Yoshimaru. Managed Futures Trading and Futures Price Volatility (1996).

Jaeger, Lars. *Managing Risk in Alternative Investment Strategies*. Upper Saddle River, NJ: Financial Times Prentice Hall, 2002

Jakiubzak, Ken. KmJ: Ready for Anything. *Futures*, Vol. 29, No. 3 (March 2000).

Kahneman, Daniel and Amos Tverksy. Prospect Theory: An Analysis of Decision Under Risk. *Econometrica*, 47 (1979): 263–291.

Kaplan, Laurie. Turning Turtles into Traders. *Managed Derivatives* (May 1996).

Karas, Robert. Looking Behind the Non-Correlation Argument. See *www. aima.org/aimasite/research/lgtoct99.htm*.

Kat, Harry M. Managed Futures and Hedge Funds: A Match Made in Heaven. Working Paper (November 2002)

Kaufman, Perry. *Trading Systems and Methods*, Third Edition. New York: John Wiley and Sons, Inc., 1998.

Klein, Gary. *Sources of Power: How People Make Decisions*. Cambridge, MA: The MIT Press, 1998.

Krauland, and Mabon, P.C. Going Once, Going Twice. *Discover* (Aug. 2002).

Le Bon, Gustave. *The Crowd: A Study of the Popular Mind*. Atlanta: Cherokee Publishing Company, 1982.

Lefevre, Edwin. *Reminiscences of a Stock Operator*. Canada: John Wiley & Sons, Inc., 1994.

Lerner, Robert L. The Mechanics of the Commodity Futures Markets, What They Are and How They Function. Mount Lucas Management Corp., 2000.

Liebovitch, L. S. *Fractals and Chaos Simplified for the Life Sciences*. New York: Oxford University Press, 1998.

Liebovitch, L. S., A. T. Todorov, M. Zochowski, D. Scheurle, L. Colgin, M. A. Wood, K. A. Ellenbogen, J.M.Herre and R.C.Bernstein. Nonlinear Properties of Cardiac Rhythm Abnormalities. *Physical Review*, 59 (1999): 3312–3319.

Livermore, Jesse L.. How to Trade in Stocks: *The Livermore Formula for Combining Time Element and Price*. New York: Duel, Sloan & Pearce, 1940.

Lukac, L. P., B. W. Brorsen, and S. H. Irwin. The Similarity of Computer Guided Technical Trading Systems. *Journal of Futures Markets*, 8 (1988): 1–13.

Lungarella, Gildo. Managed Futures: A Real Alternative. White Paper.

Mackay Charles LL.D. *Extraordinary Popular Delusions and the Madness of Crowds*. New York, 1841.

MacRae, Desmond. Dealing with Complexities. *Trading Focus* (July 1998).

Martin, George. Making Sense of Hedge Fund Returns: What Matters and What Doesn't. *Derivatives Strategies* (2002).

Mauboussin, Michael J., Alexander Schay and Stephen Kawaja. Counting What Counts. Credit Suisse First Boston Equity Research (February 4, 2000).

Mauboussin, Michael J. and Kristen Bartholdson. Stress and Short-Termism. *The Consilient Observer*, Vol. 1, No. 9 (Credit Suisse First Boston, May 2002).

Maubossin, Michael and Kristen Bartholdson. Whither Enron? Or Why Enron Withered. *The Consilient Observer*, Vol. 1, No. 1 (Credit Suisse First Boston, January 2002).

Mosser, Mike. Learning from Legends. *Futures*, Vol. 29, No. 2 (Feb. 2000).

Nacubo Endowment Study. Washington, D.C.: National Association of College and University Business Officers, 1999.

Niederhoffer, Victor and Laurel Kenner. *Practical Speculation*. Hoboken, NJ: John Wiley & Sons, 2003.

Odean, Terrance. Are Investors Reluctant to Realize Their Losses? *Journal of Finance*, 53 (October 1998), 1775–1798.

O'Donoghue, Ted and Matthew Rabin. Choice and Procrastination. University of California at Berkeley, Department of Economics. Working Paper E00-281 (June 3, 2001).

Oldest CTAs in the Industry Have Survived and Thrived. *Barclay Trading Group Roundtable*, Vol. 6, No. 3. (Third quarter, 1995).

Peltz, Lois. The Big Global Macro Debate. *Market Barometer* (April 1998): 9–13.

Peltz, Lois. *The New Investment Superstars*. Canada: John Wiley & Sons, Inc., 2001.

Peters, E.E. *Fractal Market Analysis*. New York: John Wiley & Sons, Inc., 1994.

Rand, Ayn. *Atlas Shrugged*. New York: Random House, 1957.

Rand, Ayn. *The Fountainhead*. New York: Bobbs-Merrill Company, 1943.

Rappaport, Alfred. *Creating Shareholder Value: A Guide for Managers and Investors*. New York: The Free Press, 1998.

Rappaport, Alfred and Michael J. Mauboussin. *Expectations Investing*. Boston: Harvard Business School Publishing, 2001.

Reerink, Jack. Seidler's Returns Fuel Comeback. *Futures*, Vol. 24, No. 3 (March 1995).

Rogers, Jim. *Investment Biker*. New York: Villard Books, 1994.

Russo, J. Edward and Paul J. H. Schoemaker. Managing Overconfidence. *Sloan Management Review* (Winter 1992).

Rzepczynski, Mark. The End of the Benign Economy and the New Era for Managed Funds. *MFA Reporter* (John W. Henry & Company, Inc, 2001).

Rzepczynski, Mark S. Market Vision and Investment Styles: Convergent versus Divergent Trading. *The Journal of Alternative Investments*, Vol. 2, No. 1 (Winter 1999): 77–82.

Schneeweis, Thomas, and Georgi Georgiev. The Benefits of Managed Futures. CISDM and School of Management at University of Massachusetts (2002).

Schneeweis, Thomas, and Spurgin, Richard. Quantitative Analysis of Hedge Fund and Managed Futures Return and Risk Characteristics, in *Evaluating and Implementing Hedgefund Strategies*, Second Edition, R. Lake ed., 2002.

Schwager, Jack D. *Getting Started in Technical Analysis*. New York: John Wiley & Sons, Inc., 1999.

Schwager, Jack D. *Market Wizards: Interviews with Top Traders*. New York: HarperBusiness, 1989.

Schwager, Jack D. *The New Market Wizards: Conversations with America's Top Traders*. New York: HarperBusiness, 1992.

Schwed Jr., Fred. *Where Are the Customers' Yachts?* Canada: John Wiley & Sons, Inc., 1995.

Seykota, Ed and Dave Druz. Determining Optimal Risk. *Stocks and Commodities*, Vol. 11, No. 3: 122–124.

Shapiro, Carl and Hal R. Varian. *Information Rules: A Strategic Guide to the Network Economy*. Boston: Harvard Business School Press, 1999.

Shefrin, Hersh and Meir Statman. The Disposition to Sell Winners Too Early and Ride Losers Too Long: Theory and Evidence. *Journal of Finance*, 40 (1985) 777–790.

Shekerjian, Denise. *Uncommon Genius*. New York: Penguin Books, 1990.

Shiller, Robert J. *Irrational Exuberance*. Princeton, NJ: Princeton University Press, 2000.

Robert J. Shiller. Do Stock Prices Move Too Much to Be Justified by Subsequent Changes in Dividends? *American Economic Review*, 71 (1981).

Sloan, Allen. Even With No Bull Market, Baby Boomers Can Thrive. March 2002. See *www.washingtonpost.com*.

Slywotzky, Adrian J. *Value Migration: How to Think Several Moves Ahead of the Competition*. Boston: Harvard Business School Press, 1996.

Smant, Dr. D.J.C. Famous First Bubbles, South Sea Bubble? *The Fundamentals of Early Manias*. Oct. 2001.

Soros, George. *The Alchemy of Finance: Reading the Mind of the Market*. New York: John Wiley & Sons, Inc., 1994.

Spurgin, Richard. Some Thoughts on the Source of Return to Managed Futures. CISDM and School of Management at University of Massachusetts

Steinhardt, Michael. *No Bull: My Life In and Out of Markets*. Canada: John Wiley & Sons, Inc., 2001.

Stendahl, David, Staying Afloat. *Omega Research* (1999).

Szala, Ginger. William Eckhardt: Doing by Learning. *Futures,* Vol. 21, No. 1 (January 1992).

Taleb, Nassim Nicholas. *Fooled By Randomness*. New York: Texere, 2001.

Teweles, Richard J. and Frank J. Jones. *The Futures Game. Who Wins? Who Loses? Why?* New York: McGraw-Hill, 1987.

Thaler, Richard H. Mental Accounting Matters. *Journal of Behavioral Decision Making*, 12 (1999): 183–206.

Thaler, Richard H. Saving, Fungibility, and Mental Accounts, *Journal of Economic Perspectives*, Vol. 4, No. 1 (Winter 1990): 193–205.

Tharp, Van K. *Trade Your Way to Financial Freedom*. New York: McGraw-Hill, 1999.

Thorp, Edward O. *Beat the Dealer*. New York: Vintage Books, 1966.

Toffler, Alvin. *Future Shock*. New York: Bantam Books, 1971.

Tully, Shawn. Princeton's Rich Commodity Scholars. *Fortune 9* (February 1981): 94.

Tversky, Amos and Daniel Kahneman. Belief in the Law of Small Numbers. *Psychological Bulletin*, 76 (1971) 105–110.

Tzu, Sun. *The Art of War*. Boston and London: Shambhala, 1988.

Ueland, Brenda. *If You Want to Write: A Book About Art, Independence and Spirit*. Saint Paul, MN: Graywolf Press, 1937.

Vince, Ralph. *Portfolio Management Formulas*. Canada: John Wiley & Sons, Inc., 1990.

Vince, Ralph. *The New Money Management*. New York: John Wiley & Sons, Inc., 1995.

von Mises, Ludwig. *Human Action: A Treatise on Economics*. New York: The Foundation for Economic Education, Inc., 1996. First published 1949.

Watts, Dickson G. *Speculation as a Fine Art and Thoughts on Life*. New York: Traders Press, 1965.

Where, Oh Where Are the .400 Hitters of Yesteryear. *Financial Analysts Journal* (Nov./Dec. 1998): 6–14.

Williamson, Porter B. *General Patton's Principles For Life and Leadership*. Tuscon, AZ: MSC, Inc., 1988.

Wolfram, Stephen. *A New Kind of Science*. Champaign, IL: Wolfram Media, Inc., 2002.

Wolman, William and Anne Colamosca. *The Great 401(k) Hoax*. Cambridge, Massachusetts: Perseus Publishing, 2002.

Yeung, Albert, Mika Toikka, Pankaj N. Patel, and Steve S. Kim. Quantitative Strategy. Does Technical Analysis Work? Credit Suisse First Boston. September 25, 2002.

About the Author

Michael W. Covel is the founder and President of Trend Following™. A researcher of the most successful trend-following investment managers, he has been in the alternative investments industry consulting on trend following to individual traders, hedge funds, and banks for 10 years. Covel's clients range from new and experienced individual traders and investors to multinational hedge funds and corporations.

From his writing to public speaking, Covel pulls no punches. Passionately educating his clients in order to find that "edge" has made Covel a widely respected expert in the field. He writes for numerous industry publications including *Your Trading Edge*, *SFO Magazine*, and *International Petroleum Finance* and is continually quoted and interviewed by *Barron's*, *Bloomberg*, and *Technical Analysis Magazine*, to name but a few. An experienced and successful entrepreneur, he is a frequent guest on national radio talk shows advising listeners on financial decision-making, risk management, trading, and trend following.

Fear touches everyone— even the successful people, the golden boys, the people who give the appearance of passing through life with their hands deep in their pockets, a whistle on their lips. To take on risk you need to conquer fear, at least temporarily, at least occasionally. It can be done, especially if you look outside yourself for a strong ledge to stand on.

Denise Shekerjian[1]

Michael Covel has had unparalleled face to face access with the great traders of our time. Interviewing dozens of fund managers managing collectively well over $10 billion USD has given Covel a unique understanding.

Mr. Covel is also Managing Editor at TurtleTrader.com®, the leading Trend Following news and commentary resource since 1996. TurtleTrader, one of the largest and strongest trading communities on the web, with over 7.5 million unique visitors since its inception, also functions as a resource center for the Trend Following Educational Course. Thousands of clients from more than 70 countries have engaged in years of debate and interchange, making the site the rich archive of trading information, data, and opinion that it continues to be today.

A graduate of George Mason University, Mr. Covel holds a Master's Degree in Business Administration from Florida State University.

Michael can be reached directly at info@trendfollowing.com and www.trendfollowing.com.

Index

More Praise for *Trend Following*

"Trend Following *is a great resource for all future successful traders. It covers the four bases of successful trading using real-world success stories:*

1. *Follow the trend of the market; don't waste time trying to predict it*

2. *Have sound money management rules, especially a strict loss-cutting policy*

3. *Be disciplined by implementing proven trading rules*

4. *Have the patience to wait for the right opportunity*

Michael Covel has hit for the cycle with Trend Following.*"*

> —John Boik
> author of *Lessons from the Greatest Stock Traders of All Time*

"The only two tests of a really good trading book are: Will it help you make money? Will it help you cut your losses. Trend Following *passes both tests with flying colors. It has a clarity that is compelling. While it discounts what I regard to be the useful role of macro analysis in understanding the origins of trends, it nonetheless reinforces the most important rule in sound trading— trade with the trend—in a way that triumphs. Last take: If you are a quote junkie like me, the quotes alone are worth the modest admission price."*

> —Peter Navarro
> Professor of Economics and Public Policy
> Graduate School of Management
> University of California, Irvine
> author of *When the Market Moves, Will You Be Ready?*

"The toughest play in baseball is to catch a ball hit directly at you. The toughest thing for any trader is to stay with the trend. The temptation always is to get fancy, to fade the long-term move, to pretend that you are smarter than the market somehow. The big money is made by identifying the trend and sticking with it no matter what. Michael Covel has written an indispensable work to help you do just that."

> —Howard Simons
> President, Rosewood Trading, Author and Trading Consultant

"*As a contrarian investor I have been skeptical by default of trend following models. Still, after reading Michael Covel's excellent and eye opening book about some professional traders, who with iron discipline follow market trends up and down and in the process achieve impressive capital gains, I find myself more inclined to endorse a trend following approach to investments. In fact, I wished that at times I would have had the kind of discipline the trend followers have in terms of entirely reversing their investment positions once the trend dictated such a posture.*"

—Marc Faber
Managing Director, Marc Faber Limited
Editor, "Gloom, Boom & Doom" Report

"*. . .I can safely say that this book is a classic and a must-read for anybody involved with the markets—even those of you who are just blindly plowing money into your retirement accounts . . .Covel takes no prisoners in showing why trend following is the superior trading methodology.*"

—Michael Seneadza
TraderMike.net

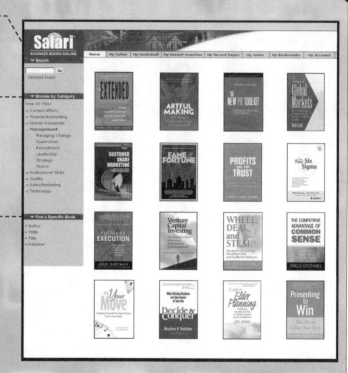

OPPORTUNITY INVESTING
How To Profit When Stocks Advance, Stocks Decline, Inflation Runs Rampant, Prices Fall, Oil Prices Hit the Roof, ... and Every Time in Between
BY GERALD APPEL

Gerald Appel, a world famous author and lecturer on investing and market timing, shows which investments provide the best returns in varying economic climates and how to recognize and take advantage of investment opportunities overseas as well as within the United States. Learn specific strategies for identifying the strongest mutual funds and stock market sectors as well as strategies for periods when interest rates either rise or fall. *Opportunity Investing* provides tools to identify periods when stocks and other investment options are likely to advance, periods when market outlooks are more cloudy, and strategies that suggest changes in portfolio allocation that may be made accordingly. Also discusses real estate, precious metals and other commodities, and investments that bring in high and steady levels of income. Readers will learn which forms of investment produce the best returns based on the general market climate. And finally, Appel identifies specific areas of investment with strategies for retirement investment. Includes coverage of foreign stocks and bonds as well as domestic securities, real estate, commodities, government issues, open and closed end mutual funds, exchange-traded funds (ETFs), and more.

ISBN 9780131721296 ▪ © 2007 ▪ 384 pp. ▪ $24.99 USA ▪ $ 29.99 CAN

TRADING CATALYSTS
How Events Move Markets and Create Trading Opportunities
BY ROBERT I. WEBB

Markets face more volatility — and more kinds of volatility — than ever before. If you can understand volatility, you can leverage enormous profit opportunities unavailable to the typical investor. If you fail to understand it, your portfolio will be buffeted constantly by shocks you weren't expecting. *Trading Catalysts* is the first complete guide to the events that spark large, rapid changes in market prices. Drawing on many recent examples, renowned futures and trading expert Robert I. Webb reveals how to anticipate market catalysts — and project the magnitude, duration, and breadth of the price changes they induce. You'll learn how to predict the impact of policymakers' comments (intentional and unintentional); elections, terrorism, and other changes in geopolitical risk; scheduled and unanticipated economic reports; even company earnings and other corporate announcements. Webb helps you decode the hidden messages in corporate press releases, and assess both the truth and market implications of unverified rumors. You'll learn how to recognize apparently inconsequential events that spark major rallies or breaks; predict positive or negative feedback loops that drive markets substantially higher or lower; even identify market overreactions. Simply put, market volatility is anything but random. You can master it and you can profit from it.

ISBN 9780130385567 ▪ © 2007 ▪ 368 pp. ▪ $39.99 USA ▪ $49.99 CAN

TREND FOLLOWING

FREE TREND FOLLOWING CDROM

CDROM contains audio MP3s you can play at home, office, car, and iPod!

Contact Information: *Please fill out all fields to receive free CDROM.*

Name _____

Company Name _____

Address _____

_____

City, State & Zip _____

Country _____

Phone _____

Fax _____

E-mail _____

How did you hear about the book "Trend Following"? _____

_____

To receive FREE Trend Following CDROM please send completed form to:

Trend Following
11654 Plaza America Drive, Suite 224
Reston, VA 20190
USA

turtletrader.com • trendfollowing.com • michaelcovel.com